GOVERNMENT OF THE METROPOLIS

Selected Readings

JOSEPH F. ZIMMERMAN

State University of New York at Albany

HOLT, RINEHART AND WINSTON, INC.

New York / Chicago / San Francisco / Atlanta
Dallas / Montreal / Toronto / London

To Margaret and Deirdre

Preface

Rampant urbanization has led to increasing concern with the ability of our governmental system, which developed in the seventeenth and eighteenth centuries, to cope with the exigencies of the space age. The literature of the past forty years abounds with warnings of impending crises and the necessity for a drastic reorganization of our governmental system to meet the metropolitan challenge.

Although there has been a fast outpouring of writings on metropolitan problems and solutions, a considerable amount of material remains scattered and relatively inaccessible to the average student. The purpose of this volume is to make readily available significant readings dealing with metropolitan problems and their solutions in the United States, Canada, and England. A special effort has been made to avoid the inclusion of readings containing material found in textbooks on American government, state and local government, and urban and metropolitan government.

In preparing these readings, I have been particularly fortunate in having access to the files of the Local Government Studies Center of the Graduate School of Public Affairs at the State University of New York at Albany. In 1962 the Local Government Studies Center incorporated the major functions of the Conference on Metropolitan Area Problems, which had been organized in 1957 to focus attention on metropolitan problems. The wealth of material contained in the Center's files makes an editor's task both easy and difficult. Space limitations unfortunately necessitated the omission of a treasure trove of material, and this forced the editor to make many difficult decisions in selecting his material.

The viewpoints finally chosen are indicative of the variety of opinions on governmental problems in metropolitan areas. No attempt has been made to favor a particular viewpoint and care has been exercised to achieve a balanced treatment of the subject matter.

J. F. Z.

ALBANY, NEW YORK
November 1967

iii

Contents

PART FOUR: SOLUTIONS FOR METROPOLITAN PROBLEMS

ROLE OF THE FEDERAL GOVERNMENT

ROLE OF THE STATE GOVERNMENT

ANNEXATION AND EXTRAMURAL JURISDICTION

CITY-COUNTY CONSOLIDATION

THE TWO-TIER APPROACH

PART ONE

Introduction

A proper appreciation of the governmental problems of metropolitan areas begins with an understanding of their development and their projected growth.

Metropolitan areas were first accorded official recognition in 1910 when the U.S. Bureau of the Census established 25 Metropolitan Districts. By 1949, four different sets of definitions—Metropolitan Districts, Metropolitan Counties, Industrial Areas, and Labor Market Areas—had been developed for various statistical series. Since each definition produced geographical areas which differed slightly, it was not possible to relate the statistics from each series to a given metropolitan area.

In consequence, a standard definition—Standard Metropolitan Area—was developed in 1949 to replace the existing sets of definitions, and thereby facilitate the analysis of metropolitan problems by having all federal statistical agencies use the same geographical boundaries in collecting and publishing data. The term "Standard Metropolitan Area" subsequently was changed to Standard Metropolitan Statistical Area (SMSA).

The general definition of an SMSA—a county or a group of contiguous counties with at least one city of 50,000 inhabitants or two cities with a combined population of at least 50,000 provided the smaller city has at least 15,000—has been criticized as an inaccurate measure of metropolitan character. The definition of an SMSA in New England— 100 persons per square mile—is considered by a number of experts to be a more accurate measure of metropolitan character. This criticism

1

becomes especially meaningful when one examines San Bernardino County, California—with thousands of square miles of desert and ranch land—which is included in the San Bernardino-Riverside-Ontario SMSA because one city with a population in excess of 50,000 is located in the southwestern corner of the county.

The trend toward metropolitanization, which commenced at the turn of the century, shows no signs of abating. Estimates reveal substantial population increases in the 55 largest SMSA's between 1960 and 1965. The greatest increase, nearly 58 percent, occurred in the Anaheim-Santa Ana-Garden Grove, California SMSA followed by a 38 percent increase in the San Jose, California SMSA. Relatively modest population growth was recorded in the Eastern SMSA's, ranging from nearly 3 percent in the Boston area to 7½ percent in the Baltimore area.

In 1960, 113 million persons lived in 212 SMSA's. By the year 2000, demographers predict a population of approximately 350 million persons for the United States, with four of every five persons living in an SMSA. Eighty percent of the projected population increase will occur in metropolitan areas.

Although metropolitan areas have been experiencing rapid population growth, centrifugal forces have resulted in a declining central core as the growing middle class has been leaving the central city and moving to the suburbs. The United States in the post-World War II period became a suburban as well as an urban nation.

As a considerable number of retail and manufacturing firms joined the exodus to the suburbs, the central city finds its problems becoming more acute. It frequently is faced with the problems of a shrinking tax base, an influx of low-income families, racial friction, traffic congestion, air and water pollution, and the need to replace obsolete capital facilities.

Metropolitanization also has created serious problems for suburban communities faced with the herculean task of accommodating newcomers by providing adequate facilities and services. The property tax rate has increased sharply in many suburban communities because the cost of capital facilities on a per capita basis often has been considerably higher than in the central city. Furthermore, most suburbs were unprepared for rapid urbanization and lacked the necessary advance planning and controls to ensure orderly development.

The seriousness of central city and suburban problems and the lack of a governmental mechanism for the resolution of critical area-wide problems have been responsible for many proposals for the reform of the governmental system of the metropolis.

In viewing the metropolitan problem in the United States, one should keep in mind the fact that the basic problem is not the same in each area. The type and seriousness of problems vary considerably from one metropolitan area to the next. In general, metropolitan problems tend to be most acute in the East as it was settled first.

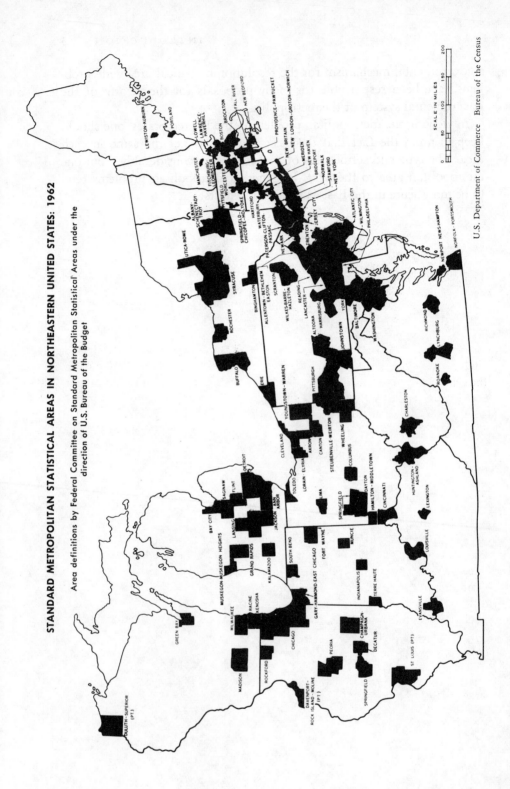

STANDARD METROPOLITAN STATISTICAL AREAS IN NORTHEASTERN UNITED STATES: 1962

Area definitions by Federal Committee on Standard Metropolitan Statistical Areas under the direction of U.S. Bureau of the Budget

SCALE IN MILES
0 50 100 150 200

U.S. Department of Commerce   Bureau of the Census

1. Criteria Followed in Establishing Standard Metropolitan Statistical Areas*

There are currently 231 Standard Metropolitan Statistical Areas ranging in population from 51,000 to 11 million. Only Alaska, Wyoming, and Vermont lack an SMSA.

Each area is defined by the U.S. Bureau of the Budget with the assistance of the Federal Committee on Standard Metropolitan Statistical Areas representing major federal statistical agencies. The criteria used in establishing SMSA's have not been revised since March 1958.

The definition of an individual SMSA involves two considerations: first, a city or cities of specified population to constitute the central city and to identify the county in which it is located as the central county; and second, economic and social relationships with contiguous counties[1] which are metropolitan in character, so that the periphery of the specific metropolitan area may be determined. SMSA's may cross state lines, if this is necessary in order to include qualified contiguous counties.

POPULATION CRITERIA

1. Each SMSA must include at least:

   (a) One city with 50,000 or more inhabitants, or

   (b) Two cities having contiguous boundaries and constituting, for general economic and social purposes, a single community with a combined population of at least 50,000, the smaller of which must have a population of at least 15,000.

2. If two or more adjacent counties each have a city of 50,000 inhabitants or

---

* From *Standard Metropolitan Statistical Areas* (Washington, D.C.: U.S. Bureau of the Budget, 1964), pp. 1–3.

[1] A "contiguous" county either adjoins the county or counties containing the largest city in the area, or adjoins an intermediate county integrated with the central county. There is no limit to the number of tiers of outlying metropolitan counties so long as all other criteria are met.

more (or twin cities under 1(*b*)) and the cities are within 20 miles of each other (city limits to city limits), they will be included in the same area unless there is definite evidence that the two cities are not economically and socially integrated.

CRITERIA OF METROPOLITAN CHARACTER

The criteria of metropolitan character relate primarily to the attributes of the county as a place of work or as a home for a concentration of nonagricultural workers. Specifically, these criteria are:

3. At least 75 percent of the labor force of the county must be in the nonagricultural labor force.[2]

4. In addition to criterion 3, the county must meet at least one of the following conditions:

(*a*) It must have 50 percent or more of its population living in contiguous minor civil divisions[3] with a density of at least 150 persons per square mile, in an unbroken chain of minor civil divisions with such density radiating from a central city[4] in the area.

(*b*) The number of nonagricultural workers employed in the county must equal at least 10 percent of the number of nonagricultural workers employed in the county containing the largest city in the area, or be the place of employment of 10,000 nonagricultural workers.

(*c*) The nonagricultural labor force living in the county must equal at least 10 percent of the number of the nonagricultural labor force living in the county containing the largest city in the area, or be the place of residence of a nonagricultural labor force of 10,000.

5. In New England, the city and town are administratively more important than the county, and data are compiled locally for such minor civil divisions. Here, towns and cities are the units used in defining SMSA's. In New England, because smaller units are used and more restricted areas result, a population density criterion of at least 100 persons per square mile is used as the measure of metropolitan character.

[2] Nonagricultural labor force is defined as those employed in nonagricultural occupations, those experienced unemployed whose last occupation was a nonagricultural occupation, members of the armed forces, and new workers.

[3] A contiguous minor civil division either adjoins a central city in a standard metropolitan statistical area or adjoins an intermediate minor civil division of qualifying population density. There is no limit to the number of tiers of contiguous minor civil divisions so long as the minimum density requirement is met in each tier.

[4] Central cities are those appearing in the standard metropolitan statistical area title.

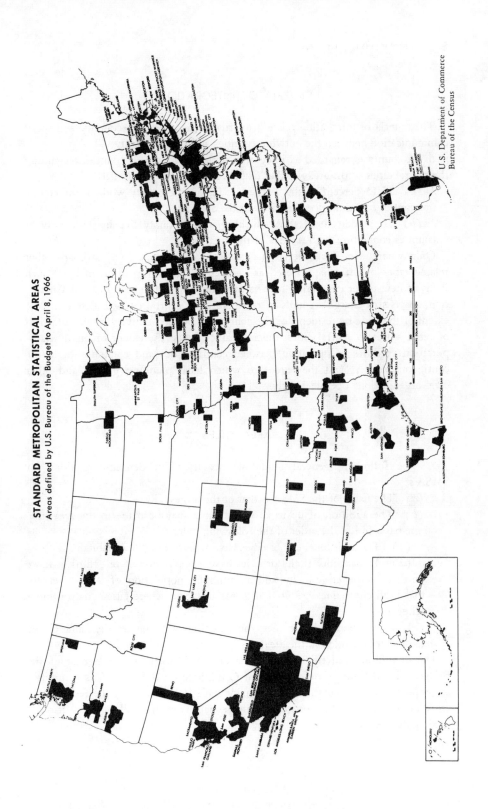

STANDARD METROPOLITAN STATISTICAL AREAS
Areas defined by U.S. Bureau of the Budget to April 8, 1966

U.S. Department of Commerce
Bureau of the Census

CRITERIA OF INTEGRATION

The criteria of integration relate primarily to the extent of economic and social communication between the outlying counties and central county.

6. A county is regarded as integrated with the county or counties containing the central cities of the area if either of the following criteria is met:

(*a*) If 15 percent of the workers living in the county work in the county or counties containing central cities of the area, or

(*b*) If 25 percent of those working in the county live in the county or counties containing central cities of the area.

Only where data for criteria 6(*a*) and 6(*b*) are not conclusive are other related types of information used as necessary. This information includes such items as newspaper circulation reports prepared by the Audit Bureau of Circulation, analysis of charge accounts in retail stores of central cities to determine the extent of their use by residents of the contiguous county, delivery service practices of retail stores in central cities, official traffic counts, the extent of public transportation facilities in operation between central cities and communities in the contiguous county, and the extent to which local planning groups and other civic organizations operate jointly.

AREA TITLES

7. The following general guidelines are used for determining titles for SMSA's:

(*a*) The name of the SMSA is that of the largest city.

(*b*) The addition of up to two city names may be made in the area title, on the basis and in the order of the following criteria:

(1) The additional city or cities have at least 250,000 inhabitants.

(2) The additional city or cities have a population of one third or more of that of the largest city and a minimum population of 25,000, except that both city names are used in those instances where cities qualify under criterion 1(*b*).

(*c*) In addition to city names, the area titles will contain the name of the state or states included in the area.

The definitions and titles of SMSA's are established by the Bureau of the Budget with the advice of the Federal Committee on SMSA's. This committee is composed of representatives of the major statistical agencies of the federal government. In applying the foregoing criteria, data from the following sources are used by the committee:

Population, labor force, density, and occupational data: Bureau of the Census, Department of Agriculture, and Bureau of Employment Security.

Employment by place of work: Bureau of Old-Age and Survivors Insurance, Department of Labor, Department of Defense, and Civil Service Commission.

Volume of commuting: Bureau of the Census.

Newspaper circulation: Audit Bureau of Circulation reports.

Data on charge accounts, delivery service practices, traffic volume, and public transportation, and related information: informed local groups.

2. Metropolitan Development and Problems*

The Committee for Economic Development, established in 1942 and composed of 200 prominent businessmen and educators, undertakes research with the objective of developing public and business policy recommendations to strengthen the economy and a free society.

The excerpt from *Guiding Metropolitan Growth* documents the continuing process of urbanization in the United States and the omnifarious problems of metropolitan areas. The seriousness of the problems helps to explain the widespread interest in a reorganization of the government of the metropolis to facilitate their resolution.

DEVELOPMENT

BACKGROUND

Within the span of a century America has gone through two great changes in its living patterns. In the last quarter of the nineteenth century and the first quarter of the twentieth century we shifted from a predominantly rural to a predominantly urban society.

The second change in American life during the twentieth century is from a basically urban to metropolitan condition. Prior to the metropolitan era cities were centers of industrial and commercial activity. The workers lived in closely built houses and tenements within walking distance of factories or of trolley car

* From *Guiding Metropolitan Growth* (New York: Committee for Economic Development, 1960), pp. 13–24.

and subway lines that went out only relatively short distances from the hub. Sanitation problems of this pattern of urban concentration were met by a central public sewer system. There was little question where the city ended and the country began. Outside of city boundaries there were no large population concentrations, and government structure outside these boundaries was designed for a basically rural condition.

The metropolitan area is in effect a new community. Its boundaries often are hard to define. In some instances they change and expand frequently. The area ignores old geographic boundaries, jumping over and around rivers and land masses. It ignores the political lines of districts, villages, towns, cities, counties, and states.

The metropolitan area reflects a new kind of society resulting from higher average incomes, the development of new tastes in living standards, and technological means for releasing people from the old patterns. The private automobile has freed many from dependence on local public transportation. The greatly increased use of septic tanks has, temporarily at least, freed dwellers from dependence on a central public sewer system. The location of industrial plants outside the core city has diffused job opportunities throughout a wide area. Suburban shopping centers have changed the marketing pattern.

These tendencies have increased rather than decreased the problems of government. As our population grows and our technology advances, the decisions about the use of land and of public revenue become increasingly complex. The governmental machinery to make these decisions, and the governmental influences on private market decisions, have not kept pace with this complexity. As a result, we are faced with increasing traffic congestion, blight in our central cities, unequal public burdens of suburban expansion, duplication of public facilities, and an inefficient use of public and private resources.

POPULATION GROWTH

Two trends have dominated the long-term growth of population in the United States: An ever-larger proportion of our people live in urban areas, and within urban areas, the suburbs and fringe are growing relatively faster than the central districts. Urbanization of our population has been in process for more than a century. In 1850 only 15 percent of our people lived in urban places. By 1900 the proportion had risen to 40 percent and 20 years later passed the halfway mark.

Today two out of three Americans live in urban areas. The growth in urban population—both relatively and in absolute terms—shows no sign of abating. It is a reflection not only of the shift of population from rural to urban areas, but of the tendency of urban populations to expand by natural increase.

Metropolitanism is a twentieth-century phenomenon. Technological advances, primarily in the field of transportation, have made possible a diffusion of plants, homes and shops in a wide expanse around the older central city. As of June 1959 the U.S. Bureau of the Census recognized 192 standard metropolitan areas —central cities of 50,000 or more together with their contiguous suburban areas. Within these areas, slightly more than half of the population still reside in the central cities, but 80 percent of the population growth in metropolitan areas since 1950 has been registered in the suburbs and the day is fast approaching when a majority of our metropolitan population will reside outside the central cities.

Where are these trends taking us? An intermediate projection by the U.S. Bureau of the Census is for a population of 220 million in 1975, an increase of roughly 40 million over 1960. If metropolitan areas continue to get three fourths of this national growth, our metropolitan population in 1975 will approximate 140 million persons. Central cities will still hold great concentrations of people —in the aggregate perhaps 60 million. But the balance will have shifted to areas outside present central-city boundaries: 80 million people will live in the suburbs and fringes of metropolitan districts.

By the year 2000, only 32 years from now, the population will exceed 300 million according to intermediate estimates of demographers, an increase of 120 million. As many as 100 million of these people will be added to the present population of our metropolitan areas.

URBANIZATION

Two large questions must be examined: First, will the forces making for urbanization be sustained? Second, how will various activities—manufacturing, wholesaling, retailing, business services, home building—be spatially distributed *within* metropolitan areas?

The forces which have transformed the United States into an urban nation within the lifetime of many of us are still ascendant. Barring several events— nuclear war, a national program for dispersal, or a pronounced shift in values— existing urban-metropolitan regions will continue to grow. For such concentrations are evidently necessary to take maximum advantage of technological opportunities that give us a high and rising standard of living. The economies of mass production and distribution which are made possible by large urban markets are widely recognized.

We are perhaps less aware of the importance of external economies of aggregation in urban areas. These are savings available to the individual concern in the form of services or facilities outside the plant and shared with other producers. Among these are middlemen and distributors, bankers, legal experts, accountants, advertising services and market analysts. Also, our transportation facilities, waterworks, sewerage plants and other massive overhead investments, and the availability of research facilities and technicians concentrated in university, library, and laboratory yield economies of this type.

Urban growth in the United States has been a cumulative process. The precondition for this growth, of course, was a marked rise in productivity on the farm with the introduction of new types of agricultural machinery in the second and third quarters of the nineteenth century. This not only yielded a surplus to feed large urban populations but released labor to the mills and shops of the city.

Meanwhile, as markets grew, mass production methods in manufacturing became more feasible. The resulting increases in output per worker were reflected in rising income for the community. This in turn made effective new consumer wants. To fill these demands a host of service industries emerged in the fields of recreation, education, personal and medical care. Commerce and industry also required more and different skills and services.

Partially offsetting the economies of urban living are certain "diseconomies" which have required additional services—building inspectors, settlement-house workers, laundries, traffic police, and window washers.

The growth in urban-type activities is revealed in the changing composition of the nation's labor force over an 80-year period. In 1870 slightly more than half of all gainfully employed workers were engaged in farming; by 1950 the proportion had dropped to one in eight workers.

Meanwhile, workers employed in trade, finance, and related industries increased from 6.4 to 21.2 percent, professional service workers rose from 1.6 to 6.3 percent, and government employees increased from 2.0 to 7.9 percent. Since 1950 the largest relative gains have continued to be registered in service type, urban-linked industries, particularly medical care, engineering and business services, public education, and other government services. These economic trends underlie the growth of urban areas at a rate considerably faster than the nation as a whole during the past half century.

The growth of urban areas continues to be fed by large-scale movements from the farms and small towns. The net migration from farms to urban areas in the United States between 1920 and 1955 amounted to about 24 million people. Most of the migrants are young adults. Many come from the rural South and Puerto Rico to the urban centers of the Northeast, the North Central region, and the West.

These migrants are a major source of unskilled and semiskilled labor and have contributed significantly to the economic expansion of the urban areas. But the movements have also entailed social costs resulting from lack of experience with urban living and frequently from insufficient income to afford decent housing.

THE PATTERN OF DEVELOPMENT

Within metropolitan regions, we are witnessing a significant redistribution of economic activities from the older central districts to the fringe areas. Home building and industrial plant construction are leading this outward movement; retail trades and household services, warehousing and other industrial services are rapidly adapting to the new patterns of development.

The statistics on home building and retailing since the end of World War II simply confirm our everyday observations. Of 13 million dwelling units erected in nonfarm areas from 1946 through 1958, approximately 11 million, or 85 percent, have been located outside of central cities.

In retailing, data for the New York region are illustrative of the national trend. Both sales and jobs in retail lines have dropped steadily in the core as a proportion of the New York region over a 25-year period with the outer rings registering the corresponding gains. In 1929 the core area accounted for about 69 percent of retail employment as well as sales; in 1954 these were down to about 60 and 55 percent, respectively.

A gradual but unremitting relative decline in manufacturing jobs located in central cities is also discernible. Of total production workers in 48 standard metropolitan areas, 66.5 percent worked in the central cities of the areas in 1929; in 1954 the ratio was down to 53.6 percent. In the postwar years between 1947 and 1954 central cities like Cleveland, Chicago, St. Louis, and San Francisco have experienced *absolute* drops in manufacturing employment of 3 to 8 percent.

Certain types of activities, however, show little inclination to deconcentrate. Business and governmental services requiring face-to-face relationships or dependent upon a large pool of female labor continue to exercise a strong preference for office space in the core of large metropolitan areas. In eight leading standard metropolitan areas[1] about 80 percent of all employment in finance, insurance, and real estate in 1956 was in the central cities.

Further evidence of this tendency for office-type activities to concentrate in or near the central business district is found in figures on office building construction. From 1946 through 1958 a total of 65 million square feet of new rentable office space was put on the market in 24 of the larger cities of the nation. Of this new space, some 27 million square feet, or 42 percent of the total, went up in the nation's leading central business district—the island of Manhattan in New York City.

Central locations have also retained their hold on manufacturers of unstan-

---

[1] Baltimore, Denver, New Orleans, New York City, Philadelphia, St. Louis, San Francisco, and Washington, D.C.

dardized products and those dependent upon a diversified mix of skills and materials. In six major central cities—Baltimore, Chicago, New York, Philadelphia, St. Louis, and San Francisco—total manufacturing employment in the central cities was 62.3 percent of manufacturing employment in the corresponding metropolitan areas in 1947, but for 19 industries central cities employment averaged 85 percent of total area employment. Among those with the highest percentages in the central city were: fur goods, 99.2 percent; footwear cut stock, 98.9 percent; printing trade services, 96.1 percent; millinery, 95.9 percent; periodicals, 95.4 percent; miscellaneous publishing, 90.1 percent.

Between the business core and the rapidly growing suburbs lies a large expanse of older districts—the "gray areas." In the more compact city of 1920 these areas housed most of our families. Increasingly since 1945, middle-income families with children have been departing for the suburbs; lower-income groups including substantial numbers of racial minorities have taken up the slack. But while there are few vacancies, physical deterioration of housing and supporting facilities is much in evidence. The gray areas are experiencing capital consumption and their economic future is in doubt.

What is the shape of things to come in metropolitan areas? In our mixed economy, investment decisions reflect a combination of factors—changes in industrial techniques, consumer preferences, and public policy. With regard to the location of new investment in metropolitan areas, the net effect of these factors in the postwar period has been to encourage a more dispersed pattern of development. For industries dealing in standardized products, the shift to horizontal-line processing in single-story plants has compelled a search for larger sites available only in the outer reaches of the metropolis. At the same time, the clustering of plants in new industrial districts has yielded some of the external economies formerly available mainly in the central city.

The strong desire for lower-density living on the part of families with children has led many to choose a suburban home. Federal policies in the field of mortgage insurance, which have generally favored single-family construction as against apartment developments, have strengthened this outward movement. So, too, have public policies in the fields of highway construction and education. On balance, these and related factors portend a more and more widely dispersed pattern of metropolitan development in the years ahead.

PROBLEMS

The large-scale breakout of residences, commercial activities, and manufacturing from the bounds of the central city has produced a number of major problems. Each part of the metropolitan area is faced with problems peculiar to itself. This diversity may strengthen the feeling of mutual antagonism between city and suburb. The area as a whole, however, faces problems which cannot be dealt with adequately on a piecemeal basis. Yet, so far, few areas have developed institutions which can adequately deal with these problems, and the prevailing antagonism between city and suburb inhibits the development of such institutions.

THE CENTRAL CITY

The public service requirements of central cities are shaped by a unique set of pressures. One is the burden of handling a daytime population 30 to 50 percent greater than the residential population. The continuous decline in use of mass transit facilities is making this task enormously more difficult. Between 1950 and 1958 transit riding in American cities fell from 17.2 billion to 9.7 billion rides per year, a drop of 43 percent. More and more people are getting to work or shopping by car.

The principal response of the cities has been to facilitate this shift by building or planning to build expressways to the core district and by adding to the supply of parking space. But discouraged by the growth of congestion, some cities like Washington, D.C., and San Francisco are considering a new emphasis on rapid transit systems. For central cities, the provision of good access to the central business district can be expected to have a high priority in capital improvement programs in the years ahead.

An historic function which the central city continues to perform is that of reception center for low-income migrants from outside the region. A steady stream of people from the rural South and Puerto Rico has replaced earlier migrations from abroad as the chief source of unskilled and semiskilled labor in urban centers. The majority of these migrants characteristically settle in the central cities.

Thus the cities carry a major share of the responsibility for helping newcomers adapt to an urban environment. It follows that city expenditures for social services, health clinics, welfare agencies, and public housing are considerably higher per capita than in suburban areas.

Another major concern of the central cities is the relentless spread of blight and obsolescence both of public and private facilities. In New York City, for example, almost half of the current capital budget is allocated to the replacement of outworn and outmoded public facilities. The prevention of excessive depreciation of private investments such as housing is a responsibility the municipality now shares with private owners.

Blight may afflict residential, commercial, or industrial areas. It involves neglect of property by owners, and it may result in the development of unsafe and unsanitary conditions. Generally, large areas are afflicted. The law of contiguity, a Gresham's law of land-use whereby poor uses drive out good, prevents private redevelopment in small parcels.

Under favorable circumstances one activity would replace another when it could make better use of the site. But thousands of acres of built-up land in the central cities of our metropolitan areas are underutilized and not filling needed functions. To restore land to sound use, redevelopment of a large acreage is generally required to overcome the impact of bad neighborhood influences.

Private ownership commonly finds it very difficult to redevelop on the scale necessary to establish new dominant uses. Owners of plots in such areas frequently have a price expectation far above market realities; many small plots must be accumulated; a few holdouts can make the cost inordinately high; and there are large demolition costs. Any major shift in land-use requires a combination of capital, foresight, willingness to risk, and the full cooperation of the local government.

The public interest in restoring land to sound use and generally to a higher taxpaying basis is considerable. Not only does this increase vital functions in parts of the central city, but it also reduces the heavy burden of providing fire protection, police protection, public health facilities, and other services which a seriously blighted area requires.

The development of effective programs to check blight and obsolescence would entail substantial increases in municipal efforts to enforce building and housing codes, relocate displaced tenants, prepare community-wide and neighborhood plans and zoning ordinances, and related activities. Few, if any, cities are yet geared to handle this immense job. Thus, continuous pressure on city budgets may be expected from this field of municipal activity.

While the needs of central cities are growing, their revenue sources are not keeping pace. Property tax income is checked by the exodus of upper and middle-income families and the establishment of retail shopping centers, new factories, and "clean" industries such as research laboratories outside the city limits. The resulting squeeze on taxpayers in some cases has sent property taxes so high as to make new private construction almost uneconomic. Without new construction to support and encourage new economic activity, the city finds it increasingly difficult to meet its revenue needs.

SUBURBAN NEEDS

With more than eight out of ten new homes being erected in suburban communities, it is these places which are feeling the brunt of demand for new schools, water systems, sewage disposal plants, fire stations, streets, and utility lines. Each new house in a suburban development requires a package of public services that entail capital outlays ranging in cost from $2500 to $3500 or more depending upon the density of development and degree of utilization.

Thus, capital expenditures run substantially higher in suburban communities than in the central city or nonmetropolitan areas. In the New York region, for example, suburbs made capital outlays in 1955 of $68 per capita compared with $44 in the central city and $38 in the nonmetropolitan sections. Considering these expenditures, it is no surprise that many communities try to effect their own salvation by screening out moderate-priced housing and forestalling a need for public sewerage systems and other facilities through such devices as two-acre zoning.

For rapidly growing suburbs the good design of neighborhoods that will provide long-term amenities and sound capital values is a problem that can be solved by intelligent local use of planning and zoning. The requirement is local awareness and willingness to use tested techniques. Since most residential construction occurs in new suburbs, they present the easiest and greatest opportunity for steps to provide long-lived improvement at minimum cost. Failure to take these steps now will prove very costly in 10 to 20 years.

AREA-WIDE PROBLEMS

Some services essential to metropolitan living cannot be provided separately by each municipality. The size and geographic extent of the capital investment, the economic forces at work, the nature of the physical environment, or the claims for use by the residents of the area make it almost impossible for communities to provide services or meet these needs separately. Among these are the provision of area-wide transportation systems, the control of air and water pollution, the reservation of open land for outdoor recreation, broad land-use planning, a fair distribution of tax resources, and the stimulation of growth in the economy of the area.

Transportation

The transportation of goods and people is basic to the life of a metropolitan area. The most important transportation problem is the movement of people within the area to places of employment and for shopping. Recreational and other personal travel needs are generally adequately met by the facilities provided for the first two purposes.

Historically, public transportation and rail commuter travel developed in our older metropolitan areas before the general use of the automobile. In these areas increased use of private automobiles has put financial strain on mass transit and rail commuter facilities. Some of our newer metropolitan areas have come to rely predominantly or almost exclusively on the private automobile supplemented by bus systems. In all areas increased use of the automobile has posed a serious congestion problem.

In the allocation of land and public revenues to various means of transportation three questions arise:

1. How shall facilities and travel be divided among highway, transit, and rail commuter?
2. Where shall facilities be located?
3. How shall the cost be covered?

In planning for population growth and higher incomes, public agencies need to determine how to strike a balance among programs which expand highways, provide mass transportation or shore up commuter facilities. At some point the additional space required for private automobile travel will so encroach on other land uses that mass transportation will have to be provided, or improved to handle the additional travel.

In some major metropolitan areas rail commuter services transport a significant number of people into the central city daily. Yet the abandonment of commuter lines under the provisions of the Transportation Act of 1958 is forcing more people to turn to the private automobile. A wholesale abandonment of commuter runs by railroads would greatly increase the expenditure and the land required for the highway system.

Commuter lines are suffering financial difficulties, with no easy solution. The property tax on roadbed and terminal facilities used by commuter lines is a competitive burden, for the highways used by alternative forms of travel are tax-free public facilities.[2] But rail commuter facilities share roadbed with rail freight and long-distance passenger traffic.

Public responsibility for the problems of the commuter railroads is divided among the federal government, the state governments, and the many communities through which the rights of way run. As with mass-transit systems, the benefits are enjoyed by users, businesses dependent on commuter travel for employees and customers, and the general public.

Transportation networks within metropolitan areas are basic, the capital costs of new construction are high, and the operating costs of rail and mass transportation are heavy. Yet in most metropolitan areas there is no single public agency able to study the relative needs for highway, mass transit, or rail. There is no single body able to allocate costs among users, businesses, and the general tax funds. No authoritative body is able to balance transportation capacity and the traffic generating uses of land.

Under these circumstances many ills are apparent: undue congestion, dupli-

[2] *Memorandum of Comment, Reservation, or Dissent* by Alan H. Temple in which Emilio G. Collado and Theodore O. Yntema have asked to be associated: "Highways can hardly be considered tax-free as long as the highway user is burdened with high gasoline taxes and federal automotive excises."

cated facilities, poor service, financial difficulties, inequitable sharing of burdens, and inadequate anticipation of future needs and costs.

Control of Air and Water Pollution

The winds that blow across the Hudson River are no observer of municipal or state boundary lines. Any program to control smoke or other pollution of the air in and around New York obviously must be area-wide. Each metropolitan area has a similar problem. The same holds true for control of the degree of contamination in fresh or salt water bodies in or on the boundaries of metropolitan areas. A river may serve as a source of water supply or as a means of waste disposal. No individual municipality can influence the water flowing into it or washing its shores except by cooperative effort with other municipalities or through an area-wide or state governmental body.

Land-use Planning and Open Land

Vacant land on the fringe of metropolitan areas is being absorbed at a rate of approximately 1 million acres a year. Current investments in housing, shopping centers, plants, streets, and public facilities are fixing the environment for two generations or more. But in few, if any, metropolitan areas is the magnitude of this responsibility matched by adequate preparation, planning, and land development controls on a metropolitan scale. In consequence, transport facilities, sewerage and water systems, and schools have been overtaxed in many areas; commercial ribbon-developments have sprung up alongside metropolitan highways, choking traffic and blighting the countryside.

Equally important, few areas have reserved sufficient space for parks and recreational needs, and rights of way have not been set aside for future expressways and utility lines. All too frequently, land only recently developed in the outskirts of a metropolis has had to be purchased for a right of way at a price five to ten times as much as the cost of the raw parcels. These costs as well as the uprooting of families and businesses are avoidable through advance planning and acquisition by the government of rights in land.

Industrial Development

The expansion of income-generating activities is desired by practically all metropolitan areas—both to provide more jobs and to provide an expansion in the tax base. The most important economic activities generally sought are expanded or new manufacturing plants.

The success of local communities in attracting new industry is partly dependent upon the expansion of the national economy and the region's economy, and some factors in industrial location are beyond the control of individual localities. But other influential factors can be controlled within the metropolitan area. Among these are space for industry, traffic, public services, the attractiveness of the community as a place to live, and local taxes.

Allocation of space for industrial use takes place partly through the free workings of the real estate market. It can be strongly influenced by industrial-zoning provisions which limit or exclude other uses. Thus the small percentage of land in a metropolitan area which is most suitable for industrial use can be reserved for such use. Where a clear conflict exists between two good uses not easily satisfied by most land, such as waterside industrial and recreational uses, some mechanism for careful decision should exist so that allocation is not made by default.

Taxes in any community in a metropolitan area may become an influence on industrial location when they are excessively high or abnormally low. Abnormally high taxes may be the result of inequitable assessment or of an inefficient local government, but they may also be the result of the community having to carry an undue share of the metropolitan area costs for welfare, highway maintenance, mass transit, schools, or other public purposes.

Abnormally low taxes in some areas may result from an avoidance of responsibilities which are passed on to others to carry; or they may reflect a reluctance to provide positive services in the nature of good schools, recreational facilities and the like. The absence of good public services of this type may reduce a community's attractiveness for new industry.

3. Local Governments
in Metropolitan Areas*

The metropolitan problem has been diagnosed as too many units of local government. This selection from the *Census of Governments: 1962* lends support to the diagnosis; the presence of 18,442 governmental units within metropolitan areas is suggestive of the degree of fragmentation and the difficulty of securing a consensus among the units for joint action to solve area-wide problems.

* From U. S. Bureau of the Census, *Census of Governments: 1962,* vol. 1, "Governmental Organization" (Washington, D.C.: Government Printing Office, 1963), pp. 11–12.

For this report, a distinction has been made in certain tabulations between the "central portions" of SMSA's and their "outlying portions." In general, the central portion consists of each county that includes the central city or cities of the area, that is, the city or cities named in the title of the area. Each metropolitan area in New England is treated as though it were a single-county area with no outlying portion, except for the "out-of-state" parts of the three interstate areas there. Altogether, each of 139 SMSA's is considered here to consist of only a central portion, the 18 entirely intrastate areas in New England and the 121 single-county areas located in other parts of the country. Statistics here on outlying portions of metropolitan areas thus pertain to the noncentral-county parts of the 70 multiple-county SMSA's located outside New England, plus the out-of-state parts of the three interstate New England areas.

The 1960 Census of Population showed nearly two thirds of the population of the United States residing within SMSA's, 113 million persons of the nationwide total of 179 million. There were 18,442 governments within these 212 areas in early 1962, or 20 percent of all local governments in the nation. This number included 6004 independent school districts, while an additional 601 school systems operated in metropolitan areas as adjuncts of other governments.

Table 1 contains a summary of the 1962 data on numbers of local governments, by type, within and outside of metropolitan areas.

TABLE 1

TYPE OF GOVERNMENT	UNITED STATES, TOTAL	WITHIN SMSA's	OUTSIDE SMSA's	PERCENT IN SMSA's
All local governments	91,185	18,442	72,743	20.2
School districts	34,678	6,004	28,674	17.3
Other	56,507	12,438	44,069	22.0
Counties	3,043	310	2,733	10.2
Municipalities	17,997	4,142	13,855	23.0
Townships	17,144	2,575	14,569	15.0
Special districts	18,323	5,411	12,912	29.5
Dependent school systems[a]	2,341	601	1,740	25.7

[a] Not included in count of governments.

Table 2 distributes metropolitan areas and their population and local governments by population-size groups of areas.

Metropolitan areas have participated, but to only a rather limited extent, in the reduction which has occurred since 1957 in the number of school districts in the nation as a whole. During this interval, the SMSA's have experienced a material net increase in other types of local governments, as shown in Table 3.

A considerable fraction of all special district governments in the nation are found in SMSA's, and this is particularly true for those units concerned with certain functions. Table 4 is a summary of special districts, by functional class. . . .

TABLE 2

SMSA SIZE GROUP (1960 POPULATION)	NUMBER OF SMSA's	POPULATION, 1960 (000)	LOCAL GOVERNMENTS, 1962
All SMSA's	212	112,885	18,442
1,000,000 or more	24	61,582	7,227
500,000 to 999,999	29	19,215	2,857
300,000 to 499,999	28	10,373	2,146
200,000 to 299,999	41	10,182	3,141
100,000 to 199,999	68	9,772	2,540
50,000 to 99,999	22	1,761	531

TABLE 3

TYPE OF LOCAL GOVERNMENTS	LOCAL GOVERNMENTS IN THE 212 SMSA's		INCREASE OR DECREASE (—), 1957 TO 1962	
	1962	1957	Number	Percent
Total	18,442	17,984	458	3
School districts	6,004	7,486	—1,482	—20
Other	12,438	10,498	1,940	18
Counties	310	311	— 1	a
Municipalities	4,142	3,844	298	8
Townships	2,575	2,607	— 32	— 1
Special districts	b5,411	3,736	b1,675	45

a Less than 0.5 percent.
b Including some types of entities not formerly subject to classification as independent governmental units.

TABLE 4

TYPE OF SPECIAL DISTRICT	UNITED STATES, TOTAL	WITHIN SMSA's	OUTSIDE SMSA's	PERCENT IN SMSA's
Total	18,323	5,411	12,912	30
Natural resources	6,158	946	5,212	15
Other than natural resources	12,165	4,465	7,700	37
Fire protection	3,229	1,174	2,055	36
Housing	1,099	391	708	36
Sewerage	937	570	367	61
Water supply	1,502	764	738	51
Other single-function districts	5,088	1,388	3,700	27
Multiple-function districts	310	178	132	57

Twenty-three percent of the municipal governments in the entire nation, and about three fourths of all municipal residents, were located in SMSA's in 1962. These areas include all municipalities of 50,000 or more inhabitants, as well as a considerable proportion of all other sizable municipalities. However, within SMSA's as well as elsewhere, the majority of municipal governments are units of relatively small population. About half of the 4142 municipalities in these areas had fewer than 2500 inhabitants each in 1960; these 2105 minor units altogether served only two million persons, or 1.7 percent of the total population of SMSA's. Another 28 million metropolitan-area residents, or 24.8 percent of the total in 1960, lived outside of any municipally governed area.

The 6605 public school systems in SMSA's represented only 18 percent of all such systems in the nation in 1962, but had 22.4 million pupils enrolled, or about 59 percent of the nationwide total. The metropolitan areas have a considerable fraction of all relatively large school systems—with 2557 of the United States total of 5838 systems enrolling 1200 pupils or more in the 1961–1962 school year—and the bulk of public school enrollment within SMSA's is accounted for by such systems. However, there are large numbers of small school units in the SMSA's—2638 with fewer than 300 pupils each in the 1961–1962 school year, including 120 with from one to 50 pupils and 912 nonoperating school systems. . . .

Individual metropolitan areas differ widely in complexity of local government structure. The number of local governments per area ranges from only a few each in several single-county SMSA's (mainly in the South) up to a total of 250 or more in each of 11 areas, as is shown in Table 5.

TABLE 5

STANDARD METROPOLITAN STATISTICAL AREA	LOCAL GOVERNMENTS, 1962			POPULATION, 1960 (000)
	Total	Central portion	Outlying portions	
Chicago, Ill.	1,060	460	600	6,221
Philadelphia, Pa.	963	4	959	4,343
Pittsburgh, Pa.	806	358	448	2,405
New York, N.Y.	555	3	552	10,695
St. Louis, Mo.	439	4	435	2,060
San Francisco-Oakland, Calif.	398	84	314	2,783
Portland, Ore.	374	137	237	822
Los Angeles-Long Beach, Calif.	348	234	114	6,743
Seattle, Wash.	281	190	91	1,107
Minneapolis-St. Paul, Minn.	261	113	148	1,482
San Bernardino-Riverside-Ontario, Calif.	250	250		810

These 11 areas include 9 to the 24 SMSA's that had at least 1 million inhabitants in 1960. Together, they account for 5735 local governments, or about 1 in 17 of the nationwide total. From 200 to 249 local governments are reported for each of 13 other SMSA's.

PART TWO

Rationale
of Metropolitan
Reform

Rampant urbanization early in the twentieth century brought to the forefront a question which is still a major political issue: Is a fractionated system of local government, which originated in the seventeenth and eighteenth centuries as a system of rural government, capable of coping with metropolitan exigencies resulting from the urbanization of the areas beyond the political boundaries of central cities? Metropolitan reformers have found the system of local government to be anachronistic and unable to meet the needs of vastly different economic, social, and physical conditions.

The rationale of the early metropolitan reformers was simple. They tended to view the metropolitan problem as one of a multiplicity of local governments. Reading 5 is evidence that a recent study group agrees with the early reformers' diagnosis. The fragmented governmental system has been held responsible for a long ballot, conflicts of authority, duplication of services, inadequate service levels, lack of area-wide planning and programming, financial inequities, and other problems as indicated in Readings 2 and 4. The reformers were convinced metropolitan areas possessed adequate resources to solve their problems provided the resources could be mobilized on an area-wide basis. To strengthen the case for the reform of what they considered to be an immensely complex and irrational governmental system, the reformers catalogued the omnifarious problems of metropolitan areas which are not respecters of artificial political boundaries.

The early metropolitan reformers were influenced greatly by the scientific management movement and advocated the use of the most efficient organizational structure which would permit the achievement of economies of scale. In their eyes, the fragmented government of the metropolis was dysfunctional and met the service needs of its citizens in an uneven fashion, and in some cases failed entirely to meet the service needs. Furthermore, the reformers were disturbed by the relatively small size of many units of local government which prevented them from achieving economies of scale in rendering public services.

Metropolitan reformers acknowledge that the system of fragmented government was adequate for a rural society, but are dismayed by the inability of the system of local government to solve area-wide problems in an age when over 50 percent of the population lives in suburban communities and the line of demarcation between the central city and the suburbs is no longer sharp. The reformers stress the interdependence of the central city and the suburbs, and they are convinced that metropolitan areas are faced with serious problems of an area-wide nature. These problems cannot be solved within a governmental framework which fragments authority and responsibility and places nearly insuperable barriers in the path of proposals for area-wide action. Furthermore, the reformers maintain that a problem of metropolitan responsibility exists because citizens have no one government in a balkanized political system to hold responsible for metropolitan failures.

Reformers recommend a comprehensive approach to the solution of metropolitan problems and the devising of rational governmental structures adequate to deal with the problems of urban growth. The prescription for improved metropolitan health issued by reformers has varied from one metropolitan area to another and has included annexation of suburbs by the central city, central-city exercise of extraterritorial powers, city-county consolidation, conversion of the traditional county government into a metropolitan county government, metropolitan federation, and the creation of metropolitan special districts. Not all metropolitan reformers have been united on a given prescription for a given area. Many, for example, object to the creation of metropolitan special districts as they would fragment further the governmental system of the metropolis.

In recent years, there has been a growing awareness of the complexity of metropolitan problems and a questioning of the assumptions of the early metropolitan reformers and the desirability of a wholesale consolidation of local governments. A number of study groups have concluded that the government of the metropolis can be made functional without the creation of a single government for the metropolitan area.

In general, recent reform proposals have not been offering a "cut-and-dried" prescription for the improvement of all metropolitan areas or advocating a wholesale consolidation of governments. Nevertheless, there are still a number of individuals and organizations who are convinced it is not possible to solve certain area-wide problems without a fundamental reorganization of the governmental system of the metropolis. In 1966, for example, the Committee for Economic Development called for a revolutionary readjustment of local government in the United States which included the reduction of 80,000 local governments to 16,000.

Many reformers in recent years have included political acceptability in the calculus of a proposal for the reorganization of a metropolitan area. That the incremental approach to organization change in metropolitan areas has the best prospect for political success has become apparent and is reflected in proposals for restructuring the existing county government as a metropolitan government, as suggested in Reading 4, in lieu of creating a new metropolitan government.

4. The Communities' Decisions*

The Cleveland Metropolitan Services Commission prepared 31 separate reports as background material in support of a proposed Cuyahoga County Home Rule Charter which was defeated by the voters in November 1959. The excerpts from the commission's report—*Government Costs: Questions for Community Decision*—identifies fiscal weakness, inefficient governments, and lack of metropolitan budgetary control as the basic metropolitan financial problems. The commission believes the problems of the metropolitan Cleveland area are not of such serious proportion as to warrant the wholesale consolidation of the 105 local governments, but it does advocate selective consolidation of functions and governments, reallocation of revenue, and the transfer of responsibility for certain functions to the county level.

THE BASIC PROBLEMS

The three basic problems of metropolitan area finance in Greater Cleveland can be restated in the following terms:

Problem Number 1

Fiscal inadequacy in the local unit. A combination in some government units of high density of population and low assessed valuation per capita; a size in other government units too small to provide for even the minimum needs of their citizens.

We must question whether, over the long term, we are willing to permit some communities to continue as second and third class citizens as far as a reasonable level of municipal services and public education are concerned.

Problem Number 2

Costs and inefficiencies of fragmented government. The high per unit costs of small units of government, the risks of expensive duplications when several different governments are performing the same type of service in a limited area,

---

* From *Government Costs: Questions for Community Decision* (Cleveland: Cleveland Metropolitan Services Commission, 1959), pp. 34–37 and 43–46.

and the premium price we must pay for several small public works projects as an alternative to a single larger one.

We must question whether the small government which is said to be "close to the people" is really providing the special values with which we credit it and whether the extra price we pay for it—in time and money—is justified.

Problem Number 3

Lack of metropolitan planning and budgetary control. No machinery for area-wide planning, administration, and financing of such major public works projects as sanitary sewerage and storm drainage which cannot be handled within geographical and financial limitations of the single municipality. No comprehensive provisions for balancing area-wide governmental service needs against available tax resources.

We must question whether or not we wish to perpetuate a fiscal and administrative pattern which inhibits the metropolitan area's capacity to move ahead because it does not have a governmental base adequately equipped to take the leadership in meeting area-wide problems.

These are the basic problems. . . . What are the more basic solutions?

WAIT AND SEE?

There are many who say that the present system has stood the test of time. No single governmental unit in Cuyahoga County faces the immediate prospect of financial bankruptcy and governmental chaos. The central city, while its needs are tremendous, is in stable financial shape, thanks to its 70 percent industrial and commercial tax duplicate, no city income tax, no bonded debt in the school system, and a tax rate still within reasonable bounds.

Although there are some notable weak spots, our suburban governments (albeit treading a financial tight rope) are getting by on a day-to-day basis and can probably expect to do so for some time to come. There are some wastes and inefficiencies in the present system of doing business, but they are hardly critical.

The county government, with some difficulty, has found it possible to assume new responsibilities in recent years and has somehow managed to make financial ends meet. To be sure, it has been unable to tackle some important jobs, but it has done others quite well. We can recognize "wait and see" as an alternative, but it is not the one that a progressive metropolitan area can select as satisfactory.

WHOLESALE CONSOLIDATION?

The opposite extreme is the insistence that the real answer to our problems is wholesale consolidation—either through annexation to the central city or through merging of all governments under the county.

Superficially, such an alternative is rational because it recognizes the under-lying unity of purpose and self-interest in the Cleveland metropolitan area. It might assure the people of the whole community of a voice in all the govern-mental decisions that affect their daily lives. But then you must ask—who? how? and when? The rational, neat answer becomes nonrational because it flies in the face of political tradition and tears down long-standing channels of communica-tion and action. Wholesale consolidation may produce mere bigness and may dilute even further popular participation in local governmental decisions.

It would hardly seem that the disease is so acute as to demand a treatment so drastic.

THE MIDDLE ROAD?

The obvious course, it seems to us, is to seek out the "middle road," attempt to reduce or eliminate our most serious governmental deficiencies, and yet still retain some of the values of our present way of doing things. The basic element in such a course is developing a realistic balance between the interests of the metropolitan area and the interests of the individual units—a realistic allocation of administrative and financial powers between their regional government and the local governments.

Such a course would recognize the importance of voluntary action on the part of individual communities on the one hand and of real and effective leadership at the metropolitan level on the other. It would attempt to eliminate weaknesses without forcing uniformity.

In charting this "middle road," we should recall again the three major finan-cial problems that we face: fiscal inadequacy in the local unit; costs and inefficien-cies of fragmented government; lack of metropolitan planning and budgetary control.

To meet these problems will require a series of basic policy decisions on the part of the whole community and its many parts. It is not our purpose to set forth a rigid accounting of what these decisions should be but rather to identify the principal steps which might be taken to solve these problems. With the possibilities before them, the communities must make the decisions.

The three avenues are:

1. Selective Consolidation
2. Reallocation of Revenues
3. Transfers of Governmental Responsibility

Each one of these alternatives can help meet one or more of the three main problems that have been outlined. The possibilities outlined below are offered as suggestive examples rather than as specific recommendations.

SELECTIVE CONSOLIDATION

Selective consolidation can include: (1) consolidation of particular governmental functions by service contract or, (2) consolidation of neighboring governmental units in order to achieve a broader financial base.

The *selective service consolidation* has the obvious advantage of spreading what may be a large financial burden over an area large enough to bear that burden. For example, the Metro reports on police services and fire services suggested that consolidations among small communities for public safety purposes only might be one useful means of meeting the financial problems of the small community. A suggested minimum standard of five full-time policemen in each municipal department—one policeman around-the-clock—would be an intolerable financial burden for a good many communities in Cuyahoga County. . . . The minimum cost of such a department would be about $35,000 a year. This figure is larger than the entire operating budgets of *eight* communities in Cuyahoga County.

It is possible that some communities can realize financial and governmental service benefits from developing further the technique of selective service consolidation.

The second alternative—*selective consolidation of neighboring governmental units*—has been less widely used in Cuyahoga County. In fact, the trend over the years has been toward further fragmentation of government rather than consolidation.

We can, however, see a number of cases in which the development of school districts—either by accident or design—has tended to relieve what could be difficult financial problems. In each of these examples, we see a grouping of high valuation communities with their less wealthy neighbors—and thus a more equitable distribution of a heavy financial burden. . . .

Quite recently four eastern suburbs—Chagrin Falls, Chagrin Falls Township, Moreland Hills, and Bentleyville—have been discussing seriously the possibility of a consolidation. Such a consolidation, if it were effected, would produce a city of 5500 population with a comfortable municipal tax base of $3400 per capita. Already these four communities, whose combined area is 12½ square miles, are closely tied together with police mutual aid contracts, fire service contracts, and inclusion within the same municipal court district. In every case, their per capita expenditures for municipal operations are at least 30 percent above the median for all the villages of Cuyahoga County. It is possible that such a consolidation might bring noticeable reductions in the per unit costs of government and would decidedly benefit each one in terms of better quality services.

Selective and voluntary consolidations of communities can relieve problems of the *fiscal inadequacy of the local unit* and problems of the *costs and inefficiencies of fragmented government*. . . .

The possibility of selective consolidation among neighboring units can also be applied on a countywide scale—as in the case of the nine library districts. The Main Branch of the Cleveland Public Library in one respect serves as an area-wide facility; more than half the library cards issued by the main branch are held by suburban residents. With respect to its branch libraries, however, it serves a purely local function in the separate neighborhood. Likewise, other library systems—Lakewood and East Cleveland, for example—fill a metropolitan function in providing services to residents of neighboring communities as well as serving their own residents. All the libraries of Cuyahoga County are dependent upon the same source of funds—the intangible tax revenues, which are collected throughout the county. Serious discussions have been held in recent weeks about the feasibility of consolidating some or all the library systems—in the interests of lessening competition among libraries for the available funds, of spreading administrative costs over a larger area, and of eliminating duplications of services and facilities. Such a program of consolidation need not weaken the special neighborhood role that is filled by suburban and branch libraries in their own particular areas.

There is undoubtedly a sound financial case in favor of many of the consolidations which have been discussed in this section. It is obvious, however, that decisions on possible consolidations are highly charged political questions.

Notwithstanding the political problems involved, the people of Cuyahoga County should consider very seriously the potential benefits that can accrue. In situations where the officials of neighboring jurisdictions show an unreasonable unwillingness to explore the possibilities of what seem to be logical and desirable consolidations, this attitude should perhaps be taken into account in the allocation of money from the local government fund and any other funds whose allocation may become subject to the discretion of the County Budget Commission. In such a way we might gradually develop a metropolitan public policy that would actively encourage sensible consolidations in the interests of governmental economy and fiscal stability.

REALLOCATION OF REVENUES

Reallocation of revenues can be accomplished by (1) revision of the allocation base for the local government fund as established by the county budget commission or, (2) distribution of a county-wide levy of a given millage back to the local governments on a per capita or per student basis.

In considering the first alternative, we have noted that there is no clear-cut relationship between the tax effort of a community and the amount it receives from the local government fund. The amount of money available for distribution from this source is comparatively small—about 7 percent of all local revenues—but a revised allocation system which gives greater consideration to the low valuation, high density communities might serve to lessen some individual problems of fiscal inadequacy.

We recognize, however, that any reallocations should be carried out on a gradual basis. Otherwise, imbalance problems might be aggravated rather than alleviated in certain communities.

The second alternative can best be illustrated by presenting a specific example and illustrating its financial impact upon the various government units of Cuyahoga County. The particular county-wide levy that is analyzed here is a 10-mill levy against the entire tax duplicate of the county. Receipts from this tax would be distributed to each of the 32 school districts on a per pupil basis. The main purpose of such a technique would be to assist the financially pressed school districts.

In considering any proposal of this sort, it is essential to remember that the state of Ohio accomplishes a certain amount of equalization of resources in school districts through its School Foundation Program. If any local equalization program were to be adopted, it should be structured so as to avoid jeopardizing the status of Cuyahoga County schools districts under the state program.

These alternatives are offered to illustrate *principles* rather than to serve as specific proposals. In evaluating them for their possible applicability to the fiscal problems of the Cleveland metropolitan area, we should keep four basic principles in mind:

1. The aim of any such alternatives should be the achievement of a *minimum level of local services* through the metropolitan area rather than uniformity of service level. Communities with above average taxable resources should not be penalized needlessly.

2. Communities should not be permitted to become a financial liability to other communities if their financial problems are primarily the result of deliberate decision—that is, either the refusal to approve reasonable tax levies for services or the unreasonable exclusion of commercial and industrial development.

3. Decisions based on these alternatives should as much as possible be decisions of local option, with the metropolitan agency primarily providing leadership, encouragement, and financial and planning analysis.

4. A metropolitan agency should take an active role in reviewing and making recommendations on proposed changes in governmental boundaries that would tend to create further uneconomic "fragmentation" of the more than 100 government units in Cuyahoga County.

TRANSFERS OF GOVERNMENTAL RESPONSIBILITY

Many Metro reports have presented an irrefutable basis of fact to support the proposition that some governmental services cannot be adequately provided on a purely *local* basis. The summary below indicates those services which have been identified as "metropolitan":

1. Fire protection
   Basic protection*
   Specialized services
   (1) Communications
   (2) Training*
   (3) Fire prevention*
   (4) Investigation*
2. Land use planning
   Planning of county projects
   Advisory local planning services*
3. Libraries
   All library services (except school libraries)
4. Police services
   Basic patrol and protection*
   Specialized services
   (1) Criminal investigation*
   (2) Crime laboratories*
   (3) Communications and teletype
   (4) Records
   (5) Advanced training*
5. Public health
   Preventive public health programs
   County hospitals and nursing homes
6. Public recreation
   Advisory Office of Recreation*
7. Public welfare
   All local public assistance programs
8. Rubbish collection and disposal
   Refuse disposal facilities*
9. Transportation
   Main highways
   Mass transit

* Available only upon the request of the local municipality.

       Ports and terminals
       Carrier regulation (intermunicipal)
       Traffic engineering (main highways only)
10. Public utilities (regional)
       Water
       Sanitary sewerage
       Storm drainage

The prime justification of a transfer of governmental responsibility from the local to the metropolitan level is to increase the total community's capacity to move ahead. We know, for example, that it will be impossible to meet our sanitary sewerage and storm drainage needs in the next few years without tackling the problem on at least a county-wide basis. Topography and finances make any other course of action extravagant. Likewise, a strong metropolitan leadership role is needed in other fields such as main highway transportation, public health, and public welfare. If we are to follow the prudent course of assigning area-wide services and facilities to the metropolitan level while keeping local services and facilities at the local level, this entails wide utilization of the technique of transferring governmental responsibility.

In many instances, such transfers can materially lessen problems of fiscal inadequacy in the local unit through broadening the base of financial support. The two-year-old transfer of Cleveland City Hospital to Cuyahoga County is a case in point. Through its assumption of the annual operating deficit, the county relieved the city of Cleveland from a burden that threatened to create a serious financial problem in the central city. At the same time, the transfer made easier the broader availability of the hospital's services and placed the ownership and control of the institution with the people of the entire area which could be expected to be served by the hospital.

The passage of a special welfare levy (to provide funds to meet the hospital's annual deficit) by the people of Cuyahoga County provided the county with the necessary funds to discharge this new responsibility. Without that provision, the transfer of the hospital might have only shifted an imbalance problem from the city of Cleveland to the county—particularly in view of the county's limited share of the non-voted millage.

We would suggest the following general principles which should guide discussions of any proposed transfer of governmental responsibility:

1. When a facility or program is transferred from one unit of government to another, the corresponding outstanding indebtedness and financial resources should likewise be transferred.

2. Before one government succeeds to the properties or obligations of another, a *mutually* acceptable plan of transfer should be developed—including

provision for compensation for partially-paid-for facilities, or preferential rates as an alternative, and equitable arrangements about the assumption of debt.

3. Further compensation for already paid-for facilities only after considera-tion of the burdens contemplated for the development of new and similar facilities and of the beneficial effects to the total community.

In considering transfer of governmental responsibility as an alternative, we must recognize the county government's need for an administrative structure and a financial flexibility that can assure its ability to carry on the added responsibilities.

5. City and Suburb:
Community or Chaos*

The Washington State Legislature in 1961 established a Joint Com-mittee on Urban Area Government and authorized it to appoint a citizens advisory committee composed of representatives of small and large urban communities. The advisory committee's 1962 report to the joint com-mittee succinctly itemizes the manifold problems associated with a multi-plicity of governments in metropolitan areas and concludes that the system of local government is politically unsound and fiscally inequitable. In advancing basic principles as guidelines for the improvement of govern-mental structure, the advisory committee rejects interlocal contracts because they perpetuate fragmented local government. It favors regional coopera-tion, however, as exemplified by the Puget Sound Governmental Con-ference, a metropolitan council of governments. Other councils are dis-cussed in Readings 31 and 32.

TOO MANY GOVERNMENTS . . .

Local government in Washington was designed for a simpler day when people were fewer and the line between city and country was clear. It has grown by patchwork additions of cities and special purpose districts and is now a crazy quilt of overlapping jurisdictions, costly in higher taxes to the homeowner and businessman alike.

---

* From *Report of the Citizens Advisory Committee to the Joint Committee on Urban Area Government* (Legislature of the State of Washington, June 1962), pp. 4–12.

Most of the governmental units, like most of the people, are in the metropolitan areas. In King County there are now over 200 units, more than any other county in the United States except one. At least 15 local units have been added in the last three years, and proceedings are now pending for the creation of three more small cities and a special purpose district. Similarly, in 1959, Spokane County had 135 units; Yakima, 119; Pierce and Snohomish, each 93; and Clark County, 44.

. . . FOR EACH PART.

The profusion of "little governments" is well illustrated by the Highline School District, south of Seattle, whose 100,000 residents are governed, taxed, or served by King County, the school district, the Port of Seattle, four small cities (Kent, Tukwila, Des Moines and Normandy Park), eight sewer districts, eleven water districts, six fire districts, a library district, a road district, a drainage district and the County Housing Authority—36 local governments, with over one hundred elected officials.

The suburbs east of Lake Washington show a similar patchwork of cities and special districts, with, for example, two islands of unincorporated territory inside the city of Bellevue, and 26 units of local government having jurisdiction over part or all of the Bellevue School District.

The Tacoma metropolitan area is following the same pattern, with Pierce County, 11 cities, and 57 districts electing 299 officials in the urbanized area.

The Spokane area adds townships to county, cities, and districts, and has special problems from the 43 domestic water suppliers of suburban Spokane.

. . . NONE FOR THE WHOLE.

A large urban area is more than the sum of its separate parts. It is a complex system for production, recreation, education, worship, play, and rest. All its people share a common interest in the efficiency, order, and livability of the whole. A dust-producing manufacturing plant can be located in an industrial zone of one city adjacent to residences in the next. Poor streets in one area can shift traffic to another community ill prepared or situated for the load. Wastes from one community can pollute the waters or air of another. Residents of a densely populated area without parks can overcrowd the playgrounds and picnic spots of neighboring communities. Small sewage treatment plants side by side can unnecessarily raise everyone's costs. There is in economic and social fact a metropolitan community, but in government there is none.

FRAGMENTED GOVERNMENT IS POLITICALLY UNSOUND . . .

Such fragmentation is sapping the strength of local government. No citizen, no matter how civic minded, can inform himself of the affairs of a dozen or more local governments. No voter can keep track of the performance of 50 or more local elected officials. Citizens have lost control of their local affairs when they are unable to place responsibility for faulty decisions or inaction.

Nor is this divided government responsive, for it cannot respond to major problems which ignore its boundary lines. Time, energy, and money are being wasted in mounting traffic congestion; water and air pollution grow; downtowns are in trouble, older neighborhoods blighted, and social problems rise. Each of the hundreds of local officials of the metropolitan areas is alert to see that no action to remedy these ills falls too heavily on his jurisdiction; none is responsible to see that there *is* action. Frustrated by local inertia and confusion, the citizen turns increasingly to state and federal programs for urban needs.

. . . AND FINANCIALLY UNFAIR.

Fragmentation damages the financial as well as the political health of local government. Traditionally it was assumed that a family lived, worked, shopped, and sent its children to school within the boundaries of one unit of local government. But such is rarely the case today when, for example, a man living in Lynnwood may drive through Seattle to and from work at a plant in south King County, while his family shops in Everett. Property taxes on the family's house are paid to the city of Lynnwood and to Snohomish County, while the street, police, and other costs of rush-hour traffic are borne by the city of Seattle. The plant, moreover, pays property taxes neither to the city, county, nor school district which serves the employee's family, nor to the city whose facilities bring its worker to his job. Fragmentation of the metropolitan areas separates benefits and burdens in ways which are often basically unfair.

In general, it is the central cities which suffer most to provide extra streets, police protection, parks, libraries and other facilities for expanded daytime populations of suburban residents they cannot tax. There is, moreover, in our local property tax system a built-in inequity between city and county residents. City residents tax their property to pay for their police, parks, garbage dumps, and other services; they are taxed again by the county partly to furnish some of these urban services for the residents of unincorporated areas. In King County, where property within the city of Seattle constitutes two thirds of the county's assessed valuation, and property within all cities and towns constitutes four fifths, city and town property owners are paying 80 cents of every dollar spent by the county on local urban services for tens of thousands of county residents. In 1962, this amounted to a subsidy of about $2,300,000 from Seattle property, about $2,775,000 from all the cities taken together. Ironically, elderly and low-income property owners struggling to rehabilitate their property in Seattle's Yesler-Atlantic urban renewal area are subsidizing residents of expensive suburban communities.

A similar inequity appears to exist in other populous counties where the county general fund supports police protection, local parks, garbage dumps and other urban services for densely settled unincorporated areas. In Pierce County, city of Tacoma property is 54 percent of the total assessed valuation, and property within all cities and towns represents 63.4 percent; in Spokane County, corresponding figures for the city of Spokane and all cities are 62.8 percent and 65 percent, respectively. In these counties, as in King, city property owners pay most of the cost of the local urban services received by county residents from the county general fund.

TO MOVE PEOPLE AND GOODS . . .

To function, an urban community must move people and goods quickly and economically between areas for work, recreation, and rest. Transportation is everybody's problem—the downtown merchant wants easier movement for his shoppers and places for them to park; city residents are taxed to pay for wide arterials used to capacity only twice a day; the manufacturer suffers higher costs from late employees, delayed raw materials, slow deliveries, and valuable land tied up in parking lots; the distributor needs extra salesmen to serve the urban area. Suburban residents spend precious hours meant for children and gardens in autos and buses on congested highways and bridges, wasting the gain of shorter working hours on longer travel time. For many, commuting is a twice daily ordeal through a miles-long alley of used car lots, junk yards, service stations, and billboards. To all of us, inadequate transportation means higher costs of what we buy.

For years transportation in our metropolitan areas has meant more and more automobiles, more and still more highways, fewer and still fewer riders on public buses, longer and longer commuting times. We have only to look at Los Angeles to see the futility of sole reliance on the automobile-highway answer. There, over $2 billion have been spent on freeways, and the automobile has consumed two thirds of the downtown land for highways, streets, and parking facilities—without ending congestion.

The peak hours are the critical times, the times which overtax facilities, pocketbooks, nerves, and patience. There is growing agreement that we must supplement the automobile with improved mass transportation, growing recognition that capital facilities of such a system will require tax support from the whole "commuter shed," growing realization that other alternatives are still more costly.

It is now too late to design mass transit facilities into Seattle's $175-million central freeway or the $30-million Evergreen Point Bridge, but this lack of coordination should not be allowed to continue. We cannot afford more single-purpose structures when multiple needs must be met. About $½ billion will be spent by the state, county, and cities in King County in the next decade on highways and bridges, many of which are presently being designed. They must be planned and coordinated for the requirements of a mass transit system as well as private automobiles. There is, however, no unit of government presently making such plans, none coordinating state and local activities into a balanced urban transportation system.

. . . KEEP PARKS AND OTHER OPEN SPACE . . .

Of all the problems of the metropolitan area, none is more urgent than the acquisition of parks and recreation sites and the preservation of other open land. In the words of a recent editorial, we are witnessing a "voracious gulping of the land," an urban sprawl so rapid that if present suburban land-use patterns continue, the more than 1 million additional people expected in King County by the end of this century could fill it from Puget Sound to the foothills of the Cascades.

Recreational use of land is growing even faster than population, for we have more leisure time each year, more opportunity to enjoy walking, boating, sports, and family outings. For parks and waterfront, however, we are living largely on the generosity of our parents and grandparents. Seattle's 315,312 people of 1920 had 2209 acres of parks, about 144 persons per park acre; its 558,000 people of 1960 had only 2646 park acres, or 211 persons per acre. In the suburbs where population has boomed since World War II, local park acquisition has not kept pace with population growth. King County's recent purchase of Marymoor Farm adds its first new large park to serve the entire area in many years. Public support of this purchase shows the rising awareness of open space needs.

The Spokane and Tacoma urban areas must also act now to preserve parks, waterfront, and other accessible open land for the thousands of new residents coming each year. The city of Spokane has many large parks, almost all acquired half a century ago, but there are already few sites of ten acres or more left in the fast growing valley to the east. In the Tacoma suburbs, too, concern over parks is rising. But action is slow in coming, and action cannot be delayed. Each piece of land is unique; once developed, it is lost to the general public. Indeed, experience shows that park land must be acquired beyond the developed areas, for land prices rise quickly once subdivision begins nearby.

Washington's large urban communities are peculiarly blessed with forests, lakes, and mountain views. But woodlands can be cut, lakes shut off from public access, views blocked. The first resident of a hillside may enjoy watching the construction of a house in the valley below, but he is shocked as woods and farms change to rooftops, wires, and television antennae. The fisherman is not concerned over the first summer house along his favorite stream, but is confused and angry when a solid row of houses blocks him from the banks. Our grand-parents looked ahead to keep green space, beaches, and beauty for us, but our vision has been short in recent times. We are taking our landscape for granted; its beauty is being mined, not tended.

. . . PROVIDE CLEAN WATER FOR ALL . . .

Like transportation and open land, the provision of clean water, the disposal of wastes, and the preservation of clean air are tasks increasingly difficult for each local unit to perform. Seattle's water lines and Seattle Metro's sewage disposal plan demonstrate, however, the effectiveness and economy of metro-politan-wide systems. Both have anticipated the needs of an entire urban area; both demonstrate that metropolitan problems can be solved when attacked comprehensively, and with the courage to plan for decades ahead.

Seattle brings pure mountain water from the Cascades at low cost to about 735,000 people of the metropolitan area, serving not only its residents, but selling wholesale water to 30 water districts and municipalities as well. Present projects, when fully developed, will guarantee mountain water for a future metropolitan population of more than 2 million. In contrast, the city of Tacoma brings its water from the Green River watershed of the Cascades but does not supply the needs of its suburbs. The nearby community of University Place suffers from inadequate water supply and distribution. A metropolitan-wide system would benefit Tacoma and its suburbs alike.

There is a natural water supply under most of the Spokane metropolitan area which is easily reached by wells. As a result, there are 43 domestic water distributors in suburban Spokane. Many of these districts, co-ops, and companies are doing an excellent job within their areas, but duplication of facilities, differ-ing pipe sizes and pressures, and no means for systematic interconnection are shortcomings paid for by suburban residents in increased costs, sometimes in-adequate service, and higher fire insurance rates.

DISPOSE OF WASTES . . .

Sewage disposal presents a still gloomier story in which the structural defects of fragmented local government are sharply exposed. In King County, before establishment of the Municipality of Metropolitan Seattle, raw sewage was being discharged into the Duwamish River, Elliott Bay, and Puget Sound at about 60 places, and 10 to 15 million gallons of treated and untreated wastes went into Lake Washington every day. Effluent from thousands of malfunctioning septic tanks was rising to ground surface and, in some areas, flowing in open ditches. Health agencies necessarily stopped construction in some areas, while elsewhere citizens invested millions of dollars in septic tanks which became more inadequate each day.

Within the metropolitan area, not a single foot of salt water shoreline, and very little fresh water, was safe for recreational use. Lake Washington was degraded and rapidly approaching permanent impairment from algal growth. In brief, water resources were being ruined, health dangers created, orderly growth stunted, millions of dollars wasted, but even after years of discussion, the 19 cities and 22 sewer districts of the Lake Washington watershed could not agree on any joint solution. Fragmented government could not act.

Only state enabling legislation for a metropolitan-wide unit and the voters' establishment of the Municipality of Metropolitan Seattle saved this appalling situation. Since its formation in 1958, Seattle Metro has planned and is now constructing a trunk sewer and treatment system for the entire Lake Washington watershed, a system which will end pollution in the watershed over the next ten years, most of it in the next five. The Metro trunk lines will also permit cities and districts throughout the area to develop orderly and economical sewer systems during the next 75 to 100 years.

Danger signals are growing now in the Spokane metropolitan area where more than 200,000 people literally live on top of their water supply. Blessed by nature with a giant underground river of clean water flowing slowly from the Idaho border beneath valley and city until it empties into the Spokane River, the metropolitan community may spoil this magnificent asset by pollution. The 181,000 people of the city of Spokane discharge wastes through sewers and treatment plant to a spot downstream on the Spokane River. The 46,500 residents of the Valley, however, have only septic tanks draining through gravel and boulders toward the water below. New people arrive every day, new septic tanks are built, and the concentration of effluent in the earth increases. Health authorities have repeatedly warned citizens and local officials that action should begin now, for once pollution is discovered, it will be too late. The water, if contaminated, will not be pure again for years.

Here, also, fragmented government poses barriers to action. The city of

Spokane has no jurisdiction in the Valley; neither county nor township has authority to build sewers; and a proper answer might require action by the entire metropolitan community. Everyone's water supply is threatened, but "everyone" has no government to act.

Tacoma has sewers and treatment plants adequate to handle its own problems of sewage disposal, but problems are accumulating in the suburbs. The drainage area around Lake Steilacoom and that of Clover Creek are reaching an acute state in which not even treated sewage can be safely added. The Lakewood area has problems ahead. There is a clear need for a comprehensive sewage system in the Tacoma area, but there is no unit of government authorized to construct or finance such a system.

. . . AND KEEP CLEAN THE AIR WE BREATHE.

Wastes of the urban community not buried in the earth or discharged into the waters are thrown into the air. Tons of material go up daily from thousands of smokestacks, chimneys, exhaust pipes, and incinerators. Serious health, agricultural, economic, and nuisance effects result—a heavy burden of respiratory ills, dirty buildings, expensive air purification systems, crop damage, and cleaning bills.

Air pollution grows with population, and public patience is already growing short. In December 1961, 1323 residents of Tacoma and Pierce County petitioned the Governor to put a stop to air pollution from a smelter in the city of Ruston, surrounded by Tacoma. Angry housewives of South Seattle forced an end to city burning of refuse at the South Park dump. On February 1, 1962, air pollution made front page headlines in Seattle, for air and sunlight conditions brought serious smog to the Puget Sound region and a new record of air pollution. Smog is rare in western Washington, but the stable air and abundant sunlight of the Spokane area lend themselves to its formation.

That a serious problem exists is clear. Equally clear is the inadequacy of present efforts to manage the problem. Seattle and Tacoma have modest pollution-control ordinances, but air does not respect city boundaries. Pollution-control districts were authorized by the legislature some years ago, but none has been established to date. No authority exists, moreover, for applying controls within any jurisdiction which does not voluntarily agree.

BASIC PRINCIPLES . . .

Blight in cities, inadequate services in the suburbs, jammed highways, polluted water and air—these are warning signals of sickness in our urban communities.

The cure for these ills lies, in the first instance, in major changes in the finances, structure, and powers of local government. Also essential are an informed and active citizenry and good men in office, but they are not enough, for the present structure defeats the efforts of citizens and officials alike. Good men with poor tools work hard to produce little; good men with good tools accomplish much for all.

Authority for contracts between local units is sometimes urged as an alternative to structural reform, but contracts are inadequate for the problems of our metropolitan areas. Agreements for one local unit to provide services for residents of another may be valuable to handle a single or unusual problem, but they perpetuate the political and financial ills of fragmented local government, and may even encourage the formation of more single-purpose cities. Contracts with a monopoly supplier are not always satisfactory for the local government dependent on another unit. Experience leading to the formation of the Municipality of Metropolitan Seattle shows the difficulty of reaching agreement among many local units, and experience elsewhere is similar. In the Los Angeles area, where the contract system is so widely used that many small cities receive almost all their services from Los Angeles County, the transportation situation became so bad that a state organized and directed transportation district had to be imposed. Contracts provide no overall plan for the metropolitan area. They are not as flexible as proper government structure in meeting changing needs. They do nothing to coordinate state and local activities. They perpetuate, and even increase, the separation of the local citizen from control of his local affairs. More than contract power is necessary for our urban areas; the structure of their government must be improved.

Certain basic principles should be guidelines for this improvement:

1. Urban functions of government should be divided among local, metropolitan, and state levels with the alternative of a combined local-metropolitan unit made available. Each level should carry out those functions appropriate to its jurisdiction. Regional cooperation should be enabled and encouraged where regional problems exist.

2. Where local and metropolitan levels are separate, local units should be governments of general powers, furnishing the full range of local urban services, with metropolitan level functions carried out by a multipurpose unit of specified functions.

3. Governments performing urban functions should be representative of and politically responsive to the people within their jurisdiction.

4. There should be a separation of executive, legislative and quasi-judicial power in each unit of government. Executive power should be vested in a single person; legislative power, in a representative body; quasi-judicial power in administrative bodies independent of the legislative and executive authorities. Appeal from decisions of the quasi-judicial bodies should be to the courts.

5. Each unit of urban government should have legal authority and financing resources adequate for its responsibilities.

6. Those who benefit from an urban service should pay for it.

7. There should be no territorial overlapping of governmental units capable of performing the same urban functions at the same level.

8. Maximum provision should be made for future adjustment of units of urban government to meet changing urban conditions.

9. Adequately sized local units of urban government should have all powers of self-government not specifically denied them by the constitution or state law.

. . . AND GOALS

FOR GOVERNMENT

IN METROPOLITAN AREAS . . .

Government in the metropolitan areas should be organized in either of two alternate ways—separate local and metropolitan level governments or a single government for the entire metropolitan area.

SEPARATE LOCAL AND METROPOLITAN LEVELS . . .

Under the first alternative, government at the local level should be cities large enough to economically provide all local urban services—police and fire protection, streets, parks, water, sewers, sidewalks,—and so situated as to cover natural geographic areas or whole communities. Ultimately, these cities of varying sizes should cover the entire territory of the urban area, with parks, forests, farms, and other open space preserved within and between the developed portions to protect the livability and beauty of the environment.

Cities are recommended because they are traditional self-governing units of general powers, able to perform urban services in a planned, integrated, responsive, and democratic fashion. By performing the great bulk of urban services through cities, local government would be kept as close as possible to the citizen. A variety of sizes and kinds of cities within one urban area would be possible, allowing the diversity of development and local attachments which enrich our lives and our democratic process.

For some time, however, there will be parts of the metropolitan area in transition from rural to urban conditions and not yet part of any city. In these areas, all locals services should be provided so as to prepare the area for inclusion in a city at the earliest appropriate time. The county and special districts furnishing these services would be, in this sense, transition governments for these areas.

At the metropolitan level, there should be a government limited to specific functions of area-wide concern, and encompassing for these functions the entire metropolitan area. Such a government could provide planning, transportation, parks and open space, and the "wholesale" or trunk line facilities for water supply and waste disposal.

. . . OR A COMBINED METROPOLITAN COUNTY-CITY

Alternatively to separate local and metropolitan governments, there should be made available to the people the possibility of merging cities and county into a single simplified government for the entire metropolitan area. Authority for such merger exists in our state constitution, but no enabling legislation has been provided.

Under either alternative, urbanized areas should not sprawl forever, merging one into the other. Their growth should be guided. They should be separated by parks, forests, farms, and other open space.

REGIONS . . .

At the regional level, the committee favors cooperation of cities, counties, and metropolitan units, rather than a regional government. We commend the work of voluntary cooperation exemplified by the Puget Sound Governmental Conference. This organization of King, Pierce, Snohomish, and Kitsap Counties, together with the cities of Seattle, Tacoma, and Bremerton, has demonstrated the possibility and flexibility of regional solutions of problems extending beyond one metropolitan area. The Puget Sound Regional Transportation Study, a proposed regional study of open space assets and needs, a proposal for a regional jail district, and many cooperative planning projects show the value of regional cooperation without the necessity of a regional government. Such regional cooperation should be encouraged, and legal authority provided where it may be lacking.

AND THE STATE . . .

Under the American system of government, the state constitution and laws are the source of authority for local governments. The people traditionally seek from the legislature legal authority for forms of local government suitable to their needs. In recent years citizens have sought and the legislature has provided specific solutions for specific problems. But this is no longer enough; the legislature must now provide a goal and a direction for government in the urban areas. It must become more responsive to the needs of the metropolitan areas and equip citizens of those areas to better govern themselves. In addition, the state government should coordinate its own activities affecting the urban areas, and carry out its programs so as to cooperate with local and metropolitan units in the achievement of their goals.

BY EVOLUTION THROUGH LOCAL ACTION

The best method to achieve this desired structure is by changes of law allowing evolution toward the goal over a period of years. In our recommendations, all changes in governmental structure of the urban areas would be initiated by action of local units of government or residents of the area affected. The pace of change would be determined by local needs. Our recommendations would preserve the maximum degree of local control consistent with orderly and effective government in large urban areas. They allow local choice among alternatives while ensuring order and effectiveness.

PART THREE

Politics
of Metropolitan
Reform

Metropolitan reformers have prepared what appear to be convincing arguments in favor of a reorganization of the system of local government, yet voters in referenda generally have been conservative and have rejected proposals for the creation of a metropolitan government by means of annexation, city-county consolidation, federation, or a restructured metropolitan county government.

The failure of reorganization proposals to win voter approval has led to a number of studies to determine why voters generally have been ill disposed toward reform proposals. Most analysts have concluded it is nearly impossible to achieve a major metropolitan governmental reorganization in the United States in the face of political realities: a generally indifferent and lethargic electorate and the strength of groups opposed to changes in the status quo. The obstacles to the implementation of reorganization proposals are described in Reading 6.

In the typical referendum, only 25 percent of the voters exercise their franchise and they are likely to be individuals who believe they will be affected adversely by the proposed reorganization. Public indifference to the metropolitan problem is attributable, at least in part, to the fact that there generally has been no acute governmental crisis within a metropolitan area. The system of fragmented local government may be unable to solve satisfactorily the manifold metropolitan problems documented by the reformers, but on the other hand, the system has not collapsed and a crisis has been avoided. Studies of voter behavior—Readings 8 and 10—reveal that arguments stressing the need for economy and efficiency in the provision of public services and the cor-

49

rection of service inadequacies often are less potent than arguments stressing the importance of keeping the government close to the citizens and free of corruption, and keeping the tax rate low.

A serious obstacle to reform in a number of metropolitan areas is the requirement for concurrent referenda majorities in the central city and the suburban communities. If there is a long history of animosity between the central city and the suburbs, a reform proposal may receive a popular majority in the central city but not in the suburbs or vice versa.

In general, metropolitan reform is supported by the League of Women Voters, metropolitan news media, chambers of commerce, banks and utilities, "good government" associations, and government research bureaus. Upon advancement of a proposal for metropolitan restructuring, a coalition of opposition groups usually is formed with little difficulty. Metropolitan reform commonly is opposed by central-city politicians, organized labor, and minority groups which fear the dilution of their political power. Negroes, in particular, fear their political power will be reduced if the central city is merged with the predominantly white suburbs. Organized labor tends to be distrustful of reform movements that have the strong support of businessmen, and the business community usually is one of the strongest supporters of metropolitan reform. Many government employees and special interest groups fear a restructuring will affect them adversely and, consequently, oppose the reform. Voters of conservative persuasion are fearful of big government, and suburbs may fear domination by the central city.

The precise nature of a reform proposal and the political traditions of the various communities within a metropolitan area will influence the nature of the opposition to the proposal as indicated in Readings 8, 9, and 10. Opposition groups often concede that a readjustment of the system of local government is needed, but object to the particular proposal that has been advanced. Suburban communities often oppose the complete consolidation of local governments with the contention that the central city generally has not been well governed and governmental failures would be compounded by merging the well-governed suburban municipalities with the inefficient and possibly corrupt central city. Metropolitan federation is opposed by individuals and organizations who object to the creation of another unit of local government—the "Metro" government.

One should not assume that the attitude of all suburban communities within a given metropolitan area will be the same on a given reform proposal, or that all central cities will react in the same manner to a given reform proposal. Contrary to the assumption that all suburban municipalities are opposed to reorganization of the government of the metropolis, Reading 7 reveals a split in the ranks of suburban communities in the Cleveland area. In general, proposals which build upon the existing system, such as the reform of county government, appear to have the best chance of winning public acceptance.

The preparation of a socioeconomic profile of the metropolitan area and a dispassionate analysis of the potential support for and opposition to various proposals designed to restructure the governmental system of the metropolis would appear to be one of the first steps that should be undertaken by the promoters of reform. The identification of potential opposition elements will assist in the determination of campaign strategy and suggest the promotion of a particular reform proposal which would mollify potential opposition. To achieve any restructuring of the governmental system, reformers may have to settle for "half a loaf."

6. Voter Reactions
to Governmental
Reorganization
in Metropolitan Areas*

The Advisory Commission on Intergovernmental Relations was established by Congress in 1959 as a permanent bipartisan commission of 26 members to study intergovernmental problems. It has performed an important service by its perceptive analysis of the response of the electorate to proposed governmental reorganization plans in 18 metropolitan areas between 1950 and 1961. This dispassionate study helps to explain why many widely heralded metropolitan reform movements have come to naught and suggests approaches to facilitate reform. Detailed studies of the politics of metropolitan reform in Cleveland, Saint Louis, Miami, and Nashville are contained in Readings 7, 8, 9, and 10, respectively.

From 1950 to 1961, proposals for significant change in local government structure were subjected to popular referendum within 18 of the nation's 212 SMSA's. In 6 instances the proposal and the related referendum involved all of a single-county metropolitan area. In the other 12 cases something less than the entire area was involved—generally, the one most populous county.

For the present report, these 18 reorganization efforts have been reviewed to determine the extent to which common patterns appear concerning the kinds of issues involved, the role of various community elements, and the promotional methods used for and against the reorganization plans. The purpose of this inquiry has been to throw some light on the question: "What factors seem to affect voter reaction toward plans for local government reorganization in metropolitan areas?"

Eight of the 18 surveyed plans passed the referendum hurdle, while the other 10 failed of adoption at the polls—including 2 which received a favorable majority in the overall vote but did not meet a legal requirement for approval by various component portions of the total area involved. From this diverse background, it is hoped, some lessons may be drawn about factors that. con-

* From *Factors affecting Voter Reactions to Governmental Reorganization in Metropolitan Areas* (Washington, D.C.: Advisory Commission on Intergovernmental Relations, May 1962), pp. 1–5 and 24–33.

tribute to the success or failure of referendum-based efforts to change local government in major urban areas.

It should not be inferred that the reorganization plans surveyed have been considered "desirable," so that the proponents were "right" and the opponents "wrong." As has been emphasized in an earlier report of the advisory commission[1] as well as in numerous other writings, there probably is no one ideal pattern of local government structure for metropolitan communities. Furthermore, each of the reorganization proposals covered in this survey was evolved locally by a process of compromise and selection from among alternative approaches. In all or most instances, no doubt, a part of the electorate was ready to concede the need for some change but opposed these particular proposals on the ground that something different would be better.

The question being explored is nonetheless of great importance. Inherited patterns of local government which fail to meet new conditions and needs must somehow be subject to considered review and alteration. Furthermore, changes in local government structure need to have the consent of the governed. To the ordinary run of legislation and operations of state, county, and municipal governments, the consent of the governed is exercised mainly through the voters' power to choose at the polls from among alternative candidates for membership in legislative or governing bodies and for key executive positions. But since commonly there is no one elective body broadly representative of an entire metropolitan area, and since major elements of the local government pattern may have long-range effects, the direct expression of public consent through a popular referendum is typically a condition for significant structural changes in metropolitan local government. From recent experience in nearly a score of areas, we may observe some of the challenges and opportunities involved in seeking such consent.

COVERAGE

Reviewed here are proposals subject to popular referendum, from 1950 to 1961, which aimed at significant change in the structure or powers of local governments within any of the 212 metropolitan areas in the United States. The study does not extend, even where a referendum vote occurred, to proposals involving only annexation of territory by municipalities,[2] incorporation of new

[1] *Governmental Structure, Organization, and Planning in Metropolitan Areas* (Washington, D.C.: House Committee on Government Operations, 1961).

[2] The phrase "involving only annexation of territory by municipalities" is not intended to minimize the importance or potential value of this means for adapting local government

municipalities, school district consolidation or reorganization, municipal charter adoptions and amendments, county charter proposals that involve only one county of a multicounty metropolitan area,[3] or only tax and debt propositions. Also excluded are changes in local government structure that were accomplished directly by state legislation (such as the establishment of some new special districts), or by action of local governing bodies (for example, through intergovernmental contract arrangements). While most of the reorganization proposals studied were to affect more than a single unit of government, four of them were county charter propositions that directly involved only the county government. Each of the latter, however, concerned a county that comprises an entire metropolitan area, so that these particular efforts at restructuring of the county government were considered relevant for inclusion in the present study.

The particular reorganization efforts subject to review, in accordance with these criteria, were as follows:[4]

> Albuquerque-Bernalillo County Consolidation, October 1959: Defeated
> Atlanta-Fulton County "Plan of Improvement," June 1950: Adopted
> Cuyahoga County (Cleveland) Home Rule Charter, November 1959: Defeated
> Denver Metropolitan Capital Improvements District, September 1961: Adopted (Declared unconstitutional, February 13, 1962)
> Durham-Durham County - "Durham County Unified," January 1961: Defeated
> Erie County (Buffalo) Home Rule Charter, November 1959: Adopted
> Knoxville-Knox County Metropolitan Charter—Consolidation, April 1959: Defeated
> Louisville, Ky. "Plan for Improvement," November 1956: Defeated

to metropolitan development, but to distinguish it from the kinds of structural change which were sought in the proposals reviewed in this study. (It may be noted that two of these—the Atlanta and Louisville proposals—contemplated some annexation of territory by the central city as part of a "package" of related actions.) As pointed out in the earlier commission report on metropolitan areas which is cited in footnote 1, some major cities accomplished sizable annexations during the past decade. However, the variety of annexation methods precluded review of these actions in the present study.

[3] There were seven such proposals subject to referendum during the 11-year period covered in this study. Of these, four were adopted (St. Louis County, Mo., 1950; Baltimore County, 1956; Jefferson Parish, La., 1957; and Suffolk County, N. Y., 1958). The other three failed of adoption, all in 1958: Jackson County, Mo.; Marin County, Calif.; and Riverside County, Calif.

[4] It was also decided that reporting here should be limited to one reorganization effort per area. Accordingly, no separate analysis has been made of additional referenda pertaining to local government structure which occurred at other times during this period in three of these areas. These involved establishment of the Metropolitan St. Louis Sewer District in 1954; defeat of a proposal for a Metropolitan St. Louis Transit District in 1955; an unsuccessful "Metropolitan Seattle" referendum in the spring of 1958; and an unsuccessful effort to cut back the Dade County metropolitan system in 1961.

Lucas County (Toledo) Home Rule Charter, November 1959: Defeated
Macon-Bibb County Consolidation, June 1960: Defeated
Miami-Dade County Metropolitan Federation, May 1957: Adopted
Nashville-Davidson County Metropolitan Charter—Consolidation, June 1958: Defeated
Newport News-Warwick Consolidation, July 1957: Adopted
Oneida County (Utica) Home Rule Charter, November 1961: Adopted
Onondaga County (Syracuse) Home Rule Charter, November 1961: Adopted
Richmond City-Henrico County Merger, December 1961: Defeated
Saint Louis "Greater Saint Louis City-County District," November 1959: Defeated
Seattle Special Purpose District, "Municipality of Metropolitan Seattle," September 1958: Adopted

Of these 18 reorganization efforts, only 1 came to a vote before 1956 (Atlanta-Fulton County, 1950), and only 5 others from 1956 to 1958; the 12 remaining fall within the three years, 1959–1961. Half of all these proposals involved a metropolitan area in the South, with the remainder scattered among other parts of the country.

The metropolitan areas where these reorganization plans came to a vote altogether include about one ninth of the population of all metropolitan areas in the nation. Of the ten most populous metropolitan areas—each having at least two million inhabitants in 1960—only the St. Louis area was involved in a significant reorganization effort as defined for study here. Of the 14 next-ranking areas, each with between 1 and 2 million inhabitants, there were four with a reorganization effort during this period—Cleveland, Buffalo, Seattle, and Atlanta. Of the 29 metropolitan areas having a 1960 population of 500,000 to a million, only four—Miami, Denver, Louisville, and Syracuse—were involved. Taking these several groups altogether, then, half of the 18 reorganization efforts covered in this study related to a metropolitan area with a population of at least a ½ million inhabitants, while the others concerned nine of the 159 less populous metropolitan areas. . . .

CONCLUSIONS AND INFERENCES

A number of generalizations with regard to problems of governmental reorganization in metropolitan areas seem to be justified by the record of the 18 area efforts which have been subject to review.

Proposals for governmental reorganization in metropolitan areas have faced a largely apathetic public. Typically, within the 18 areas studied, only one in four persons of voting age bothered to cast a vote on the reorganization proposal.

In only two instances was there voting participation by as much as one third of the adult population. The 18 areas were distributed as follows:

TOTAL REFERENDUM VOTE AS PERCENT OF VOTING-AGE POPULATION	NUMBER OF AREAS
40 to 45	2
30 to 35	2
25 to 29	5
20 to 24	4
15 to 19	3
10 to 14	2

In any sizable community, of course, the total population of voting age includes some persons not entitled to vote—for example, through lack of citizenship, recency of moving into the area, or (generally most important) failure to register. In the absence of uniform registration figures, one may measure public concern with metropolitan reorganization by comparing the vote on such proposals with balloting in Presidential elections. Again a marked divergence appears: the turnout on reorganization matters was typically less than one-half the vote cast for President at the national election of a nearby date. In only two of the 18 areas was the referendum vote more than two thirds of the local vote for President, and in three instances it was less than one-third. The 18 areas were distributed as follows:

TOTAL REFERENDUM VOTE AS PERCENT OF VOTE CAST FOR PRESIDENT IN ELECTION OF NEARBY DATE	NUMBER OF AREAS
70 to 79	2
60 to 69	2
50 to 59	3
40 to 49	5
30 to 39	4
20 to 29	2

It is not being suggested, of course, that an increased turnout at the polls would automatically assure adoption of any particular reorganization proposal. In fact, the 18 efforts studied offer no clear evidence on this score: some obtained a favorable majority with a rather limited turnout of voters, and some lost in spite of a relatively high percentage of voter participation. The following array shows voter participation for the two groups of proposals—the ten which received an over-all popular majority and the eight which failed to do so:

Total Referendum Vote as Percent of Vote Cast for President in Election of Nearby Date	AREAS WHERE MAJORITY OF VOTE CAST WAS	
	For Proposal	Against Proposal
60 or more	2	2
50 to 59		3
40 to 49	4	1
30 to 39	4	
Less than 30		2

However, a big turnout at the polls at least provides an *opportunity* to over-come relatively limited elements opposing change in the status quo. And *whatever the outcome,* the expression of the "consent of the governed" by a considerable fraction rather than by only a minor part of the electorate is likely to have clear advantages. If reorganization is thus authorized, the new arrangements start with a better chance of general community acceptance than if they could be "blamed" upon a limited, though active and effective, minority of the electorate. Furthermore, even though defeat of a particular proposal will generally leave unsolved the problems that led to its development, widespread popular participation in the action is more likely than a sparsely shared referendum to "clear the air" and perhaps to suggest what alternative kinds of change might be more likely to obtain popular approval.

Reorganization efforts should not be undertaken lightly, but with full recognition of obstacles to their success. One kind of problem has been widely noted: the difficulty of obtaining concurrence on desirable change from a majority of voters in various parts of the entire area concerned. The requirements of concurrent majorities has often been cited as a major barrier to local government reorganization.

It is frequently averred that proposals for local government reorganization in metropolitan areas are likely to carry in the central city but lose in the suburbs, giving rise to arguments against requirements for "concurrent majorities." The following tabulation shows how each plan fared in this respect:

Of the 18 proposals surveyed here, only two of the ten which failed of adoption owed their defeat directly to the demand for concurrent majorities—that is, the Louisville "Plan for Improvement," and the Richmond-Henrico merger proposal. Of the reorganization efforts adopted, there were two, Denver and Miami, which depended only upon an areawide majority and would have lost if concurrent majorities within subareas had also been legally necessary. And there were two defeated plans which received a favorable majority in a central city but lost in outlying territory as well as in total (Macon-Bibb County, and Nashville-Davidson County). In the other 12 of the 18 reorganization efforts

PROPOSAL	AREA-WIDE	CENTRAL CITY	OUTSIDE C. C.	NET RESULT
Albuquerque-Bernalillo Co.	Lost	Lost	Lost	Defeated
Atlanta-Fulton Co.	Won	Won	Won	Adopted
Cuyahoga Co. (Cleveland)	Lost	Lost	Lost	Defeated
Denver Metropolitan Area	Won	Won	Lost	Adopted
Durham-Durham Co.	Lost	Lost	Lost	Defeated
Erie Co. (Buffalo) N. Y.	Won	Won	Won	Adopted
Knoxville-Knox Co.	Lost	Lost	Lost	Defeated
Louisville, Ky.	Won	Won	Lost	Defeated
Lucas Co. (Toledo)	Lost	Lost	Lost	Defeated
Macon-Bibb Co.	Lost	Won	Lost	Defeated
Miami-Dade Co.	Won	Won	Lost	Adopted
Nashville-Davidson Co.	Lost	Won	Lost	Defeated
Newport News-Warwick	Won	Won	Won	Adopted
Oneida Co., N. Y.	Won	Won	Won	Adopted
Onondaga Co., N. Y.	Won	Won	Won	Adopted
Richmond-Henrico Co.	Won	Won	Lost	Defeated
St. Louis Metropolitan Area	Lost	Lost	Lost	Defeated
Seattle Metropolitan Area	Won	Won	Won	Adopted

studied, pluralities ran parallel in the central and outlying parts of the area concerned, favorably in six instances and unfavorably in the other six. Altogether, this record suggests a somewhat less forbidding cleavage of public attitudes, geographically, than some discussions of metropolitan problems might suggest. Nonetheless, the common requirement for multiple majorities for adoption of a large-area reorganization proposal must be recognized as a difficult hurdle to surmount.

But there is an even more troublesome problem which has not been widely emphasized. Any particular reorganization plan submitted to referendum is typically competing for public favor not merely against the status quo ("this particular change versus no change at all"), but potentially also against alternative ways of dealing with the problems that gave rise to the proposal. The difficulty of this assignment may be suggested by analogy: it is as if, in order to replace the incumbent of an elective office, some one opposing candidate had to obtain more votes than the total cast for the incumbent *and* all other candidates combined, in a single election open to any number of candidates and without any primary or run-off arangement.

In several of the reorganization efforts surveyed, some of the most effective and telling opposition emphasized the limitations of the change that was being urged as compared with a different kind of structural adjustment. For example, the St. Louis proposal was attacked on the ground that it contemplated the creation of an additional layer of local government, which might be avoided by another kind of change; and some of the proposals elsewhere for city-county combination met the charge that the fixity of county boundaries made this a less desirable reform than extensive use of the municipal annexation approach. Perhaps in certain instances the preference expressed for "something else" is not entirely sincere, but the variety of problems commonly involved in a restructuring of local government in metropolitan areas makes this a plausible basis for opposing any particular proposition.

Thus, the task of the would-be reorganizer is not merely to arouse public concern with existing conditions that are undesirable, nor even besides this to provide a convincing case that his particular plan would provide a reasonable remedy, but also to be prepared to demonstrate that his proposal is better than any available alternative.

Any consequential local government reorganization in a metropolitan area will inevitably involve "political" issues. It is folly to expect that some proposal or approach will have such overwhelming logic from the standpoint of equity or "economy and efficiency" that it can avoid or readily withstand attack from individuals, groups, neighborhoods, or population elements whose position in the area it may seem to jeopardize. Herein, perhaps, lies the most serious limitation of the "outside" adviser, however technically knowledgeable he may be, in developing a reorganization proposal sufficiently oriented to the political facts of life of a particular area that popular acceptability may reasonably be expected.

The 18 efforts which have been reviewed for this study offer numerous illustrations of various kinds of political issues likely to be encountered. For example:

1. The status of individual elective officials and other communities is usually involved. This is obvious where two or more independent governments are proposed to be consolidated, but it is inherent even in a proposal to change the size of a governing body, to eliminate or combine existing offices, or to subordinate some officials or agencies more fully to a governing body or a chief executive, as may be sought in a single-government charter plan. The incumbents affected and at least some of their subordinates are understandably likely to have reservations about such proposed changes.

2. Another difficult political problem pertains to the size and nature of constituencies for members of governing bodies, and for other elective officers. In general, metropolitan reorganization looks toward the development or strengthening of some large-area instrumentality. If the governing body is to be reasonably limited in size, the issue of its members' remoteness or limited accessibility to the public automatically arises. Where the proposed change involves some shift of responsibility from other bodies which have previously served areas of differing population characteristics, an especially difficult problem may exist. Some of the reorganization plans reviewed took explicit account of

this kind of situation, and included provisions that were designed to safeguard the future representation interests of diverse subareas.

3. Numerous other groups in the area are likely to have some attachment to existing arrangements which might be affected by the proposed change in the status quo—local government employees, contractors, suppliers, and the like. Several of the reorganization plans reviewed had certain provisions to minimize this prospective issue insofar as local government personnel were concerned—for example, explicit protection of their employment and retirement rights, in the event of intergovernmental or interagency transfers. Defeat of at least one or two of the proposals studied has been attributed by observers to the vigorous opposition of firms and organizations supplying certain urban-type services (such as refuse collection) on a contract basis in suburban areas.

As the foregoing paragraphs may suggest, the reference here to "political" issues does not mainly involve partisan politics. Among the 18 reorganization efforts reviewed, there was only one (Lucas County, Ohio) where, according to observers, opposing positions by the major political parties played a highly significant part in the referendum campaign. It should be noted, however, that nine of the eighteen areas involved are in the South, where major controversial issues are often fought out within a dominant party rather than between two closely matched parties. Where there is strong divergence in prevailing party loyalty, among various portions of the total area involved in a particular reorganization effort (for example, between a central city and outlying areas), the chance is increased that pro and con attitudes may be taken locally by the opposing parties, or at least by certain of their recognized leaders.

One condition for success in metropolitan reorganization is an intensive and deliberate effort to develop a broad consensus on the best attainable alternative to the status quo. This point follows obviously from those stated above, concerning the many barriers to accomplishment of change. It points toward the application of time and effort not only to assemble information about problems which need solution but also to develop a particular plan which has some reasonable prospect of predominant area support. This does not necessarily dictate a willingness to settle for such a low common denominator approach that most of the problems involved are left untouched, although there undoubtedly are situations where a realistic preliminary appraisal will suggest that efforts at desirable change should be postponed.

The record reviewed here tends to support the understandable presumption that a proposal for major structural change has less chance of popular acceptance than would something less extensive. As already pointed out, only one of the five least drastic reorganization proposals subject to survey was defeated, as compared with three of the "intermediate" proposals and six of the seven proposals involving the greatest structural change. On the other hand, some proposals were attacked in local referendum campaigns on the ground that they were inadequate or palliative in nature. Perhaps one important consideration as to a "best" approach involves looking beyond immediate effects to consider the question: Would the accomplishment of this particular change tend to facilitate —or, on the other hand, to prevent or hamper—adaptations likely to be needed in the future?

It is not to be expected that all elements of potential opposition to reorganization can be avoided or mollified. But it is important: that there be an early, realistic, and hard-headed consideration of the implications of structural change for key groups and leaders in the area; that these implications enter into the choice among possible alternatives in the development of a particular reorganization proposal; and that the process by which a specific proposal is developed be such as to enlist the interest and expression of views by a diverse range of community elements.

Some of the successful reorganization efforts studied, and some others which approached success, were relatively unusual in the degree to which the plan-preparing body was able to obtain expressions of opinion and attitude from a wide spectrum of groups and citizens. In numerous instances elsewhere, however, shortage of time or other factors severely limited the opportunity for advisory civic participation in the design of the reorganization proposal later submitted to referendum.

At least three important purposes may be served by a deliberate effort, through hearings or otherwise, to enlist the views of potential opponents as well as probable supporters of metropolitan reorganization: this should provide further insight on the political feasibility of alternative kinds of structural change; it is likely to develop certain of the arguments that will arise in the subsequent referendum campaign, on issues not subject to compromise or adjustment in the proposal as finally developed; and it may serve to win potential backing or at least neutrality from some individuals and groups that might otherwise be hostile through lack of information or through suspicion of the motives of the plan-preparing body.

An alternative point of view might be urged—that the development of a particular reorganization proposal should be handled "close to the chest," to avoid "advance warning" to prospective opponents—if it appeared that the attitudes of various elements are fixed in a rigid and predictable pattern. Fortunately, the record of the various reorganization efforts which have been surveyed tend to discount such a presumption. With due allowance for the variety of proposals involved, it is possible to find examples of differing reactions by some kinds of community elements from one area to another, and many examples of cleavage of opinion within particular groups. . . .

Enlistment of popular support for governmental change in a metropolitan area calls for the use of a variety of promotional methods, suited to the diverse composition of the electorate. This point sounds like a truism, but failure to take it adequately into account was apparently a major limiting factor in several of the reorganization efforts which have been reviewed. . . . The problems of local government structure in a metropolitan area are complex and the design of feasible improvements is an arduous task which calls for analysis and judgment, rather than emotion. Individuals have the capacity and temperament to wrestle with such problems, and individuals who identify themselves with areawide rather than localized interests—that is, those commonly in the forefront of efforts toward metropolitan reorganization—are unlikely also to comprehend the attitudes of many rank-and-file voters having a markedly different background and exposure. It is not reasonable to expect the initial instigators of "reform" to be skillful also in the strategy and tactics of enlisting broad-based popular support.

This suggests, in turn, how important it is for efforts at metropolitan reorganization to have the active participation of experienced politicians. Less generally than civic "amateurs" are such individuals likely to underestimate the need to summarize issues simply for many voters; to fall into the error of overconfidence; or to overlook the importance of localized and face-to-face methods of enlisting popular support.

7. Metropolitan Government
for Metropolitan Cleveland:
An Analysis
of the Voting Records*

RICHARD A. WATSON AND JOHN H. ROMANI

John H. Romani, University of Michigan, and Richard A. Watson, University of Missouri, are former staff members of the Cleveland Metropolitan Services Commission. Here they analyze voter reaction to metropolitan reorganization proposals in the Cleveland area over a period of 28 years, and conclude there has been no trend in the direction of

* Reprinted from "Metropolitan Government for Metropolitan Cleveland: An Analysis of the Voting Records," *Midwest Journal of Political Science*, November 1961, vol. 5, no. 4 by Richard A. Watson and John H. Romani, by permission of Wayne State University Press. Copyright 1961 by Wayne State University Press.

metropolitan reform. Contrary to the hypothesis that the central city tends to support reform and the suburban municipalities tend to oppose it, Romani and Watson found that suburbanites in seven cases out of ten gave stronger support to reform than did central-city residents. The authors' findings should be contrasted with the St. Louis findings described in Reading 8.

Reading 4 contains the rationale of governmental reform in the Cleveland area as developed by the Cleveland Metropolitan Services Commission.

The following investigation of electoral behavior in the Cleveland area is divided into two major parts. The first is a broad trend analysis of voting over the years on . . . various metropolitan charter issues. . . . The second focuses on the 1950 charter proposal alone and attempts to identify more precisely the specific factors associated with positive and negative voting in that particular election.[1]

TREND ANALYSIS

In this portion of the analysis we were interested in testing very broad hypotheses about the attitudes of the electorate on metropolitan reform in Cleveland. We were particularly concerned with determining general patterns of voting behavior on metropolitan issues and ascertaining to what extent changes have occurred over the years in this behavior. The specific criteria we employed to test voting attitudes was the percentage of the total vote that was cast in favor of metropolitan reform. Hereafter this figure will be referred to more simply as the percentage of positive vote.

The data available for the Cleveland area are particularly fruitful for a trend analysis. Since the electorate has expressed itself on some aspect of metropolitan charter reform on no less than ten separate occasions over the period of the last 28 years, there is an extensive electoral record for analysis.[2] Moreover, . . . there

[1] The authors would like to acknowledge persons who offered valuable assistance in the statistical analysis for this article. Included are Mrs. Barbara Haley of the staff of the Cleveland Metropolitan Services Commission and James Hobbs, a graduate student in political science at the University of Missouri.

[2] It is doubtful if such a situation exists in many, if any, other metropolitan areas, and if this is the case, this will hinder the application of trend analyses to voting on metropolitan reform efforts elsewhere.

have been virtually no changes in the governmental boundaries of the area—either by way of annexations or incorporations—during the period under analysis, and thus attitudes of communities can be compared meaningfully over the years.

We first focused attention on the overall vote on metropolitan issues over the years to ascertain what trends, if any, appeared in the electorate's attitude on reform. Had the almost continuous agitation for change been successful in winning progressively more support for reform? Or instead, had individual community loyalties deepened, making the voters more and more hostile to the concept of metropolitan government? Or did such factors tend to cancel each other, leaving no perceptible trend in either direction? Recognizing all these as possibilities, we expected to find that the "education" process—coupled with the worsening of some of the conditions giving rise to "metropolitan" problems (lack of adequate facilities for water supply, sewage, transportation, etc.)—would tip the electoral scales increasingly in favor of reform.

To aid our analysis, we divided the votes into the three separate categories of referenda referred to previously and examined trends within these categories. This was done on the premise that the more specific an election issue was, the lower the positive vote on it would be. For example, one could not meaningfully compare voting results on actual charter proposals with electoral expressions on enabling constitutional amendments since the former would naturally involve more concrete matters over which there would be considerable controversy.

Contrary to our expectations, there has been no overall trend in favor of metropolitan reform in metropolitan Cleveland. The only significant electoral pattern that emerges is the relationship between *favorable* charter commission elections and subsequent votes on charters themselves. The 1934, 1949, and 1958 elections showed an increasingly favorable vote for the selection of a commission to propose changes in the government of metropolitan Cleveland, yet votes on actual charter proposals in 1935, 1950, and 1959 respectively found less and less support from the electorate. Thus the gap progressively widened between a positive vote on the selection of a commission and the subsequent vote on the commission's charter recommendations. This may suggest that as metropolitan "problems" intensify and are given more and more publicity,[3] voters are willing to *consider changes* in government organization. At the same time, other factors such as community commitments to certain governmental programs, that is, the fact that actual changes proposed affect more and more status quo interests, may make it progressively more difficult to get the electorate to agree upon the specific provisions of a charter.

[3] Some 30 reports were issued by the Cleveland Metropolitan Services Commission on various governmental matters in the metropolitan area; many of the Commission's recommendations were incorporated in the county charter proposed in 1959.

As a part of our trend analysis we were interested in testing the assumption one often hears that voters in the central city tend to support metropolitan reform, whereas suburbanites generally oppose it. We were not convinced that this difference actually existed some years ago in light of Victor Jones' comment in 1940 that it would be foolhardy to view the voters in either the central city or the suburbs as being of a single mind on metropolitan integration.[4] However, we knew of the post-war influx of low income groups demanding governmental services into Cleveland proper at the very time that middle class elements of the population, as well as new commercial—and in some cases, industrial—ventures are locating outside its borders. We expected that this situation would be reflected in increasingly favorable votes on metropolitan reform by central city residents in recent years as a means of tapping suburban financial resources for public programs, and a progressively more negative suburban vote as a means of resisting such a development. Table 1 contains the necessary data for testing our hypothesis.

The data in this table indicate that over the years the central city has not voted more affirmatively on metropolitan charter issues than have the suburbs. In fact, if anything, the tendency has been just the opposite: in seven of the ten instances studied, suburbanites favored metropolitan reform more than residents of the central city. Nor has the recent trend appeared which we expected to find; in the five postwar elections, the central city led the suburbs only once in terms of percentage of positive vote. If any general principle appears at all, it lies in the tendency of central city and suburban voters to view the question of metropolitan reform somewhat similarly: only twice, in 1935, and again in 1936, did one group of voters favor a proposition while the other opposed it.

When the expected trend toward more favorable voting in the central city failed to appear, we sought to determine what factors might be contributing to the negative attitude of city residents on metropolitan reform. Since so many of the recent migrants to Cleveland are Negroes, we reasoned that this group might have a considerable influence on the central city electoral record. We were also aware of Professor Banfield's observation that metropolitan government would mean the transfer of power over the central cities from largely lower class elements, of which the Negro population is a prominent part, to the largely middle class white elements who dominate the suburbs.[5] Moreover, we noted that some of the Negro leaders in Cleveland, possibly acting upon this premise, had begun to oppose reform.

We examined the voting record of the Negro community over the years on

[4] Victor Jones, "Politics of Integration in Metropolitan Areas," *The Annals of the American Academy of Political and Social Science,* 207 (January, 1940), 161.

[5] Edward Banfield, "The Politics of Metropolitan Organization," *Midwest Journal of Political Science,* 1 (May, 1957), p. 81.

TABLE 1

PERCENTAGE OF POSITIVE VOTE CAST BY CENTRAL CITY
AND SUBURBAN RESIDENTS OF CUYAHOGA COUNTY
ON METROPOLITAN ISSUES, 1933–1959

Year	PERCENTAGE OF POSITIVE VOTE Central City	PERCENTAGE OF POSITIVE VOTE Suburbs
1933	69.5	58.8
1934	58.5	61.5
1935	54.0	49.8
1936	48.2	51.8
1941	42.8	46.9
1949	57.4	67.7
1950	47.1	48.7
1957	58.1	55.6
1958	61.0	68.7
1959	42.4	46.7

metropolitan issues, expecting to find that as the Negroes in the city increased—
particularly as their numbers gave them a reasonable chance of exerting effective
political power—their vote on metropolitan reform would become progressively
more negative. At least this would be the case if enough of the Negro leaders
perceived the development Banfield described, and were successful in persuading
the rank and file Negro voters that the transfer of power from the central city
to a metropolitan government would mean a diminution of their political influence as a result of its being merged with that of the predominantly white
voters located in the suburbs.

In attempting to test our hypothesis on Negro voting behavior, we were
faced with the difficulty of separating the ballots on the basis of race. Only in
census years is there any accurate information on the exact location of Negroes
within the central city, and even then it is difficult, if not impossible, to relate
this information to electoral behavior because the boundaries of census and election districts do not coincide. Therefore, for our trend analysis we decided to
focus attention on the voting of wards represented by Negro councilmen. We
realize that some whites live in these areas, and that some Negroes live in wards
represented by white councilmen. Nevertheless, given the general residential
segregation pattern of Cleveland, we feel that it is reasonable to assume that
wards with a Negro councilman are populated primarily by Negroes. Table 2
shows the voting behavior of these wards on metropolitan issues over the years,
as compared with that of wards represented by white councilmen.

The information in this table reveals the development we expected to find;
namely, as the Negro political strength in the central city increased significantly,

the attitude of Negro voters on metropolitan reform changed. Negro wards voted more positively than white wards during the first eight elections examined, indicating that the Negro community felt it had no stake in the political status quo and that it might even benefit from change. However, beginning with the 1958 election, the pattern altered. It is significant that this change took place between 1957 and 1958 at the time when Negroes made their greatest political gains, going from 4 to 7 Negro councilmen, and from casting some 6 percent of the total city vote cast on the metropolitan issue under examination, to two and one half times that percentage the following year. The trend continued in 1959 when additional advances in Negro political strength were accompanied by a further decline in support for metropolitan reform. Of course it is possible that other factors may also have contributed to the change in Negro voting habits, but the data are clearly consistent with our hypothesis.

We were also interested in testing whether any voting differences exist between general classes of communities in Cuyahoga County with respect to metropolitan reorganization. We decided to exclude townships from consideration because . . . they number only four, contain less than one half of one per cent of the county's population, and are, therefore, too small to be statistically significant. Moreover, their governmental powers are far more limited than those of municipal corporations, and we wanted to hold this factor constant and test the element of size as a possible determinant of voting behavior. We, therefore, con-

TABLE 2

PERCENTAGE OF POSITIVE VOTE CAST IN CITY OF CLEVELAND
ON METROPOLITAN ISSUES, 1933–1959,
BY RESIDENTS OF WARDS
REPRESENTED BY NEGRO AND WHITE COUNCILMEN

Year	Number of Negro Wards*	Percentage of City-Wide Vote Cast in Negro Wards	PERCENTAGE OF POSITIVE VOTE Negro Wards	PERCENTAGE OF POSITIVE VOTE White Wards
1933	3	5.4	79.3	69.0
1934	3	5.3	63.4	58.3
1935	3	7.9	77.0	52.1
1936	3	5.2	59.4	47.6
1941	3	2.3	57.2	42.2
1949	3	5.8	72.1	56.5
1950	3	5.2	64.8	46.2
1957	4	6.0	72.1	57.2
1958	7	15.0	50.2	62.7
1959	8	21.2	29.3	45.9

* There were 33 wards in Cleveland during each of the years under study.

fined our analysis to a comparison of the electoral records of cities and villages, the former constituting municipal corporations with over 5,000 residents (including the central city), and the latter being those entities with lesser populations.

In making this analysis we are drawing on information in some studies that size of place correlates with voting behavior.[6] Moreover, Robert Wood has traced the impetus for modern suburbia to a romantic desire to recreate the "miniature republics" so eulogized in the folklore of early American political institutions.[7] We reasoned that persons residing in small village communities might be more inclined than city residents to regard metropolitan integration as a kind of subtle annexation process designed to destroy their experiments with "grass roots" government and to place them under the control of "Big Democracy." Therefore, we expected to find the aggregate city vote on metropolitan issues more favorable to metropolitan reform than that of the villages.

The data in Table 3 generally verify our hypothesis that village residents are

TABLE 3

PERCENTAGE OF POSITIVE VOTES CAST BY CITY
AND VILLAGE RESIDENTS OF CUYAHOGA COUNTY
ON METROPOLITAN ISSUES, 1933–1959

Year	PERCENTAGE OF POSITIVE VOTE Cities	PERCENTAGE OF POSITIVE VOTE Villages
1933	67.8	48.7
1934	60.5	49.8
1935	53.9	38.4
1936	50.0	39.8
1941	44.7	35.4
1949	61.6	60.8
1950	48.4	38.3
1957	57.3	52.4
1958	65.4	65.1
1959	44.5	46.8

more opposed to metropolitan reform than city dwellers. At least this was the case in 9 of the 10 referenda examined. However, it should be noted that the gap between the two groups has narrowed in recent years, the difference being

[6] For example, Professor Epstein found differences in partisan voting among voters of different-sized cities in Wisconsin. See Leon D. Epstein, "Size of Place and the Division of the Two-Party Vote in Wisconsin," *Western Political Quarterly,* 9 (March, 1956), 138–150.

[7] Robert C. Wood, *Suburbia: Its People and Their Politics* (Boston: Houghton-Mifflin, 1958), ch. 2.

important only once in the last five referenda, namely, in 1950 when the favorable vote of city dwellers exceeded that of village residents by some 10 percenage points. Moreover, in the most recent instance (1959) village voters were somewhat more favorably disposed towards the charter than were those living in the cities of Cuyahoga County. Thus forces are at work in cities and villages in Cuyahoga County which are bringing the attitudes of their respective residents closer together on the matter of metropolitan reorganization.

CORRELATES OF VOTING ON THE 1950 CHARTER

In this part of the analysis we were interested in determining the variables associated with positive and negative voting on the 1950 charter. This particular election was chosen because it coincided with the year in which census data were gathered in the Cleveland area. In addition to population figures, studies published by the Real Property Inventory of Cleveland, a private research agency, provided us with detailed information on the social and economic characteristics of the residents of each of the communities in the Cuyahoga County.[8] Moreover, excellent financial information was developed by the Cost Analysis Project of the Cleveland Metropolitan Services Commission.[9] Thus we had access to exceptionally rich data on individual communities, and this, coupled with the 1950 voting record of these municipalities,[10] enabled us to explore correlations between certain community characteristics and election results.

In working with these correlations, we assumed that attitudes of voters on metropolitan reform would, to some extent at least, be shaped by the particular kind of community in which they lived. Or even if community identification itself was not the crucial determinant in the voter's decision, we expected to find residents with similar social and economic backgrounds viewing metropolitan reform efforts somewhat similarly. In either case, comparing characteristics of communities with the voting record of their residents promised to be fruitful.

The statistical tool we employed in our analysis was simple linear correlation. Product-moment correlations were calculated between certain community characteristics designated as independent variables, and community voting records,

[8] The publications are *Family Income by Tracts* and *Census Facts and Trends by Tracts*, published by Real Property Inventory of Metropolitan Cleveland in 1953 and 1954 respectively.

[9] See Seymour Sachs, Leo Egand, and William Hellmuth, Jr., *The Cleveland Metropolitan Area—A Fiscal Profile* (Cleveland: The Cleveland Metropolitan Services Commission, 1958).

[10] No voting results for 1950 were available for the village of North Randall. Individual records of each of the other 54 municipalities in existence that year were analyzed.

our dependent variable. In each case the specific measurement employed for the latter variable is the same one we used for our trend analysis, namely, the percentage of positive vote. The measurements used for independent variables vary with the particular community characteristic under analysis; each of them will be explained in the discussion that follows.

POPULATION AND DENSITY

The first kind of community characteristic we investigated was population and density. . . . We felt that there were legitimate reasons for thinking that size of place might affect resident attitudes on metropolitan reform. In our trend analysis, we did find some differences existing between aggregate city and village voting on metropolitan issues. In this instance we were interested in exploring the population determinant in more detail by investigating possible variations in voting among different-sized communities within each of these two major categories. In addition, we also introduced the element of community physical size into the analysis by calculating the density of each community (population divided by area) in order to determine whether population concentration correlated with voting behavior on the 1950 proposed charter.

The analysis in Table 4 shows some positive correlation between population

TABLE 4

COEFFICIENTS OF CORRELATION:
POPULATION SIZE AND DENSITY
WITH PERCENTAGE OF POSITIVE VOTE ON 1950 CHARTER:
CITIES AND VILLAGES

CLASSIFICATION	NUMBER OF UNITS	SIZE AND POSITIVE VOTE	DENSITY AND POSITIVE VOTE
Cities	20	.04*	.33
Villages	34	—.17	—.22
Total	54	.09	.23

* The large population of Cleveland vis-à-vis the other communities tends to distort this correlation somewhat. If this extreme value is removed, and a correlation computed for the 19 remaining cities, the coefficient of correlation is .33.

size and density and percentage of positive vote among the cities analyzed. In other words, the larger the city and the more densely it is populated, the higher the percentage of positive vote it tended to cast. However, these coefficients of correlation are not statistically significant at the .01 level of significance.[11] The

[11] At this level of significance with 20 groups under observation, a correlation of .56

correlates which existed between population size and density of villages and the positive vote were of a negative character, that is, generally, the greater the village population and the higher its density, the lower the percentage of positive vote it tended to cast. However, this negative correlation was also too low to be statistically significant.[12] Therefore, we concluded that neither population size nor density was a factor of importance in the voting on the 1950 charter.

TAXABLE WEALTH

Another general community characteristic we explored was that of tax resources. It is often thought that economic self-interest leads poor communities to favor, and wealthy communities to resist, efforts to consolidate their govern-

TABLE 5

COEFFICIENTS OF CORRELATION:
TOTAL TAXABLE WEALTH AND INDUSTRIALIZATION
WITH PERCENTAGE OF POSITIVE VOTE ON 1950 CHARTER:
CITIES AND VILLAGES.

CLASSIFICATION	NUMBER OF UNITS	TOTAL TAXABLE WEALTH AND POSITIVE VOTE	INDUSTRIALIZATION AND POSITIVE VOTE
Cities	20	.63	—.10
Villages	34	—.32	—.56
Total	54	—.27	—.32

mental programs. We reasoned that voters might view attempts to transfer functions from municipalities to a metropolitan government as a kind of consolidation of the governmental services so affected. Therefore, we expected to find inhabitants of communities with lesser tax bases more favorably disposed to the 1950 charter than those with more affluent resources. In testing this proposition, we used assessed valuation per capita as our measure of total community taxable wealth.

We refined our analysis by examining different kinds of taxable wealth as possible sources of variation in voting behavior. We knew that public officials of

or greater is significant. This means that there is less than one chance in a 100 that such a correlation would result from mere chance. (This statistical test is employed on the assumption that the Cleveland situation constitutes a kind of "sample" of the general phenomena under study.)

12 At the .01 level of significance a correlation of .42 or greater is significant when there are 34 groups under observation.

some of the industrial enclaves in the Cleveland area were openly hostile to the idea of metropolitan reform, and we expected to find this attitude also reflected in the voting record of the residents of these communities. If this were the case, a negative correlation should exist between community industrialization and percentage of positive vote on the 1950 charter. As our measurement of industrialization, we employed the tax on tangibles—such items as machinery, equipment, etc.—calculating the percentage of the total tax base of each community which was derived from this revenue source.

Our first hypothesis with respect to taxable wealth and community voting on the 1950 charter proved to be incorrect with respect to the cities in Cuyahoga County. We expected to find a negative correlation, but instead a positive one existed, that is, cities with good tax bases tended to vote more positively than did those with lesser resources. Moreover, this correlation is statistically significant at the .01 level of significance. Our hypothesis did tend to be borne out in the villages, where a negative correlation appeared; but it is not a significant one.

Our second hypothesis, that industrial communities would tend to oppose the charter, proved to be true in the villages, where the negative correlation was relatively high. However, the correlation in the cities, though negative, was too low to be considered significant. Thus the industrial enclaves most opposed to the 1950 charter in Cleveland were the ones with small day-time populations; residents of the larger industrial communities were not as disposed to oppose metropolitan reform.

SOCIAL AND ECONOMIC BACKGROUND OF RESIDENTS

Our final major area of correlation analysis deals with the general social and economic background of community residents. The tendency of communities with good tax resources to vote affirmatively on the charter led us to believe that persons of means might generally be disposed to favor metropolitan reform. We reasoned that since industrialization is related to an opposite voting attitude, it must be the non-industrial sector of the community revenue which is associated with positive voting on the charter. The major element of that sector being residential property, we anticipated that high-income persons, who furnish such taxable wealth, must generally favor metropolitan reform. The yardstick we used to measure personal affluence in our correlation analysis is median family income.

We also tested the factor of education as a possible source of variation in voting behavior. Our knowledge of the elements of the Cleveland community most clearly identified with metropolitan reform led us to anticipate that level of education would correlate fairly well with positive vote on the charter. As our measure of educational level, we used the median number of school years completed by the residents of each community.

The hypothesis with respect to income and voting on the charter proved to be correct in both the cities and the villages, with the correlations in each case being relatively high. Education also correlated positively with the charter vote in both the cities and villages, but only in the latter was it statistically significant. However, when the two groups are combined, the coefficient of correlation for all 54 units becomes significant.[13]

TABLE 6

COEFFICIENTS OF CORRELATION:
INCOME AND EDUCATION
WITH PERCENTAGE OF POSITIVE VOTE ON 1950 CHARTER:
CITIES AND VILLAGES.

CLASSIFICATION	NUMBER OF UNITS	INCOME AND POSITIVE VOTE	EDUCATION AND POSITIVE VOTE
Cities	20	.61	.36
Villages	34	.68	.64
Total	54	.67	.58

As the final element of our correlation analysis, we examined the relationship between occupational status and voting on the 1950 charter. We knew that Masters and Wright found this factor to be significant in partisan voting in Michigan;[14] moreover, Victor Jones referred to the split between business and labor on metropolitan reform.[15] To measure this factor we examined the voting record of two general occupational groups: one composed of managers, proprietors, professionals, and technicians; the other of laborers and operatives. (Hereafter these groups are referred to more simply as managerial and laboring.) We hypothesized that communities in which the former group was numerous would tend to support the charter, and, conversely, that those in which there were many residents from the second group would tend to oppose it. For our correlation involving occupational status, we used the percentage of the labor force of each community which was composed of persons in each of these two general categories.

Our expectations with respect to occupation and voting were generally con-

[13] At the .01 level of significance a correlation of .35 or greater is significant when there are 54 groups under observation.

[14] See Nicholas A. Masters and Deil S. Wright, "Trends and Variations in the Two-Party Vote: The Case of Michigan," *American Political Science Review*, 54 (December, 1958), 1085 ff.

[15] See Jones, "Politics of Integration in Metropolitan Areas," *loc. cit.,* pp. 162 ff.

firmed. The relationships we expected to find, that is, positive correlation between managerial status and the positive vote and a negative correlation between laboring status and this same vote, were statistically significant in the villages and for all 54 units under observation, and fell just short of significance in the city group.

TABLE 7

COEFFICIENTS OF CORRELATION:

OCCUPATIONAL STATUS

WITH PERCENTAGE OF POSITIVE VOTE ON 1950 CHARTER:

CITIES AND VILLAGES.

CLASSIFICATION	NUMBER OF UNITS	MANAGERS AND POSITIVE VOTE	LABORERS AND POSITIVE VOTE
Cities	20	.49	—.42
Villages	34	.67	—.64
Total	54	.60	—.60

Thus our investigation of eight independent variables indicated that median family income was the most significant factor analyzed, correlating .61 and .68 respectively with the positive vote of the cities and villages on the 1950 charter. When these two groups are combined, the coefficient of correlation for all 54 units (20 cities and 34 villages) is .67. By squaring this statistic we arrived at a coefficient of determination of .45. This figure indicates that some 45% of the variation in the vote on the charter by municipalities in Cuyahoga County can be explained by the factor of median family income. The remaining 55% of the variation is unexplained.

Of course our analysis indicated other pertinent variables. For example, education and occupational status each correlated significantly with voting on the 1950 charter. We therefore proceeded to a multiple correlation analysis to determine the cumulative effect of four independent variables on the 1950 vote; included were median family income, median school year completed, and percentage of managers and percentage of laborers in the labor force.[16]

The resulting coefficient of multiple correlation, .69, is statistically significant. When this figure is squared, the coefficient of determination becomes .48. This means that 48% of the variation in the vote on the 1950 charter is explained by the combined effect of the four variables, while the remaining 52% is unexplained. The fact that the multiple correlation is only slightly higher than that of the single variable, median income, suggests that the four independent variables are highly correlated with each other. In other words, those communities whose

---

[16] The necessary computations were done by the Computer Center at the University of Missouri, Roy F. Keller, Acting Director.

residents have high incomes also tend to come from the managerial group and are well educated; the municipalities with a low level of income also contain persons with a low educational level who tend to come from the laboring group. An analysis of the interrelationship of these factors confirms that this is indeed the case.

Thus our correlation analysis gave us some indication of the factors associated with positive and negative voting on the 1950 charter. We were able to identify at least some of the significant factors by computing simple linear correlations; moreover, our multiple correlation analysis revealed the cumulative effect of individually-significant variables on the 1950 vote. While this latter analysis left more than half the variation in this vote unexplained, it did point up the close interrelationships existing between such factors as income, education and occupational status. These three elements are prominently identified with social class; and therefore the essential division in the electorate in this election was along class lines.

8. Metropolitan Post-Mortem*

HENRY J. SCHMANDT, PAUL G. STEINBICKER, AND GEORGE D. WENDEL

Henry J. Schmandt, University of Wisconsin-Milwaukee, and Paul G. Steinbicker and George D. Wendel, St. Louis University, evaluate the influence of a survey of metropolitan problems conducted by St. Louis University and Washington University on the metropolitan reform movement culminating in a 1959 referendum which rejected a proposal to create a "Greater St. Louis City-County District." The authors conclude that politicians generally see little in the way of rewards and face great political risks in supporting metropolitan reform, particularly in view of citizen indifference with metropolitan problems.

The uniqueness of the political environment of each metropolitan area becomes apparent when the St. Louis experience is contrasted with the Cleveland experience, described in Reading 7, the Miami experience, described in Reading 9, and the Nashville experience, described in Reading 10.

The St. Louis experiment adds to the long list of failures to win governmental reorganization battles in the nation's metropolitan areas. In retrospect, the move-

* From *Metropolitan Reform in St. Louis,* by H. J. Schmandt, Paul G. Steinbicker, and George D. Wendel. Copyright © 1961 by Holt, Rinehart and Winston, Inc.

ment could not possibly have succeeded. The forces at work against it were too powerful, and the groups for it too uncommitted to bring about the proposed changes. Reshaping the governmental pattern of the metropolis is a complex task that impinges upon a variety of change-resistant interests and clusters of power. The St. Louis election once again demonstrated the ease with which these interests can be mobilized into an effective army of opposition through use of the existing network of relationships among public officials and interest cliques. It also gave added emphasis to the shopworn truism that it will take more than metropolitan surveys and public pronouncements by the civic elite to modify the present system of local government in any significant fashion.

The welter of confusing facts and circumstances that surround a metropolitan reform effort such as that in St. Louis seems to defy analysis. Yet each of these attempts provides new insights, new perspectives, and hopefully better understanding of the political processes at work in our urban centers. The abortive St. Louis venture into the field of area-wide constitution making was not altogether in vain. From the standpoint of practical accomplishments it stimulated thinking and minor action on several problems and led to some governmental readjustments of lesser scope. More importantly, from the standpoint of knowledge it contributed to clearer understanding of several facets of the metropolitan-reorganization issue. This latter result is discussed within the framework of three questions:

1. Why was the degree of commitment or involvement by the majority of citizens and many major interest groups relatively low, and what effect did this factor have on the outcome of the referendum?

2. What impact did the comprehensive study conducted by the universities have on the charter drafters and the general public?

3. What are the minimum essentials or preconditions that must exist in a metropolitan area before broad-scale reorganization is possible?

THE PATHOLOGY OF METROPOLITAN ACTION PROGRAMS

Ironically, the metropolitan reorganization proposal in St. Louis was caught in a heavy cross fire from opposite extremes. On the one hand it was attacked because it was too timid; on the other, because it was too far-reaching. The uncongenial union of these two dichotomous forces is symptomatic of the factors that impede restructuring of metropolitan governmental patterns. There are always individuals and groups who see personal advantages and opportunities in changing the system. There are others who have vested interests in preserving the existing arrangements. Finally, there are still others who have no personal stake in the system other than that of citizens concerned with its proper operation. Supporters of metropolitan reform fall predominantly into this last category—a fact that helps to explain the weaknesses of the reorganization movement.

The most highly motivated proponents of change are those who anticipate personal rewards from a restructured system. If the prize is attractive enough, they are willing to commit time, money, and effort in order to achieve the desired alteration. Normally this group includes politicians and interest groupings of various economic, social, and racial dimensions. Those in this classification usually play negative roles in metropolitan reform. When not in active opposition, they have been lukewarm or neutral toward reorganization proposals. Their lack of enthusiasm can be explained by several factors, particularly the nature of the reform plans and the unresponsiveness of the general public.

For some years now, the common approach to metropolitan reorganization has been based on the gospel of management efficiency and the dogma of local autonomy tempered by the transfer of certain nonlocal powers to an area-wide agency. Discarding political consolidation as unrealistic or undesirable, the mid-twentieth-century movement to "save the cities" continues to view the metropolitan problem as essentially one of relating sound engineering and administrative solutions to matters of sewage disposal, traffic control, water supply, and like functions. And by concentrating its attention on organizational efficiency, reformist activity has assiduously avoided the deeper and more controversial questions of the metropolis such as racial assimilation, housing, economic segregation, and even public education.

The consequences of this approach are not difficult to ascertain. To couch metropolitan reform in purely administrative terms is to divorce it from those issues motivating large interest coalitions. These groups are unwilling to expend their resources on a cause that skirts the problems concerning them. On those occasions when they are enlisted in the cause by the proponents of reform, these interest groups give little more than nominal support. Similarly, when they are attracted into the ranks of the opposition, as in St. Louis, they put only minimal effort into the task.

A central-city mayor, a political party, and possibly labor may visualize distinct political rewards in a merger of local governments, but they normally see little payoff in lesser schemes. Cervantes deviated from the general behavior pattern of core-city politicians, perhaps because he saw in the reorganization movement an issue that would further his political ambitions. But Tucker and not Cervantes was the political leader of the area, a fact which seriously impeded Cervantes' ability to mobilize widespread support for metropolitan reform. Suburban politicians have likewise seen only risks and little reward in espousing the reorganization movement. Some of them at the county level have occasionally supported plans that utilize the county government as the metropolitan vehicle, but here again they are attracted by the anticipated rewards.

One major reason for the largely negative attitude of the political leaders and parties toward metropolitan reorganization lies in the unresponsiveness of the citizenry toward the issue. It is frequently assumed that the impetus for governmental change in metropolitan areas is generated by widespread dissatisfaction with services. But this great ground swell of popular dissatisfaction is more mythical than real. The direction of urban growth may be such as to "negate the rich promise of American life," but the average citizen remains unconvinced of this awesome possibility. In St. Louis, and more recently in Dayton, attitude surveys clearly demonstrated that most people are relatively well satisfied with their local governments and have few service complaints. St. Louis residents had no strong criticism of any of their governments. Only 1 unit of more than 150 was considered to be performing poorly by as many as 10 percent of the residents —and ironically, this was the sewer district, a metropolitan agency. In answer to questions about various local governmental services, only recreation, traffic, and transportation drew responses of dissatisfaction from more than 17 percent of those interviewed.[1]

The results in Dayton were similar. There, only about one in ten persons believed that his local government was poor in either efficiency or responsiveness to the people. Less than one half of the respondents had either felt like complaining or had complained about a local governmental service. Almost 60 percent could name no more than one service with which they were dissatisfied.[2] It is unrealistic to believe that those in charge of the local governmental machinery will support major changes under such circumstances. Until popular concern or dissatisfaction with the existing system is made more evident, few local political leaders can be expected to champion the cause of metropolitan government. Many of them look upon it as an issue devoid of popular appeal. Some of them take advantage of it in a negative sense by assuming the role of St. George and protecting the "little governments" against the voracious dragon. Others portray themselves as political Pasteurs, defending the central city against the suburban parasites.

If party leaders generally and mass-based interest groups particularly evidence only mild concern over the reorganization issue, the same cannot be said for the administrative bureaucracy and the officeholders who have high personal stakes in the retention of the existing system. This group includes the central-city mayor as well as the suburban official. The first will accept an enhancement of his power through political merger but fight against a dilution of it by functional consolidation of selected services, such as envisaged by the St. Louis plan. The

[1] John C. Bollens, ed., *Exploring the Metropolitan Community*, Berkeley, Calif.: University of California Press, 1961, pp. 188–190.

[2] *Metropolitan Challenge*, Dayton: Metropolitan Community Studies, 1959, pp. 241–251.

second looks with suspicion on all change as a possible threat to his interest. Only in those instances in which existing arrangements are damaging his position of leadership—a sewer or water crisis for example—is he willing to accept minimal modification of the structure. It is the members of this officeholding group who are the most strongly motivated by the risks and rewards of metropolitan reform and usually the most active in campaigns involving this issue.

The third group—the civic reformers—includes the economic elite, the "good government" people, the metropolitan press, and a sprinkling of other community-minded individuals and organizations. The prize they seek is an efficient system of local government; there are few personal stakes. Even the economic leaders do not feel that a change in the existing system will enhance their business interests in any material fashion. Hence, while they are willing to play their role as symbols of civic virtue and champions of progressive local government, their motivation is seldom strong enough to commit them to an all-out effort for metropolitan reorganization.

This coalition of good-government forces and business is further handicapped in issues requiring popular referendum by lack of a constituency that can be readily mobilized. The group's effectiveness in winning electoral support is therefore severely limited unless it can entice into the cause such mass-based groups as the political parties and labor. The press is similarly handicapped. Although it has a mass audience, its ability to mobilize the public in a civic cause is restricted by the interests and predispositions of its readers, their readiness to listen, and their capacity to understand the issues.

A division somewhat parallel to the three categories of interest groups can also be identified among the general citizenry. These three types might be plotted on a continuum as mergerites, or metropolitanites, moderate integrationists, and local autonomists, or localists. They appear in sharp contrast in the attitude interviews conducted by the universities. The findings of the survey study prompted the conclusion in the final public report that a majority of both city and county residents "favor a plan of government that will vest control over area-wide functions in a metropolitan agency,"[3] a conclusion that found little support in the election returns. The results of the interviews are of some relevancy here.

Respondents were presented with a simplified statement of the various alternatives for governmental change possible under existing laws and were asked if they liked or disliked each alternative. Retention of the status quo was included in the list. Although the variations in responses were not striking, the metropolitan-district system was the most generally favored (by 53.5 percent of those interviewed) and the status quo the most generally disapproved (54.4

[3] *Path of Progress,* St. Louis: Metropolitan St. Louis Survey, August 1957, p. 68.

percent). More significantly, however, were the responses to a succeeding question: "Which of these proposals do you like best and which do you dislike the most?" As Table 1 shows, a relatively high degree of polarization existed among the residents of the area with a majority (54.5 percent) preferring either total merger or no change in the existing system. The balance of the answers were divided among three proposals of a more moderate nature.

The respondents who preferred merger generally favored the status quo least, while a majority of the localists disliked merger most. Since the district system was the only alternative that elicited a clear majority of favorable responses to

TABLE 1

RESPONSES TO VARIOUS ALTERNATIVES FOR GOVERNMENTAL CHANGE
IN ST. LOUIS AREA
(EXPRESSED IN PERCENTAGES)

PROPOSAL	LIKED THIS PROPOSAL MOST	DISLIKED THIS PROPOSAL MOST
Merger of all governmental units	33.5	26.9
Consolidate the two county governments but retain all local units	13.4	13.8
Create a local federal system by establishing a metropolitan district government	15.3	9.8
Consolidate the suburban municipalities into a smaller number	10.3	10.9
Leave present governments just as they are	21.0	28.8
Don't know	6.5	9.8
	100.0	100.0

the initial question of likes and dislikes, and since it was the least disliked of all the listed changes, it appeared to be the solution with the most political appeal. This analysis, however, did not anticipate the union of the two extremist groups—the metropolitanites and the localists. It wrongly assumed that a majority of those who favored merger most but did not express a dislike for the district plan would also accept the lesser solution.

The interviews suggest that those who favor complete consolidation and those who support the status quo are more firmly committed to these views than are the moderates to any particular lesser remedy. The latter, although expressing their general approval of a metropolitan district, were almost equally divided as to which intermediate proposal they liked best. These findings also suggest that the stronger commitment of those in the two polar positions will likely motivate them to greater activity than the moderates in a campaign for metropolitan reorganization. The situation might be summarized in this fashion: the localists are prone to resist any change of consequence; the metropolitanites are inclined to be hostile or disinterested in any proposal that does not embrace political merger; the moderates are likely to remain apathetic, confused, and uncertain as to the proper remedy.

Several interesting points of contrast between the St. Louis election and the Cuyahoga County (Cleveland) referendums serve to underscore these general observations and assumptions. On the same day that the St. Louis plan was submitted to the electorate, residents of Cuyahoga County rejected a metropolitan reorganization proposal (in the form of a county home-rule charter) that had been drafted by an official commission. Unlike the overwhelming defeat in St. Louis, the Cleveland charter was turned down by a much smaller margin, losing in the central city by approximately 29,000 votes out of 193,000 cast and in the remainder of the county by only 8,000 out of almost 226,000. Unlike the St. Louis proposal also, the Cleveland plan at least had the formal approval of the political parties while several top politicians, particularly those who stood to gain from a refurbished county government, worked actively for the charter. The business leaders also were active in support of the cause.

Leading the opposition in Cleveland, as in St. Louis, were the central-city mayor, the administrative bureaucracy, and suburban officialdom. The most active and effective campaigners among the opponents were the heads of two city departments whose functions were to be transferred to the county under the reorganization plan. Their colorful appeals repeatedly captured public attention away from the charter proponents.[4] The only large-scale interest bloc to oppose the plan actively was the Negro community which saw in it a threat to its growing political power within the central city. (In St. Louis the Negro opposition was much less active, possibly because the district proposal involved only functions of peripheral concern to the Negro leaders.) By enlisting the support of many of the politicians and motivating the civic leaders, the Cleveland plan made a better showing at the polls. It might have succeeded had the central-city mayor espoused it. The same cannot be said of the St. Louis charter.

THE SURVEY INFLUENCE

The St. Louis Board of Freeholders and the metropolitan charter election had been preceded by an extensive university study designed to ascertain the facts,

[4] See E. E. Sparlin, "Cleveland Seeks New Metro Solution," *National Civic Review*, March 1960.

identify the problems, and work out realistic remedies. Generously financed, this diagnostic and prescriptive study had been staffed by professionally competent personnel and conducted with civic approbation. The sponsorship was unimpeachable—both universities were highly respected in the community. Preceding sections of the present case study have already indicated that the survey's findings and recommendations greatly influenced the "moderate" faction on the Board of Freeholders, and that the plan ultimately presented to the voters was in effect the plan of the first researchers.

Members of the merger bloc on the board were not happy with the recommendations, and while they could not openly repudiate the study because of its prestigious sponsorship, they insisted from the beginning that the survey group could not be substituted for the freeholders' staff. This strategy of disassociation was evident throughout the board's deliberations, appearing particularly whenever survey staff members were called upon to testify. The attempt, however, was far from successful because the district bloc repeatedly referred to the survey report in support of its position. It is doubtful, in fact, that the district proposal could have prevailed in the board without the authority and rationale of the report in support of the position.

The dilemma posed here is one constantly faced by researchers whose findings will lead to specific proposals for action. Should such fact finders make recommendations that necessarily involve value judgments and assessments of political realities, or should they merely present the facts with possible alternative solutions? In the St. Louis case the recommendations of independent "experts" attached to no official or citizens' committee were presented to the public in anticipation of a charter commission. Following the report, a Board of Freeholders, presumably representative of the people, was called into existence to draft a plan of government. Members of the board whose judgments or views differed from those of the "experts" found themselves at a disadvantage in disputing the wisdom of a highly respected group.

Several freeholders in the promerger faction bitterly complained that the survey recommendations had placed the board in the unenviable position of ratifying an already formulated plan or risking public disapprobation for repudiating the universities. They contended that the survey report's disclaimer of intention to present a charter while offering "working proposals" for broad consideration was meaningless—the fact is that a plan *was* presented and that it carried the imprimatur of the study group. In their view the survey staff should have confined itself to the assembling of facts and problems and left the board unhandicapped in order to perform its constitutional duty of determining which remedy should be presented to the people. As Shewmaker expressed it, "The people in their wisdom have decided that it is boards like ours rather than political scientists that are best able to make the decisions." But he continued plaintively, "I realize that to talk about political scientists at all is . . . somewhat like talking about motherhood."[5]

The metropolitan expert's role, however, is not so simple as the mergerites describe it. As a specialist, he is expected not only to diagnose but also to prescribe for the ills of the community. Metropolitan reformers want this kind of assistance—not merely a delineation of problems. Had the survey limited itself to the role of the community's fact finder and not its mentor, it would have failed to meet the expectations of many of its supporters.

Although it is difficult to see how any metropolitan study can remain neutral in the recommendations, there are points at which a report can judiciously be uncommitted. The question of election types provides one such instance in the St. Louis plan. The survey's recommendation of nonpartisan elections for metropolitan councilmen and the chief executive was severely criticized by labor and political leaders, and the plan ultimately presented to the voters rejected the proposal in favor of partisan elections. By leaving questions of this type unanswered the survey could have avoided peripheral issues that diverted attention from the main recommendations and needlessly aroused opposition to or raised doubts about the survey in general.

Once the campaign got under way, the survey report was forgotten as an issue. Proponents of the plan referred to it in their talks and debates, and the metropolitan press often supported its editorials in behalf of the proposal by citing the "experts" on the survey staff. On the other side of the fence, a few extremists among the opposition spoke caustically of the survey, one of them remarking that it was "a shame the Ford Foundation could not have given $300,000 to an able group of people who would sincerely try to find what makes the multiplicity of governments work better and cheaper."[6] Other than these occasional references, there is no indication that the survey played an important role in the campaign. It is doubtful that a highly technical study of an exceedingly complex issue can have any direct influence on the mass of citizens. Its impact, if any, will be on the opinion formulators, and in the St. Louis area many of these people were unwilling to accept the judgments of the survey because the proposals differed from their own views and interests.

A second question concerning the survey's impact relates to the character of the sponsorship. Is a university-conducted study designed as the basis for an action program actually an effective medium for action? Here further comparison with the Cleveland experience is helpful. As in St. Louis, the creation of an official charter commission in Cleveland had been preceded by a compre-

[5] Transcript of meeting of the Committee of the Whole, Metropolitan Board of Freeholders, November 13, 1958.
[6] Quoted in the *St. Louis Globe-Democrat,* September 23, 1959.

hensive study. Unlike the St. Louis survey, however, the Cleveland study was conducted under the direction of a lay citizens' board. Throughout the research period, every effort was made to secure wide community involvement in the work and to keep the public fully informed. Numerous subcommittees consisting of civic leaders, government officials, politicians, labor representatives, and businessmen were appointed to work with the professional staff. Over 250 influential citizens and public officials actively participated in the study groups.[7]

The Cleveland procedure ensured the existence of a large nucleus of influential community leaders who were wholly or partially committed to the findings and recommendations of the study and intellectually and emotionally prepared to push for action once the work was completed. The St. Louis study, on the other hand, was conducted with no formal public participation or citizen committees. Under this arrangement, the scholar was relieved of the task of educating and guiding a lay committee and bringing about consensus among its members. This approach afforded the researcher more time and greater freedom in order to make his basic study without using time on administrative or public relations work characteristic of many metropolitan surveys. That the research in the St. Louis venture profited and the subsequent action program suffered as a consequence is a likely hypothesis. While other factors, particularly strong political support, contributed to a more favorable vote in Cleveland, the campaign activity of the civic elite was considerably more pronounced there than in St. Louis—a participation no doubt encouraged by the active involvement of the community leaders in the research program.

METROPOLITAN PROGNOSIS

In both the St. Louis and Cleveland cases the reorganization plans met defeat in the central city as well as in the suburbs. Noteworthy also are two other defeats of reorganization proposals in the same year. In Knox County, Tennessee, a consolidation plan was decisively voted down by core-city residents and suburbanites; and in New Mexico a proposed merger of the City of Albuquerque and Bernalillo County was similarly rejected by top-heavy votes both inside and outside the city. The chaste suburbs have generally been regarded as balky brides-to-be in metropolitan marriages but now the rakish central cities have also assumed the role of reluctant grooms. This series of setbacks may indicate that metropolitan governmental relations are becoming more inflexible,

---

[7] For an account of the vast effort that went into this process, see J. A. Norton, "The Natural History of Metropolitan Surveys," paper delivered at the 1959 annual meeting of the American Political Science Association.

and that instead of progressing closer to agreement, the present pattern of local political pluralism had become institutionalized to the point where only catastrophe or the imminent threat of it will bring radical readjustment.

In addition to the usual handicaps, the metropolitan-reform movement in St. Louis suffers from other congenital defects. The long divorcement of the city from the county has created a traditional chasm of "separateness" that will be difficult to bridge. Mayor Tucker, for obvious fiscal reasons, would have been willing to see the city return to the county, but reentry itself offers no solution to the problems of the area. Although such an approach would provide a ready-made metropolitan vehicle in the form of the county government, it is highly improbable that Tucker and the central-city bureaucracy would consent to a power loss to this unit any more than they would to a metropolitan district. Use of the reentry proposal would have negated one telling argument used by the opposition—creation of an expensive new level of government—but it would have touched off another sensitive issue among suburban voters, that of saddling county residents with the fiscal burdens of the city.

The political isolation of the two jurisdictions has, moreover, created another disunifying element that militates against reentry or, for that matter, any other significant metropolitan remedy. Because of the legal division, each area has separate political party organizations, each with its own leadership structure and individual spheres of influence. As a result, leaders of both parties in the county look with disfavor on any arrangement that would throw them together structurally with the city organizations (as reentry presumably would). Enrollment of the political parties in the metropolitan-reform cause is thus a far more difficult task in St. Louis than in Cleveland or other areas where the party organizations are coterminous with the county.

A third impediment to governmental reorganization in St. Louis lies in the nature of the enabling provisions for adjusting city-county relations. Generally, a metropolitan area that has constitutional authorization to accomplish structural and functional reform on its own initiative is considered fortunate. However, the rigid demarcation and inflexibility of the alternatives open to the St. Louis reformers are more of a handicap than blessing. So long as the enabling grant exists, the natural tendency is to employ it rather than seek other constitutional or statutory authorization. Yet these provisions place those endeavoring to work out a satisfactory solution to the area's problems in a serious bind, as the deliberations of the freeholders so graphically illustrated. Had the board, for example, been able to use the county government as the metropolitan vehicle, the possibility of reaching broader agreement among its members would have been greatly enhanced—a possibility clearly indicated by the paired voting analyses. Reorganization under any circumstances involves legal problems; in metropolitan St. Louis these are blown up out of all proportion by the intricacies of the enabling provisions. Confusion and uncertainty among community leaders as well as the general public are the inevitable results.

Where then does all this leave the cause of metropolitan reform in the St. Louis area? When Cervantes was asked for his reactions to the defeat, he replied that the community simply was not "ready" for metropolitan government. He stated further that even if the proponents had spent several times as much as they had "the plan would still have been soundly defeated." In similar vein, another political leader observed that reorganization will be possible only when an obviously bad breakdown in existing local government occurs or when there is a manifest economic interest at stake for the voters. In the St. Louis case, the only acute problem of a readily visible nature was traffic, but traffic in St. Louis is no worse than in most other large metropolitan centers. Nor was there any immediate concern about the local economic situation. Proponents of reform did argue that the economic future of the area was being jeopardized by an irrational political structure with its inability to control growth, but most voters respond only to the economic facts of the present, and in 1959 these caused no alarm.

It is unlikely that any serious effort at comprehensive reorganization in the St. Louis metropolis will be instituted in the near future. Shortly after the district election, the promerger group announced plans to campaign for political consolidation, but few seemed to have any taste for this attempt and the movement soon dissipated. The picture, however, is not one of unmitigated bleakness. Progress in the form of lesser remedies will undoubtedly take place during the next decade—certainly a transit authority, partial reorganization of the county government, further school-district consolidation, and perhaps even merger of some suburban municipalities. But if broader reform is to be accomplished it will require far greater interest among the general citizenry than now exists, the support of key political leaders in both city and county, a genuine rather than token commitment on the part of the economic and civic elite, and assistance from some of the mass-based interest groups. That these conditions will materialize in the forseeable future is a possibility highly remote.

9. Reflections
on the Creation
of Metro*
EDWARD SOFEN

A trenchant analysis of the reasons for the birth of a metropolitan government in Dade County, Florida—one of the few examples of a successful metropolitan reform movement in the United States—is contained in this selection by Edward Sofen, University of Miami.

Sofen contrasts the Dade County milieu with the environments of other metropolitan areas and attributes the referendum victory to a set of unique conditions not found in other metropolitan areas.

A fuller appreciation of the atypical political environment of Dade County can be gained by comparing this selection with Readings 7, 8, and 10. For a consideration of the problems and accomplishments of the metropolitan Dade County government, see Readings 19 and 20.

To explain the success of the campaign for metropolitan government in Greater Miami, it is necessary to examine the relationship of the central city to the remainder of Dade County, the socioeconomic environment of Greater Miami, the people and forces who worked for the charter, and the methods that were used.

THE MIAMI MILIEU

The difference between the central city and the suburbs in Greater Miami is probably not as great as in other metropolitan areas in the nation. Dade County, because of its youth, its many homeowners, its relatively few apartment dwellers, and its unusual physical and geographical setting, is in many respects one big suburbia. Suburbanites of Dade County are not an "overspill" from the core city seeking greener pastures, but are primarily *émigrés* from many different sections of the United States. These newcomers have not had sufficient time to develop deep roots or, often, even firm friendships, and thus have few emo-

* From *The Miami Metropolitan Experiment* (Bloomington: Indiana University Press, 1963), pp. 71–86.

tional ties to the Miami area. (It would seem that the longer the residency the greater the emotional attachment to a community.)[1]

Nevertheless, these characteristics do not vitiate the reality of the struggle between the core city and its satellites. City of Miami officials, as well as spokesmen for the city's organized business groups, have consistently maintained that central city residents have to bear the financial burden of county-wide facilities. These sentiments were dramatically asserted at a 1957 Congressional subcommittee hearing in Dade County. Robert M. Morgan, civic leader, certified public accountant, and a member of the executive board of the Miami-Dade Chamber of Commerce, blasted the various "parasite communities," which, he said, owed their very existence to the central City of Miami. Replying to a denunciation of Metro by the mayor of Miami Beach, Mr. Morgan declared that Miami Beach was about the least self-sufficient city in the nation. "We Miamians furnish them with water, we burn their garbage, we house their servants, we furnish them with roads leading to Miami Beach . . . we even carry it to the ultimate extreme, we bury their dead."[2]

Some observers contend that the charter, from its inception to its adoption, was a conspiracy of the "downtown Miami merchants." Undoubtedly, this group played one of the more important roles in the genesis of the consolidation movement, but its activities can hardly be classified as a conspiracy. Nor can the general dissatisfaction of a large number of the residents of the City of Miami be traced to the influence of the merchants. The political difficulties that plagued the city for many years might well have disillusioned even the most stouthearted. Despite—or because of—a council-manager form of government, with many nonprofessional managers over the years, the City of Miami was in constant political turmoil. Charges of corruption filled the air, and the police force was under perpetual attack for its failure to enforce the laws against gambling and

---

[1] A September 1958 poll (Beiler Survey No. 12) indicated that the attitude of 433 registered voters towards the autonomy amendment, a pro-city amendment to the home rule charter, varied with the length of residence.
The statistics were as follows (*percentage*):

	7 MONTHS TO 5 YEARS (88 PERSONS)	5 YEARS TO 13 YEARS (144 PERSONS)	13 YEARS AND LONGER (201 PERSONS)
For	22.5	23.0	30.5
Against	60.0	53.5	50.0
Uncertain	17.0	23.5	19.5

[2] U. S., Congress, House, Subcommittee of the Committee on Government Operations, *Hearings, Federal-State-Local Relations, Dade County (Florida) Metropolitan Government,* 85th Cong., 1st sess., Nov. 21 and 22, 1957, p. 114.

other forms of vice. It was to counteract this state of affairs that the Greater Miami Crime Commission, a citizens' group, was formed in 1948.[3] At about the same time the Dade County Research Foundation was created to serve as a "watchdog" over governmental activities and to give assistance to the governments of the area whenever possible.[4]

At the very time that critics of the government of the City of Miami were strongly condemning the city council, these same critics had only the highest praise for the County Commission. The satisfaction with the County Commission can be attributed to its unanimity of outlook, its peace and harmony, and its fairly impressive handling, at least in the public mind, of the county parks, hospital, and Port Authority. The County Commissioners, who had had long experience in their elected offices, were acting as both administrators and policy makers under a commission form of government. The existence of this dichotomy of a "good" county government and an "evil" city government, together with the desire of the city's businessmen to have the county assume the financial burdens of metropolitan functions, helps to explain the transfer to the county of the City of Miami Port Authority and Jackson Memorial Hospital. The transfer of the hospital shifted the costs of support from the city to the county. The designation of the highly respected Board of County Commissioners as the governing board of the Port Authority was seen, by the supporters of the move, as a distinct advantage to the Port Authority in its negotiations with banks. The better credit standing of the county plus the high repute in which the County Commission was held may help to explain why the airlines and the businesses dealing with the airlines preferred county to city control of the airport. Moreover, since the spokesmen for most organized business groups in the central city see Greater Miami as a single unified area, it is to be expected that the central city businessmen would favor a governmental entity that had, in fact and in law, the power to deal with the problem of airports, harbors, and seaports.

From 1945 to 1953 all plans for geographical consolidation could be traced, in part, to the efforts of the powerful business elements within the City of Miami. The 1945 plan was abortive for a number of reasons. The members of the City of Miami Commission, at the time, were of high caliber, and there appeared to be no urgency to save the city. Moreover, the strong bond that was

[3] The Crime Commission was founded on March 31, 1948. It was approved by 250 delegates representing some 90 Dade County civic, patriotic, and business organizations at a three-day law enforcement convention at the Mayfair Theater in the City of Miami. (*The Crime Commission of Greater Miami,* undated pamphlet.)

[4] *Miami Herald,* Jan. 12, 1947, p. 1A. Businessmen were responsible for creating and financially supporting both the Crime Commission and the Research Foundation.

later forged between the Dade delegates to the state legislature and the City of
Miami businessmen had not as yet materialized. Even the *Miami Herald* had
not at this time realized its position of power.

In the 1948 and 1953 elections,[5] a solid alliance was established between the
Dade legislators and the proconsolidation elements in Dade County. Among
the latter were the *Miami Herald,* the Dade County Research Foundation, the
Miami Chamber of Commerce, the Junior Chamber of Commerce, and many
members of the League of Women Voters. The near victory of the 1953 move
to consolidate the City of Miami with the county led to the introduction, by the
localists,[6] of a modified scheme of consolidation aimed at saving the cities from
destruction. Even this proposal, however, was only a counteraction to the pressures from the consolidationists.[7]

The socio-political setting of Greater Miami also was conducive to the
development of a metropolitan government because of a combination of characteristics peculiar to the area: the tremendous growth of population, the perva-
sive tourist atmosphere, the rapid population turnover, the existence of a
no-party political system, the absence of relatively strong racial or religious
minorities committed to the status quo, and the lack of a strong labor movement.

One student of politics has observed that for many years to come it will be
difficult, if not impossible, to integrate local governments in areas where there
is a two-party system.[8] Miami with its "every man for himself" type of politics
has, in effect, a no-party system and, consequently, was spared the kind of
struggle that might have occurred if the fate of political parties had hinged on
the outcome of the move to create a new metropolitan government. By contrast,
certain other metropolitan areas with more formalized party structures, such as
Cuyahoga County in the Cleveland area, have reflected sharp divisions between
the parties as well as within the parties on the issue of metropolitanization.[9]
One can expect a similar response in other areas where political parties stand
to gain or lose power as a result of disrupting the political status quo. While
stressing the logic of efficiency, economy, and unification, the advocates of
integrated metropolitan government elsewhere in the nation, have generally
failed to give sufficient consideration to the concrete factors of power relationships.

[5] Regular elections are held in the Miami area in even-numbered years; special elections
in odd-numbered years.

[6] The localists insisted upon maintaining the autonomy of the municipalities.

[7] The consolidationists espoused the abolition of the municipalities and the creation of
a single government for the Greater Miami area.

[8] Edward C. Banfield, "The Politics of Metropolitan Area Organization," 1 *Midwest
Journal of Political Science* 86 (May 1957).

[9] Governmental Affairs Foundation, Inc., *Metropolitan Surveys: A Digest* (Chicago:
Public Administration Service, 1958), p. 163.

The opposition to recent movements to establish metropolitan governments in the United States stemmed not only from political parties but also from various pressure groups that considered themselves threatened. Minority groups which have found a *modus vivendi* in an existing government are particularly loath to change the political structure. Thus one finds that there were Negro leaders in both Cleveland and St. Louis who strongly opposed changing the existing governmental framework because of the fear that they would lose their personal influence in a larger, more rationalized government.

In Miami, Negroes constitute only 6.8 per cent of the registered voters.[10] Of those voting in the predominantly Negro precincts, an estimated 60 per cent have generally opposed the creation of a metropolitan government. Although there may have been rare instances when the Negro vote on metropolitan or consolidation issues has been crucial to the outcome of certain municipal elections, this has not been the case in Dade's county elections.

In the St. Louis area, however, approximately 25 per cent of the registered voters are Negroes, and it has been estimated that as many as 80 per cent of the Negroes vote as a Democratic bloc.[11] One member of the Board of Education and six aldermen are Negroes. (Of the six Negro aldermen, four serve on the local board of the National Association for the Advancement of Colored People.) Prominent Negroes fill other important positions in the city government and are influential in the labor union movement. Obviously, if Negroes as a group oppose metropolitan government in St. Louis, it has little chance of being adopted.

The Jewish population of Miami Beach is another minority group that may have been reluctant in the past to disturb a political power setting in which it enjoyed a relatively important position. And yet, despite the overwhelming opposition to Metro from Miami Beach, Jewish leaders from that city as well as from other municipalities played important roles on the Metropolitan Charter Boards. In addition, the Jewish population in the southwest section of the City of Miami has been pro-Metro and in no way reflects the insularity of the Jewish residents of Miami Beach. Finally, it must be noted that the anti-Metro attitude of Miami Beach might better be explained by its peculiar economic interests than by its ethnic considerations.

The powerful labor unions which are found in most metropolitan areas constitute yet another political force vitally concerned with any threat to its power status. Greater Miami, however, has a relatively small number of industrial

---

[10] Interview with Dr. Thomas J. Wood, Department of Government, University of Miami.

[11] Kenneth E. Gray, *A Report on Politics in St. Louis* (Cambridge: Center for Urban Studies, 1959. Mimeographed), ch. II, pp. 20–21; ch. V, p. 5.

workers,[12] and although there are some 50,000 union members in the area,[13] unions have played a relatively unimportant role in Dade County politics. By contrast again, in St. Louis there are 35,000 workers in the teamsters' union alone.[14] Also, the Teamsters Local 688 is a vitally significant force in St. Louis. Labor for the most part opposed the metropolitan-oriented District Plan in St. Louis.

In a number of industrial areas throughout the nation, the businessman, or at least an important segment of the business community, has been acutely conscious of the need for the establishment of county-wide metropolitan government. Although prometropolitan business organizations in such cities as Boston, Cleveland, and Dayton generally were ineffectual and ill designed for political action, large sums of money were raised by business groups in conjunction with Ford Foundation and other organizational grants, to advance the metropolitan cause. In Miami, on the other hand, the business leaders allowed the Dade County Research Foundation, a business-sponsored "good government" group, to expire for want of funds.

It may be that the "countervailing power theory" of big business begetting big unions also works in reverse. In the case of Miami, the lack of countervailing organizations, in the form of cohesive labor or minority groups, meant that the business community had no real competitors in the political arena. Moreover, since the cause of "good government" groups coincided with the desires of the more powerful Miami business organizations, the latter were quite content to allow the newspapers, professional groups, university professors, and the League of Women Voters to assume the positions of catalytic leadership in civic affairs.

To these variables revolving about the amorphous power setting of Miami one must add two other factors: the lack of a real crisis situation in Miami except, perhaps, in the minds of the more knowledgeable, and the deep political apathy of most Miami citizens. From what we know of other studies, these conditions are probably typical of most metropolitan areas. The extent of the

---

[12] In 1958 only 13 percent of Greater Miami's nonagricultural labor force were employed by manufacturing concerns, while approximately 30 percent of the national labor force were so employed. See University of Miami Bureau of Business and Economic Research, *Economic Almanac of Southeastern Florida, 1959* (Coral Gables: University of Miami, 1959), p. 25; United States Department of Commerce, *Statistical Abstract of the United States, 1959* (Washington, D. C.: U. S. Government Printing Office, 1959), p. 210.

[13] *Miami Herald,* Oct. 18, 1959, p. 1G.

[14] The city-wide distribution of its members and the aggressive leadership of its secretary-treasurer have made this union the most active and effective interest group in St. Louis. Once a month, assemblies of union stewards are held to discuss city problems and implement requests that have arisen at ward meetings. Their actions are confined primarily to endorsements of candidates and of issues in city, state, and national elections. See Gray, *Report on Politics,* chapter V, pp. 7–12.

existence of citizen apathy in Miami is made clear by the following observations:

> Any testing of levels of thought and feeling in the political substructure inevitably yields new evidence of abject apathy and gross ignorance in the citizen mass. This is particularly true in dealing with the subject of local government. To find, as we did in Survey #10, that only 15% of our registered citizens could think of anything good that the county commission had done in the preceding year, or that 24% could name something blameworthy that they had done (9% named a parks concession scandel) is routine.
>
> However, somehow one expects a thing as big as Metro to make an impression. When only 32% say they have heard or read about a new county charter and had a sliver of a correct idea about it while 13% have a quite wrong idea about it, that sinking sensation returns. It was not only in the telephone poll that 64½% said they did not know of any big change in the county government in the last couple of years. The same question had produced the identical 64½% shrugging response when asked in Survey #10.[15]

The authors of the above quotation concluded that those persons possessing little local political interest did not embrace a strong Metro position and, if low enough in interest, held a distinctly "neutral" position. There was also a definite correlation between high local political interest and a pro-Metro position. At first glance one might get the impression that apathy contributed to Metro's success by keeping the "neutral" and anti-Metro voter away from the polls. However, a statistical breakdown of voter turnout in the various precincts in Greater Miami refutes this. Surprisingly, it shows that there was no marked difference in voter turnout in the high socio-economic precincts, with a high degree of local political interest, and the lower socio-economic precincts with a low degree of local political interest.[16]

PEOPLE, FORCES, AND METHODS

Although the Miami environment and the political process as explained above may have created a setting conducive to the acceptance of metropolitan government, they scarcely account for the positive actions which were necessary to plan, promote, and push Metro to successful adoption. The political environment, in short, provided a favorable matrix; it did *not* provide the "catalytic action-spark." In the following pages the roles of the main actors involved in

[15] Ross C. Beiler and Thomas J. Wood, *Metropolitan Politics,* p. 13.

[16] The information was obtained from an interview with Dr. Thomas J. Wood, professor of government, University of Miami, December 31, 1959.

the formation of Metro will be examined and analyzed. The taxonomy of activists includes the newspapers, the business organizations, the civic groups, the Charter Board, and the professionals.

As already noted, the political vacuum in Miami was filled to a considerable extent by the *Miami Herald,* the influence of which in crystallizing public opinion has been recognized by friends and foes alike.[17] The formulation of the *Herald* editorial policy is attributed by most civic leaders to Associate Editor John D. Pennekamp. Aspirants for political office eagerly seek the *Herald's* endorsement, which is extremely important in this no-party area. Some of Miami's most important businessmen, elected officials, and administrative officers meet and consult with Mr. Pennekamp on important community problems. A few of the associate editor's close contacts are characterized by their enemies as "errand boys," with Mr. Pennekamp portrayed as a puppeteer pulling the strings.

The characterization of Mr. Pennekamp and the *Miami Herald* might well be compared to that of publisher Paul Block, Jr., and the *Toledo Blade* in the following:

> Although . . . Paul Block, Jr. . . . . would win no popularity contest in Toledo, *The Blade* is by all odds the most potent political force in Toledo. It certainly does not run the city in arbitrary, single-handed fashion. No newspaper could. But it wields immense influence. It has made, broken and chastened many a politician. It has pushed through or blocked many a public policy. . . .[18]

Mr. Pennekamp has successfully used the power of the *Herald* to crusade for many civic reforms. He has an almost artistic touch in the manner in which he gradually builds a case for or against an issue. His sense of righteousness makes him a devoted ally—and an extremely dangerous foe. The *Herald,* under the editorial guidance of Mr. Pennekamp, has fulfilled an important leadership role in the Miami area, and the legend of Pennekamp has become part of Miami's folklore.[19]

The emphasis upon the *Herald* is not intended to belittle the role of Miami's evening newspaper, the *Miami News.* During the campaign for the home rule amendment, the editorial staffs of both the *News* and the *Herald* toured the state and persuaded fellow editors to support the amendment. Both papers also strongly supported the home rule charter.

[17] See above, p. 60.

[18] Reo M. Christenson, "The Power of the Press: The Case of 'The Toledo Blade,'" 3 *Midwest Journal of Political Science* 227–28 (Aug. 1959).

[19] In August 1958, Don Shoemaker, former editor of the *Southern School News,* was appointed editor of the *Miami Herald's* editorial page. On January 17, 1962, Mr. Shoemaker became editor of the *Miami Herald.* Mr. Pennekamp continues as associate editor.

Candidates and others seeking public favor appeal to the *News* as well as to the *Herald*. The *News,* although less influential than the *Herald,* has supported candidates who have carried an election without the *Herald's* endorsement. However, while most persons who read the evening *News* also read the *Herald,* the reverse is not true.[20]

A majority of the downtown City of Miami business elements constitute another faction that has consistently supported consolidation movements. The efforts of this group to win public support for Metro were centered around the activities of the Miami Chamber of Commerce. In 1955 the chamber changed its name to the Miami-Dade Chamber of Commerce and invited each of the chambers in the suburbs to appoint an associate director to the Miami-Dade board of directors.[21] The move was considered presumptuous and few chambers cooperated. It is significant that most of the local chambers of commerce, with the exception of the Miami-Dade chamber, have opposed geographical consolidation.

The Miami-Dade chamber, despite schisms within its membership, has played a significant role in all consolidation movements. The organization's support of the 1948 and 1953 drives lacked the fervor that was evident in later years, however. Despite the fact that chamber members were well represented on the 3M Board and the first and second Charter Boards . . . , the movement for metropolitan government was never closely identified in the public mind with the Miami-Dade Chamber of Commerce.[22] The organization was considered by the

[20] As of September 1961, the daily circulation of the *Miami Herald* was 299,689 and that of the *Miami News,* 138,753; the Sunday circulation was 351,222 for the *Herald* and 117,716 for the *News.*

[21] The information was obtained from an interview with Alfred Canel, executive vice-president of the Miami-Dade Chamber of Commerce.

[22] In a late 1957 and early 1958 poll (Beiler Survey No. 10) respondents were asked what individuals or groups they would name as most influential in the decisions shaping the new county government. Out of 723 persons questioned (422 registered, 301 unregistered), only 5.5 percent alluded to a category that included the Chamber of Commerce, the Junior Chamber of Commerce, neighborhood groups, clubs and fraternal organizations. The other responses were as follows (*percentage*):

1.	No group indicated	82.0
2.	Municipal (city commissioners, city officials, Dade League of Municipalities, police, municipal employee groups)	3.5
3.	County Commission and Port Authority	6.5
4.	Newspapers	4.5
5.	Television	1.0
6.	Charter Board and other advisory boards	1.5

The response to the question on which individuals were most influential was practically nil. One would have to conclude that the "average" resident was unaware of the identity of the decision makers in the Greater Miami area.

public to be just another "civic" group supporting metropolitan government. This was probably fortunate, for if the Metro movement had been thought to be a chamber "conspiracy" aimed at shifting taxes from the City of Miami to the county, it would undoubtedly have failed. This is not to suggest that the chamber was in reality the moving force behind Metro and that it managed successfully to disguise the fact. At most, the chamber was part of a loosely aligned group that, along with the *Miami Herald* and the Dade legislative delegation, was responsible, before appointment of the 3M Board, for initiating geographical consolidation movements—none of which succeeded. As already indicated, the initial step toward metropolitan government was a countermovement by the enemies of consolidation, who were concerned primarily with the preservation of the cities. The consolidationists joined the "localists" in support of a federal type of metropolitan government and, according to some observers, may have succeeded in leaving their consolidationist imprint on the charter.

The Dade County Research Foundation was created in 1947 primarily by business groups in the City of Miami to help bring about more economical and efficient government. The director and fulltime staff of the organization was responsible for keeping its members informed of the foundation's findings and recommendations. The foundation enjoyed the respect of the community and the support of the newspapers. It reported on matters of integrity and efficiency in the operations of the City of Miami government and later of the Dade County government. John F. Willmott, first executive director of the foundation, met with opposition when he attempted to criticize the omnipotent County Commission, and in March, 1956, he thought it best to resign.[23] It was somewhat later that the *Herald* and the *News* also began to take the County Commissioners to task.

The foundation *Newsletter* was used to inform not only the members of the organization but also the newspapers, the Miami-Dade Chamber of Commerce, and the League of Women Voters. Under the direction of Harry T. Toulmin, Mr. Willmott's successor, the *Newsletter* also was a source of information for members of the 3M Board and the first and second Charter Boards. During the campaigns for the home rule amendment and the home rule charter, thousands of copies of the publication were distributed by the Miami-Dade Chamber of Commerce and the Dade League of Women Voters. Indeed, the main function of the Dade County Research Foundation was to provide facts for those drawing up the charter and for the organizations trying to influence public opinion.

Although the League of Women Voters, prior to 1957, took no official position on consolidation movements, its members individually gave strong

[23] The position of executive director remained vacant until filled by Harry T. Toulmin on August 19, 1956.

support to such movements. The league, at the time of the charter referendum, however, officially supported the home rule charter.[24] League members were strong allies and formidable opponents. They centered their efforts on distributing pamphlets, ringing doorbells, making phone calls, holding parades, and carrying on other old-fashioned but effective means of "politicking." This group, which is most successful if it is provided with political leadership by a "nonpartisan, good government" organization, maintained such a symbiotic relationship with the Dade County Research Foundation.

The activities on behalf of consolidation by good government groups, as well as by newspapers and business groups would have come to naught without the introduction of appropriate bills by the Dade delegation in the Florida Legislature. . . . Management of both the 1948 and 1953 consolidation bills was assumed by Dade Senator R. Bunn Gautier, who, because of his experience, his strong personality, and his political leadership might well be called the father of consolidation.[25]

Considering the role of Senator Gautier in the consolidation movement, a number of questions come to mind: Was the Senator a tool of the Miami Chamber of Commerce? Was he dictated to by the *Miami Herald?* Or was it purely fortuitous that the Senator's aims were compatible with those of the chamber and the *Herald?* The answers to all of these questions must be in the negative. It would seem that Senator Gautier at times had to rally the members of the chamber to support consolidation, rather than the reverse. Although a concord did exist between him and the *Herald,* it was hardly what one would describe as a case of follow the leader.[26] On the whole, the relationship between Senator Gautier and the consolidationist organizations evolved from interaction and a mutual concern; Senator Gautier's leadership was not merely an individual manifestation but rather a reflection of the group process at work.[27]

A brief examination of some of the preliminaries to the drafting of the 1953

[24] There were actually four separate leagues at the time—City of Miami, Miami Beach, Hialeah and Coral Gables—with a total membership of 450. The information was obtained from an interview with Mrs. John Baker, former president of the League of Women Voters of (the City of) Miami. League activities in promoting the home rule amendment were previously mentioned in ch. 4.

[25] Mr. Gautier was a member of the Florida Legislature from 1947 through 1956. He served one term in the House and four in the Senate.

[26] The information was obtained from interviews with members of the Miami-Dade Chamber of Commerce, with representatives of the *Miami Herald,* and with R. Bunn Gautier.

[27] "It appears, then, that the group experiences and affiliations of an individual are the primary, though not the exclusive, means by which the individual knows, interprets, and reacts to the society in which he exists." David Bicknell Truman, *The Governmental Process* (New York: Alfred A. Knopf, 1951), p. 21.

consolidation bill may reveal some interesting sidelights on the interaction of groups and the individual. Senator Gautier was assisted in drawing up the bill by a prominent attorney, who represented the *Miami Herald* in important litigation and who also was retained by Florida Power and Light. This latter corporation, which preferred to deal with municipalities individually, had consistently opposed consolidation; and from all evidence such was the case in 1953. The attorney for Florida Power and Light, despite his close relationship with the company, agreed to take the assignment. Senator Gautier, on the other hand, was legal counsel for Dade's major transit company, a utility favorably disposed toward, if not eager for, consolidation. Unlike the power company, the transit interests welcomed the prospect of dealing with a single governmental unit legally and financially able to purchase and consolidate the different bus systems. It should be noted, however, that the Senator was an ardent consolidationist before his association with the transit company.

In summary, Senator Gautier seemed to have the characteristics of what James MacGregor Burns calls a "pressure politician":[28] that is, he subconsciously and unconsciously tends to reflect the views of the dominant interests of the community. He may even be ahead of them, but at all times he is a member of the fraternity. He is somewhat of an alter ego of these groups. This observation, according to the writer, is not meant to be disparaging since most successful politicians are "pressure politicians."

Although Senator Gautier was the prime initiator of the early consolidation movements, he was not involved in launching the 3M Board. As mentioned before, the impetus to create the 3M Board came from the "localists" who were intent upon preserving the autonomy of the cities.

The history of the 3M Board and the first and second Charter Boards illustrates Robert Michels' concept of oligarchical leadership as a component of all organized group activity.[29] In the 3M Board the leadership was assumed by an advisory committee composed of Donald R. Larson, chairman of the Government Department of the University of Miami; William L. Pallot, attorney; and Joseph J. Orr, plumbing contractor. While Mr. Pallot and Mr. Orr were "federalists" with a city orientation, Dr. Larson might be described as a "federalist" with consolidationist leanings. To win support for Metro, however, Dr. Larson was quite willing to adopt a conciliatory position and let the future take care of consolidation. These three men worked hand in hand with the PAS consultants in planning strategy, directing public relations, and administering the 3M Board.

[28] James McGregor Burns, *Congress on Trial* (New York: Harper & Brothers, 1949), pp. 18–31.

[29] Robert Michels, *Political Parties* (Glencoe, Ill.: The Free Press, 1949).

The same three men were the nucleus of a 5-man Executive Committee of the first Charter Board. Here, too, they consulted with the experts, directed administration, and took charge of public relations. They gave generously of time, effort, and energy. Professor Larson, experienced in the ways of government, emerged as a dominant figure of both the Advisory Committee of the 3M Board and the Executive Committee of the Charter Board.

The second Charter Board, although it did not include Dr. Larson, also had a number of influential men such as Mitchell Wolfson, owner of a chain of motion picture theaters and a television station; J. D. Ryan, town administrator of Miami Springs; George S. Okell, Sr., attorney and former legislator; and Kurt Peiser, business executive. While Mr. Okell adopted the view of the Dade League of Municipalities and refused to support the charter, Mr. Wolfson and Mr. Ryan endorsed the federal formula. Although the board had no official executive committee, Mrs. Katherine Hudson, executive secretary, often consulted with S. D. Phillips, Jr., chairman of the second Charter Board, and with Mr. Wolfson, Mr. Pallot, and Mr. Orr. Mrs. Hudson and a number of the board members also discussed their problems with Harry T. Toulmin, executive director of the Dade County Research Foundation.

As work on the charter neared completion, the board called in John D. Corcoran, PAS consultant, to assist in evaluating the "Tentative Draft of the Proposed Charter," dated February 28, 1957. In addition to Mr. Corcoran's recommendations, the board, in the final revision of the charter, relied too upon the advice of Charter Board Attorney Daniel Paul. Thus it appears that the professionals played an important role in the final stages of charter development as well as in the early and intermediate stages.

To explain the importance of professionals in molding the charter and in gaining public support for its adoption, it is necessary to examine what might be called the "expert syndrome." Before interpreting this term, however, there should be some clarification of the different types of experts. Mr. Corcoran, in an interesting article,[30] makes a rather invidious comparison between the costs and results of the PAS studies on the one hand and the "probing research" of the foundation-endowed scholars on the other. Obviously, there is need for both types of research, but it would also seem fairly evident that the PAS study was far more productive of results than the work of the scholars. The "syndrome" developed, therefore, around the "practical" expert rather than the "theoretical" expert. The practical expert's laboratory is middle-class suburbia, which has its Book-of-the-Month, its Record-of-the-Month, even its Frozen-Food-of-the-Month, and may at any moment produce its Expert-of-the-Month.

[30] John D. Corcoran, "Seeking Better Government for Metropolitan Areas," 40 *Public Management* 82 (April 1958).

The typical suburbanite, with a better than average education and fairly high socio-economic status, has escaped from the unclean realm of politics to the antiseptic atmosphere of the expert. The appeal for good government, non-partisanship, economy, and efficiency has found a favorable response in what might be characterized as "League of Women Voters" communities. Irrational loyalties to the old and established ways of doing things have not as yet taken root in suburbia.

In Miami the image of the PAS staff as nonpartisan experts provided the symbol of good government. Public Administration Service is not only a research group but a prestige organization as well. As expert consultants analyzing the Miami area, PAS staff members were able, through their recommendations, to keep a number of issues from becoming controversial. The authority of ideas emanating from PAS influenced both the newspapers and the Charter Boards, and PAS representatives worked closely with the Advisory Committee of the 3M Board and the Executive Committee of the first Charter Board. The PAS endorsement of the charter, a sort of *Good Housekeeping* "Seal of Approval," was repeatedly emphasized by the second Charter Board in its campaign for adoption of the home rule charter.

Still another important factor in the promotion of Metro was the symbol of a nonpartisanship with which the public most closely identified the Charter Board. The members of the second Charter Board, appointed by the governor at the behest of the Dade delegation, were not representative of the Greater Miami community either geographically or economically. There were 7 members from Coral Gables, 4 from the City of Miami, 3 from Miami Beach, and 1 each from Miami Springs, Miami Shores, and the unincorporated area. The members, other than those from Coral Gables and the City of Miami, did not reflect the sentiments of the voters of their communities.

A significant number of Charter Board members were men of great wealth in agriculture, business, or finance; at least 6 of the 17 members were in this category. Among the members of the board were 6 experienced officeholders, 3 attorneys, 2 educators, 1 labor leader, and 1 housewife who was a civic leader . . . . On the basis of economic status alone, the board hardly appears to be representative of the people of Dade County. The board, however, was not intended to represent narrow geographic and economic interests. Nor were the board members conscious of strong identification with any specific area or group. For example, two board members—one a labor leader and the other a prominent agriculturist—were able to disregard the sharp anti-Metro feeling of their respective groups. Similarly, those members residing in Miami Beach, as well as a very intense partisan of local government from Coral Gables, joined wholeheartedly in the support of the home rule charter.

It was not the second Charter Board but rather the 3M Board, with its representatives from the Dade League of Municipalities, that first achieved a consensus on the basic principle of federalism. Without this initial impetus, the plan for metropolitan government might have been stillborn. Strategically, "federalism" in Miami appears to have been an accommodation to both groups of antagonists: a shelter for localists against the "terror" of total consolidation, and a half-way house toward integration for the centralists. Indeed, the principle of a federal type of government that permeated the thinking of the 3M Board preconditioned the members of both Charter Boards.

The function of "representativeness" has been defined as the ability to win community consent or to gain the assent of the major power elements.[31] In Greater Miami the Charter Board was confronted with the problem of winning community consent. The board members were looked upon as public-spirited citizens sacrificing freely their time and energy. They had the respect of the community and thus they were able, despite a hard core of opposition from city officials, municipal employees, and beneficiaries of city business, to contribute to the charter referendum victory. The emphasis upon the "virtue" of the board members, made by the public relations firm assisting the board, was an extremely important selling point in the campaign for the charter.

Excerpts from a bulletin sent to the board by its public relations counsel are quoted below:

> On the basis of information gained in vote research a campaign of PRELIMINARY education can be tailored with two goals:
>
> First: to increase and solidify existing support.
>
> Second: to hammer away with the *truth* about the Charter in simplified SLOGAN form; and the trustworthiness of its authors . . . so consistently that as the election nears the opposition will be discredited as irresponsible spreaders of confusion.
>
> In aiming at these two goals, the PRELIMINARY campaign would:
>
> (a) Play up the background of members of the Charter Board as the ablest and most trustworthy men and women in the community. The public must develop the utmost confidence in the Board members, because the Board will CONDUCT the final campaign for the Charter. The public must have full confidence in them.
>
> This confidence would then outweigh and discredit self-seeking motives of most opposition from present officeholders and their spokesmen.
>
> (b) Educate the public on Charter matters as early as possible and continuously. Members of the Charter Board should speak before clubs

---

[31] James R. Jensen, *The Politics of Metropolitan Integration: An Interim Report from Houston* (Houston: Nov. 6–8, 1958. Mimeographed), p. 7. (Paper delivered at the annual meeting of the Southern Political Science Association at Gatlinburg, Tenn., Nov. 6–8, 1958.)

and at other meetings while they are still writing the Charter, and also on radio and TV. It is true that they may not yet be able to present conclusions of the Board, but they can discuss the problems of the Charter, and set forth intelligently the various alternatives being considered. They can invite their audience to present suggestions and points of view to the Board.

The Board may decide this should not be done. The decision rests with the Board, and I would abide by that decision. But it is a calculated risk on the basis of information I have been at great pains to gather on other campaigns of similar nature throughout the nation.[32]

SUMMARY

Miami was able to create a metropolitan government with the very type of support that failed in other parts of the nation because of the ecological conditions earlier considered—particularly the absence of powerfully established political parties, labor organizations, and ethnic groups—and because Miamians have long been accustomed to depend on such non-party sources as the newspapers for political leadership. These factors, together with the astuteness of Dade's legislative delegation to the state legislature, the practical orientation of the 3M Board, the high caliber and independence of the Charter Board members, and the prestige of the Public Administration Service experts, were all responsible for the birth of Miami's metropolitan government.

10. Public Opinion
and Metropolitan
Reorganization
in Nashville*

BRETT W. HAWKINS

The successful consolidation of the city of Nashville and Davidson County, Tennessee, in 1962 is analyzed by Brett W. Hawkins, University of Georgia, who tests four voter attitude hypotheses and attempts to formulate the conditions which must be present if a reform proposal is to achieve success.

[32] The information was obtained from Charter Board files. The memorandum was signed by Robert P. Daly, co-director of public information for the Metropolitan Charter Board.

* The Journal of Politics (May 1966), pp. 408–18.

Hawkins found greater support for metropolitan reform among citizens dissatisfied with existing governmental services, citizens who did not anticipate higher taxes as the result of the consolidation, suburban citizens who were not suspicious of the central city, and citizens with more than a grade school education.

For a consideration of the accomplishments of the metropolitan government of Nashville and Davidson County, see Reading 18.

Recent years have witnessed an enormous outpouring of literature on the nation's metropolitan areas, much of it designed to offer solutions to the problems of governing such areas. In spite of extensive interest in reform, however, few major structural changes have occurred when a vote was required. From 1950 to 1961, for example, there were six failures in seven attempts that contemplated the consolidation of two previously independent governments.[1]

Why have metropolitan area voters been so reluctant to approve reorganization proposals? What kinds of voter attitudes underlie opposition and support? These are the fundamental questions of this study. Its focus is on voter attitudes toward metropolitan reorganization; and the author's purpose is to contribute to an understanding of the conditions under which major reorganizations are probable and the conditions under which they are improbable. It is also hoped that the following analysis will help to meet the objections of those students of metropolitics who are critical of reform-oriented research, and who complain that there has been little systematic research into voter attitudes for and against reorganization.[2]

On June 28, 1962, the voters of Nashville and Davidson County, Tennessee attracted nationwide attention by approving a consolidation charter. In 1958 they had rejected a similar charter despite the heavy support of the area's civic and business leaders.[3] Following the 1958 defeat the City of Nashville annexed some 85,000 county residents. The city's morning newspaper, the *Tennessean*— a long time foe of Nashville Mayor West—portrayed the annexation as an assault on county residents and began a crusade for another vote on consolidation. Supported by the *Tennessean* and a well-organized (though heterogeneous

[1] Advisory Commission on Intergovernmental Relations, *Factors Affecting Voter Reactions to Governmental Reorganization in Metropolitan Areas* (Washington, 1962), pp. 7, 26.

[2] See for example Scott Greer, "Dilemmas of Action Research on the 'Metropolitan Program,'" *Community Political Systems,* ed. Morris Janowitz (Glencoe, Illinois: The Free Press, 1961), p. 188.

[3] See David A. Booth (ed.) *Metropolitics: The Nashville Consolidation* (East Lansing, Michigan: Institute for Community Development and Services, 1963).

and unstable) citizens' committee, the proponents of "Metro" soon succeeded in placing a second consolidation charter before the voters.

The campaign that followed was marked by the efforts of Metro's proponents to stigmatize the governmental status quo and to personalize the issue by attacking Mayor West. The proponents also conducted a block-by-block canvas for votes. Metro's opponents, on the other hand, hoped to use the reputedly well-oiled West organization to obtain a "no" vote in the city. (West himself believed that the adoption of Metro would spell the end of his tenure as Mayor, as indeed it did.) The opponents also expected a heavy "no" vote from city Negroes who feared the dilution of their influence in a consolidated city-county.

Subsequently the city voters approved the charter by 56 percent and the county voters by 58 percent.

VOTER ATTITUDE HYPOTHESES

In this section, four voter attitude hypotheses gleaned from the relevant literature are compared with data from 181 interviews in the Nashville area. Only the data from the 181 interviews are considered. "Don't know" and "no answer" responses are discarded in all cases, and for purposes of this paper null hypotheses are rejected when the probability value for chi square is less than .05.[4] It is also important to understand that the present research was conducted *after* the 1962 consolidation vote. Consequently, in addition to any sampling error that might be present, the *ex post facto* nature of the research was likely to introduce a bias in favor of the actual outcome of the referendum (in this case on the pro-Metro side). Such discrepancies are common in *ex post facto* research.[5]

DISSATISFACTION WITH PUBLIC SERVICES UNDER FRAGMENTED STRUCTURE

"It is frequently assumed that the impetus for governmental change in metropolitan areas is generated by widespread dissatisfaction with services."[6]

[4] The interview schedule used in this study was precoded for punch card tabulation and included both open and fixed alternative questions. The sample was drawn randomly from the official list of registered voters in Davidson County. Inasmuch as the hypotheses tested relate to the attitudes of voters, only those registrants whose cards indicated that they had actually voted in the referendum were chosen. (If the choice happened to fall on a nonvoter, the next card was chosen, and so on.)

[5] Herbert Hyman, *Survey Design and Analysis* (Free Press of Glencoe, Illinois, 1955), p. 151. See also F. Mosteller *et al.*, *The Pre-Election Polls of 1948* (New York: Social Science Research Bulletin #6, 1949), p. 213.

[6] Henry J. Schmandt *et al.*, *Metropolitan Reform in St. Louis: A Case Study* (New York: Holt, Rinehart and Winston, 1961), p. 63.

In St. Louis a large proportion indicated some dissatisfaction (approximately 80 percent had some suggestion for change) but there was very little consensus as to changes desired and there was no significant criticism of most major services.[7]

One hypothesis implied by findings of dissatisfaction is that *voters who are dissatisfied with services are more likely to support reorganization than voters who are satisfied*. This is perhaps the most common hypothesis and is the one tested here.

Each Nashville area respondent was first asked what he thought of his services at the present time. The question was intentionally left open-ended in order to provide a measure of the saliency of this issue among respondents. Fifty-four percent answered "inadequate."[8] These results were then compared with answers to the question on how the respondents voted. Table 1 shows this relationship.

TABLE 1

RELATIONSHIP BETWEEN DISSATISFACTION
WITH SERVICES AND SUPPORT FOR REORGANIZATION
IN NASHVILLE, 1962 (PERCENTAGE)

	SATISFIED WITH SERVICES	NOT SATISFIED WITH SERVICES
Vote:		
For reorganization	52.6	81.1
Against reorganization	47.4	18.9
N(= 100%)	76	90

$$X^2 = 14.09, df = 1, p < .001$$

These data show much greater support for reorganization among voters not satisfied with their services than among satisfied voters, and thus the data confirm the hypothesis as stated. It is worth emphasizing, however, that even among those expressing satisfaction more than half voted for consolidation.

ANTICIPATION OF HIGHER TAXES WITH REORGANIZATION

It seems likely that voters will oppose reorganization when they feel that higher taxes will follow. Other attitudes are possible, however, including the belief that reorganization will save money by ending duplication and waste. It is nonetheless generally assumed in the literature that voter anticipation of

[7] Scott Greer, *op. cit.*, pp. 197, 198.

[8] Sewage disposal and street and road maintenance were most often mentioned as needing improvement.

higher taxes is associated with opposition to reorganization. Thus the hypothesis tested here is that *voters who anticipate higher taxes with reorganization are more likely to oppose it than those who do not anticipate higher taxes.*

To discover something of the saliency of this issue compared with others, all Nashville area respondents were asked to state the most important reason causing them to vote either for or against Metro. Among those voting against it, 23.7 percent said that their decision was based on the belief that consolidation would cost them more in taxes. Although this percentage is not large (76.3 percent expressed other reasons), it was the modal reason.

Each respondent was also asked to say what he thought would happen to taxes "as a result of Metro." In Table 2 these responses are compared with those from the question on how the respondents voted.

It is clear from Table 2 that a majority of those who indicated that they anticipated higher taxes with reorganization voted "no," whereas those who did not anticipate higher taxes voted "yes." The sample data therefore support the hypothesis.

The author also considered the possibility that this correlation represents as much the satisfaction or dissatisfaction with services variable as the anticipation or nonanticipation of higher taxes. If this were true it would suggest that opposition to metropolitan reorganization can be explained equally well with either variable.

TABLE 2

RELATIONSHIP BETWEEN ANTICIPATION
OF HIGHER TAXES
WITH REORGANIZATION AND OPPOSITION TO REORGANIZATION
IN NASHVILLE, 1962 (PERCENTAGE)

	ANTICIPATING HIGHER TAXES	NOT ANTICIPATING HIGHER TAXES
Vote:		
For reorganization	41.4	85.7
Against reorganization	58.6	14.3
N(= 100%)	70	98
$X^2 = 34.38, df = 1, p < .001$		

The data in Table 3 lend some support to this hunch. Thus 92.7 percent of those both dissatisfied with their services and *not* anticipating higher taxes were "yes" voters, whereas only 26.3 percent of those both satisfied with their services and anticipating higher taxes were "yes" voters. In the latter group more than 7 out of 10 were "no" voters.

On the other hand, it appears that the anticipation of higher taxes variable is still relevant when the satisfaction with services variable is held constant, because among all voters dissatisfied with their services a much higher percentage of those not anticipating higher taxes (NAT) were for reorganization than those anticipating higher taxes (AT). Furthermore, among all satisfied voters a much higher percentage of NAT's were "yes" voters than of AT's. Thus given the wording of the hypothesis, it is not required that the hypothesis be rejected from these data.

In any case, the Nashville data do suggest that more research is needed into these relationships.

TABLE 3

RELATIONSHIP OF SATISFACTION
WITH SERVICES TO ANTICIPATION OF HIGHER TAXES
IN NASHVILLE, 1962 (PERCENTAGE)

	SATISFIED WITH SERVICES			DISSATISFIED WITH SERVICES		
	Antici-pating Higher Taxes	Not Antici-pating Higher Taxes	Total	Antici-pating Higher Taxes	Not Antici-pating Higher Taxes	Total
Vote:						
For reorganization	26.3	87.5	52.6	63.3	92.7	81.1
Against reorgani- zation	73.7	12.5	47.4	36.7	7.3	18.9
$N (= 100\%)$	38	32	76	30	55	90
	$X^2 = 24.79, df = 1, p < .001$			$X^2 = 9.61, df = 1, p < .01$		

RURAL AND SUBURBAN SUSPICION OF THE CITY

It is frequently assumed that fringe distaste for the central city is fairly widespread, thus providing a base for anti-reorganization sentiment where reorganization can be viewed as a device for enabling the city to reach out and swallow up the fringe. Survey research in this area suggests that such distaste is in fact widespread. It turned up in Flint, Michigan, for example.[9]

The hypothesis implied from such findings is that where there is suspicion there will be resistance to reorganization. The hypothesis tested here therefore is that *fringe voters who are suspicious of the central city are more likely to oppose reorganization than those who are not.* (This hypothesis uses the word

[9] Amos H. Hawley and Basil G. Zimmer, "Resistance to Unification in a Metropolitan Community," *Community Political Systems,* ed. Morris Janowitz (Glencoe, Illinois: The Free Press, 1961), pp. 170, 182.

"suspicious" only to convey the anti-city attitudes widely attributed in the literature to fringe residents.)

All respondents outside the City of Nashville were asked to indicate whether they agreed or disagreed with the following statements printed on a card:

1. This community (or area) is really a separate community from Nashville and should have a separate government.

2. On the whole, big city politics are more corrupt than smaller city politics.

3. As a rule, it is better to live in small communities with small governments than large communities with large governments.

Responses of agreement were regarded as indicating some degree of suspicion. These data were then compared with those from the question on how respondents voted. Space prohibits a complete presentation of results, but they were very similar from all three measures of suspicion. Table 4 presents the results using measure number 3.

TABLE 4

RELATIONSHIP BETWEEN SUSPICION
OF THE CENTRAL CITY AMONG FRINGE VOTERS
AND OPPOSITION TO REORGANIZATION
IN NASHVILLE, 1962 (PERCENTAGE)

VOTE	SUSPICIOUS	NOT SUSPICIOUS
For reorganization	37.5	75.0
Against reorganization	62.5	25.0
(N = 100%)	32	40

$$X^2 = 8.80, df = 1, p < .01$$

If our measures of suspicion are valid there is clearly a higher incidence of opposition to reorganization among those who expressed suspicion than among those who did not. These data therefore support the hypothesis.

VOTER IGNORANCE AND UNFAMILIARITY WITH LOCAL GOVERNMENT

In the literature there is strong documentation for the conclusion that many voters are ignorant about government. In Flint, Hawley and Zimmer were brought to the tentative conclusion that resistance to unification rested largely in ignorance of government and what to expect from it.[10] The proposition implied from such findings is that voter ignorance is associated with resistance to reorganization. The hypothesis tested here is that *less knowledgeable voters are more likely to oppose reorganization than more knowledgeable voters.*

[10] Hawley and Zimmer, p. 182.

Among the measures of knowledgeability used in Nashville were two fixed-alternative questions designed to test the respondents' familiarity with the proposed consolidation charter.

The data from these two questions, compared with those on how the respondents voted, were in conflict as to their support for the hypothesis. In the first case the less knowledgeable voters (LKV's), 26 in all, split evenly in their support for the charter, whereas the more knowledgeable voters (MKV), 104 in all, supported it. Thus although the LKV's did not oppose reorganization they did vote against it proportionately more than the knowledgeable voters. In the second case, however, the LKV's heavily supported the proposal and the MKV's split evenly. The data from the second measure, therefore, offer nothing in the way of confirmation of the hypothesis.

A third measure of voter ignorance was an open-ended question asking the respondents what other courses of action, beside Metro, might metropolitan areas take to deal with some of their problems.[11] Of those whose answers were knowledgeable (only 29 in all) an overwhelming 86.2 percent supported reorganization. The "unknowledgeable" also supported it, however, although in less striking fashion.

A final test of the hypothesis was to compare education (measured by last grade in school) to voting. The results are presented in Table 5.

TABLE 5

RELATIONSHIP BETWEEN VOTER EDUCATION LEVEL
AND OPPOSITION TO REORGANIZATION
IN NASHVILLE, 1962 (PERCENTAGE)

VOTE	GRADES 1–8	GRADES 9–11	HIGH SCHOOL GRADUATE	SOME COLLEGE	COLLEGE GRADUATE
For reorganization	33.3	57.7	71.4	80.8	95.7
Against reorganization	66.7	42.3	28.6	19.2	4.3
	30	26	63	26	23

$X^2 = 25.36$, $df = 4$, $p < .001$

Except for those in the grade school category, all groups supported Metro in a clear pattern of increasing support with increasing education and decreasing support with decreasing education. Clearly this is some support for the hy-

[11] Answers coded by the author as "knowledgeable" included annexation by the central city, partial consolidation, and intergovernmental co-operation. "Unknowledgeable" answers included "make studies," more civic spirit by the citizenry, better leadership, and the levying of higher city taxes.

pothesis, although the measure used (years in school) is not a measure of knowledge about government.

The author also considered the possibility that this correlation is as much "income" as "education." If this were true the poorly educated voters (anti-Metro) would be predominately the same persons as those in the very low income brackets. Table 6 shows the support for Metro at each intersection of the two stratified populations.

TABLE 6

RELATIONSHIP OF INCOME
TO EDUCATION LEVEL AND SUPPORT FOR METRO
IN NASHVILLE, 1962

| | PRESENT SUPPORT FOR METRO | | | | |
Reported Annual Income	Grades 1–8	Grades 9–11	High School Graduate	Some College	College Graduate
Under $3,000	($n = 13$) 38.5	($n = 3$) 66.7	($n = 1$) 100	($n = 2$) 100	($n = 1$) 100
3,000– 5,999	($n = 9$) 33.3	($n = 10$) 60.0	($n = 20$) 70.0	($n = 3$) 66.7	($n = 5$) 100
6,000– 9,999	($n = 3$) 66.7	($n = 10$) 50.0	($n = 23$) 60.9	($n = 12$) 75.0	($n = 7$) 100
10,000– 14,999	($n = 4$) 0.0	($n = 3$) 66.7	($n = 7$) 57.1	($n = 6$) 83.3	($n = 6$) 83.3
15,000– and over	($n = 1$) 0.0	($n = 0$)	($n = 4$) 100	($n = 3$) 100	($n = 4$) 100

Since the pro-Metro percentages generally increase across the rows and not down the columns—that is, the percentages increase with increasing education—these data suggest that education was a more relevant variable than income. Even so the income categories used in this study were probably too broad to permit any very meaningful conclusions as to whether it is "really" low income or low education that is primarily associated with opposition to metropolitan reorganization.

No consistent pattern emerges from all these data on voter knowledgeability and attitude toward reorganization. It therefore seems possible to conclude that voter ignorance (at least of government) and opposition are not significantly associated, perhaps because ignorance is subject to manipulation and can go either way. On the other hand, the sample data do suggest that voter support is associated with greater knowledge about local government and with higher education.

AGGREGATE VOTING BEHAVIOR

A breakdown of the aggregate voting figure reveals some important geographic variations. Thus when the central city is broken down into old city (7 wards) and annexed area (3 wards) the results are striking. And when the county outside (15 civil districts) is then broken down into unincorporated suburban areas, rural areas, and incorporated cities further important variations appear. See Table 7.

There are a number of plausible explanations for these figures. In the old city it appears that West's political organization carried the day, with assistance from most Negro voters (the 13 city precincts with a nonwhite majority voted "no" by 56.8 percent in aggregate). Of course the whites in the city also voted "no," and by a very similar margin (55.6 percent in 29 precincts). Thus while the data provide little evidence that the racial factor was of great importance, it is quite possible that whites and Negroes voted similarly for different reasons; the whites in support of West and the Negroes in fear of losing their voting power.

In the recently annexed areas it is possible that anti-city and anti-West sentiments, whether clearly separated by the voters or not, resulted in the 72 percent "yes" vote. In the county it appears that the unincorporated suburban areas, which may have felt threatened by further annexations, played a part comparable to that of the annexed areas in the city; that is, they pushed the entire area into the "yes" column. Annexation, one can argue, made it possible for the proponents of change to stigmatize successfully the status quo and to champion Metro as a device for eliminating not only future annexations but also the fomentor of such evils—namely, Mayor West. In a word, most county residents perhaps voted for consolidation to fend off being annexed involuntarily.

The reader will recall, however, that the sample data presented above showed not support but opposition from fringe area residents who were suspicious of the central city. Possible explanations for this are that the sample may have been off and that the questionnaire measures of suspicion may have uncovered only the extraordinarily "suspicious" who would not vote for governmental integration under any circumstances.

Turning to incorporated cities, it is interesting to note that the three high income cities voted "yes" whereas the three lower income cities voted "no." Two of the latter, however, were several miles from the central city. It is therefore possible that the higher education or income levels in the former, plus their perhaps less locally oriented populations, were the deciding factors.

TABLE 7

RELATIONSHIP BETWEEN GEOGRAPHIC AREA, BY GROUPS OF PRECINCTS, AND 1962 METRO VOTE (PERCENTAGE)

| | WITHIN CITY | | | OUTSIDE CITY | | | |
	Old City	Annexed Area	Total	Unincorporated Suburban Area	Rural Area	Incorporated Suburban Cities	Total
NUMBER OF PRECINCTS	42	27	69	53	20	6	79
Vote:							
For reorganization	45.2	72.2	57.4	62.6	34.0	47.3	56.0
Against reorganization	54.8	27.8	42.6	37.4	66.0	52.7	44.0
Number of voters (= 100%)	19,960	16,726	36,686	19,706	4,040	4,662	28,408

CONCLUSIONS

The outcome in Nashville of a proposed reorganization was not the usual one. Therefore voter attitudes underlying support for metropolitan reorganization are perhaps the most important findings of this study. The interview data suggest that such support is associated with (1) voter dissatisfaction with services, (2) the nonanticipation by voters of higher taxes stemming from reorganization, (3) voter education levels higher than grade school, and (4) voter understanding of "metropolitan problems."

A common sense conclusion from the aggregate voting data, in addition, is that annexation transformed the usual "no" vote of fringe residents (an anti-city vote) into a "yes" vote. The relevant interview data contradict this conclusion, however. Doubtless more research is required into the character and correlates of fringe "suspicion."

Scott Greer has suggested that the available alternatives for bringing about metropolitan reform are (1) to manipulate the electorate through redefining (or misdefining) the issues and (2) to bring about change through *fiat*. The former course, he finds, was taken in Dade County, the latter in Toronto.[12]

The Nashville experience perhaps falls into the Dade County category. Certainly the annexation of 85,000 county residents helped Metro's proponents to put the issue on a personal, barely relevant, nonrational basis—namely, for or against Mayor West. The insertion of a "devil," moreover, simplified the task of selling a highly complicated governmental reorganization. It is certainly true, in any case, that the circumstances that pertained to Nashville from 1958 to 1962 have not been common to proposals for governmental reorganization in metropolitan areas. This in turn lends some support to Robert C. Woods' proposition that "program expansion of urban governments" not initiated from without the system, nor by highly mobilized elite groups, is random—"the result of accident, not design."[13]

[12] Scott Greer, *Metropolitics: A Study of Political Culture* (New York: John Wiley and Sons, 1963), p. 199.

[13] Robert C. Wood, "The Contributions of Political Science to Urban Form," *Urban Life and Form,* ed. Werner Z. Hirsch (New York: Holt, Rinehart and Winston, 1963), p. 113.

PART FOUR

Solutions
for Metropolitan
Problems

ROLE
OF THE FEDERAL GOVERNMENT

One of the most significant governmental developments of the twentieth century has been the emerging metropolitan role of the federal government. This is attributed by several observers to the failure of the typical state government to take energetic action to alleviate metropolitan problems.

The increasing federal involvement in metropolitan affairs has been highlighted by a number of developments in the 1960s including the creation of the Department of Housing and Urban Development in 1965 and the Department of Transportation in 1966, and the enactment of the Demonstration Cities and Metropolitan Development Act in 1966. One of the most interesting federal responses to metropolitan challenges is the use of the federal-state compact whereby the federal government becomes a direct partner in a program designed to solve various metropolitan problems. The best known federal-state compact is the Delaware River Basin Compact.

The increasing federal involvement in the problems of the metropolis has not been welcomed universally. Conservatives fear a trend toward the centralization of decision-making power in Washington which will destroy local initiative, and many state officials are disturbed by federal grant-in-aid programs which bypass the state governments and deal directly with the local governments. The apparent alliance between the federal government and mayors is resented by state officials who are convinced that the states have an important metropolitan role to play in a system of "creative federalism." Reading 13 identifies several undesirable consequences of relying upon massive federal grants-in-aid.

The federal government has assisted the resolution of metropolitan problems primarily through conditional grants-in-aid to state and local governments which increased from $894 million in 1946 to nearly $15 billion in 1967; most grants are administered in metropolitan areas.

Considerable sharp criticism of the federal involvement in metropolitan affairs has been directed at the apparent conflict in objectives of various federal programs which are in part a reflection of the federal response to different interest groups. The interstate highway program favors the private automobile and appears to conflict with the mass transportation program. The insurance of home mortgages by the Federal Housing Administration and the Veterans Administration has facilitated the flight of the middle class to the suburbs at the same time the urban renewal program is designed to make the central city more attractive to the middle class. Mortgage insurance has encouraged metropolitan sprawl and appears to be in conflict with the open space program.

Several critics have suggested that new federal programs designed to solve metropolitan problems are not needed, but better coordination and management of existing programs are needed. Senator Edmund S. Muskie of Maine in particular has been critical of the administration of federal grant programs and refers to a "management muddle." In Reading 11, the senator questions how it will be possible to effectuate coordination of local government programs if coordination of the various federal grant programs is lacking. Senator Abraham A. Ribicoff of Connecticut agrees with Senator Muskie's criticisms and also criticizes the federal administration as "frozen and afraid of new ideas" in the urban field.

Perhaps one of the most promising federal programs is the $2.3 billion "Demonstration Cities" program designed to overcome much of the criticism directed against uncoordinated federal grant programs. Reading 12 contains President Lyndon B. Johnson's message to Congress proposing the program. Officials of the Department of Housing and Urban Development maintain that the new program is designed to place physical and social programs in one coordinated package, and to encourage experimentation and innovations. Nevertheless, the program has been criticized as too small and a patchwork of aid programs; others have suggested that more could be accomplished by allocating the "Demonstration Cities" funds to the urban renewal program. Still others advocate tax sharing by the federal government and the use of block grants which would accord recipient governments a maximum of flexibility in spending the grant funds in the attack upon metropolitan problems.

Although the federal government has not utilized conditional grants-in-aid to force a restructuring of the government of the metropolis, it is insisting upon comprehensive planning for metropolitan areas and requiring review—by a metropolitan planning commission or council of governments responsible for metropolitan planning—of requests by local government for airport, highway, land conservation, library, mass transportation, open space, and sewer and water facilities grants. The purpose of the requirement is to foster cooperation and coordinated decision making in a fragmented political system, thereby promoting the orderly development of the metropolitan area. If the federal effort to solve pressing area-wide service problems is successful, the fragmented government of the metropolis probably will be perpetuated as reformers will be deprived of some of their most compelling arguments.

11. Coordination
at the Federal Level*
EDMUND S. MUSKIE

The increasing involvement of the federal government in metropolitan affairs has created phenomenal problems of coordinating the manifold federal programs. An astute observer of the federal system is Senator Edmund S. Muskie of Maine, Chairman of the Subcommittee on Intergovernmental Relations, who advances several major proposals to improve federal program coordination and intergovernmental relations. This selection should be read in conjunction with Reading 12 which contains President Johnson's proposals to improve program coordination.

We can hardly expect state and local jurisdictions to coordinate their programs and services if the federal house is not in better order. Thus, one of the first items of business should be a wholly new policy of coordinating federal aid, and working with state and local governments to help them improve their financial resources and administrative effectiveness. It is now quite apparent that the present use of interagency committees and councils is just not sufficient to meet this need. Most of these coordinating agencies are understaffed—if staffed at all—meet too infrequently, and concern themselves too often with vague pronouncements rather than specific ground rules for integrating programs. In addition, while many departments and agencies have designated officials to handle their own intergovernmental relations, those officials are too far down the chain of command to be effective. The two areas—better program coordination and better interlevel cooperation—should be the major concern today of top domestic policymakers in the executive branch.

First. Consideration should be given to designating a special assistant to the President for program coordination and intergovernmental relations who would keep abreast of interdepartmental and interlevel conflicts and assist the President in solving them. At the same time, he could establish a more direct liaison between the White House and state and local leaders to improve state and local relations.

Second. This special assistant should, in turn, be aided by a topflight U.S. Bureau of the Budget official, equipped with a sufficient staff, which would make

---

* From "The Challenge of Creative Federalism," *Congressional Record* (March 25, 1966), pp. 6504–06.

continuing investigations of intergovernmental problems and recommend policies for improving federal-aid administration.

Third. To help both the special assistant and the President, the bureau should develop—far more than it is presently planning—a computerized information clearinghouse system which could provide immediate information to the President and others concerning: (a) social, economic, and other basic characteristics of individual states and local areas; (b) efforts on the part of these jurisdictions to meet their growth problems and projected needs; (c) federal aid programs which now are assisting specific state and local jurisdictions; and (d) those available federal assistance programs which have not been utilized but could improve state and local programs.

Such a clearinghouse system would be of great benefit if it were linked to regional, departmental, and Bureau of the Budget levels, with each providing pertinent information concerning its particular jurisdiction. The U.S. Civil Service Commission has recently initiated federal information centers in 55 major communities throughout the country. Regional computerized clearinghouses could be located at these offices, thus providing a meaningful "one-stop shopping center" for local officials and others.

Fourth. At the department and agency level, a deputy undersecretary—or his equivalent—should be given a full-time responsibility for the coordinating of aid programs on a departmental, interdepartmental, and intergovernmental basis, and he should work directly with the special assistant to the President in formulating coordination guidelines and in identifying the more serious problem areas. To assist him in this task, a special staff should be assigned. Placing the responsibility for coordination and federal-state-local relations in the office of the undersecretary puts muscle into the program, and brings the machinery for coordinating the coordinators much closer to the Secretaries and to the President. One wonders how many Watts-type riots might be avoided—or at least mitigated—with this new approach. As a matter of fact, I had expected that HUD would put its Office of Urban Program Coordination in the immediate charge of the undersecretary, and—as I have stated—I think it has made a strategic mistake in not doing so.

Fifth. What about federal coordination in the field? Here HUD is to be commended. According to its new organizational scheme, it has brought all of its functions at the regional level under a regional administrator from whom it expects "strong local-level program leadership and coordination through decentralization of operations"—Secretary's Organization Order No. 2, February 24, 1966.

But federal departments with key aid programs would do well to follow its example. In particular, regional offices should be set up in accordance with standard geographical boundaries. Each should be headed by a regional director who would represent the secretary or agency chief on all matters in the area, and be responsible for coordinating all departmental activities at the regional level, and for achieving similar coordination with other agencies. The regional director should be given sufficient decision-making powers to implement this coordination, and to the largest extent possible, resolve intergovernmental conflicts. This regional director and his staff could be a very important information source to the Secretaries, Bureau of Budget, and the President with respect to interlevel problems and possible solutions.

Sixth. Ideas for developing improved intergovernmental relations at the local level are finding their way into recent administration proposals. Here again HUD has paved the way with its proposal for local program coordinators located in metropolitan areas to work with local government administrators to help them find their way through the maze of federal programs, expedite applications for assistance, stimulate areawide planning, assist in resolving intergovernmental conflicts at the local level.

Seventh. Also to be commended is the proposal to establish one-stop shopping centers for local officials and others to get up-to-date program and planning information, government publications, statistical data, administrative counseling and data processing services.

Eighth. Consideration, however, should be given to creating federal coordinators and services in state capitals for the benefit of state planners and the nonmetropolitan communities. To some extent, this has been done, but there must be more emphasis on federal planning and technical assistance to encourage areawide and regional planning as it effects the broad scope of economic and social development.

Ninth. For long-range action, serious thought should be given to establishing permanent operating machinery in the Executive Office of the President for enforcing coordination guidelines laid down by the President, and for establishing working relationships with state and local leaders for a continuing assessment of their needs and for a speedy resolution of administrative conflicts.

One suggestion—which I think makes a tremendous amount of sense—would be the creation of a National Intergovernmental Affairs Council—NIAC—chaired by the President and composed of those Cabinet officials and agency heads whose activities have a major impact on domestic grant-in-aid programs and intergovernmental relationships. Its membership would include the Secretaries of HUD, HEW, Labor, Agriculture, Commerce, the Attorney General, the Director of OEO, the head of the Bureau of the Budget, the Chairman of the Advisory Commission on Intergovernmental Relations, and others.

Patterned somewhat after the National Security Council, this body would have an executive director, and a working secretariat composed of the deputy under-secretaries representing the departments and agencies, and top-level executives independently selected and responsible to the executive director.

The council would go far beyond the advisory responsibilities of the Bureau of the Budget and the Council of Economic Advisors. It would be an operating mechanism for developing the President's policies of program coordination, and overseeing their implementation. It would provide the forum for determining basic intergovernmental policies and provide the President with an immediate liaison with state and local governments.

At the same time, it could be the President's ombudsman, a watchdog for crises, a central domestic information agency and an inspector general for program effectiveness. It would be concerned with both urban and rural development as a multidepartmental responsibility involving education, housing, transportation, public facilities, law enforcement, civil rights, and other issues. It would play a strategic role in long-range planning, and assist states and local governments in regional planning.

NIAC could also provide the leadership and the organization for calling conferences of governors, mayors, and other leaders for a review of national and regional problems and for the development of new approaches to meet economic and social needs. Such conferences and special meetings with the council's secretariat would be very helpful to the federal government in getting an up-to-date review of regional, state, and local problems. They would be helpful to the states and local governments because they would provide a forum for the airing of complaints and the discussion of new ideas.

Such a domestic security council could well be called on to use its experience and expertise in the domestic field to assist foreign countries in their own development programs. For instance, a national council of this nature might have been brought into immediate action by the President in his recent promotion of economic and social development assistance for certain Asian countries. Although there may be differences between the United States and our foreign friends in terms of traditions and political and social outlooks, the technical lessons learned in building communities, cleaning up rivers, developing transportation systems, providing health facilities, and improving agriculture can be applied advantageously in most areas. Therefore, what we learn in America through basic and applied research, through industrial development and through the development of more efficient coordinated planning, we can apply to our commitments overseas to obtain maximum effectiveness.

As I see it, a National Council for Intergovernmental Affairs could be an effective substitute for various interdepartmental committees and councils that presently exist under various pieces of legislation.

I am presently preparing legislation which would embody the concepts of this suggestion of a National Intergovernmental Council, and I expect to introduce it within the next few weeks.

Tenth. Long-range action concerning federal field management should also be considered. Just as a National Council for Intergovernmental Affairs would provide the President with greater control over federal programs at the national level, a similar overall coordinating mechanism should be created in each of the various regions of the country. Many competent observers feel that a large percentage of intergovernmental conflicts could be resolved at this level.

The suggestion is made that a Federal Regional Coordinator—not connected with any department or agency—be established to obtain across-the-board implementation of federal programs in accordance with state and local comprehensive plans—of course consistent with national objectives and standards. He would be the President's man in the field, concerned with effective interrelationships of programs, the efficiency of administration, the cooperation of federal officials with their state and local counterparts, and the developing problem areas. He should have a competent staff to assist him, and a status which would be above all other federal regional officials in his area.

If a National Council for Intergovernmental Affairs is established, this regional coordinator should be paid by it, and made immediately responsible to its executive director. Prior to such establishment, he should be paid by the Executive Office of the President, and be directly responsible to a special assistant to the President and to the Bureau of the Budget.

The Public Works and Economic Development Act of 1965, provides for the creation of regional planning commissions each with a federal cochairman and governors—or designates—as members from the states involved. At the moment, this federal member is responsible to the Secretary of Commerce. As these commissions develop, consideration might well be given to making these federal cochairmen regional coordinators. If this is feasible, they should be transferred from the Department of Commerce and put in the Executive Office of the President.

Another long-range alternative which deserves attention is the suggestion that the Bureau of the Budget return to its system of regional field offices which was abandoned in 1953 as part of an economy move. In this situation, the Bureau of the Budget's regional director could be the President's Regional Coordinator, both with respect to federal aid programs and planning, and to obtaining and providing essential information about regional needs, plans and trouble spots. He could also serve in the role as the President's intergovernmental liaison in the field.

Before leaving the matter of federal field management, mention should be made of the federal executive boards. Up to now, these organizations—made up of department and agency chiefs in each region—have been ineffective in coordinating federal programs, except as they may apply to personnel or administrative expenditures. FEB chairmen have no meaningful powers, or separate staffing, and, except in limited situations, they have been given no real mandate to integrate substantive programs. There is much doubt as to whether the FEB's should be continued, but if they are to remain, they certainly should be strengthened, and used as active boards for coordinating federal policy with respect to federal aid, improvement in administrative practices, technical and planning assistance to state and local governments and problem identification. Chairmen should be assigned by the President on the basis of their ability and knowledge of federal economic and social programs. . . .

12. A Demonstration Cities Program*

LYNDON B. JOHNSON

President Lyndon B. Johnson's message to Congress proposing a $2.3 billion "Demonstration Cities Program" for a six-year period reveals not only the extent and magnitude of federal involvement in metropolitan affairs, but also federal leadership in solving metropolitan problems. The program is designed to encourage experimentation to solve major urban problems. Congress responded to the President's message with the Demonstration Cities and Metropolitan Development Act which President Johnson signed on November 3, 1966. Eligible cities receive regular federal grants-in-aid and a special grant of 80 percent of the nonfederal share of the various grant programs to help finance a coordinated program to eliminate urban blight.

I propose a demonstration cities program that will offer qualifying cities of all sizes the promise of a new life for their people.

I propose that we make massive additions to the supply of low- and moderate-cost housing.

I propose that we combine physical reconstruction and rehabilitation with effective social programs throughout the rebuilding process.

* From *City Demonstration Programs,* Message from the President of the United States, January 26, 1966, House Document No. 368, 89th Congress, 2d Session, pp. 4–11.

I propose that we achieve new flexibility in administrative procedures.

I propose that we focus all the techniques and talents within our society on the crisis of the American city.

It will not be simple to qualify for such a program. We have neither the means nor the desire to invest public funds in an expensive program whose net effects will be marginal, wasteful, or visible only after protracted delay. We intend to help only those cities who help themselves. I propose these guidelines for determining a city's qualifications for the benefits—and achievements—of this program.

1. The demonstration should be of sufficient magnitude both in its physical and social dimensions to arrest blight and decay in entire neighborhoods. It must make a substantial impact within the coming few years on the development of the entire city.

2. The demonstration should bring about a change in the total environment of the area affected. It must provide schools, parks, playgrounds, community centers, and access to all necessary community facilities.

3. The demonstration—from its beginning—should make use of every available social program. The human cost of reconstruction and relocation must be reduced. New opportunities for work and training must be offered.

4. The demonstration should contribute to narrowing the housing gap between the deprived and the rest of the community. Major additions must be made to the supply of sound dwellings. Equal opportunity in the choice of housing must be assured to every race.

5. The demonstration should offer maximum occasions for employing residents of the demonstration area in all phases of the program.

6. The demonstration should foster the development of local and private initiative and widespread citizen participation—especially from the demonstration area—in the planning and execution of the program.

7. The demonstration should take advantage of modern cost-reducing technologies without reducing the quality of the work. Neither the structure of real estate taxation, cumbersome building codes, nor inefficient building practices should deter rehabilitation or inflate project costs.

8. The demonstration should make major improvements in the quality of the environment. There must be a high quality of design in new buildings, and attention to man's need for open spaces and attractive landscaping.

9. The demonstration should make relocation housing available at costs commensurate with the incomes of those displaced by the project. Counseling services, moving expenses, and small business loans should be provided, together with assistance in job placement and retraining.

10. The demonstration should be managed in each demonstration city by a single authority with adequate powers to carry out and coordinate all phases of

the program. There must be a serious commitment to the project on the part of local, and where appropriate, state authorities. Where required to carry out the plan, agreements should be reached with neighboring communities.

11. The demonstration proposal should offer proof that adequate municipal appropriations and services are available and will be sustained throughout the demonstration period.

12. The demonstration should maintain or establish a residential character in the area.

13. The demonstration should be consistent with existing development plans for the metropolitan areas involved. Transportation plans should coordinate every appropriate mode of city and regional transportation.

14. The demonstration should extend for an initial six-year period. It should maintain a schedule for the expeditious completion of the project.

These guidelines will demand the full cooperation of government at every level and of private citizens in each area. I believe our federal system is creative enough to inspire that cooperative effort. I know it must be so creative if it is to prosper and flourish.

SIZE OF THE PROGRAM

The program I recommend is intended to eliminate blight in the entire demonstration area. Through efficient rebuilding it must replace that blight with attractive and economic housing, social services, and community facilities.

There are many ways by which this can be done, once the commitment has been made to do it. Total clearance and reconstruction; partial clearance and rehabilitation; rehabilitation alone—any of these methods may be chosen by local citizens. Whatever approach is selected, however, must be comprehensive enough to be effective and economic.

There are few cities or towns in America which could not participate in the demonstration cities program. We shall take special care to see that urban communities of all sizes are included. For each such community, the impact of the program will be significant, involving as much as 15 to 20 percent of the existing substandard structures.

For the largest qualifying cities a relatively modest program could provide decent housing for approximately 5000 families now living in substandard dwelling units. It could rehabilitate other marginal housing sufficient to affect 50,000 people. A typical program could well involve a total of 35,000 units or 100,000 people.

For cities of approximately 100,000 people, 1000 families could be rehoused and 3000 units rehabilitated, affecting a total of 10,000 people.

BENEFITS OF THE PROGRAM

I recommend that participating cities receive two types of federal assistance:

First, *the complete array of all available grants and urban aids* in the fields of housing, renewal, transportation, education, welfare, economic opportunity, and related programs.

Second, *special grants amounting to 80 percent of the nonfederal cost of our grant-in-aid programs included in the demonstration.* These grants are to supplement the efforts of local communities. They are not to be substituted for those efforts.

In every qualifying city, a federal coordinator would be assigned to assist local officials in bringing together all the relevant federal resources.

Once authorized, the supplemental funds would be made available in a common account. They would be drawn at the discretion of the community to support the program. They would be certified by the federal coordinator.

It is vital that incentives be granted for cost reductions achieved during the performance of the program.

At least as vital as the dollar commitment for rebuilding and rehabilitation is the social program commitment. We must link our concern for the total welfare of the person, with our desire to improve the physical city in which he lives. For the first time, social and construction agencies would be joined in a massive common effort, responsive to a common local authority. . . .

FEDERAL COST

Funds are required in the first year to assist our cities in the preparation of demonstration plans. We should not underestimate the problems involved in achieving such a plan. The very scale of the demonstration, its widespread and profound effects on the social and physical structure of the city, calls for marshaling the city's planning and administrative resources on an unprecedented scale.

I estimate the appropriate federal contribution to this planning effort at $12 million. For the supplemental demonstration grants I will recommend appropriations, over a six-year period, totaling over $2.3 billion, or an average of some $400 million per year.

It is impossible to estimate exactly—but it is necessary to consider—the rising cost of welfare services, crime prevention, unemployment, and declining property values that will plague all governments, local, state, and federal, if we do not move quickly to heal and revitalize our cities.

METROPOLITAN PLANNING

The success of each demonstration will depend on the quality of its planning, and the degree of cooperation it elicits from the various governmental bodies concerned, as well as from private interests.

Most metropolitan areas conduct some degree of metropolitan planning now. The federal government has made funds available throughout the country so that state and local planning agencies might devise—many for the first time—comprehensive plans for metropolitan areas.

I recommend improvements and extensions of this program. The Congress enacted them recognizing that the problems of growth, transportation, housing, and public services cannot be considered by one entity of government alone.

The absence of cooperation between contiguous areas is wasteful. It is also blind to the reality of urban life. What happens in the central city, or the suburb, is certain to affect the quality of life in the other.

The widespread demand for these funds has resulted in their being spread thinly across the 50 states. Thus, the benefits of a truly coordinated attack on metropolitan problems have not generally been realized.

INCENTIVES TO ORDERLY METROPOLITAN DEVELOPMENT

Over the past five years, the Congress has authorized federal grants for urban mass transportation, open space, and sewer and water facilities. The Congress has required that such projects be consistent with comprehensive planning for an entire urban or metropolitan area. The federal government has thus not only helped our localities to provide the facilities they need; it has also stimulated cooperation and joint planning among neighboring jurisdictions.

But more remains to be done. The powerful forces of urban growth threaten to overwhelm efforts of achieve orderly development. A metropolitan plan should be an instrument for shaping sound urban growth—not a neglected document.

I now propose a new incentive to help assure that metropolitan plans achieve their potential.

The federal government should bear a larger share of the total cost of related federal aid programs. This share would be borne where local jurisdictions show that they are ready to be guided by their own plans in working out the patterns of their own development and where they establish the joint institutional arrangements necessary to carry out those plans.

DEMONSTRATIONS OF EFFECTIVE PLANNING

I propose that a series of demonstrations in effective metropolitan planning be undertaken promptly.

Metropolitan areas would be selected to return the broadest possible data and experience to federal, state, and local governments. They should therefore be of varying size and environment, in widely separated locations. They would be selected to assure that their benefits reach small communities surrounding the large cities.

Advanced techniques and approaches should be employed. There must be—

Balanced consideration of physical and human development programs.

Coordinated treatment of the regional transportation network.

Technical innovations, such as metropolitan data banks and systems analysis.

New educational and training programs.

New arrangements for coordinating decisions of the various local governments involved.

I estimate the cost of the demonstrations at $6,500,000.

I shall impose on the new Department of Housing and Urban Development the continuing responsibility to stimulate effective planning. If local governments do not plan cooperatively and sufficiently in advance of inevitable urban growth, even adequate funds and an aggressive determination to improve our cities cannot succeed.

HOUSING FOR ALL

The programs I have proposed—in rebuilding large areas of our cities, and in metropolitan planning—are essential for the rebirth of urban America.

Yet at the center of the cities' housing problem lies racial discrimination. Crowded miles of inadequate dwellings—poorly maintained and frequently overpriced—is the lot of most Negro Americans in many of our cities. Their avenue of escape to a more attractive neighborhood is often closed, because of their color.

The Negro suffers from this, as do his children. So does the community at large. Where housing is poor, schools are generally poor. Unemployment is widespread. Family life is threatened. The community's welfare burden is steadily magnified. These are the links in the chain of racial discrimination.

This administration is working to break that chain—through aid to education, medical care, community action programs, job retraining, and the maintenance of a vigorous economy.

The time has come when we should break one of its strongest links—the often subtle but always effective force of housing discrimination. The impacted racial ghetto will become a thing of the past only when the Negro American can move his family wherever he can afford to do so.

I shall, therefore, present to the Congress at an early date legislation to bar racial discrimination in the sale or rental of housing.

NEW COMMUNITIES

Our existing urban centers, however revitalized, cannot accommodate all the urban Americans of the next generation.

Three million new residents are added each year to our present urban population. The growth of new communities is inevitable. Unless they are to be casual parts of a general urban sprawl, a new approach to their design is required.

We must:

1. Enlarge the entire scale of the building process;
2. Make possible new efficiencies in construction, land development, and municipal services;
3. Relieve population densities;
4. Offer a variety of homes to a wide range of incomes.

These communities must also provide an environment harmonious to man's needs. They must offer adequate transportation systems, attractive community buildings, and open spaces free from pollution. They must retain much of the natural beauty of the landscape.

The private sector must continue its prominent role in new community development. As I recommended to the Congress last year, mortgage insurance should be made available for sites and community facilities for entire new communities.

It is apparent that new communities will spring into being near an increasing number of major metropolitan areas. Some, already in existence, promise dramatic efficiencies through size and new construction techniques, without sacrificing beauty. Obviously such a development should be encouraged. I recommend that the Congress provide the means of doing so.

RENT SUPPLEMENT PROGRAM

Rarely has a new housing program evoked such a dramatic and positive response as the rent supplement program. The Department of Housing and Urban Affairs has already received preliminary proposals from sponsors to construct nearly 70,000 low-income units under this program as soon as funds become available. The proposals involve 424 projects in 265 localities in 43 States, the District of Columbia, and Puerto Rico. The sponsors have already selected sites for some 40,000 of these units. The interested groups are about equally divided between nonprofit organizations and private limited dividend developers.

The need for this program is obvious. It is the need of the poor and the disadvantaged. The demand for the means to meet this need by private enterprise is demonstrated by the figures I have just cited.

I strongly urge the Congress to pass a supplementary appropriation to fund the rent supplement program at the $30 million level it has authorized in the Housing and Urban Development Act of 1965.

MASS TRANSPORTATION PROGRAM

We must continue to help our communities meet their increasing needs for mass transportation facilities. For this purpose, I propose an additional one-year authorization for the urban mass transportation program.

THE NEW DEPARTMENT

No federal program can be effective unless the agency that administers it is efficient. This is even more crucial for programs that call for comprehensive approaches at both the federal and local level.

Progress was made after 1961 toward unifying the Housing and Home Finance Agency. But the very nature of that agency limited the extent to which its several parts could be welded into a truly unified whole. Its administrator lacked the statutory basis for gaining full control over partially independent agencies.

With this in mind, I requested—and you enacted—legislation to create a Department of Housing and Urban Development. As a result, the Secretary of the new department now has the authority and the machinery for implementing the new programs I have asked for. I see five ways by which he can do this:

1. He can organize the department so that its emphasis will be upon meeting modern urban needs—rather than fitting new programs into old and outworn patterns.

2. He can strengthen the regional structure so that more decisions can be made in the field.

3. He can assert effective leadership throughout the department.

4. He can mesh together all our social and physical efforts to improve urban living.

5. He can assume leadership among intergovernmental agencies dealing with urban problems. . . .

I believe these are among the most profound aspirations of our people. I want to make them part of our destiny.

I urge the Congress promptly to adopt the Demonstration Cities Act of 1966. If we begin now the planning from which action will flow, the hopes of the twentieth century will become the realities of the twenty-first.

13. A Mayor
Tells How to Modernize
America's Cities*

HERMAN W. GOLDNER

In contrast to those who look to the federal government to rescue cities, Mayor Herman W. Goldner of St. Petersburg, Florida—a businessman-lawyer and a member of the Advisory Commission on Intergovernmental Relations—maintains that cities have the resources to solve their problems, but are hindered by antiquated laws and thinking. He suggests criteria for the granting and receiving of federal funds, and cites state and local personal income taxes as a potential revenue source to supplant partially federal grants-in-aid.

Too many of our ailing cities today are calling for massive doses of federal aid as a cure-all, complaining bitterly that they do not have the resources to heal their own maladies.

They are wrong. They have potential cures at hand if they will honestly seek them out.

Most of our urban areas are stopped tantalizingly near to solutions by archaic laws and equally out-of-date thinking. They need not only more money but new systems and tools—from super-cities to computers—to help meet people's needs.

If most of the nation's municipal governments were private corporations, they would be out of business when the next payroll comes due because they cannot

* © 1966, *Nation's Business*—the Chamber of Commerce of the United States. Reprinted from the April issue with permission of publisher and author.

build the fiscal and organizational resources needed to carry on.

No sane businessman would dream of structuring a corporation which has obligated itself to provide millions of dollars in services, maintenance and capital improvements without adequate income.

No sane businessman would consider forming a corporation which must rely upon its "competitors" for revenue.

Yet municipal governments, as they exist today, are comparable to private firms which have gone into business without the ability to sustain their endeavors financially.

Our cities and urban areas must rely primarily upon sources of income already tapped by their "competitors" in government—the county, state and federal systems.

And when our cities find they cannot function fiscally, they begin to call loudly for help and too often the first call is for federal cash and lots of it.

Our cities, often neglected in the past by unsympathetic state legislatures, expect some return on the federal taxes paid by their citizens.

Massive federal aid, however, can mean an atrophying of municipal self-reliance. It causes a breakdown in planning to meet future needs; the feeling is that "if we run into trouble we can always go to Washington and hook onto some program or other."

It leads, furthermore, to a distortion in allocation of local resources on a sound priority basis. The temptation is great to concentrate local spending on projects for which federal grants are available, regardless of need.

Urban problems must be solved at the urban level. The federal government should lend financial assistance only in those areas meeting basic criteria, the most important being that an honest local effort has failed.

This is not to deny Washington's responsibility, which exists if only because federal spending ultimately taps the same till as local government. But straight substitution of federal programs for local programs is wrong.

The true federal responsibility, it seems to me, is to create an environment wherein the cities can better solve their own problems with their own resources.

Municipal officials, myself included, jump at the opportunity to testify before congressional committees and point out that the 220 Standard Metropolitan Statistical Areas (SMSA's) as defined by the Bureau of the Census contain over three fourths of our people. We emphasize that in these areas occur most of the poverty, delinquency and traffic congestion in the country and that these are national problems requiring financial aid in large doses.

However, there are some other shattering facts about these SMSA's and their own financial potentials which we mayors fail to mention:

- They account for three quarters of our bank clearings.
- They account for four fifths of all value added by manufacture.
- They contain four fifths of all bank deposits.

• And most important of all, at least 80 per cent of all federal personal income taxes are collected from people within their boundaries. The personal income tax is the major source of federal revenue from which federal grants-in-aid are financed.

Of course, the difficulty is that within the SMSA's the problems (poverty, crime, etc.) are not in the same jurisdiction as the fiscal resources. Combined action by state and local governments is essential to meet these disparities. One of the questions we in municipal government must honestly begin to ask our-selves is:

Are federal funds too often taken by local governments simply because they are available?

We must soon seek the establishment of realistic criteria for the giving and receiving of federal funds by local governmental units. I suggest some of the points to be considered are:

1. Is there a real need for federal funds for the particular local program for which they are sought? How urgent is that need and what is the honest ability of the local government to meet that need?

2. What realistic formula can we agree upon to indicate the amount of local effort being brought to bear upon the particular problem for which federal funds are sought?

3. Can this formula include an honest appraisal of the tax base in use by the local unit and can it determine the extent to which the local unit is taxing, or otherwise seeking to raise money, to meet its needs?

In addition, I believe we must have some hard and fast guidelines outlining the scope of federally funded local programs. When do they begin, how broad an area do they encompass and—most importantly—when do they end?

As one of four mayors serving on the President's Advisory Commission on Intergovernmental Relations and now nearing my fifth year of service in a metropolitan city, I find myself becoming increasingly aware of some municipal facts of life.

My fellow members in the U.S. Conference of Mayors, I find, also are be-coming more aware of these facts.

NEEDED: COURAGE

Most of us have the revenue potential to enable us to survive without massive federal aid. Few of us have the political courage sincerely to use this potential.

This revenue potential is available to us in the form of state or municipal personal income taxes. It is almost the only local level tax which can grow with the economy. It can be a revenue source to supplant, in part, massive federal aid.

The federal government—if it is sincere and honestly means what it seems to say about assisting urban areas to meet their problems—must provide a realistic tax break to enable these state and local governments to consider some form of personal income tax to finance programs.

Such a cutback, or refund to persons in areas in which local governments are levying an income tax, would permit greater use of what is almost the only really untapped tax source left to the lower echelons of government.

It also would permit local governments, in effect, to levy taxes for greater local use. And, conversely, it would permit greater taxpayer control over expenditure of tax dollars.

Without a reduction in federal income tax rates to those taxpayers contributing to state and local income levies, the individual burden would be oppressive and grossly unfair.

This is the only approach that recognizes the facts of political life. The taxpayer, who feels that he has little or no control over federal spending levels, is hardly to be blamed if he votes down a local bond issue or opposes a local tax increase. Doing so he feels he can exercise direct influence on spending for public purposes.

Now, with federal taxes levied for urban programs, it is hard for the local official confronted with real needs to resist pressure to ask for his "share."

With creative administration, local governments can solve a good part of their problems. Proper zoning can, in many instances, ease the need for massive urban renewal programs; proper housing code enforcement, more often than not, can lessen the crises of slum clearance; sensible taxing practices can permit a return of investment and risk capital to our central city core areas.

In any event, we must not—indeed, we cannot—increase the tax burden upon real estate or land.

In most urban areas, and particularly in the heart of the city, land taxes must be reduced.

High land taxes in these older central city areas actually cause blight and decay, in many instances. Because of a prohibitive tax structure, owners of older properties there are reluctant to keep up, or improve, existing buildings.

This tends to encourage blight and decay—the very things most of us are seeking to halt, and usually are seeking federal funds to help us halt it.

A recent study by the Advisory Commission on Intergovernmental Relations showed these changes and reductions are necessary because historically the federal government's intensive use of the personal income tax is the single most important deterrent to its expanded use by states and cities.

Our research showed that between 1937 and 1960 not a single state adopted a personal income tax. During this period 13 states did adopt general sales taxes.

A relative handful of the nation's cities are given a share of state income taxes for their needs. . . .

ROLE
OF THE STATE GOVERNMENT

The salubrity of their metropolitan areas should be a paramount concern of state governments, yet their role in resolving metropolitan problems until the middle of the twentieth century generally was relatively minor and often limited to the creation of a special district to solve a critical service problem. Pungent critics accuse the states of failing to meet their responsibilities to their metropolitan areas. And a call is issued in Reading 14 for constitutional amendments, new legislation, and new administrative actions which will facilitate the resolution of metropolitan problems.

In the late 1950s the states began to exhibit increasing concern with metropolitan problems. The states' response has taken many forms. A common course of action has been the appointment by the governor of a commission to study area-wide problems and submit recommendations designed to modernize local government. Several governors have appointed an assistant for urban and metropolitan affairs, and Massachusetts has a coordinator of intergovernmental relations in the Department of Administration. The California Intergovernmental Council on Urban Growth, an advisory body to the governor, seeks to develop policies to assist state and local officials in meeting the problems of urban growth, and to encourage interlocal cooperation and regional planning.

Although Pennsylvania established a state agency for local affairs in

1919, it was not until the New York State Office for Local Government was established in 1959 that interest in a state agency for local affairs was revived. Currently, 17 states have organized such agencies and several other states have expressed interest in creating one.

The functions of a state agency for local affairs differ from state to state, but commonly include providing technical assistance to local governments, coordinating federal grants-in-aid programs, operating an information clearinghouse, drafting and reviewing proposed legislation, and training local officials. Recently several state agencies have been given additional responsibilities. The New Jersey Department of Community Affairs, for example, has been made responsible for state housing and urban renewal programs.

If the metropolitan problem is one of a multiplicity of local governments, the fact that more than 50 percent of the 1074 municipal incorporations in the period 1950 to 1960 occurred in the 10 percent of the counties located within SMSA's supports the contention that the problem is becoming more critical. Defensive incorporations to forestall annexation have not been uncommon. Since municipalities are incorporated under the provisions of state statutes, the states obviously possess the power to prevent further political fragmentation by repealing permissive incorporation laws. Several states—Oregon and Kansas in 1965 and Colorado in 1966—have established stricter standards for incorporation.

A related development has been the creation of a state agency to restrict new incorporations and thereby facilitate the resolution of problems attendant to rapid metropolitan growth. The Minnesota Municipal Commission, for example, was established in 1959 to regulate the creation of new municipalities in metropolitan areas. The commission occasionally has recommended that the remaining unincorporated territory in a metropolitan area be annexed to cities and villages. The Alaska Local Boundary Commission has been operating since 1959 and has the power to propose boundary changes to the legislature and determine whether an area wishing to incorporate as a borough meets the necessary standards.

State law not only governs incorporation of new municipalities, but also regulates annexation procedures. Antiannexation laws have come under review in recent years to see if they unduly impede the resolution of metropolitan problems. In 1965, Alabama, Georgia, New Mexico, and West Virginia liberalized their annexation procedures.

In recent years, the states have been placing greater emphasis upon the enactment of laws designed to encourage metropolitan planning, joint exercise of powers by local governments, provision of services by means of interlocal contracts, formation of regional districts, and transfer of functions to counties. Because of the diversity of metropolitan areas within many states, a state-wide approach to the resolution of metropolitan problems cannot be standardized.

14. Vigorous Action Required:
Recommendations
to the States*

In 1961, the Advisory Commission on Intergovernmental Relations, established by Congress in 1959 as a permanent bipartisan commission of 26 members to study intergovernmental problems, recommended the enactment by each legislature of " 'a package' of permissive powers to be utilized by the residents of the metropolitan areas as they see fit." While it is apparent the adoption of the commission's recommendations would not be a cure-all for the complex problems of metropolitan areas, these areas would be in a position to initiate action that would alleviate many of their most acute problems.

In the recommendations which follow, the commission sets forth no single "pat" solution for easing the problems of political and structural complexity at the local government level. The commission is convinced that no single approach can be identified as the most desirable, whether from a national standpoint or within a given state. Neither does the commission believe it can be a profitable effort for the legislature of any state having within its borders a number of metropolitan areas to endeavor to legislate a single solution; rather, the approach recommended in this report is one of legislative provision by the state of permissive authority to all of its metropolitan areas to employ whichever of these principal methods is determined by the residents of the areas and their political leaders to be the preferable one in the light of all the attendant circumstances. . . .

In brief, the commission is proposing the enactment by state legislatures of a "package" of permissive powers to be utilized by the residents of the metropolitan areas as they see fit. Additionally, the commission is proposing that states establish within the structure of state government a dual function of oversight and technical assistance to local units of government, thereby asserting a determination to assist continually and to intervene where necessary in ameliorating political jurisdictional problems in the metropolitan areas.

---

* From *Governmental Structure, Organization, and Planning in Metropolitan Areas* (Washington, D.C.: Government Printing Office, 1961), pp. 19–21, 24, 26, 30–33, 37, and 39–41. Footnotes in original omitted.

PROVISION BY THE STATE OF "ARSENAL"
OF REMEDIAL WEAPONS TO BE DRAWN UPON
BY METROPOLITAN AREAS

ASSERTION OF LEGISLATIVE AUTHORITY REGARDING METROPOLITAN AREAS

The commission subscribes firmly to the principle of maximum flexibility and freedom of action for local units of government in meeting the needs of their citizens; however, the commission also believes that certain limitations must be introduced against the historical concepts of home rule as applied to political subdivisions located within metropolitan areas. The commission recommends that the states, when considering either general constitutional revision or undertaking constitutional changes with regard to local home rule, reserve sufficient authority in the legislature to enable legislative action where necessary to modify responsibilities of and relationships among local units of government located within metropolitan areas in the best interests of the people of the area as a whole. . . .

AUTHORIZATION OF MUNICIPAL ANNEXATION
OF UNINCORPORATED AREAS WITHOUT CONSENT OF AREAS ANNEXED

The commission recommends that the states examine critically their present constitutional and statutory provisions governing annexation of territory to municipalities, and that they act promptly to eliminate or amend—at least with regard to metropolitan areas—provisions that now hamper the orderly and equitable extension of municipal boundaries so as to embrace unincorporated territory in which urban development is underway or in prospect. As a minimum, authority to initiate annexation proceedings should not rest solely with the area or residents desiring annexation but should also be available to city governing bodies. There is also merit to the proposition that the inhabitants of minor outlying unincorporated territory should not possess an absolute power to veto a proposed annexation which meets appropriate standards of equity. The commission further urges states generally to examine types of legislation which in certain states have already been adopted to facilitate desirable municipal annexations, with a view to enacting such facilitative provisions as may be suitable to their respective needs and circumstances. . . .

AUTHORIZATION OF INTERLOCAL CONTRACTING AND JOINT ENTERPRISES

The commission recommends the enactment of legislation by the states authorizing, at least within the confines of the metropolitan areas, two or more units of local government to exercise jointly or cooperatively any power possessed by one or more of the units concerned and to contract with one another for the rendering of governmental services. . . .

AUTHORIZATION FOR THE CREATION OF FUNCTIONAL AUTHORITIES

The commission recommends that states consider the enactment of legislation authorizing local units of government within metropolitan areas to establish, in accordance with statutory requirements, metropolitan service corporations or authorities for the performance of governmental services necessitating areawide handling, such corporations to have appropriate borrowing and taxing power, but with the initial establishment and any subsequent broadening of functions and responsibilities being subject to voter approval on the basis of an areawide majority. . . .

AUTHORIZATION FOR VOLUNTARY TRANSFER
OF FUNCTIONS FROM MUNICIPALITIES TO COUNTIES AND VICE VERSA

The commission recommends the enactment of legislation by the states authorizing the legislative bodies of municipalities and counties located within metropolitan areas to take mutual and coordinate action to transfer responsibility for specified governmental services from one unit of government to the other. . . .

AUTHORIZATION FOR CREATION
OF METROPOLITAN AREA STUDY COMMISSIONS

The commission recommends that where such authority does not now exist, states enact legislation authorizing the establishment of metropolitan area commissions on local government structure and services, for the purpose of developing proposals for revising and improving local government structure and services in the metropolitan areas concerned, such commissions to be created, optionally, by either mutual and concurrent action of the governing bodies of the local units of government within the area or by initiative petition and election of the voters of the metropolitan area, and with the proposals developed by such commissions to become effective if approved at a special election held for the purpose. The enabling legislation should contain provisions designed to assure that the membership of such commssions is balanced in such a way as to provide general equity of representation to the population groups and governmental constituencies making up the metropolitan area as a whole. . . .

AUTHORIZATION FOR CREATION
OF METROPOLITAN AREA PLANNING BODIES

The commission recommends the enactment of legislation by the states authorizing the establishment of metropolitan area planning bodies to comprise representatives from the political subdivisions of the metropolitan area. The functions of such a planning body should consist at least in providing advisory recommendations to the local units of government in the area with respect to the planned development of the metropolitan area; desirably they should include the development of areawide plans for land use and capital facilities and the review of zoning ordinances proposed by the component units of government in the area. . . .

DIRECT STATE ACTION: ASSISTANCE AND CONTROL

ESTABLISHMENT OF UNIT OF STATE GOVERNMENT
FOR METROPOLITAN AREA AFFAIRS

The commission recommends the enactment of legislation by the states to establish (or adapt) an agency of the state government for continuing attention, review, and assistance with respect to the metropolitan areas of the state and associated problems of local government, planning, structure, organization, and finance. . . .

ESTABLISHMENT OF STATE PROGRAM
OF FINANCIAL AND TECHNICAL ASSISTANCE TO METROPOLITAN AREAS

The commission recommends that the states take legislative and administrative action to establish a program (or to expand existing programs) of financial and technical assistance to metropolitan areas in such fields as urban planning, urban renewal, building code modernization, and local government organization and finance. . . .

CONTROL OF NEW INCORPORATIONS

The commission recommends that where such authority does not now exist, states enact legislation providing rigorous statutory standards for the establishment of new municipal corporations within the geographic boundaries of metropolitan areas and providing further for the administrative review and approval of such proposed new incorporations by the unit of state government concerned with responsibility for local government or metropolitan area affairs. . . .

FINANCIAL AND REGULATORY ACTION
TO SECURE AND PRESERVE OPEN LAND

The commission recommends the enactment of legislation by the states (a) to provide for acquisition by the state of conservation easements designed to remove from urban development key tracts of land in and around existing and potential metropolitan areas and (b) to authorize local units of government to acquire interests and rights in real property within existing metropolitan areas for the purpose of preserving appropriate open areas and spaces within the pattern of metropolitan development. . . .

RESOLUTION OF DISPUTES
AMONG LOCAL UNITS OF GOVERNMENT IN METROPOLITAN AREAS

The commission recommends that the states, where necessary, take legislative or administrative action to encourage and facilitate exercise of discretionary authority by the governor and his office, to resolve those disputes among local units of government within metropolitan areas which (a) cannot be resolved at the local level by mutual agreement, (b) are not of sufficient scope or subject matter to warrant special legislative action and (c) which, however, in the determination of the governor, are of such moment as to impede the effective performance of governmental functions in the area. . . .

ANNEXATION AND EXTRAMURAL JURISDICTION

Annexation often has been used to solve certain metropolitan problems and has several advantages. It simplifies the governmental structure by inhibiting new incorporations and consolidating responsibility; eliminates duplication of services; and raises service standards. It also may permit the achievement of economies of scale in the provision of governmental services.

Early metropolitan reformers favored the use of annexation as the most effective means to create a metropolitan community. The suggestion has been made that a root cause of the metropolitan problem was the failure of annexation to keep pace with urbanization. Although central cities commonly annexed suburban territory as it became urbanized in the nineteenth century, annexation was little used in the twentieth century until the post-World War II period.

Most recent annexations have been small. In 1965, 756 cities with populations of over 5000 annexed 530.4 square miles of territory, but only 141 cities annexed territory in excess of one-half square mile. And only five cities annexed in excess of ten square miles: Albuquerque, New Mexico; Houston, Texas; Huntsville, Alabama; Kansas City, Kansas; and Phoenix, Arizona.

The political integration authorized by annexation laws may be either full or partial. In several states, the legislature has granted central cities a partial annexation power by allowing the cities to regulate extraterritorially the development of contiguous land within a specified distance of the municipal boundaries. The Advisory Commission on Intergovernmental Relations in Reading 16 recommends that state legislatures grant certain extramural powers to municipalities to enable them to prevent the development of problem areas immediately beyond their boundary lines.

In a number of metropolitan areas, annexation has been frustrated by new incorporations and the requirement of a concurrent majority in the annexing city and the territory to be annexed. In other states, the law facilitates annexation by authorizing a city council by passage of an ordinance to annex territory without the consent of its residents. The Texas law is described in Reading 15.

If state law requires that a referendum be held on the question of annexation and a majority affirmative vote in the city and the territory in question, the voters in the suburban territory may block annexation for fear that taxes would be increased and the city would fail to provide services to the territory. On the other hand, there have been cases where the need for water or sewage disposal facilities has prompted a suburban area to seek annexation to the central city.

Annexation raises a question of equity. The central city has a need to control the development of land contiguous to its boundaries, yet the interests of the residents of the annexed territory must be protected. To minimize the impact of annexation, some laws freeze the tax rate in the annexed area for a period of years and require the central city to extend services to the annexed area. Residents of annexed areas should not be required to pay regular city taxes in the absence of city services.

Annexation is not always an unmixed blessing to the central city as it is saddled with the responsibility of controlling the development of and extending services to the annexed territory. There are diseconomies as well as economies of scale and it may be costly for the central city to service the annexed territory. Expenditures for highways and sanitation, in particular, frequently rise sharply as the result of annexation.

Annexation is not a panacea for metropolitan problems, yet it is of value in helping to solve certain problems. Its limitations—such as its inability to solve the problems of an interstate metropolitan area and rival cities' claims to the same territory—must be recognized.

15. The Municipal Annexation Law of 1963*

STUART A. MacCORKLE

Stuart A. MacCorkle, Director of the Institute of Public Affairs of The University of Texas, describes the Texas laws authorizing full and partial annexation, discusses recent annexations, and makes a preliminary appraisal of the Municipal Annexation Act of 1963. In his opinion, the new law appears to have stopped certain undesirable annexation practices, assisted cities to attact new industry, and provided a mechanism to settle rival cities' claims to land to be annexed.

The law, H.B. 137, both added to and subtracted from previous annexation powers of both general and law and home-rule cities.[1] One of the traditional requests of Texas municipalities has been authority to control fringe-area development by maintaining standards of health, safety, and welfare comparable to those existing within the corporate limits. Texas cities now have the power by ordinance to govern the development of plots and subdivisions through the grant of extraterritorial jurisdiction over unincorporated land contiguous to their corporate limits. This power is enforceable through the courts. The width of these extraterritorial bands or strips varies according to the population of the municipality. For cities under 5,000 population, the jurisdiction extends for a half-mile from the city's corporate limits; for those of 5,000 but less than 25,000, one mile; for cities of 25,000 but less than 50,000, it is two miles; for those of 50,000 but less than 100,000, three and one-half miles; and for cities in excess of 100,000, five miles. As a city acquires more land through annexation, gift, or purchase, the external limits of its extraterritorial jurisdiction will expand in conformity with the increase in city area. In addition, as a city passes from one population bracket into the next, it is entitled to claim a wider area under its jurisdiction.

In cases where the extraterritorial jurisdiction of one city overlaps the authority of one or more other cities, the governing bodies of the cities involved may

* From *Municipal Annexation in Texas* (Austin, Tex.: Institute of Public Affairs, The University of Texas, 1965), pp. 28–36.

[1] Vernon's Annotated Revised Civil Statutes of the State of Texas (1963), art. 970a. Hereafter cited as V.A.C.S.

apportion the land by mutual agreement. If no agreement is reached, or if one of the parties to the disputed area so desires, any of the cities may file a claim in the district court of the judicial district in which the largest city laying claim to the territory is located. The courts are required to consider the population densities and patterns of growth, transportation, topography, and land utilization in the cities concerned and in the overlapped area in making their apportionments. The apportioned area must be contiguous to the city receiving it. If the extraterritorial area of a city is totally overlapped, the courts are directed by the act to apportion the land according to the population ratios among the contesting cities and to apportion the territory in a "substantially compact shape," but in such apportionment no city shall receive less than one tenth of such overlapping area. Consideration must be given to existing property lines, and single-owner tracts of less than 160 acres cannot be divided between two municipalities without the consent of the owner.

Finally, land included in the extraterritorial jurisdiction of a city is not subject to municipal taxation.

INDUSTRIAL DISTRICTS

The additional increase in municipal power is found in section 5 of the new law, which provides for the designation of any part of the area in the extraterritorial ring as a tax-exempt industrial district for a period up to seven years. The municipal governing body and the owner or owners of the affected property enter into a contractual agreement to establish the period up to seven years for which the industrial property shall be immune from annexation. Moreover, the contract can be renegotiated for successive periods not to exceed seven years each.

Some contend that the provision for industrial parks has a two-fold advantage. A city may now attract new industry by guaranteeing nonannexation during the period of company development. The city, however, may protect its own residents by extending regulatory ordinances, such as planning and zoning laws, into the areas surrounding the industrial park. On the other hand, this provision of the law in effect sets up a subsidiary for industry located within the created industrial area.

ANNEXATION

Whereas advantages such as subdivision regulation accrue to the cities with the grant of extraterritorial jurisdiction, their authority is in another way limited by the rings encircling the periphery of the city. A city may annex new territory only with the confines of the extraterritorial jurisdiction and during a single calendar year may annex land equivalent in size only up to 10 per cent of the total corporate area of the city on the previous January 1. However, a city may carry over any unused portion of a 10 per cent allocation as long as annexation acquisitions do not exceed 30 per cent of the January 1 land area during a given year. There are significant exceptions to the 10 per cent rule:

1. Territory caused to be annexed by a request of a majority of the qualified resident voters in the territory and the owners of 50 per cent or more of the land in the territory.

2. Territory annexed which is owned by the city, the county, the State, or the Federal Government which is used for a public purpose.

3. Territory annexed at the request of the owner or owners thereof.[2]

The procedures of annexation have been substantially changed. Formerly, once an annexation proceeding was underway, it could be suspended indefinitely. Under the new law, a city must complete any annexation of territory within ninety days after proceedings are begun, or such proceedings shall be considered null and void. Moreover, a public hearing must be held not more than twenty and not less than ten days before annexation proceedings are begun.

In any case where there is judicial intervention during the ninety-day completion period, the time involved in the injunction shall not be considered a part of the ninety days. . . .

POLITICAL SUBDIVISIONS

Another advantage given to the cities by the new law is found in section 8, which states that "no city may be incorporated within the area of the extraterritorial jurisdiction of any city without the written consent of the governing body of such city." Neither may a political subdivision whose purpose is water supply or sanitary sewer service be created without written permission from the municipality which has extraterritorial jurisdiction over the area in which the subdivision is sought to be created.

Should a city refuse to grant permission for the incorporation, a majority of the resident voters and the owners of 50 per cent or more of the land may request annexation by the city. It should be recalled that such annexations do not count against the 10 per cent allocation. If the city refuses or fails to grant such annexation within six months of the request, proof of such failure or refusal shall constitute authority to proceed with incorporation. Similarly, if a city fails or refuses to grant permission for the creation of a political subdivision within sixty days of a request, a majority of the qualified voting residents and owners of 50 per cent or more of the land in the territory may request provision

---

[2] *V.A.C.S.*, art. 970a, section 7B.

of water and sewer services from the city. Again, refusal or failure to supply service constitutes authorization to proceed with formation of the necessary water and sewer districts. Either incorporation procedures or creation of political subdivisions must be begun within six months of the authorization and must be completed within eighteen months, or the authorization is terminated.

SERVICES-DISANNEXATION

Any city annexing a particular area is required to provide or cause to be provided within three years governmental and proprietary services, "the standard and scope of which are substantially equivalent to the standard and scope of . . . services furnished by such city in other areas of such city which have characteristics of topography, patterns of land utilization, and population density similar to that of the particular area annexed." Should a city fail or refuse to provide these services or to cause them to be provided, a majority of the qualified resident voters and the owners of 50 per cent or more of the property may petition the governing body of the city for disannexation. If the city does not grant the disannexation within ninety days, any signer of the disannexation petition may within sixty days after the refusal file an action praying for disannexation in the district court of the judicial district in which the city is located.

A disannexed area may not be re-annexed within one year of the disannexation, and if it is re-annexed within three years of the disannexation, the period for the provision of services is reduced from three years to one year.

However, there are two important limitations to the disannexation section (section 10) of the law. First, the right of disannexation is not available to "any particular annexed area which was lawfully within the city limits of a city at the time of the approval or sale of any general obligation bonds of the city if proceeds therefrom have been expended for capital improvements to serve such particular annexed area, so long as any such bonds are outstanding." Secondly, for the residents and owners of an area to petition for disannexation, the area must adjoin the outer boundaries of the city. In other words, once the area has become surrounded by other corporate territory, it is no longer eligible for disannexation.

PRESENT STANDING OF CITIES

Where do the cities of Texas stand now with regard to annexation powers? According to the Municipal Annexation Act of 1963, Texas cities may now insure that fringe-area development will meet with the standards set by the city for in-city building and construction and land use, and they may seek injunctive relief from the courts for violations of such ordinances.[3] They may negotiate with industry for the establishment of tax-free industrial parks for a time period amenable to both parties. The statute restricts the development of new cities on the edge of their own corporate limits.

On the other hand, the restrictions that have been placed on the cities are several. A city is limited in the amount of land it can annex during a calendar year, although there are exceptions to the limitation in the form of resident or owner requests and annexation of governmental property. A city is also limited in the direction of its annexation by the bounds of its extraterritorial jurisdiction, but the extraterritorial band prevents other cities from annexing to its doorstep. This provision, plus the time limit of 90 days, should prevent abuses such as the first reading privilege and should also reduce the effects of intercity competition for land. The provisions for disannexation and those regarding authorization for incorporation or the creation of special districts will doubtless raise administrative and legal questions. The statute supposedly protects residents and property owners from being brought into the municipal territorial limits only to be left without the services enjoyed by other taxpayers. Furthermore, an annexed area cannot leave the city once bonded indebtedness has been incurred or once the area has become encircled by the city and is no longer on its perimeter.

Carrying out the law will cause some administrative headaches. How are the extraterritorial bands to be drawn or determined? What shape must the area under extraterritorial jurisdiction take? Exactly how will "services substantially equal in scope and standard" be decided? As of this writing, no court cases had been decided on the basis of the new law. To present, many questions remained unanswered.

PRACTICE

During the first year the 1963 law was operable, cities were able to settle disputes about overlapping jurisdictions among themselves without employing the provision of the statute which provides for access to the district court in the judicial district in which the largest party to the suit is located. However, later years should see some court decisions.

[3] However, Mr. S. G. Johndroe, Jr., City Attorney of Fort Worth, in Opinion No. 107, June 4, 1964, to Mr. J. L. Brownlee, City Manager, stated, "It is the opinion of this department that the City Council of the City of Fort Worth has no power to control the use of land outside the city limits and within its extraterritorial jurisdiction except through contracts made voluntarily by the landowners."

The North Texas cities of Denison and Sherman, both in Grayson County, desired to annex the same parcel of land in the summer of 1964. According to the 1960 U. S. Census, Denison had just under 23,000 and Sherman a little less than 25,000 in population. Consequently, each city was entitled to extend its extraterritorial jurisdiction not more than one mile from the incorporated city limits. However, on the basis of 1964 population estimates, Sherman has now exceeded the 25,000 population mark and is entitled to extend its jurisdiction in a two-mile radius. This population growth points out another ambiguity in the law. Unlike most statutes governing municipalities the Municipal Annexation Law does not specifically state that population figures will be based on the last preceding federal census. The governing body of Denison passed an annexation ordinance incorporating the land it considered to be under its jurisdiction. Then the mayor of Sherman announced that his city planned to file suit to nullify the Denison ordinance because Denison "is fudging a little by inching over the boundary line."[4] The prospects of this suit were announced in late summer of 1964.

Another example of the practice of cities under the new law concerns a dispute settled between the involved cities without the necessity of court assistance. In Harris County, the community of Seabrook and the new bay-shore town of El Lago in the Manned Spacecraft Center area are only a half-mile apart, and, as towns under 5,000 population, each was entitled to a half-mile of extraterritorial jurisdiction. Both wanted to annex the same 58-acre tract which their respective jurisdictions overlapped. El Lago quietly annexed the tract July 27, 1964, the day before Seabrook planned to announce its intention to annex 300 acres, including the disputed territory. City officials and attorneys of the two cities met to discuss the dispute[5] and negotiated a settlement on August 25 whereby El Lago kept the 58-acre tract it had annexed and Seabrook received the remaining 242 acres in the territory to which both had claims.[6]

The City of Houston employed the new annexation statute in a different manner. Earlier in this discussion it was noted that Houston had not followed through on a first-reading annexation of the 1,150 remaining square miles of unincorporated land in Harris County. However, Houston took advantage of subsection B of section 7 of the Municipal Annexation Law to take in much of the land it had previously placed under first reading. That particular subsection of the law provides that territory annexed by a city which is owned by "the city, the county, the State, or the Federal Government and which is used for a public

---

[4] Stuart Long (ed.), *Austin Report*, XVI (August 9, 1964), 3.

[5] As an act of good faith on August 20, El Lago voted to send a $1600 check to the Seabrook Volunteer Fire Department for services rendered in El Lago and called together councilmen from those two cities plus Taylor Lake Village to work out future financial arrangements for fire services.

[6] *Houston Chronicle,* August 20, 21, and 26, 1964.

purpose" is not subject to the 10 per cent per year rule. Houston annexed a strip of land down both sides of the right-of-way along county, state, and federal roads and highways in the county. A map of the city now looks like a huge body with many spidery legs going forth from it. This annexation of right-of-way land offers several advantages: (1) the extraterritorial jurisdiction of the city is substantially increased since the city's five-mile limit is extended from its furthest boundaries, and, thus, the area from which potential annexations can be made is also enlarged; (2) concurrently, the size of future annexations is increased because 10 per cent of the land area of the city is now greater; (3) there is little danger of incorporations, desires for establishment of special districts, or requests for services along these roads.

Finally, there are two interesting examples of recent annexation in Tarrant County. The City of Arlington, entitled to three and one-half miles of extra-territorial jurisdiction because it is in the 50,000–99,999 population bracket, began a protective annexation program in mid-1964. The city council planned to annex a 10-foot strip southward to the Ellis County line, eastward to the Dallas County line, and northward to Arlington's present boundaries, thus en-compassing about 20 square miles of territory.[7] The proposal did not come to any noticeable conflict with the plans of other cities, but rather is cited as an example of how one city may use its extraterritorial prerogatives over a period of time to secure its future growth.

The other Tarrant County incident is more complex. In 1963 the City of Fort Worth annexed a residential tract known as Greenfield Acres which was composed of mixed rural and urban characteristics near one of the local lakes. The city supplied fire and police, garbage, weed control, library bookmobile, and animal control services; enforced building, plumbing, air-conditioning and electrical codes and providing zoning protection; and expended money on street maintenance and engineering and on street and traffic signs. It also constructed a water main adjacent to the addition from which some of the tract's residents have purchased water at regular city rates.

However, 75 per cent of the area's residents signed a petition brought to the city council during the summer of 1964 asking that the area be disannexed. One of the principal reasons was the fact that most of the water supply has been provided by the developers of the addition and not by the City of Fort Worth. The city planning department and the city attorney recommended to the council that the petition be refused. The fireworks began, with one side contending that the disputed area is not integrated with the city and the other that part of the council has financial interests in the area.[8]

Mr. S. G. Johndroe, Jr., City Attorney, contended that Fort Worth in annex-

[7] *Dallas Morning News,* August 23, 1964.
[8] *Fort Worth Star-Telegram,* August 15, 1964.

ing Greenfield Acres has expended considerable funds in making available city facilities and services to the residents of the area. He further pointed out that funds expended and those to be expended in providing these facilities and services were raised, and were to be raised, through the sale of City of Fort Worth bonds. He emphatically called to the attention of the City Council, "that no particular area should be allowed to escape its share of city debt when such area, along with other areas of the city, shares the benefits derived from the creation of such debt."[9] Mr. Johndroe expressed the opinion that an ordinance detaching Greenfield Acres would be a violation of existing state law.

Apparently the matter has been set at rest. The City Council as of this writing has taken no action to de-annex the area.

SUMMARY

The socio-economic complexion of Texas has changed considerably in the past decade, bringing with it rapid urbanization and a need by cities for some means of controlling fringe-area development. At the same time, some protection needed to be given to residents and owners of property outside the city limits. The legal answer to these problems was attempted in the Municipal Annexation Law, which allows both general law and home-rule cities more control over suburban development while affording some measure of protection to the people living on the edge of the city boundaries. The new law curbs some of the old practices which many persons considered abusive, such as the indetermination of the first-reading proceeding and the annexing of land without any hope on the part of owners for gaining compensatory services. On the other hand, cities seem to have gained a means of encouraging industry, and a method of settling disputes between cities over land to be annexed. More than that, through interpretations in the law already made they have a considerable amount of leeway through such provisions as those exempting from the annexation property used for a governmental purpose and through the exemption from disannexation of areas not on the perimeter of the city or for which bond monies have been voted. Not until practice has tested and the courts have interpreted the law can a true evaluation be made of it.

[9] S. G. Johndroe, Jr., City of Fort Worth, Opinion No. 0–110, July 31, 1964.

16. The Use
of Extraterritorial Powers*

Extramural or extraterritorial powers refer to the powers a city may exercise outside its boundaries. In 1962, the Advisory Commission on Intergovernmental Relations issued a report that catalogues the uses of extraterritorial powers, assesses their strengths and weaknesses, and recommends that state legislatures grant extraterritorial planning, zoning, and subdivision regulation powers to municipalities where effective county powers do not exist in unincorporated areas.

Extraterritorial powers as defined in this report are powers which a city exercises outside its ordinary territorial limits to regulate activity there or to assist in providing services to its citizens within its own boundaries.

Regulatory powers of an extraterritorial nature commonly include control over possible threats to health and safety, abatement of nuisances, and regulation of zoning and subdivisions. The use of extraterritoriality for providing services to the city's residents is most commonly connected with water supply, sewage treatment, recreation areas, and rubbish dumping sites outside city boundaries. The term "extraterritoriality" is also frequently used to refer to the power of a city to furnish services to areas outside the city. In this report such action is covered in the next section on intergovernmental agreements.

SCOPE AND TREND OF USE

Use of extraterritorial powers by cities varies among the states and by the type of power authorized. State legislatures have been relatively generous in granting cities power to go outside their boundaries to help in providing a service to their residents. In most states cities are particularly allowed to obtain their water and treat and dispose of sewage outside their boundaries, because of the frequent difficulties of providing these important utility services within their own boundaries.

* From *Alternative Approaches to Governmental Reorganization in Metropolitan Areas* (Washington, D.C.: Government Printing Office, 1962), pp. 20–25. Footnotes in original omitted.

Cities quite commonly exercise police power beyond their borders for health purposes—the protection of milk and meat supply, especially. About one third of the states authorize cities to exercise extraterritorial powers to abate nuisances, such as slaughterhouses and soap factories. However, only a small portion of the cities exercise their nuisance abatement authority, leaving regulation mostly to the state. Few states grant localities the power of extraterritorial regulation of morals, such as gambling and the sale and use of liquor, and fewer cities exercise such powers. These are generally regarded as state-wide problems.

About 30 states have given cities jurisdiction beyond their boundaries for regulating subdivisions. To some extent, the increased establishment of county planning and zoning in unincorporated areas is reducing the need for such extraterritorial power. Few states have given cities power of extraterritorial zoning.

As a method of helping to meet governmental problems in metropolitan areas, the planning, zoning and subdivision regulation facets of extraterritoriality have received most attention in recent years. They can be effective in dealing with the problems of haphazard growth in the unincorporated fringe areas of municipalities, particularly where counties do not have such regulation in unincorporated areas. Thus, zoning divides an area (usually a municipality) into districts and within those districts regulates the height and bulk of buildings and other structures, the percentage of a lot that may be occupied, the size of required yards and other open spaces, the density of population, and the use of buildings and land for trade, industry, residence, or other purposes. Subdivision regulation controls the arrangement and width of streets, length and depth of blocks, provision of public open space, provision of sewer and water distribution systems, grading and surfacing of streets, and sufficiency of easements for utility installations. Such subdivision regulations are frequently required to conform with the provisions of the comprehensive plan of the municipality concerned, as in Wisconsin, in order to assure orderly development of the entire area.

A survey conducted for the *Municipal Year Book 1954* gave an indication of the extent of use of extraterritorial zoning and subdivision regulation powers. The survey covered 174 cities over 5000 population out of a total of 2527 cities.

While about 85 percent of the responding cities had zoning ordinances in effect within their boundaries, only about 10 percent had such ordinances effective outside their boundaries. Of the latter, only one-half were effective up to three miles outside the boundaries, one-fourth up to five miles, and one-fourth up to one or two miles. The principal reason for this relatively small use of zoning outside the city boundaries was the lack of statutory permission. To some extent the cities' lack of extraterritorial zoning was offset by county zoning laws in the unincorporated areas, particularly around big cities, but county zoning tended to be less comprehensive.

Extraterritorial subdivision regulation was more common than zoning. Seventy-seven percent of the cities surveyed had subdivision regulation within their borders, and 37 percent had extraterritorial authority. Of those with the power, two-fifths exercised it up to five or six miles beyond the city limits, another one-third exercised it up to three miles, and the remainder exercised it up to one or two miles. Counties participated only slightly more often in the areas not touched by extraterritorial subdivision controls than they did in areas not touched by extraterritorial zoning controls.

STRENGTH AND WEAKNESS

AS AN AID TO PROVIDING SERVICE

A city's use of extraterritorial power is a way of extending its geographical jurisdiction. As a means of providing or improving city services, as in the case of water supply or recreation sites, it is a logical and frequently necessary way for a city to discharge its responsibility to its citizens. From the standpoint of the metropolitan area as a whole this may prove a disadvantage if it deters the city from cooperating with other communities in an area-wide approach yielding greater overall benefits. This approach also raises the possibility of creating intergovernmental friction if the city is not careful to be a "good citizen" in the way it carries on its activity in the outside area. The maintenance of refuse dumps and correctional institutions are examples of activities susceptible to complaints by the outside areas.

AS A REGULATORY DEVICE

The use of extraterritoriality as a means of extending a city's geographical boundaries can be more important in the regulatory field, particularly in planning, zoning and subdivision regulation in unincorporated areas. Uncontrolled development at the fringes can have deteriorating effects on property values in the established neighboring areas of the central city, and can complicate the provision of certain services within the municipality, such as fire protection, crime control, traffic control and disease prevention. The use of extraterritorial zoning and subdivision regulation in unincorporated fringe areas can bring these conditions under better control by the adjoining municipality. By so doing it strengthens the movement toward area-wide land use planning.

Extraterritorial planning, zoning and subdivision regulation may also serve as a step toward annexation by giving the fringe area characteristics harmonious with those of the adjacent city. Such an effect seems most likely in such states as Virginia, North Carolina, and Texas where the cities have considerable initiative in annexation proceedings and fringe areas cannot exercise a veto over annexations. On the other hand, the threat of extraterritorial controls may stimulate hasty and ill-advised incorporations as a "defensive" measure, particularly in states where incorporations are easily accomplished.

From the standpoint of political feasibility, the use of extraterritorial controls has the advantage of creating relatively little disturbance in the political status quo. Unincorporated territories usually have only "rudimentary government," so that the officials and employees whose positions are threatened are few. Moreover, while the extraterritorial controls represent an exercise of governmental power from outside, it is the very lack of exercise of such power by the residents of the territory which frequently moves the adjoining city to exercise its power there. Thus extraterritorial regulation represents a new exercise of power, rather than a shift of an existing power.

A major weakness of extraterritorial regulation as an approach to reorganizing local government structure in metropolitan areas is its limited applicability. Many states do not give localities adequate authorization for the most important regulatory powers from the standpoint of dealing with metropolitan growth: planning, zoning and subdivision regulations. Even where the powers exist they are useful only when there are unincorporated areas adjacent to municipalities, a condition which is long past for many urban centers. Moreover, to the extent that these controls help ease the problems of fringe areas, they relieve the pressure for more basic solutions, except where the fringe area cannot veto a proposed annexation initiated by the adjoining city.

While extraterritorial regulation as presently authorized in most states enables the central city to protect itself it deprives the residents of the outside areas of a voice in determining their own affairs. This is contrary to the principle of local self-determination. It also can generate resentment, to the detriment of the cooperation required for satisfactory intergovernmental relations in metropolitan areas, as well as continued working for more comprehensive approaches to reorganization.

RECOMMENDATIONS

The commission recommends that where effective county planning, zoning and subdivision regulation do not exist in the fringe area, State legislatures enact legislation making extraterritorial planning, zoning and subdivision regulation of unincorporated fringe areas available to their municipalities, with provision for the residents of the unincorporated areas to have a voice in the imposition of the regulations.

It is the commission's view, that while extraterritorial power holds no great potential for resolving basic intergovernmental problems in metropolitan areas, such potential as it has should be made available to localities. Where counties are not already exercising effective control of the unincorporated fringe areas, extraterritorial planning, zoning and subdivision regulation can be important tools for preventing the development of problem areas around individual cities, and for easing the transition to a sound governmental structure.

The content of legislation authorizing municipalities to exercise such extra-territorial powers is suggested by the model draft statute attached in the form of an amendment to existing state statutes on planning, zoning and subdivision regulation. The proposed statute is adapted from a 1959 North Carolina statute on extraterritorial zoning recommended by the Municipal Government Study Commission of the North Carolina General Assembly and an earlier North Carolina statute on extraterritorial subdivision regulation. The suggested draft provides for the inclusion of residents of the unincorporated territory on the planning commission and zoning adjustment board for participation in making recommendations on planning, zoning and subdivision regulation matters apply-ing to the "extramural" territory in which they reside. The fact that the municipality and unincorporated area have equal representation on the extra-territorial matters gives the unincorporated area some protection against arbi-trary action by the municipality. Adoption of the zoning ordinance and approval of zoning adjustments, however, are still left to the municipal governing body.

Even with the provision for equal fringe area representation on the planning commission and the zoning adjustment board, the granting of extraterritorial zoning authority might stimulate a movement toward "defensive" incorpora-tions. This is a risk that seems worth taking in view of the possible advantages to be gained by orderly fringe development and the stimulation of greater county-wide interest in zoning. Also, as the commission pointed out in its report on *Governmental Structure,* any action directed toward greater control over the unincorporated area, whether it be giving municipalities greater initiative in annexation proceedings or, as in this case, greater control through extraterri-torial zoning, should be accompanied by simultaneous strengthening of the State's regulation of new incorporations.

The minimum size of municipality and the distance of extraterritorial juris-diction from the municipality's boundary for the zoning and subdivision regula-tion statute is not specified in the draft legislation because of varying State needs and conditions.

CITY-COUNTY CONSOLIDATION

City-county consolidation may be complete or partial. In a complete consolidation, a new government is formed by the amalgamation of the county and municipal governments. Partial consolidation may involve the merger of most county functions with the cities to form a new consolidated government, but the county government continues to exist for the performance of a few functions which may be required by the state constitution. A second form of partial consolidation involves the merger of several but not all municipalities with the county.

City-county consolidation takes place under the provisions of a state law which usually provides for a popular referendum on the question of consolidation and requires a majority in both the central city and the balance of the county to effectuate the consolidation. State laws did not require a popular referendum to implement city-county consolidation in the nineteenth century and consolidation occurred in four areas: New Orleans (1813), Boston (1822), Philadelphia (1854), and New York City (1898).

Complete city-county consolidation has the advantages of simplifying the governmental structure, consolidating responsibility, increasing popular control, and eliminating duplication. If the metropolitan area falls entirely within the confines of a single county, complete city-county consolidation provides a single government with adequate powers to ensure the orderly development of the metropolitan area and the resolution of its problems. Yet only three proposals for city-county consolidation reached the ballot in the twentieth century prior to 1947 and all were defeated. City-county consolidation has been implemented in only three areas in the United States—Baton Rouge, Jacksonville, and Nashville—since 1947.

In 1946, Louisiana voters approved a constitutional amendment authorizing the drafting of a county home rule charter for the Baton Rouge area. In a 1947 referendum with one third of the voters participating, a charter providing for the semiconsolidation of the city of Baton Rouge and the parish of East Baton Rouge was approved effective in 1949.

The new charter retains the city government, parish government, and two small municipal governments. The city-parish council is composed of the seven members of the city council and two members from the outlying areas. The chief executive of the city and the city-parish is the mayor-president. An evaluation of the success of the consolidation is contained in Reading 17.

The Metropolitan Government of Nashville and Davidson County was established on April 1, 1963, as the result of popular approval of a charter providing for city-county consolidation.

The first attempt to restructure the governments in the Nashville area was made in 1951 when the Tennessee Legislature established the Community Services Commission to study the problems of Nashville and Davidson County. The commission's report of June 1, 1952, recommended the functional consolidation of the health and welfare programs and that Nashville should annex a sizable amount of territory.

In 1953, the Tennessee constitution was amended to permit home rule and the consolidation of city and county functions. The implementation of city-county consolidation, however, requires concurrent majorities in the central city and the remainder of the county.

In 1957, the legislature created the Metropolitan Government Charter Commission to draft a charter for submission to the voters. On March 28, 1958, the commission proposed a charter which would (1) consolidate Nashville and Davidson County, (2) create a 21-member metropolitan council, (3) establish an expandable urban services district and a general services district, and (4) establish a tax rate for each district based upon services rendered. The chief executive would be a metropolitan mayor elected for a four year term.

On June 17, 1958, the proposed charter was approved by Nashville by a vote of 7802 to 4803, but was rejected by the remainder of the county by a vote of 19,235 to 13,794. In consequence, Nashville turned to annexation as a solution for its problems and annexed seven square miles of territory on July 16, 1958, and 42.46 square miles on April 29, 1960.

A new charter commission was created in 1961; on April 6, 1962, it filed a proposed charter that closely resembled the 1958 charter. The new charter was approved on June 28, 1962 by a vote of 21,064 to 15,599 in Nashville and 15,914 to 12,514 in the remainder of the county. The consolidation of the city of Nashville and Davidson County did not affect six small cities in the general services district other than to forbid them to expand their boundaries by annexation. The cities are given the option of disincorporating and joining the urban services district when it expands to their area.

Reading 10 contains an analysis of voter attitudes toward metropolitan reform in Davidson County, and Reading 18 evaluates the results of the city-county consolidation and concludes it is not the answer for the problems of metropolitan areas in Texas.

17. The Merger of Governments in the Baton Rouge Area*

WILLIAM C. HAVARD, JR., AND FLOYD C. CORTY

William C. Havard, Jr., University of Massachusetts, and Floyd C. Corty, Louisiana State University, describe and analyze the partially consolidated city of Baton Rouge and East Baton Rouge Parish (county). The authors acknowledge the Baton Rouge area still has a number of governmental problems—including two governing councils, a large number of special districts, under-representation of the rural wards, and a multiplicity of popularly elected officials. Nevertheless, they maintain that the merger generally has been a success during its first 15 years and may serve as an example for similar communities elsewhere.

THE PLAN IN SUMMARY

The consolidated city-parish government which came into effect for Baton Rouge and East Baton Rouge Parish on January 1, 1949, contained the following general features. The political geography of the parish was extensively altered. The city was expanded to more than six times its former size to include virtually all of the densely populated portion of the parish outside the two small municipalities of Baker and Zachary, both of which continued to exist as separate corporations, (Figure 1.). The new city-parish charter forbade the incorporation of any new city, town, or village within the parish, although special districts could still be created as provided by law. In order to protect outstanding financial obligations, existing special districts were continued under the plan of government, although they would henceforth be more effectively unified under the general government with its consolidated finance and line departments (especially the department of public works).

Three general jurisdictional areas were recognized within the parish, with correlative tax structures and service responsibilities. The City of Baton Rouge, with its expanded boundaries, was vested with the usual municipal powers and service responsibilities; its residents would pay all parish property taxes and would additionally be assessed the general city levy in order to meet the costs

---

* From *Rural-Urban Consolidation: The Merger of Governments in the Baton Rouge Area* (Baton Rouge, La.: Louisiana State University Press, 1964), pp. 32–44 and 139–47. Footnotes in original omitted.

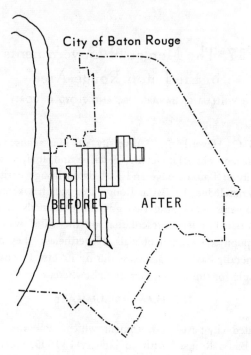

FIGURE 1. Relative areas within Baton Rouge city limits before and after consolidation.

of specifically urban services (garbage collection, street lighting, sidewalks, police and fire protection, etc.), which were extended throughout the area embraced by the new city boundaries. The industrial areas (Figure 2.), from which all residential property was to be excluded, were assessed only at the parish rate, on the stipulation that they were to furnish their own services of a municipal type. Failure to maintain these services within the industrial zone would result in a reversion of the offending sectors to urban status. A portion of the parish general tax in the industrial area was eventually distributed to the three municipalities on the basis of a population formula. The remainder of the parish was to be a rural area, subject to parish taxes and beneficiary of services extended by the general parish government. For electoral purposes Baton Rouge was designated as Ward One, and the rural area was divided into two additional wards (Figure 3.).

Special provisions were included for expanding the boundaries of the city and for creating new industrial areas. Municipal annexation depended on the initiative of the area to be annexed; if a majority in number and amount of property taxpayers in a compact body of land adjoining the city (but outside an industrial area) petitioned for annexation, the city council could, after public

East Baton Rouge Parish

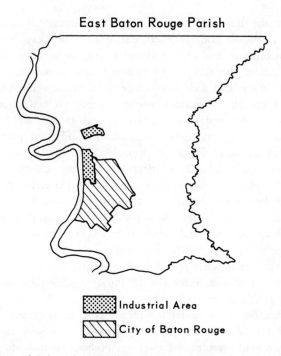

FIGURE 2.   City and industrial areas of East Baton Rouge Parish under consolidated plan of government.

East Baton Rouge Parish

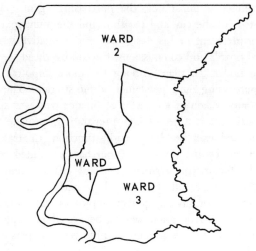

FIGURE 3.   Ward divisions of East Baton Rouge Parish after consolidation.

hearings, annex the territory by ordinance. New industrial areas could be formed out of a compact body of rural area land of not less than 320 acres. Petitions for establishment of these industrial areas were to be filed with the parish council, under the stipulations that the area would be devoted predominantly to industry, that a substantial industrial plant would be constructed within five years, and that provisions would be made (at petitioner's expense) for streets, sewerage, fire and police protection, and garbage and refuse collection and disposal. The general governing authority under the plan of government consisted of two councils, a city council and a parish council, but with the membership of the two bodies overlapping. The city council was composed of seven members elected at large from the City of Baton Rouge; the parish council included these seven councilmen plus two rural members, elected from Wards Two and Three. Although the councils were to function separately insofar as governing the city and the parish was concerned (including the separate adoption of budgets and passing ordinances relating to city and parish functions), the concurrent memberships were designed to assist the coordination of their respective activities, especially in those functional areas which had hitherto been separate and were now to be unified.

The main executive officer under the plan was a mayor-president who, like the members of the council, was popularly elected for a four-year term. The mayor-president was to preside over meetings of both councils, to prepare the executive budgets for the city and parish, and to prepare an annual report for submission to the councils. He was to be chief administrator and was given the power to appoint the director of the department of public works, the finance director, the personnel administrator, the purchasing agent (all largely functionally consolidated for the city and parish), and the municipal fire and police chiefs. The mayor-president or his designated representative was also expected to serve on several boards and commissions. Certain overhead, or staff, functions were consolidated under the plan. Among the more important of these were finance, central purchasing, and personnel administration. The department of finance under the supervision of a director of finance who was appointed by the mayor-president was to assist in budget preparation, provide for a uniform accounting system, and exercise the preaudit function. Centralized purchasing was to be carried out by the division of purchasing headed by a purchasing agent appointed by the mayor-president, and the charter contained provisions which required this office to effect a central property control system. A comprehensive merit system for city and parish employees was outlined in the plan. The administration of this program was to be vested in a personnel director appointed by the mayor-president and a three-member personnel board appointed by the parish council.

Three other consolidated staff offices were to be filled by appointment by the parish council: the attorney, the clerk, and the treasurer. The attorney was assigned responsibility as legal counsel to both councils, to the mayor-president, and to the various departments of the city-parish government. In addition, he was to prepare ordinances and resolutions and to represent the city and parish in litigation in which they might be involved. The clerk, whose office could be combined with that of the treasurer (but was not), was made responsible for city and parish journals, thus establishing his office as the central records office of the two councils. The treasurer was made custodian of all city-parish funds and was responsible for disbursing funds properly certified for expenditure by the director of finance. The organization for consolidated city-parish government is illustrated in Figure 4.

Of the departments performing line functions, consolidation was most fully effected under the charter in the departments of planning and public works. Since these agencies are treated fully in chapters three and four, only brief mention will be made of them here. The planning function, which is both a staff and a line activity, was a new one for the city and parish. Its administration was vested in a nine-member commission, with provision for a professional staff to work under its direction. The commission was made responsible for both general planning and the preparation of capital improvement programs. In addition, the planning commission was to serve as a zoning commission for the city (and later for the parish when comprehensive zoning was made legally possible). A single department of public works was established under the plan to replace the old parish department under the police jury and the various units of the old city commission concerned with public works activities. Certain divisions of the department were prescribed in the plan of government, apparently in the interest of separating strictly municipal functions (such as garbage collection, sewer maintenance, and inspections) from public works functions that were to be performed over the entire parish. A central garage was established for the service and repair of vehicles and equipment used throughout the parish. One of the more interesting aspects of the consolidation was the fact that Baton Rouge city streets were declared to be parish roads. This consolidation of the street and road system offered certain tangible benefits. In addition to unified maintenance under the consolidated department of public works, the change enabled the homestead exemption to be applied against the entire four mills of parish tax; and, since the state reimburses the parishes out of the property tax relief fund for revenues lost to the parishes through this exemption, a considerable financial advantage was realized by this change. Other divisions or costs between city and parish budgets that were affected by provisions in the plan of government are discussed in chapter five.

The remaining functions of government touched upon by the new charter represented continuations of old programs under much the same conditions as

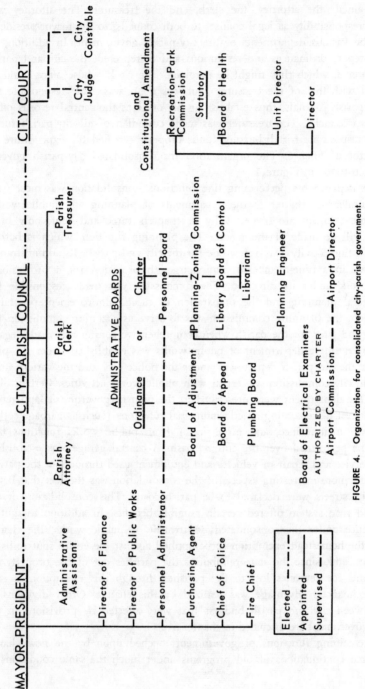

FIGURE 4. Organization for consolidated city-parish government.

previously and are not especially pertinent here. Fire and police departments were included within the sections of the plan applicable to the city; and the recreation and park commission was recognized as a continuing agency of independent status and was authorized to use certain services of the public works department (engineering, building maintenance, and the central garage), the purchasing division, and the personnel system. The parish library was continued and its board was given charter status under the plan; in point of fact, the city was later to include substantial items in its budget to help defray the cost of the library, although technically the library is an institution of the parish. The "constitutional offices" of the old parish government—the sheriff, assessor, clerk of court, and coroner—could not have been abolished without extensive amendment of the state constitution (and for that matter without arousing such political controversy as to endanger plans for consolidation), so they continued to perform their established functions. By the same token, such functions as education, the already consolidated public health activities, and the judicial offices in general were affected only indirectly, if at all, by the change in the local system of government in the Baton Rouge area.

THE PLAN IN EFFECT

Although the plan of government had been ratified by a narrow popular margin, its success was by no means assured. In addition to the normal transitional problems involved in so substantial a governmental change, the lingering hostility of the adamant opponents of consolidation constituted a threat, as did the possibility that, in the long run and from a practical standpoint, the merger might prove unworkable. As is normal in many jurisdictions, the validity of the new charter had to be adjudicated before the governing authority under it could borrow money or issue bonds. A test suit was accordingly entered by the state's attorney general early in 1949, shortly after the city attempted to issue bonds of indebtedness. The attorney general's brief raised virtually all of the legal arguments that might have been construed as grounds for invalidating the charter, either on procedural or substantive constitutional grounds. The district court, however, upheld the charter against all contesting issues and its decision was affirmed by the state supreme court.

Following the legal validation of the charter, opposition to the plan showed increasing signs of solidification. A series of meetings culminated in the draft of a proposed charter designed to abolish the city government and establish a parish-wide three member commission form of government. This charter, known as the "Webb plan," received its name from the parish assessor, Jesse Webb, Sr., who had emerged as the leader of the unreconciled opposition to the new government. In the fall of 1949, Webb and approximately fifty other opponents of the consolidated plan of government attended a parish council meeting to present a proposal which was held to be a means of effecting a budgetary saving to the parish of some $300,000. Accompanying the Webb charter proposal was a petition requesting that the council call an election on the issue. Since the plan of government contains a clause (sec. 11.09) under which amendments may be proposed upon petition of qualified voters equal in number to 10 per cent of the votes cast for sheriff at the preceding election, the council pledged an amendment election based on the Webb plan. The election was to be carried out despite severe doubts about the constitutionality of the proposal and despite the fact that the names of about 40 per cent of the petitioners had to be removed from the petition because they were not registered voters.

The controversy was intensified when twenty-seven proponents of the charter petitioned the district court for an injunction prohibiting the council's call for an election. The district court permanently enjoined the amendment referendum on the grounds that the proposals violated the state constitution; but when the appeals reached the state supreme court, that body refused to intervene on the grounds that the calling of an election was a legislative function. In the interim, however, the parish council reversed its previous position and refused to call the amendment referendum, whereupon the opponents of the plan of government sued for a writ of mandamus to force the election. This case, too, followed the now familiar path to the state supreme court where it was finally dismissed on the grounds that the election for sheriff, on which the number of petitioners required to propose an amendment depended, was the primary and not the general election (the difference was that 27,000 votes had been cast in the primary as against 1,000 in the general election) and only 212 registered voters had signed the amendment petition. This action brought an end to the litigation involved in the inception period of the city-parish consolidation.

Approximately two years after the plan of government came into effect, however, it was recognized, both as a matter of concern about the plan and as a result of the pressures of proponents and opponents of the new government, that an objective evaluation of the effectiveness of the new charter was in order. Consequently, the mayor-president proposed, and the parish council adopted, a motion to create a "Plan of Government Study and Recommendation Committee." The eleven-member committee was composed of a mixture of citizen members and officials from the city-parish government. Although Webb was invited to participate and the Independent Taxpayers' Association (largely made up of opponents of the plan from the old Third Ward) was asked to name a representative to the committee, both refused to take part directly. The committee met weekly from late November, 1950, through May, 1951. The committee's deliberations ranged widely, but three general possibilities were considered in detail. One of these was a complete revision of the plan of government in the form of a change to a parish-wide commission form of government. Two proposals were made along these lines: one of them was the "Webb plan"; the other called for a five-man commission for the city, with two additional commissioners from the rural wards. A second set of proposals would have had the effect of amending the charter to restore most of the provisions of the original Reed proposals, including the city-parish manager, which had been struck out of the plan during the course of its development. The third approach, and the one which eventually received greatest support, involved the consideration of a series of amendments which were designed to remedy observable defects in the plan of government.

Toward the close of deliberations, the committee decided to present to the parish council one plan for each type of government—the commission form, the mayor-president and council form (the type already in existence under the plan) with amendments, and the city-parish manager form—with the recommendation that an unofficial ("straw" ballot) election be held so that the people of the parish might express their preference. The plans submitted were those which the committee considered to embody the best features of each of the three types, and were thus not simply the specific proposals brought before the committee by Webb and others. After presentation to the council, the committee's report was turned over to the parish attorney for legal analysis. About a year later, the parish council proposed seven amendments based on some of the changes recommended by the study committee in relation to the existing plan of government. These seven proposals were voted on in July, 1952, and the electorate ratified all but one of them. The defeated proposal, which lost by a narrow margin, would have instituted the most far-reaching change of any of the proposed amendments; it would have had the effect of merging the city and parish councils into a single body, with all members participating in both city and parish decisions, provided the state constitution could be amended to permit this action. The other amendments embodied structural, procedural, and financial changes of less consequence—a change in the distribution of the industrial area's parish tax, alteration in the procedure for passing ordinances and resolutions, an adjustment in the membership of the planning commission, a slight alteration in the membership of the recreation and parks commission, and minor changes in the charter provisions for the city court and city judge, as well as in the office of the city constable.

The study committee did much to alleviate both minor and major objections to the new government: it allowed all parties an opportunity to bring their grievances into the open; the city-parish government was broadly discussed by a prestigious body; some adjusting amendments were made; and public understanding of the rather complex system was enhanced. In fact, the study committee idea was so successful that two other plan of government review committees have been created since that time. The first of these made its report in 1956, and its four proposals for change were subsequently adopted by amendment. These included the addition of the office of administrative assistant to the mayor-president, an increase in the per diem of the council members, provision for a limited veto by the mayor-president, and further alteration of the planning commission's membership. The last review committee sat for eight months in 1959-60 and briefly reconvened in 1961. A number of proposals for change appeared in its report, some of which were put into effect by council or administrative action without the necessity for charter amendment.

At the time of this writing, those committee recommendations that would require charter amendment have not been proposed by the parish council, although these include some substantial recommendations, such as alterations in the personnel system, the absorption of the fire and police civil service by the over-all parish system, some additional qualifications for certain administrative officials in the city-parish government, and the incorporation of the independent recreation and parks commission into the general government of the parish. Several other events further strengthened the position of the newly consolidated government. The adoption of a one per cent city sales tax in 1950 put the experiment on a sound financial basis by enabling services—particularly fire and police—to be extended rapidly to the newly annexed municipal areas and greatly intensified these services in all parts of the city. The surpluses which were reported in the city budget as a result of this step also produced a flexibility in fiscal matters that favorably affected the entire parish. With the election of the late Jesse Webb, Jr. (son of the assessor) as mayor-president in 1952, important dividends were yielded for the new system. The younger Webb had been brought up, and at the time of his election, still lived in old Ward Three, so that much of the opposition from that sector was pacified by his assumption of the highest office of the new government. Furthermore, Webb carried out his administrative duties with vigor and dispatch, whereas the previous (and first) mayor-president had unfortunately suffered a prolonged illness which removed him from active participation in the new government at the very time when energetic executive leadership was greatly needed. A candid appraisal five years after the adoption of the plan of government revealed that the system was effectively in operation and had the tacit, and perhaps the enthusiastic, support of the great bulk of parish residents.

Each of the last two review committees affirmed the increased confidence in the consolidation that came with experience in operating the new government. The 1956 committee indicated that the system was sound and that, because of it, ". . . the City of Baton Rouge and the Parish of East Baton Rouge are better equipped for the ever increasing problems of a metropolitan area than any other local government in the country." In less extravagant terms, the more recent committee noted that ". . . this plan appears to be eminently well suited to the efficient and responsible conduct of local government in the area. The Committee is well aware that the future growth and development of this Parish will necessitate adjustments and we believe that the Charter provides an excellent framework within which this development can take place." . . .

CONSOLIDATION: A REAL OR DEFERRED SOLUTION?

The modified consolidation of the City of Baton Rouge and East Baton Rouge Parish which was inaugurated with the adoption of the *Plan of Government* now has approximately fifteen years of experience behind it. From an organizational standpoint, the plan undoubtedly provided a substantial basis from which to approach the problems of the metropolitan area on a unified basis. Measured by almost any criteria, the pre-1949 delineations of community types within the parish and the general governing bodies responsible for local public services were inadequate. The boundaries of the old city bore no relation to the extent of urbanization, the relation of both city and "rural" areas to the major industrial sites within the parish was undefined, and coordination between the parish and city governing authorities was haphazard to say the least. A geographical entity which was socially and economically interdependent was almost totally lacking in the governmental institutions necessary to effect the public services implied by this interdependence or to play its appropriate role in the creation of a larger measure of community identity among the residents of the metropolitan area. If consolidation did not produce a single government for the entire metropolitan complex, it did create the conditions for coordinating rural, urban, and industrial area government by means of governing councils with overlapping memberships and a single executive. The personalized and fragmented administrative system previously in operation was effectively displaced; and the new government could easily be conceived to be *the* government upon which responsibility could be fixed.

From a standpoint of the orthodox precepts of local government organization some important deficiencies still exist in the Baton Rouge consolidation. In the first place, the metropolitan area continues to be governed by two councils rather than by a unified local authority. Although the councils overlap in membership, the rural area councilmen have shown increasing signs of being restive under a plan which precludes their participation in decisions relating to the incorporated area, decisions which they consider as directly affecting the areas outside the city. As early as 1951, the first study committee actually approved a motion recommending that "city-parish council members vote on all the issues of both the city and parish, and have a common council for both city and parish." At a later meeting of the committee, however, it was pointed out that Art. VIII, Sec. thirteen of the Louisiana constitution (making ineligible for office persons who are not qualified electors of the state, district, parish, municipality, or ward in which the functions of the office are performed) apparently prevented such a merger. . . . The proposed charter amendment to accomplish the complete merger of the two councils was defeated by the voters in 1952. The action necessary to implement complete consolidation of the two councils has been deliberated in subsequent study committees, but was deferred in each instance. Even if a constitutional amendment permitting the merger were approved, problems concerning the constitutional authority of taxation and eligibility for homestead tax exemption, which were previously indicated, would have to be approached cautiously in order not to jeopardize either existing municipal tax sources or state rebates to the parish in lieu of homestead exemptions. Despite these thorny legal issues, both incumbent rural council members (from Wards Two and Three) strongly express the view that their areas require many more city-type services than can presently be extended to them and both seem to feel that a unified council might make an extension of such services possible on a less costly basis than is now afforded through special districts. However, unless the unified council had the authority to levy both parish and municipal taxes in any part of the parish, and unless corporate municipal powers could be extended to cover any areas needing municipal services (either complete or piecemeal) outside the present incorporated area, it is difficult to see how the problems that they indicate could be effectively solved. A mere merger of the councils, without breaking down existing boundaries within the parish, would not do the job.

Other closely related problems arise from the continuation of a substantial measure of separation between city and parish. Although the city has expanded by annexation since consolidation, this expansion has been slight in terms of the growth of the suburban fringe. The method of annexation provided in the plan has not encouraged the type of municipal expansion or general extension of urban services necessary to keep pace with urban growth. The proliferation of special tax districts for the purpose of providing municipal-type services on a service-by-service basis to urbanized communities in the "rural" area is symptomatic of the difficulty. It may be argued that the street lighting districts, garbage districts, and fire districts in the parish do not present the same type of problem that special districts do in some other governmental jurisdictions. They do not involve, for example, additional governing authorities, administrative overhead, or special work crews and equipment because these are supplied through the existing local governmental institutions. The justification for continued use of this fractionated special district system is that residents have the opportunity to acquire additional public services if they are willing to pay the price. It is not necessary for an entire city to agree on having the service before it can be made available. Even so, it is apparent that the costs to residents of the special districts for these piecemeal services is quite high in comparison with the unified provision of comparable services within the city. The time seems appropriate to consider a further wholesale annexation or a broader extension of the compound-functional consolidation in order to meet service needs on a more systematic basis and halt the proliferation of special districts.

The problem of representation is also a factor of increasing importance. The rural wards, which were slightly over-represented in terms of proportionality of population when consolidation was achieved, are now seriously under-represented. On a strict population basis, Ward Two would already be entitled to a minimum of two councilmen. Attempts at reapportioning the councils undoubtedly will re-open such questions as the single-member district versus at-large memberships and might very well exacerbate some of the old area conflicts and tendencies toward administrative dispersal that experience with the plan has muted. The concentration of administrative responsibility in the office of the mayor-president was one of the outstanding accomplishments of the consolidated plan of government. The establishment of unified executive control over major line functions, budgetary matters, and staff activities has undoubtedly helped to systematize and coordinate the administration of major functions of local government in both parish and city. A personnel merit system has been introduced, an effective central records management program established, and fiscal and accounting responsibilities have been unified. The city-parish government now has a chief executive who is equipped with the authority and tools to plan and manage the administrative affairs assigned to him; in turn this concentration of authority makes it possible for the mayor-president to be held accountable for deficiencies of administration.

These favorable developments are conditioned by the fact that there is still a considerable dispersal of control over some functions of local government. In consequence, there is also duplication, either of function or staff activity, at some points. A large part of this problem results from the compromise necessitated by the entrenchment of the parish constitutional officers. The direct election of a multiplicity of officials, each of whom is separately and directly accountable to the public, certainly violates the standard proverbs of administrative organization, expands administrative overhead, tends toward duplication of functions (as in the case of law enforcement), and increases the difficulty of coordination. Short of a complete revamping of existing local government boundaries and administrative structures, however, it is difficult to visualize a means of dealing with these intransigent factors. It is readily apparent that consolidation did not eliminate all duplication of agencies and services. The city and parish still prepare separate budgets and maintain separate accounts of revenues and expenditures. In effect, most of the city functions that prevailed before consolidation are continued as city functions. Likewise, most of the parish functions retain their former identities.

Much of the financial support for constitutional offices comes from fees and commissions directly related to the services they provide. Nevertheless, the city-parish government contributes office space and considerable financial support to many of the constitutional offices, particularly for care and feeding of prisoners, clerk of court, family court, district attorney, coroner, district court and registrar of voters. One unit of local government that retained its independent status and was not included in the city-parish consolidation was the school board. Its powers and duties are granted by state law and neither the city nor the parish councils have jurisdiction over school board revenues and expenditures. The audit of school board records continues to be a responsibility of the state supervisor of public funds. Other problems of an administrative nature persist, too. As a matter of logic, there does not seem to be any reason for the fire and police civil service system to be administered separately from the general personnel system of the city-parish. By the same token, it is not easy to understand the continued independence of the recreation and parks commission, which is not directly accountable to any elective legislative or executive agency. There are, of course, legal obstacles to the merger of these two functions into the general government, but these apparently could be overcome fairly easily if the urge to continued separation on the part of those most directly involved were not so strong.

In terms of the development of new services and expansion of existing services to meet piled-up needs, the record under consolidation is impressive. The most important new services have been those furnished by the planning department. Even if it is conceded that a planning program might have been developed under the pre-1949 governmental system, there is no reason to assume that its services would have extended beyond the boundaries of the city, with the result that many of the tangible, and even more of the intangible, benefits of planning (such as the coordinating effects produced by planning the development of facilities on a parish-wide basis) would have been lost. Even with the availability of planning services, the problems of maintaining an orderly basis for the rapid growth that the parish has undergone have taxed the administrative and fiscal resources of the area so heavily that the imagination balks at the thought of what might have occurred without them. It is difficult to determine with any great degree of precision whether local government administration is at a more efficient level as a result of consolidation. Local conditions are not the same as before consolidation. Capital investments made earlier serve as a base for continued growth and development. Public needs have changed, new standards of living have been achieved, and fringe benefits to employees have added considerably to costs.

In appraising the local government services which antedated the consolidation, we have concentrated most of our attention on the department of public works. This course was followed for two reasons: in the first place, this research project was designed primarily to explore the effects of consolidation on the rural sector of the parish, and the department of public works is the department which is responsible for the overwhelming proportion of local government functions in the unincorporated area; secondly, public works is the line department whose organization and operations are most fully consolidated under the plan of government. It should be emphasized at this point that, on balance, the city (including the areas newly incorporated under the plan) derived the most immediate benefits from the consolidated government. Both the municipal fire and police departments have undergone complete renovations, and substantial improvements have been made in traffic circulation, garbage collection, street maintenance and development, and street lighting in the incorporated area. The attention accorded the city during the earliest period of the plan's operation was not simply a matter of the city's having made a better bargain in moving toward consolidation than the rural areas; the city was the area of most urgent need insofar as public services were concerned, and five-sixths of the new city consisted of sectors of the parish previously under a rural-type government. Even before the most crucial needs of the city were met, however, programs were underway to improve rural area roads and drainage. And while these projects have been somewhat limited by conditions described in the chapter on public works, the volume and quality of service in these fields of primary interest to the rural residents completely outstrip the efforts prior to 1949. But even if the measurable differences in service levels are left aside, there is an impressive record, under consolidation, of preparation of the rural area for the increasing urbanization that it has undergone and is undergoing. Strict lines of separation once marked out local boundaries within the parish, but these have largely been swept away in the interest of unifying the whole community physically; and the physical unification has led to a stronger sense of local identity in terms of the larger dimension. Accessibility by road from any part of the parish to any other part has been greatly facilitated, and the mere presence on road and drainage works of *city-parish* crews in *city-parish* vehicles is sufficient to call attention to the interdependence of the entire metropolitan community. The extension of planning and subdivision regulation to the entire parish was another government activity which had the dual effect of preparing for sound future growth and bringing the entire parish into closer unity. Finally, the consolidation of the sanitary sewer system and the expansion of its facilities beyond the limits of the heavily built-up areas and into the areas of greatest potential growth is a significant physical symbol of the civic maturation of an urbanized area that retains some rural components.

Neither the scope nor the resources of this research project on city-parish consolidation permitted a survey of the attitudes of local residents toward the plan of government. Such a survey should be well worth the effort from the standpoint of the knowledge it might yield about the responses of citizens to the change and their perceptions of existing service standards and deficiencies. Even in the absence of such a survey, it is possible to conjecture that the plan works to the reasonable satisfaction of most of the area's residents, including those in the sections from which most of the original opposition came. There is no reason to suppose that this is a mere matter of passive adjustment to an innovation that was originally resisted. On the contrary, the obvious physical changes that have taken place under the plan seem to have produced a favorable public reaction, and a considerable amount of retrospective pride is evidenced among many sectors of the community in the uniqueness of the plan and its successful installation in the face of considerable odds. Each of the last two committees established to review the system has expressed strong confidence in the plan; and despite discontent on the part of the rural members of the parish council with some of its details, neither of them would want to abandon the consolidated plan. As the councilman who has served for more than eleven years from Ward Two has said, "the prime factor to keep in mind is that under this plan even today more money is being spent in the rural areas than ever would have been under the old system. The Police Jury system . . . just won't work in a highly industrialized parish such as ours." Several rural taxpayers have also stated that the consolidation has resulted in effective coordination of public works in rural areas. For example, ward boundaries formerly marked the abrupt halt of road construction or road maintenance. Now the work is planned and carried out on a parish-wide basis, without segmented control by smaller political subdivisions.

As an object lesson in an approach to the metropolitan area problem in communities which combine urban sprawl with substantial surrounding rural sectors, the Baton Rouge consolidation is as valuable for its demonstration of the limits on what is possible in local government change as it is for the display of the more positive effects of the experiment. No matter how urgent the need for change may appear to those closest to the local government scene, and however logical the recommended solution may be, it is important not to discount the inertia produced by the innate political conservatism of an existing community. This natural tendency to cling to known and established government, even when its utility lags in the face of social change, provides a cautionary note which is strongly underlined by the Baton Rouge experience. Only the most careful advance planning, followed by an intensive public relations campaign, enabled the plan to succeed, and even then a considerable amount of sheer good luck was involved. The proponents of the plan were able to take advantage of some highly favorable conditions in the particular situation facing them. The state constitution could be amended fairly easily to accommodate the type of change desired and to permit a referendum that was less constrictive than usual; the metropolitan area was contained within the boundaries of a single parish; and there were only two small municipal corporations other than Baton Rouge in the area. Those primarily responsible for the charter's development were also willing to compromise in order not to jeopardize the possibility of some change. They did not attempt to buck insuperable odds by abolishing all vestiges of existing institutions (e.g., the parish constitutional offices), and they moderated their proposals to take account of popular antipathies in cases such as the council-manager form of government.

In the final analysis, the groups which provided the initiative for the plan did not cease their efforts once final popular and legal approvals had been attained. At the lowest points in its struggle for survival, the plans had the concerted backing of a substantial portion of influential citizens who were determined to see that it was made to work because they regarded it as the last best hope for a solution to the particular metropolitan area problems facing the city and parish. In this connection the creation of the first plan of government review committee proved to be an unexpectedly effective development. The review committee was highly regarded because it was not partisan; and its full public discussion of the strengths and weaknesses of the plan, together with possible alternatives to it, improved public understanding while acting as a sounding board for popular complaints. Furthermore, the proposed amendments which ultimately came out of the committee's actions (albeit in a watered-down version) were evidence of flexibility on the part of the new government in adjusting to the exigencies of a fluid political situation. In establishing the first review committee and in following it up with additional ones at intermittent stages, the city-parish councils opened the way for a noticeable upsurge of interest in local public affairs; every major issue in recent years has been the subject of public hearings and debate based on widespread participation and publicity.

In summary, it may be said that the Baton Rouge consolidation may, if proper restraints are applied, furnish an example for similarly situated communities throughout the country. It will do so, however, not so much in terms of the specifics of the case as in the generalities. The foremost characteristics of the reform, if it may be termed that, is its pragmatism. The Baton Rouge experiment has to be regarded as a success because the city and parish were finally consolidated whereas the history of such attempts is mainly a record of failures. What is more, the system has survived and demonstrates some capacity for the self-correction of weaknesses and possible adaptability to further consolidation. If the success is tempered by certain limitations, it is no more than may be expected, and it is unquestionably a major improvement over the condition of governmental paralysis that seems to afflict so many of the nation's areas of prodigious growth.

18. Metro Nashville:
Interesting,
But Not Exportable*

After ten years of study and agitation, voters in a referendum held on June 28, 1962, approved the complete consolidation of the city of Nashville and Davidson County, Tennessee. The Texas Research League—a citizen-supported research corporation concerned with the problems of Texas government—examined the Metropolitan Government of Nashville and Davidson County and concluded it was not a paragon for Texas metropolitan areas, but did prove that reorganization plans for metropolitan areas can be developed and successfully implemented.

For an analysis of voter attitudes toward metropolitan reform in Nashville and Davidson County, see Reading 10.

Of the 212 metropolitan areas in the United States, only three have forms of government that might—with a little stretching of the definition—be called metropolitan-wide. Many political scientists believe that the most successful of these is the Metropolitan Government of Nashville and Davidson County, Tennessee—Metro Nashville, for short. Recently League staffers assigned to the Texas metropolitan areas study visited Nashville to see this unique governmental entity at first hand.

The Verdict: Very interesting, but probably not an answer for Texas.

The staff talked to several public officials and knowledgeable private observers during their visit. Nearly everyone interviewed stressed the fact that there were many unique factors which enabled Metro Nashville to be created, and that the plan was tailor-made to the requirements of the area. One metro official made a categorical statement: "It is working fine here, but I certainly would question any attempt to transplant our plan to any other city."

* *Texas Metropolitan Study Newsletter* (April 1966), pp. 1–2.

Metro Nashville came into being April 1, 1963, after a favorable referendum vote the previous June. In effect, the City of Nashville disincorporated and merged its government with that of Davidson County. Several very small incorporated municipalities continue to exist within the County—these are, however, prohibited from annexing additional territory and most of their services are provided by the metropolitan government.

Under the Nashville plan the jurisdiction of the metro government coincides with the County boundaries. The County is divided into two broad geographic areas—a General Services District which covers the entire County and an Urban Services District which encompasses the City plus the highly urbanized but unincorporated fringe that surrounded it, less a small "doughnut hole" for the incorporated community of Berry Hill.

The Metropolitan Government provides the following services throughout the General Services District: police protection, administration of justice, health, welfare, streets and roads, schools, parks and recreation, library, planning, housing and urban renewal, refuse disposal and various regulatory functions including building codes. Within the Urban Services District, the following governmental functions are performed: "additional" police protection,[1] fire protection, water, sanitary and storm sewers, street lighting and cleaning, and refuse collection.

Metro Nashville has a strong mayor-council form of government (the council-manager form was never seriously considered), and former County Judge Beverly Briley is the incumbent mayor. (He is currently seeking reelection to the first full term and his opponents—the former mayor of Nashville and the incumbent Vice Mayor of the Metropolitan Government—have both pledged their support to metro.) The Metropolitan Council consists of 40 members—5 elected at large and 35 from districts. A number of the administrative officers heading the line departments are appointed by the mayor in conformity with civil service regulations and have civil service protection in their positions.

Remnants of the old Davidson County still exist to comply with the requirements of the Tennessee Constitution. Thus there continue to be elected administrative officials such as the Registrar, Constables, District Attorney, Trustee, Public Defender and County Court Clerk. The elective positions of Sheriff and Tax Assessor are of particular interest. The County Sheriff has been relieved of

---

[1] The distinction between the "additional" police protection provided in the urban zone and just plain police protection available everywhere is not precisely defined and is actually handled on a pragmatic basis. In the current budget, a total of $4.6 million is spent on police protection of which $2.7 million is charged against the general zone and $1.9 million is considered "additional" and charged against the urban zone. Since the urban zone has 55% of the taxable values in the general zone, it can be deduced that urban area taxpayers pay for 74% of all police services.

all law enforcement activities but continues to serve civil papers and is in charge of the metropolitan jail and workhouse. The County Tax Assessor actually came out of the reorganization with substantially increased powers. He is now known as the Metropolitan Assessor and is the sole assessing authority in Metro Nashville.

The court system—principally elective—was unchanged except that the old city courts became divisions of a Metropolitan Court.

The change made in the school system was of great importance and was one of the principal reasons why many people supported the metro plan. Under the old system there were two school districts—one with a board appointed by the Mayor of Nashville while the other was appointed by the county authorities and, in each instance, the school budget was subject to review and approval by the governing body of the city and county respectively. The two school systems operated under different standards with the result that children living on one side of a street could receive a substantially different education from those on the other. Under the Metro Nashville plan there is only one school district covering the entire county. Metropolitan Board of Education members are appointed by the Mayor with approval of the Council. The school budget is submitted to the Metropolitan Council for approval. If two-thirds of the Board of Education members feel that the budget as adopted by the Council is "insufficient and inadequate to meet the needs of public education" they can cause a public referendum to be called at which the voters can overrule the Council's action. Thus under the Metro plan the schools have some measure of fiscal independence which they did not enjoy under the old City-County arrangement.

In general, it appears that the principal results of the adoption of the Metro Nashville plan have been:

1. It has made possible the provision of needed services to a large urban population that formerly resided in unincorporated territory. Moreover, these services have been provided at a lower tax cost than these people would have had to pay had they been annexed by the City.

2. Partly because the unincorporated urban areas have been brought into the urban service tax base and partly because some services have been shifted to a countywide tax base, the tax on property in the old City of Nashville has been significantly reduced.

3. The taxes on property located in the truly rural (or non-urban) portion of the county have been substantially increased as the people in these areas have been called upon to shoulder a share of those services deemed to be of area-wide importance.

4. Duplication of management between the county and the city has been eliminated and along with it some of the problems that arose when services were divided upon largely artificial political boundary lines.

5. By consolidating the two school systems, the differential in the standard of education was eliminated.

Since the adoption of the Metro Nashville plan, one of the political science professors at Vanderbilt University has kept close tabs on developments in the area and has, with the help of his graduate students, tried to measure changes in public opinion regarding metro. His findings indicate that support for metro has continued to be very high in the formerly unincorporated fringe areas of the old city (where the affirmative vote ran close to 80% favorable) and that the margin of support in what used to be the City of Nashville has increased significantly (the plan was favored by 57% of the 1962 voters). In the unurbanized portions of the county, the people continue to oppose metro by just about the same 2-to-1 margin that they indicated in the 1962 voting—the tax increase which these people experienced was just about what they had anticipated when they went to the polls.

To those who argue against any form of areawide government, the success of the Metro Nashville plan and the popular support which it retains may come as a surprise. On the other hand, there are many features of the Nashville plan which fail to accord with some of the pet devices of metropolitan reform groups. These include the retention of a long ballot with many elected officials, the large city council, the civil service status of top administrative officials and the continuance of several tiny incorporated enclaves.

But the people of Nashville were not trying to prove anything. They had a number of specific local problems and they believe that they have solved them in a specific local manner. They like the solution, but they do not have any missionary urge to spread the plan to other metropolitan areas.

Is the Metro Nashville Plan a model for any Texas metropolitan area?

In detail—definitely NO!

In broad outline—Very unlikely!

Does Metro Nashville offer a lesson for Texas?

Yes! The success of Metro Nashville proves that acceptable plans for solving the problem of governmental organization in metropolitan areas can be devised. It further proves that a county government—for essentially that is what Metro Nashville is—can, if it has to, undertake urban functions and perform them satisfactorily.

THE TWO-TIER APPROACH

The two-tier approach to the resolution of metropolitan problems is represented by the metropolitan county, metropolitan federation, and metropolitan special district; each involves the sharing of governmental power between an area-wide government and other local governments. The metropolitan county plan differs from the other two plans in that an additional unit of government is not created. And the metropolitan special district plan usually assigns fewer responsibilities to the area-wide government than the other two plans. Each plan has the problem of determining which functions should be assigned to the area-wide government and which functions should be assigned to the other local governments.

THE METROPOLITAN COUNTY

Students of metropolitan politics are convinced that serious obstacles lie in the path of any proposal to reform the government of the metropolis by consolidating existing local governments or creating a new unit of general local government. Organized county government exists in all states except Rhode Island, Connecticut, and Alaska, and most SMSA's fall within the confines of a single county. Consequently, a number of observers have concluded that the most feasible method to create a metropolitan or area-wide government would be to reform the existing county government which generally has limited authority and an outmoded organizational structure. Counties historically have been highly resistant to reform, but the application of the United States Supreme Court's "one man, one vote" principle to county governing boards may facilitate reform.

Whereas Los Angeles County became a metropolitan government by the incremental approach as indicated in Reading 21, Dade County, Florida, suddenly was converted into a metropolitan government by the adoption of a new charter. The initial success of the reformed Dade County has spurred interest in the reform of county government to meet the challenges of metropolitan areas.

The creation of the metropolitan Dade County government in 1957 was the culmination of a 12-year attempt to cope with metropolitan growth in the Miami area. Proposals to consolidate the city of Miami and Dade County were made in 1945, 1947, and 1953, but were defeated.

The Miami City Commission in July 1953 created the Miami Municipal Board and authorized it to draft a plan for the improvement of the governmental system of Dade County. The board contracted with the Public Administration Service of Chicago for the preparation of a report. Completed in 1954, the report recommended creation of a metropolitan government. The Florida Legislature on June 23, 1955 approved the necessary constitutional amendment providing for Dade County home rule and Florida voters ratified the amendment by a vote of 244,817 to 120,343 on November 6, 1956. Less than one fourth of Dade County voters on May 21, 1957, voted in a referendum and approved, by a vote of 44,404 to 42,620, the proposed charter providing for a commission-manager county government with metropolitan powers. Reading 9 analyzes the politics of metropolitan reform in Dade County.

Voter approval of the new charter did not end the conflict over the question of a metropolitan government for the Miami area. Various cities challenged the constitutionality of the new government and a total of 155 suits affecting the operation of the new government were decided during its first three years; none was successful.

Opponents of the metropolitan county government sought to emasculate it by charter amendments. By a vote of 74,420 to 48,893, Dade County voters on September 30, 1958 defeated an autonomy amendment, proposed by the Dade County League of Municipalities, which would have denied the county government jurisdiction over functions performed by cities at the time of the adoption of the charter. Adoption of the amendment would have restricted Dade County's powers to unincorporated areas.

A more serious threat to the new government was the McLeod amendment which proposed 37 changes in the charter including popular election of the sheriff and tax assessor, replacement of the commission-manager plan by a five-member commission, and removal of the county's jurisdiction over a number of area-wide functions—sewage, water supply, and transportation. On October 17, 1961, the McLeod amendment was defeated by a slim margin: 105,097 to 97,170.

The defeat of the McLeod amendment did not terminate attempts to weaken "Metro." On August 21, 1962, the voters approved two charter amendments weakening the power of the county manager; his appointments of department heads and administrative orders combining or creating departments require the approval of the county commission. Three other proposed amendments were defeated.

On November 5, 1963, the voters approved four and defeated six proposed charter amendments. Amendments approved provide for an elective sheriff, election of one commissioner from each of eight districts by the voters of the county at large, an increase in the number of signatures required on petitions for charter amendments, and a new system for the selection of judges of the metropolitan courts.

Although many area municipalities have opposed the Dade County government, there has been a considerable amount of city-county cooperation and the county provides a number of services to various cities on a contract basis. Furthermore, cities have turned functions over to the county under the charter provision authorizing a city by a two-thirds vote of its city council to transfer functions to the county. Nevertheless, the second county manager in Reading 19 recommends the complete consolidation of the county and cities.

The appropriateness of commission-manager government for metropolitan areas has been questioned and the suggestion made that the plan is an inappropriate form of government for such areas. On the other hand, the Government Research Council of the Miami-Dade Chamber of Commerce has concluded the manager plan of administration is effective. Reading 20 attributes many of the achievements of the metropolitan Dade County government to the manager plan. The Dade County experiment with manager government is being watched carefully and undoubtedly will influence the adoption of the manager plan by other metropolitan counties.

METROPOLITAN FEDERATION

Patterned after the federal relationship which exists between the national government and the states in the United States, metropolitan federation is a compromise between the existing fragmented political system and total amalgamation of the units of local government. Metropolitan federation always involves the creation of a new area-wide government; existing local units of government may be continued or partially consolidated. Proponents stress the flexibility of federation as functions can be transferred from the local units to the area-wide government as conditions change. In the view of the early metropolitan reformers, federation was preferable to a decentralized governmental system for the metropolis if total consolidation was not possible.

Although no metropolitan area in the United States has adopted federation, it is found in the Toronto and Winnipeg areas in Canada and the greater London area in England. The New York City borough plan, in effect from 1898 to January 1963, had the superficial appearance of metropolitan federation because each of the five boroughs was responsible for a few functions: construction and maintenance of streets and sewers, maintenance of public buildings, and enforcement of the building code. However, the boroughs lacked legislative powers.

Interest in metropolitan federation in the United States predates the twentieth century. A federated plan for the greater Boston area was proposed in 1896, but the Massachusetts General Court (legislature) failed to approve a bill authorizing the electorate to vote in a referendum on the question of the adoption of federation. In a 1929 referendum, a proposal to federate Pittsburgh and Allegheny County was defeated. A similar proposal to federate St. Louis County and St. Louis was defeated in a 1930 referendum.

The creation of a metropolitan federation in the Toronto, Canada area by the unilateral action of the provincial legislature has captured the interest of students of metropolitan areas. No referendum was held to allow the citizens a voice in the determination of whether a federal plan of government should be adopted for the 240-square-mile area, six times larger than the City of Toronto.

The Toronto area experienced rapid population growth and concomitant governmental problems during the first half of the twentieth century. The population of the City of Toronto increased from 200,000 in 1900 to 665,000 in 1953; the population of the 12 suburban communities increased from 25,000 to 507,000 in the same period. There were no single purpose metropolitan authorities in the Toronto area similar to those found in the Winnipeg area and other areas, but there were several interlocal service contracts.

Although opposed to amalgamation for 25 years, the City of Toronto shifted its position in 1950 and advocated total consolidation. On February 2, 1950, the City of Toronto applied to the Ontario Municipal Board for an order amalgamating Toronto with ten of its suburbs and major portions of two other suburbs; this action led to the famous Cumming Report of January 20, 1953. The report—prepared by L. R. Cumming, Chairman of the Ontario Municipal Board, with the assistance of Vice-Chairman W. J. Moore—described federation as "the most promising avenue of approach" and served as the basis for the creation of the Municipality of Metropolitan Toronto. Bill 80, introduced by the provincial government, received royal assent on April 2, 1953, and became the Municipality of Metropolitan Toronto Act, 1953. The act became effective January 1, 1954.

Following the creation of the Municipality of Metropolitan Toronto, the City of Toronto continued to press for total amalgamation and, in 1963, the Royal Commission on Metropolitan Toronto was appointed to review the system of government. Reading 22 presents the case against total amalgamation. The commission in 1965 rejected the City of Toronto's position and recommended the continuance of the two-tier system of government with a reduction in the number of municipalities from 13 to 4 as indicated in Reading 23.

On the basis of the commission's report, the provincial government introduced legislation which became the Municipality of Metropolitan Toronto Act, 1966. The act appears to represent an evolutionary approach to total amalgamation as the number of municipalities is reduced from 13 to 6: the City of Toronto and the boroughs of East York, Etobicoke, North York, Scarborough, and York. The Metropolitan Council was increased in size from 24 to 33 members; 12 seats are allotted to the City of Toronto and 20 seats to the five boroughs. The council continues to appoint its chairman who need not be a member of the council. The powerful 11-member executive committee is composed of the chairman of the Metropolitan Council, five members from the City of Toronto, and five members from the boroughs.

In the nineteenth century, the government of rapidly growing metropolitan London was a subject of concern. The first inquiry into the government of the London area was that of the Royal Commission on Municipal Corporations which issued reports in 1835 and 1837. The 1837 report recommended expansion of the Corporation of the City of London, but no action was taken on the report by Parliament. Other royal commissions studied the government of the London area and issued reports in 1854, 1894, and 1923.

The lack of an area-wide authority and the overlapping functions of various units of local government led to the appointment, on December 10, 1957, of the Royal Commission on Local Government in Greater London 1957–1960 to study the system of local government and to recommend changes, if needed, in the structure of the governmental system and the distribution of functions. The commission's report, issued in October 1960, rejected the transference of functions to the central government and recommended reorganization of local government institutions to provide a two-tier system of government for an area with a population of over eight million or nearly one fifth of the population of England.

Reading 24 contains the Government White Paper which agrees with the basic recommendations of the Royal Commission. On the basis of the commission's report, the Government introduced legislation which became the London Government Act 1963. The act dissolved all units of local government except the ancient city of London in an area extending 38 miles east to west and 28 miles north to south; and created the Greater London Council to perform area-wide functions and 32 London boroughs ranging in population from 146,000 to 341,000.

Metropolitan federation in greater London assigns sole responsibility for a number of functions such as ambulance service, land drainage, and refuse disposal to the Greater London Council, and sole responsibility for many other functions to the London boroughs. Responsibility for still other functions—planning, roads, traffic, and housing—is shared by the Greater London Council and the London boroughs. Criticism of the plan of government for greater London is evaluated in Reading 25.

METROPOLITAN SPECIAL DISTRICTS

The failure of comprehensive metropolitan reorganization plans to win voter approval has promoted the organization of politically acceptable metropolitan special districts to solve critical area-wide service needs. Creation of a metropolitan special district is facilitated by state laws which usually do not provide for a popular referendum on the question of the district's creation. Existing local governments in a metropolitan area continue to perform all their regular functions with the exception of the one assigned to the special district.

Metropolitan special district governments are assigned responsibility for area-wide facilities and services such as airports, bridges, housing, tunnels, terminals, sewage disposal, water supply, and parks and recreational facilities. The vast majority of special district governments are unifunctional, but a few have been assigned responsibility for the performance of more than one governmental function in a metropolitan area. The Metropolitan District Commission in the Boston area, for example, is responsible for water supply, sewage disposal, and certain parks and recreational facilities. Although the Municipality of Metropolitan Seattle is responsible only for sewage disposal and water pollution abatement, it may be assigned other functions by the area's municipalities under the provisions of the enabling statute which authorized the Municipality's creation.

A metropolitan special district has several advantages. It is not restricted by traditional local government boundaries as its jurisdictional area may include an entire metropolitan area or the greater part of one. A metropolitan special district may be the only feasible mechanism for the resolution of critical area-wide problems in a metropolitan area which extends beyond the boundaries of a single county or state. Since metropolitan special districts rely upon user charges, they are not restricted by constitutional and statutory tax limits. And revenue bonds exempt from debt limits can be issued without a popular referendum. Concentration upon the provision of one service in a relatively large geographical area often allows a metropolitan special district to achieve economies of scale and specialization.

That a metropolitan special district has certain advantages is not denied by reformers who favor a comprehensive approach to the resolution of metropolitan problems. The reformers, however, raise several objections to the creation of a metropolitan special district.

A new special district further fragments an already fractionated political system and makes the government of the metropolis more complex. Within a metropolitan area, it is not unusual to have more than one special district and each one may have different geographical boundaries. The relations between metropolitan special districts and other local governments have not always been good and coordination of their activities has been less than desirable. Furthermore, a special district may make the achievement of a comprehensive approach to metropolitan development more difficult as the activities of a special district may affect adversely other government programs. A metropolitan special district, for example, may facilitate the movement of automobiles by constructing and operating bridges and tunnels, and thereby injure a mass transportation program.

Critics often charge that metropolitan special districts exceed their authority and are responsible to no one. Only a small minority of the governing bodies of metropolitan special districts are popularly elected. The members of most governing bodies are appointed or hold office by virtue of other offices they hold.

It also is charged the creation of a metropolitan special district to provide an area-wide service may deprive a central city of needed bargaining power in its relations with suburban communities. A suburban community which is dependent upon the central city for sewage disposal may be more willing to cooperate in a program designed to solve the central city's water supply problem.

The best known metropolitan special district is the Port of New York Authority, which was created in 1921 to develop and operate transportation and terminal facilities in an area radiating 25 miles out from the Statue of Liberty in New York City harbor. The Port of New York Authority has been subjected to considerable criticism over the years. Reading 26 contains an example of the pungent criticism directed against the Authority. Nevertheless, a special New Jersey Senate Investigating Committee conducted a comprehensive review of the Authority's operations and concluded in 1959 that it is a responsible organization fulfilling its statutory obligations and contributing to progress in the metropolitan area.

19. Recommendations
for Unified Government
in Dade County*

IRVING G. McNAYR

In his report to the Board of County Commissioners, Irving G. McNayr, the second manager of Dade County, Florida, makes it clear that the home rule charter has not solved all the county's metropolitan problems. In McNayr's opinion, governmental fragmentation has accentuated the problems of providing services to the public. His recommended solution for the county's governmental problems is the unification of the 27 cities and the unincorporated area of metropolitan Miami into one city. For a description and analysis of the politics of the creation of the metropolitan Dade County government, see Reading 9.

This is a report designed to bring into focus the most fundamental local issue facing us today: the role of the cities and the county in providing governmental services to our citizens. This problem has doubtless given you much thought. It has also been uppermost in the minds of other local public officials and civic leaders as well as the general public. We are asked almost daily, "When will we have a single occupational license?" "When will we have a unified police force and fire department?" "When will Metro provide the badly needed municipal services in the unincorporated area?" "Which services is the county responsible for and which are the cities responsible for?" "Why must I take out a building permit in each city as well as the county once I have passed the county-wide contractors' examination?" These problems all resolve into the fundamental question of the future role of the cities and the county in local government. . . .

MUNICIPAL BOUNDARIES

Municipal borderlines were established at a time when towns were isolated places, many of them small in size. They have now lost their meaning and new settlements have filled in the area between and around them. Further compli-

* From *A Report to the Chairman and Members of the Board of County Commissioners* (September 25, 1962).

cating the pattern was the rapid incorporation and annexation of the Florida "boom" period, and the ensuing contraction of the cities after collapse of the boom, when the cities' financial conditions left them unable to service their expansive areas.

The sizeable contractions of the municipalities rarely left logical and orderly boundary lines in their wake. Individual property owners frequently "sued out" of their respective cities, leaving jagged, often weird, boundaries—a legacy of the past that plagues governmental efficiency today. South Miami is now literally a "city in pieces," with parts of the city geographically separated from the city proper, forming islands in the unincorporated area. . . . There are unincorporated islands within the cities of Hialeah, El Portal, and North Miami Beach. The entire unincorporated area weaves in, around, about, and through the cities in an illogical and irregular path.

This haphazard pattern of jurisdictional boundaries has important effects on the government of the area. The problems of providing local services are accentuated by this fragmentation; it makes it difficult and costly for the cities to service themselves and even more difficult for Metro to service the unincorporated areas. Police patrol, fire response areas, garbage collection routes, and sewerage systems are crisscrossed, overlapping and ineffectual. The existing boundaries prevent the efficient and economical deployment of public works forces and equipment. The many small, irregularly joined governmental units make it difficult to bring the area's full resources to bear on the task of providing better services, particularly those which require large scale capital investments and central facilities such as water, sewers, garbage disposal, and so forth. Only about one third of Dade's residences are now connected to sewerage lines. The area's water supply system is a complexity of contractual arrangements, primarily with the city of Miami, with many residents still relying on their own individual wells. Several cities are presently contemplating large investments for the construction of waste composting plants and incinerators in an effort to meet their immediate problem. However, there is a strong possibility that such efforts may compound rather than solve area problems.

Numerous examples can be cited where Metro patrols one side of a street and municipal police the other side. Similarly, county waste trucks service one side of the street while city waste collectors are picking up garbage on the other side. On some streets in the South Miami maze, it was actually necessary for the city to supply the county with the house numbers of the homes they service and of those which we service.

At the present time, the only public functions which can avoid the waste and inefficiency which is imposed by these boundary patterns are those which have been removed from the jurisdiction of the municipal governments. If reasonable efficiency and economy in government is to be achieved, the existing jurisdictional boundaries must be eliminated. They presently provide only a deterrent to efficient and logical service and fail to recognize that this is one metropolitan community regardless of political boundaries. City streets are traveled by the residents of other cities, by residents of the unincorporated areas and by tourists. Nor are the thoroughfares in the unincorporated areas magically cut off from travel by municipal residents. A thief residing in one municipality may find the practice of his "trade" more lucrative in another, thereby placing the cost of his apprehension on the second municipality. South Miami residents shop in Coral Gables and vice versa. Residents from the entire metropolitan area visit the race track in Hialeah, the Orange Bowl in Miami, Crandon Park in the unincorporated area. . . .

Another impediment to progress is the multiplicity of governing jurisdictions. The frictions and areas of dispute are not limited to city-county relationships but are found among the cities themselves. Competition arises between them for attracting trade, industry and tourism without regard to the overall needs of the community. This diversity of interest has often prevented necessary action on a community-wide level. Frequently, cities have failed to cooperate in matters where we should offer a common and united front in asserting ourselves with state and federal agencies.

It is necessary also to explode several myths which are advanced by those who would attempt to retain fragmentized government. We often hear that unified government will cause "loss of community identity," or that the communities will be "swallowed up" by the larger government. Coconut Grove, Ojus, and Perrine were once cities which dissolved themselves but which retain their identity and character. Carol City, Cutler Ridge, Westwood Lake, and Key Biscayne, on the other hand, are all examples of communities which have never been incorporated yet whose residents display strong community identification and civic interest.

The statement, "Our standards will be lowered," is still another myth. There is simply no basis for this argument. Has anyone ever seen a large city where all neighborhoods had the same characteristics, standards, and amenities? One can look right here in the city of Miami where both low rent districts and luxury neighborhoods exist. Has Coconut Grove deteriorated by virtue of its consolidation with Miami? Does the luxury community of Bay Point have the same standards as the blighted areas of Miami? The same conditions exist in Miami Beach—all classes of neighborhoods, from the areas in transition to the luxury islands. This argument simply will not stand up in the light of logic and experience.

To those who say, "Our officials will no longer be responsive to us," it is believed that the reverse is true. In a single city there will be single responsibility and single accountability. No longer can there be "buck passing" and confusion over jurisdiction and responsibility. There will be one set of elected representatives and one set of appointed officials, without overlap and duplication. Community service centers will answer complaints and inquiries. Police substations will service neighborhoods. Libraries and fire stations will not be moved but will be expanded into logical service areas. Garbage routes can be districted logically for more efficient service and waste trucks can deposit their loads at the nearest disposal center rather than driving miles further as presently. The nearest fire station will respond to an alarm without regard to the present illogical political boundaries. No longer will policemen be confused over jurisdictions when accidents occur on municipal boundaries. . . .

FISCAL PROBLEMS

Over 400,000 persons now reside in the unincorporated area of Dade County. Most of these people reside in areas which have all the characteristics of cities—high population density, sizeable commercial and industrial centers, traffic congestion, and the entire spectrum of urban requirements. Yet, there is a vast difference between the levels of services offered to the residents of cities and those offered residents of the unincorporated areas. Some of the shortcomings in the unincorporated area are: police and fire protection, inadequate street maintenance, sidewalks, sewerage and water supply, no auto inspection stations and libraries, virtually no street lighting and fire hydrants.

The residents of these areas can look only to Metro to provide the public services they need. Thus, Metro is required to act as a city government in the unincorporated areas while simultaneously serving as a metropolitan-wide authority. Yet our fiscal powers, as a county, are still geared to a government designed to have primary responsibility for rural areas. In the 1940s and 1950s, a number of previously municipal functions were transferred to the county government—health, hospitals, airports, and so on. Under Metro, still more functions were turned over and many others contemplated. Unfortunately, while the Metro charter gave the county the power to carry on a central metropolitan government, it was unable to grant the new government any taxing powers other than those it previously possessed as a county. This resulted in the paradoxical situation where governmental responsibilities were shifted from municipal governments, with wider taxing powers, to the county with much narrower taxing powers.

The differences between the revenue-raising authorities of Metro as a county and its potential revenue as a city are rooted in the rights granted by the state to its counties and to its cities. The state, recognizing the additional requirements placed upon governments operating in urban (as compared to rural) environments, granted greater fund raising powers to the cities. The counties, on the other hand, were viewed essentially as agents for the performance of state functions and for governing rural areas. Its chief functions, traditionally, were judicial administration, tax assessment and collection, election administration, construction and maintenance of rural roads, and rural law enforcement. As such its financial needs were relatively small, and with less responsibility, it was reasoned that the counties needed less broad revenue raising powers.

The cities' greater revenue-raising abilities stem essentially from their powers to levy excise taxes and franchise taxes, and to regain from the state the taxes collected from the sale of cigarettes within the municipalities. Cities may impose excise taxes on utility bills. Residents of areas outside city limits are not so taxed. The state-imposed cigarette tax is a source of considerable strength to cities as 95 percent of the taxes so collected are returned to the city. The taxes on cigarettes sold in the unincorporated areas are retained in their entirety by the state, and the county receives nothing. During 1960–1961, the City of Miami alone received more than $5 million from these two sources—more than one fifth of all its general revenues. . . .

Municipalities also have greater freedom in deriving franchise taxes from utilities. Although the county has been successful in levying a similar tax on the Florida Power and Light Company for its operation in the unincorporated areas, it does not levy a franchise tax on other utility enterprises.

To illustrate the effect of such differences in taxing powers between the cities and Metro, compare the general revenue sources of Metro, the City of Miami, and the City of Hialeah. Over 90 percent of Metro's tax revenues are obtained from ad valorem taxes, as compared to 65 percent for Miami and 37 percent for Hialeah.

This vividly illustrates the financial strait jacket in which Metro is bound and brings us to a situation that further compounds the problem. Under state law, ad valorem taxes levied by the counties must be levied uniformly county-wide. In addition, the municipalities levy separate property taxes within their respective boundaries. Thus, the resident of a municipality pays property taxes to two governments, Metro and the city in which he lives, while the resident of an unincorporated section is taxed only by Metro. Since some of Metro's receipts must be used to provide strictly local services in the unincorporated areas, the residents of the municipalities are placed in the position of having to finance services from which, on the surface at least, they receive no benefits. About 70 percent of Metro's tax base is within the municipalities; thus any increase in the level of local services in the unincorporated areas must increase the subsidy the city residents are now paying to those areas. Naturally, Metro has been loathe to pursue such a course. The inevitable result has been that Metro has not provided an adequate level of local service in the unincorporated areas. Inasmuch as the unincorporated areas are growing at about four times the rate of the municipalities, the demands for local services in those sections will continue to increase, placing ever-mounting pressures on the county government.

The logical and obvious solution to these financial problems is the total incorporation of Dade County as a city, retaining also our identity as a county. As a single city, we would qualify for over $6 million in revenues not presently available to us as a county. This amount is greater than our entire present expenditures for the local services which are restricted to the unincorporated area. This additional revenue alone, available to this area as a single city, would enable us to more than double our present services to the unincorporated area.

At the same time avoidance of duplication of jobs, the ability to deploy personnel and equipment where needed without regard for municipal boundaries, the establishment of one central purchasing facility, and all the other devices for providing needed services to the whole community if under one government should greatly reduce the costs of government throughout the area.

MUNICIPAL OPPOSITION

There is still another factor concerning present city-county relationships which should be frankly faced and openly discussed. It is the political opposition that municipal officials have placed in the path of almost every area-wide endeavor attempted. They have obstructed, or attempted to obstruct, Metro's progress every step of the way, and continue to do so. The League of Municipalities has openly used taxpayers' funds to finance anti-Metro movements. In supporting the autonomy amendment which was subsequently defeated at the polls, the cities freely used municipal personnel, equipment and tax monies. . . .

This opposition has been so intense that at one point it seems that the City of Miami went so far as to release traffic violators rather than permit their trial in Metro Court. The concept of Metro Court was fought all the way to the United States Supreme Court in a two-year court battle. When that failed, the recently proposed charter amendment attempted to do at the polls what the courts refused to do. County-wide traffic engineering was attacked in the courts. Work on the Dodge Island Seaport was delayed for years by the opposition of officials of Miami Beach. The City of Miami attempted to stop the transit take-over by court action and by every other means. The cities have refused a county-wide automobile inspection system and the City of Miami Beach even refuses to use a uniform inspection sticker. City councils have openly favored charter amendments restricting Metro even though their residents have consistently voted pro-Metro. They have fought uniform hours for the sale of liquor, a uniform building code, a uniform traffic code, and virtually every effort made to implement the charter. These are the public and open areas of opposition. We daily encounter others in every area of contact.

This lack of cooperation is often laid at Metro's doorstep by city officials. But the actual record indicates that lack of cooperation tends to stem primarily from municipal officials. . . .

In every transfer of a function to the county, we have had to pay taxpayers' money for equipment and facilities already paid for by taxpayers who would still get the same benefit from it. As we increase our taxes, in assuming these new functions, the cities do not lower their taxes. . . .

There has been a standing offer to the cities to use our purchasing division, one of the best in the country and which has attracted nationwide attention through the methods it has used in bringing prices down. Not a single city has fully accepted this readily available economy.

Municipal cooperation to date in developing area-wide services has occurred only rarely, and every bit of progress by Metro has been made despite, rather than in concert with, municipal officials. If we are ever to move ahead, it must be with a unity of purpose. City officials have openly and defiantly demonstrated that they do not intend to cooperate in the development of metropolitan area government.

CONCLUSION AND RECOMMENDATION

These then are the three major obstacles to progress in this area:

1. The illogical and haphazard municipal boundaries which impede the provision of services by the cities as well as the county.

2. The financial straitjacket of both the county and the cities: the county losing millions of dollars annually due to the state restriction on its revenues as a county; and the cities due to their size, unable to finance many major improvements.

3. The political opposition created by city officials who have fought every Metro attempt to make progress.

The 27 cities and the unincorporated area of metropolitan Miami should unify into one city. It is one city in every sense of the word, except for the purposeless political boundaries now existing. As the City and County of Miami, the area would retain its identity as a county for our relationships with the state and in meeting legal requirements. As a city, the government would release itself from the financial condition which serves the rural counties adequately, but which ties the hands of an urban government serving over a million residents. Double taxation of the city residents would be eliminated. . . .

Advantages of one city-county government are vast and almost endless. The following list is not intended to be all inclusive but rather to illustrate some of the many benefits and savings to be derived through this unification:

FINANCIAL

One tax assessment; one tax bill; one purchasing system which through competitive bidding on volume buying will afford countless savings; one consolidated insurance program at huge savings; one budget for balanced programming and elimination of intergovernmental charges.

POLICE AND FIRE

One central police and fire communications system providing one emergency telephone number for immediate response regardless of political boundaries; one police and fire academy to provide minimum and uniform training; one standard uniform, insignia and vehicle; one police and fire chief; one crime laboratory providing complete county-wide modern crime investigation; one central jail and stockade system eliminating the costly expense of individual municipal jails; one police records bureau providing complete files on all known criminals regardless of political boundaries; one auto inspection system; one vice squad; one homicide division to handle all capital crimes; one juvenile bureau with properly trained personnel; one firefighting system with uniform equipment.

The lack of coordination of police services, perhaps, is the key factor in this area finding itself year after year listed by the FBI in its Uniform Crime Reports as among those areas in the nation with the highest incidence of crime in most categories.

PUBLIC WORKS

One capital improvements program properly coordinated and implemented on the basis of need rather than political boundaries and pressures; one water and sewer agency using the City of Miami system as a nucleus to serve the entire county; uniform maintenance and construction of all roads; one agency to coordinate road and expressway planning, engineering and construction; fuller utilization of heavy equipment, government facilities and forces; logical routing of waste and trash collection routes regardless of existing political boundaries; implementation of the master waste disposal plan.

GENERAL

One voice, cognizant of the areas' needs, to deal with state and federal officials for funds and programs; one governing body with the responsibility and authority to handle the Miami River problem; an area-wide library system; one county-wide industrial development and general publicity program; one standard weights and measures system; one occupational license, taxicab permit, bicycle license, liquor store license, charity drive and soliciting license; one uniform liquor law pertaining to hours of operation; uniform building and zoning inspection control; uniform personnel rules, pay plan and retirement provisions for all local government employees.

In summary, the issue of one city for Dade County has long been avoided in the face of popular support and logic. It has been and will be no doubt strongly opposed by the local municipal office holders. The problems facing this area have been generally stated as well as recommendations for their solution. Much study remains to be done in detail and with deliberation. This is the most important local issue which will face us in this decade at least. Many more facts need to be gathered, aired and discussed.

Accordingly, it is respectfully urged that the Board of County Commissioners of Dade County appoint a board of its choosing, composed of outstanding citizens representative of the various areas and elements of the community, to undertake this study, hold public hearings, and present its findings to the Board of County Commissioners and citizens of Dade County for the orderly implementation of this proposal.

20. Metropolitan
Dade County
Government:
A Review
of Accomplishments*

D. P. S. PAUL

D. P. S. Paul, a leading Miami attorney and civic leader, reviews the
attempts which have been made to reform the governmental system of
metropolitan Miami, and assesses metropolitan Dade County's first eight
years, pointing out accomplishments and continuing problems. He refutes
critics who maintain the manager plan of administration is an inappropriate form of governmental administration for a metropolitan area by
attributing many of metropolitan Dade County's achievements to the manager plan of administration. A description and analysis of the politics of
the creation of the metropolitan Dade County government is contained in
Reading 9.

   Looking back over the past eight years during which a metropolitan government in Dade County has been evolving, one is both surprised and disappointed.
Surprised to find that so much has been accomplished. Disappointed to see how
the suspicions and antagonisms of city politicians, unsuccessful lawsuits challenging every major move of Metro, and disrupting charter amendment elections,
have denied citizens the governmental amenities and services which would make
living in Dade County more pleasant.
   O. W. "Hump" Campbell, metropolitan Dade County's first county manager,
said when he first arrived in Miami eight years ago, that it would take at least
two years just to reorganize the county government which at that time was run
somewhat like the country store. Little more than a year later, he said it would
be 10 to 15 years before the benefits of metropolitan government would be
appreciated. However, people in Dade County, as well as interested spectators
across the country, constantly seek answers to the question, "What has Metro

* From an address presented to the Local Government Law Section, American Bar
Association, Miami Beach, Florida (August 8, 1965).

done in eight years?" Before answering this question, some brief history will put our new government in perspective.

"Metro," as the new form of government came to be known through the headlines, was not as revolutionary a change in local government as some view it. Given a spectacular population growth—5000 in 1900 to more than a quarter-million in 1940, a half-million by 1950, and nearly a million by 1960—it was not hard to see that the bucolic form of county government would not suffice. Given stiff municipal annexation laws and a large unincorporated area where nearly 40 percent of the county's population resided by 1960, it was apparent that core-city Miami and a scattering of station-wagon–bedroom cities could not provide the governmental services needed by a sprawling metropolitan community.

By the mid-1940s, proposals to reorganize the local government structure through legislative action were being discussed. Three attempts were made but each was unsuccessful. During this time an inevitable shifting of governmental services was taking place. A multidistrict school system was consolidated into a county-wide system in 1945. That same year a Dade County Port Authority was created by legislative action to supersede the city of Miami's unsuccessful airport endeavors. Three years later the City of Miami turned over to the county ailing Jackson Memorial Hospital, which had been plagued for years with charges of inefficiency and neglect.

Following a close vote in 1953 on consolidation of the City of Miami and Dade County, a study of local government structure was made and in 1955 the state legislature approved a home rule constitutional amendment. This amendment was ratified by the voters in a state-wide election. A charter, drafted in accordance with the amendment, was approved by the voters in a close 44,404 to 42,620 vote on May 21, 1957. By the constitutional amendment and the charter, the local government in Dade County was changed in three significant ways:

1. Broad *home rule* powers were granted to the county government and to all 26 municipal governments. Our state legislature no longer has the authority to legislate on matters solely affecting Dade County or its cities.

2. A central *metropolitan government* was devolved from the old county government with the additional power to provide a wide range of services on a county-wide basis. This replaced a county government with limited county-wide powers, designed essentially for a rural community.

3. A *county manager* form of government was established. Traditional county governments in Florida had utilized the commission form with each Commissioner responsible for the administration of a group of county departments. However, the manager form of government was commonplace in Dade

County as Miami and most of the satellite cities had had managers for many years.

WHAT HOME RULE HAS MEANT TO DADE COUNTY

More than anything else, home rule has meant an often explosive interest in the problems of local government in a burgeoning community. It is difficult to become excited, or even to know, about the laws that are enacted by a state legislature meeting biennially 500 miles away in the cow country for a brief 60 days. But the local press can and does give wide coverage to the controversy attendant on the passage of laws each week at the county courthouse.

The constitutional amendment granted the electors of Dade County the right to adopt a county charter which could:

> grant full power and authority to the Board of County Commissioners of Dade County to pass ordinances relating to the affairs, property and government of Dade County and provide suitable penalties for the violation thereof; to levy and collect such taxes as may be authorized by general law *and no other taxes,* and do everything necessary to carry on a central metropolitan government in Dade County.

Although the powers granted by the charter have been broad, the financial base has been narrow. The restriction on taxing power in the constitutional amendment quoted has limited the county to the same sources of revenue enjoyed by all other Florida counties, most of which still serve sparse populations.

Home rule has not only meant greater attention to the *county* government, it has heightened interest in *city* government among municipal residents. After the shock had worn off and citizens discovered that the power of self-government was really in their hands they began to look at their city and town governments and to devise ways of improving them. Many municipal charter changes have subsequently been approved by city voters.

WHAT METROPOLITAN GOVERNMENT MEANS

The granting of metropolitan powers to the county government has enabled the county government, which already had limited county-wide jurisdiction, to perform a wide variety of services on a county-wide basis. Traffic-choked streets were one of the most widely acknowledged problems in the mid-1950s. There were no expressways and no overpasses. Speed limits and other traffic regulations varied from town to town. No single local government had jurisdiction over arterial roadways traversing several cities. Traffic backed up at major intersections all day long. Speed traps in towns which owed their existence to extracting fines from unwary motorists were a source of annoyance to residents and of shame to a tourist-conscious community. Over the howls of the city hall politicians, which reached all the way to the United States Supreme Court, the new metropolitan government exercised its powers which transcended the municipal boundary lines.

A uniform traffic code was adopted which superseded a number of conflicting municipal traffic codes. As a Metro ordinance, violations of the code are tried in the new Metro Court. With the help of the American Bar Association, a model traffic court was established and following lengthy legal battles the cities capitulated. Today we have a uniform system of justice for traffic offenders which has received wide national attention although die-hard dissenters still propose fragmentation.

Coupled with this development was the turnover of spotty traffic engineering to Metro with resultant economies in material purchases and increased capacity of existing streets. Capacity on a main thoroughfare, U.S. Route 1 south of Miami, was increased by one half by eliminating curbside parking. Buggy-age speed limits were raised to realistic levels. Traffic signals were modernized and synchronized. Uniform traffic regulation signs were installed. Intersections were restriped to allow turns without backing up traffic for blocks. A "beefed-up" professionalized Metro engineering staff went to work on expressways and speeded completion of over 50 miles of expressways in five years, with a *minimum* of federal participation. Traffic will remain a major problem in this community which grew up and sprawled out in the age of the automobile. But today, one governmental agency, instead of 27, is dealing with it. With reapportionment now in the offing, Dade also has hope of having a 1931 formula on gas tax fund distribution revised to further alleviate road financing problems.

Of related interest, the new Metro budget includes funds for arterial street lighting and lighting of main intersections. Additionally, over 43,000 properties in the unincorporated area have been lighted through special lighting districts authorized by Metro. This program is continuing.

Municipal police chiefs notwithstanding, law enforcement is seen by many thoughtful persons as an area-wide responsibility. In Dade County today it is not. Metro has not yet fully faced up to this aspect of government in the metropolitan area. However, some steps in this direction have been taken. A central traffic accident records bureau was established by Metro and a county-wide police communications system serves 45 percent of the population but is not yet integrated with the Miami system. Miami has turned over its crime lab to Metro and several other police services have been centralized. A major roadblock to further unification of police services occurred when voters, by a slim margin, returned the office of Sheriff from appointive status to the pre-Metro elective status. Although the idea of an elective sheriff is emotionally reassuring to the politically immature, the idea of an elected head of a law enforcement agency in a community of a million-plus people is a frightening prospect.

Perhaps one of the most significant achievements of metropolitan government has been the encouragement of the County Commission and civic leaders to think in terms of total county-wide development. The Metro Dade County Planning Department has concerned itself, irrespective of present city boundaries, with the orderly development of a community $2\frac{1}{2}$ million people by 1985. This department works very closely with the Dade County Development Department which is charged with attracting industry to our area. The rural-type county government provided by the creaking constitution of Florida could not have supplied today's businessman and industrialist with the professional information supplied by these departments. A clear-cut example of the metropolitan approach to a community problem which has developed here was the decision of County Commission and the voters two years ago that urban renewal was indeed a county-wide problem—even though the first project was located within the City of Miami.

Mass transportation, clearly a county-wide function, is another achievement of Metropolitan Dade County. Metro acquired from a private owner four bus lines which were unified into a system which now carries 90 percent of the county's transit passengers. Twenty-five of the 36 transit routes have either been improved or extended, the number of air-conditioned buses has been doubled, and a third of the routes are now completely air-conditioned. As the result of unification of routes and fares, daily savings to passengers range from 10 cents to as high as 90 cents per round trip. However, many areas of the sprawling county are still without public transportation and further route extensions will be needed.

On another transportation plane, Metro undertook from the City of Miami, the operation of the Miami Seaport and the construction of a new seaport to service cruise ships and light cargo. As in the need for hospital expansion 20 years ago, the central City of Miami was not in a financial position to finance the new port which serves an area three times the size of the city proper.

One of the original concepts of the home rule charter was that a legal means would be created to enable the residents of the unincorporated area—now close to a half-million population—to obtain services through the creation of special taxing districts. A procedure has been established to create such districts on petition of the residents involved. In addition to 33 lighting districts which have been authorized, five water districts have been created to supply water to areas previously served by well water. A small parks tax district has also been formed in one subdivision.

A county-wide water and sewer system is still in the future for this community whose development preceded rather than followed the installation of water mains. However, master plans for water and sewers have been prepared and are used as a guide when extensions by municipalities or the private companies take place. In addition, the Metro Water and Sewer Board exercises regulatory control over some 50 private water companies and over municipal systems operating in the unincorporated area. An important step toward a county-wide system was taken recently through the adoption of an ordinance making hook-ups mandatory in areas served by existing water lines. Water rates, in most instances reviewed by the board, have been reduced and consideration is presently being given to a blanket order requiring all water and sewer companies to revise their rates downward to reflect tax reductions.

In an area keenly aware of the threat of hurricanes, the adoption of the South Florida building code by Metro was an important step in protecting people from property damage caused by poor construction. The code applies to all construction in the county, is enforced by Metro inspectors in the unincorporated area and by municipal inspectors within the cities. Metro also established a single competency exam for contractors, doing away with a multiplicity of separate exams for contractors doing business in more than one municipality. Still a thorn in the sides of many contractors is the continuing necessity for the payment of separate license and building permit fees to each municipality.

In addition to the uniform building code, Metro has moved to establish other uniform regulations in a variety of spheres. Uniform subdivision regulations protect the public by requiring adequate drainage, streets, water supply, sewers, and so forth. Uniform automobile inspection regulations have ended the racket previously run by a few small municipalities who looked on the inspection fee only as a lucrative source of revenue, not a safety measure. Although present pollution of Dade's air and water is low, Metro took a historic step to protect our human and natural resources through the adoption of one of the strictest pollution control ordinances in the nation. It was this Metro ordinance that has forced the major detergent manufacturers to develop a "soft" detergent which will prevent the sudsing of drinking water not only in Dade County but across the nation.

BENEFITS OF THE MANAGER FORM OF GOVERNMENT

Many of the achievements of the metropolitan form of government in Dade County are closely related to the simultaneous adoption of the manager form of government. Improvements in the internal operation of the county government under Dade's first two county managers have enabled the county to provide citizens with an extension of services which probably would have been impossible without businesslike management techniques.

A professional survey in its analysis of Dade County government in 1954 stated that "Every accepted principle of financial administration is either violated or is unattainable." The pre-Metro budget, prepared by a lay budget commission appointed by the Governor, was a poor reflection of an antiquated governmental structure. This budget commission was abolished by the charter and a budget department was established and staffed by trained personnel. Data processing equipment was installed and a multiplicity of separate accounting systems were unified for better control. A position control system was inaugurated to prevent unwarranted additions to staff. Employee attrition figures were established and when applied to the budgets have reduced them by an estimated $8 million in the past six years. Central purchasing procedures save the county an estimated $100,000 a year and have been made available—though not widely utilized—to the municipalities.

Prior to Metro, the county government was composed of a conglomeration of 35 loosely related departments with poorly defined functions, many of them with duplicated responsibilities. In addition, separately elected officials controlled tax assessing, tax collecting, purchasing, voter registration, and some law enforcement functions. Today, the haphazard departmental structure and lack of administrative accountability has been streamlined into 15 departments reporting directly to the county manager. He, of course, is responsible to the nine-member County Commission and serves at its pleasure.

This administrative streamlining and modernized financial procedures were necessary, as Dade's first county manager pointed out, before the county government could hope either to take on any metropolitan functions or provide the additional services demanded by an exploding population. Metro's success in meeting the expanding needs of the community has been considerable. Public hospital expansion has added 400 beds. Facilities for the treatment of mental illness have been constructed. Modern laboratory facilities which have enabled the hospital to serve as a teaching institution for the University of Miami are constantly being improved. Such specialized services as the Nuclear Medicine Service, one of the nation's newest medical diagnostic medias in the detection of cancer, are indicative of a high quality medical center. A child welfare program was instigated by Metro and welfare functions expanded beyond the outmoded dole to provide counseling and other services designed to keep welfare recipients from being institutionalized. Four senior citizens day centers have been developed and emergency ambulance service provided county-wide.

As you might imagine in the land of sunshine, some of the most important strides have been taken in the field of parks and recreation. Dade County had developed a fine system of regional parks prior to Metro but there were no neighborhood or recreation programs in the unincorporated area which by 1960 had a population equivalent to a city the size of Toledo. Recreational facilities have been established in 40 locations around the county and an additional ten were scheduled for opening October 1, 1965. Financing for construction for the new neighborhood parks, pools and golf courses comes from electric franchise revenues derived from the unincorporated areas.

In the field of law enforcement too, there have been major expansions. Prior to Metro, public safety responsibilities were assigned to five separate county organizations operating from seven different budgets. By the mid-1950s, when nearly a quarter-million people lived in the unincorporated area, there were only two police patrol cars to protect them. Today there are 58 officers on each of the three shifts patrolling largely the unincorporated area. Requests for police service of all kinds have doubled in the eight years of Metro. With construction of a new jail and public safety building, Metro established a fine crime lab which services Miami and most of the other municipalities.

Public works programs have expanded since Metro, not only to keep up with expanding population, but to catch up on the backlog of facilities the old county government wasn't geared to provide. In addition to the 400-bed addition to the county hospital, voters have just approved a $9-million bond issue for replacement of an old hospital in the south end of the county and for other hospital improvements. The jail, public safety building and seaport have been mentioned. In addition to engineering and acquisition of rights of way for the expressway system, Metro has rebuilt or resurfaced nearly every major thoroughfare in the county as well as improving residential streets long neglected. Two new health clinics, a museum, nine swimming pools, two public golf courses, major flood control projects and even some 3000 feet of fishing catwalks for the angling public have been built by Metro.

Many other accomplishments could be mentioned if time permitted. We have touched on the accomplishments here and not on the battles, upheavals and recalcitrance that has been encountered in the achievement process. The controversy will not subside for years to come for there are many programs and services not now provided all the citizens which are imperative to this community looking forward to being one of the great metropolitan areas of the nation. Decisions on how they will best be provided still need to be made.

21. The Rise
of Los Angeles County
as a Producer
of Municipal Services*

ROBERT O. WARREN

The development of Los Angeles County since the turn of the century
as a major producer of urban services for residents of unincorporated
territory and a number of cities illustrates the role a metropolitan county
can play in solving area-wide service problems and reducing the pressure
for incorporation of unincorporated territory. Robert O. Warren, University of Washington, ably documents the rise of Los Angeles County,
which had a 1965 population of 6.7 million, as a major producer of local
services and the ramifications of its development. Reading 30 describes
the services offered to contract cities by Los Angeles County.

Prior to 1900, Los Angeles County functioned in the traditional role of a
rurally oriented administrative arm of the state. Within thirty years, however,
the County developed a highly professional bureaucracy and was producing a
wide range of municipal-type services for over 300,000 residents in unincorporated territory, and for a number of cities as well. . . .

The extent to which the County acquired a capacity to meet the public service
needs of highly urbanized areas is reflected in the fact, between 1930 and 1950,
only one small municipality was organized, while the population in unincorporated areas increased by over 500,000 during the same period. In addition, the
range of contract services which were available from the County to municipalities also increased and became more specialized.

This development of the County into a major producer of urban services
required adequate legal authority, county officials who were willing and able
to utilize such authority, and a large enough clientele to achieve production
efficiencies. The necessary legal framework was provided by the State Constitution and the legislature which, as in other matters concerning local government,

* From *Government in Metropolitan Regions: A Reappraisal of Fractionated Political
Organization* (Davis, Calif.: Institute of Governmental Affairs, University of California,
1966), pp. 92–94, 102–05, and 110–17. Footnotes in original omitted.

proved willing to grant authority directly to county government, or to county administered special districts, for the production of municipal-type services. Locally, the early Los Angeles County Board of Supervisors adopted a policy of functional expansion. From time to time, county officials lobbied for additional powers, innovated within their existing authority, and showed a willingness to move in directions suggested by a professional staff of administrators. Finally, there was a significant number of citizens in unincorporated territory and municipalities who chose to utilize county produced services rather than to incorporate or produce the same service locally, in the case of a city.

The County's production oriented growth in municipal services followed no deliberate plan, but largely evolved from entrepreneurial administrative responses to changing patterns of demand over four decades.

COUNTY SERVICES TO MUNICIPALITIES

The rapid population increases in the County between 1900 and 1930 put great strains upon many cities in meeting service needs through local production of municipal services. The capacities of some cities proved so limited that consolidation with larger jurisdictions was required, particularly in the case of water. Under these circumstances, opportunities to obtain economies of scale in the production of services through the utilization of an external producer without substantial loss of local autonomy became increasingly attractive.

Apart from the Metropolitan Water District and Los Angeles City contracts for sewage disposal, these opportunities were primarily made available by Los Angeles County. After 1910, the administrative structure of the County was modernized under a constitutional amendment, which allowed a degree of county home rule. This, combined with a series of enactments of the state legislature authorizing a county to provide services to municipalities through voluntary agreements, laid the groundwork for Los Angeles County to assume tax collection and assessment, library and public health services for municipalities, and to participate in sewage disposal with a number of cities by 1930.

Leaders in Los Angeles County quickly utilized a 1911 constitutional authorization for home rule and drafted and adopted a charter in 1912. The charter took effect the following year and, among other things, it reduced the number of elected officials, apart from judicial officers, to a five-member board of supervisors, the district attorney, sheriff and assessor; basically centralized general governmental powers in the supervisors; and instituted a civil service system. . . .

Another constitutional amendment, passed in 1914, authorized counties to perform municipal functions for cities through contractual arrangements.

County authority to enter into certain types of service contracts with municipalities predated the amendment, but this provided a firmer legal base for such undertakings.

Los Angeles County's first service contract with a municipality involved tax assessment and collection for the City of Lordsburg (subsequently changed to LaVerne) in 1907, under an enabling statute passed in 1895. Three more municipalities contracted for these services by 1910. Many smaller cities had simply used the county assessment figures, adjusting them to conform to local evaluation policy, before contracting was widely utilized. In the case of larger cities, economies were also realized in transferring these functions to the County Assessor and Tax Collector. Consequently, every municipality which incorporated after 1907 immediately contracted with the County and, by 1950, all but three cities, Arcadia, Long Beach, and Pasadena had entered into such contracts. . . .

ADDITIONAL SERVICE CONTRACTS

In 1930, the County was providing municipalities with the option of transferring the production of health, library, and tax assessment and collection services directly to the County without loss of local autonomy. Similarly, joint participation between the County and cities in the operation of sanitation districts offered a method of providing a basic service which had become virtually impossible for communities to handle individually at the local level. In the next two decades, these County services became more urbanized and specialized to meet the needs of member or contracting cities with expanding populations and, particularly, the increasing demands from the even more rapidly growing unincorporated communities.

During the 1930's and 1940's, the County entered into contracts on a limited basis for the issuance of building permits and inspection, animal regulations, personnel, planning, and street and highway services. Los Angeles County's home rule charter was amended in 1934 to allow county officers to assume and discharge ". . . any of the municipal functions of any of the cities and towns within said county." As enabling legislation was passed at the state level for joint arrangements in particular service areas, this provision offered adequate local authority for the County to act.

An act of 1935 authorized any municipality to contract with any other city, county, or state agency for the performance of various services in the personnel field. The County's Civil Service Commission had been in existence since 1913, and was in a position to make the services of a large and professionalized staff available to municipalities. Hawthorne contracted in 1936, ten cities received County services in 1940, and twelve by 1950.

Terms of the arrangements varied widely. All municipalities contracted for examination services, and a number for complete personnel service. Several methods of assessing costs were utilized by the County until a standard system was adopted in 1941. Prices are based upon an estimate of the prorated cost of personnel administration per employee in the county system. Contract cities were billed in proportion to the number of employees they have served by the County.

Los Angeles County entered the land use planning field in 1923 with the creation of the Regional Planning Commission by the Board of Supervisors. Its technical staff first provided advisory zoning services to the City of San Gabriel in 1938 on a contract basis. Four additional cities, Torrance, Manhattan Beach, Hawthorne, and West Covina, utilized the County for zoning work by the early 1940's. Immediately after World War II, Alhambra and Glendale contracted for the employment of county personnel for general planning services.

Cost was determined by employee time plus overhead, or a flat rate per meeting attended by county consultants. By 1947, the Regional Planning Commission found that its limited staff could not satisfactorily meet the County's own planning needs and fill the demands for contract work that had developed. Consequently, contract work was discontinued in that year ". . . pending reorientation of the department to the return of the director from active military duty. . . ."

During this period, the County Road Department developed a variety of contracts with smaller cities. Two types of arrangements evolved. Many contracts were for specific projects only, and others, covering general road work, were set up on a continuing basis. By 1950, sixteen cities were utilizing the Road Department for general road work, installation, and maintenance of traffic signals or painting traffic stripes. These contracts called for reimbursement of all expenses incurred, plus an overhead charge.

Two cities, Whittier and Montebello, contracted with the County Pound Department for animal regulation services in 1947 and 1948. In each case, the city was faced with the choice of finding an alternative to a previous service arrangement which had been discontinued. The cities were billed on the basis of the number of hours county patrol trucks operated within the municipalities, and the County retained impounding and miscellaneous fees to offset the costs of night emergency calls. The patrol patterns of the County in the unincorporated territory it served were simply extended to include the two cities.

This close interrelationship between the level of services provided to municipalities and unincorporated communities by the County is reflected in agreements negotiated for the enforcement of local building, plumbing, and electrical codes. In 1939 and 1940, four cities contracted with the County Department of Building and Safety for these services. These cities were required to provide quarters, utilities, and whatever janitorial services were necessary to maintain a local office. Although it was not stipulated in the contract, residents of adjacent unincorporated areas utilized these offices to transact business with county personnel. The cities make no direct payment, but remit all fees for permits to the County. The fee schedule is based on the rates charged by the County in the unincorporated area.

These arrangements, which allowed economic benefits for municipalities, also provided the County with extensive experience in producing municipal services for residents of cities both under direct contract and district membership. This willingness of cities to transfer the production of several urban functions to the County, and the ability of the County to satisfy the service needs of quite diverse municipalities provided the basis for the subsequent development of the Lakewood Plan but also foreshadowed the competitive tendencies of the County's post-1950 relationships with contract cities.

COUNTY SERVICES IN UNINCORPORATED COMMUNITIES

In contrast to the continuous high growth rate and urbanization of unincorporated areas between 1900 and 1950 . . . a reverse trend occurred in the number of municipalities that were formed in the county. Despite rapid population increases outside of municipal boundaries after 1930, only one small city was organized. Consequently, to support this population without forming cities or annexing, which did not occur either, optional methods of obtaining municipal levels of service had to be available.

The County provided this option. The jurisdiction's ability to provide acceptable levels of animal regulation, building inspection, health, library, planning and road services to municipalities was largely a consequence of the fact that the County, particularly after 1920, consistently had responded to the needs of rapidly growing unincorporated communities by producing urban levels of services for residents outside cities. The availability of an increasing number and quality of municipal-type services to inhabitants in county territory had the effect of reducing the incentives for unincorporated communities to organize as cities, even though they had all of the demographic and economic attributes traditionally associated with a municipality. This virtual end to the formation of new cities between 1930 and 1950 was also affected by policies adopted by the County, as it became a major producer of municipal services, to inhibit the organization of cities and maintain the scope of county operations in unincorporated communities. . . .

A CHANGING INCORPORATION PATTERN

The aggressive movement of Los Angeles County into the production of municipal services during the 1920's provided the basis for supporting large concentrations of population outside city boundaries in subsequent decades. As annexation pressure from the City of Los Angeles and other municipalities subsided in the later 1920's, unincorporated territory residents had the services of a large scale jurisdiction of metropolitan scope available for the production of municipal services without organizing a city . . . seven of nine proposals to organize cities which reached the ballot stage were rejected by local voters between 1930 and 1950. In comparison, forty-three of fifty-five incorporation elections had been successful in the previous three decades.

Even prior to 1930, over forty identifiable unincorporated communities existed in the County, with populations ranging from 2,000 to 75,000 in one case. While finding the lack of a formally unified government in the area unsatisfactory, Studenski concluded, in 1930, that Los Angeles County represented the one example in the country of a county which had utilized its power to draft a home rule charter to ". . . reconstruct itself to meet the demands of a metropolitan area." He goes on to describe the supervisors as functioning: ". . . in every way as do city commissioners in a commission-governed city. The impression which a visitor to the county offices carries away with him is that of a city government operating at full speed."

During the next twenty years, the number of residents in unincorporated territory grew to nearly 900,000, putting Los Angeles County in the position of producing municipal services for a population equivalent to "the eighth largest city in the nation," in addition to services provided to municipalities. . . .

The policies of Los Angeles County had two basic effects in influencing this modification in the traditional pattern of utilizing municipal status to obtain urban levels of service. The range and level of services available from the County and districts meant that cities no longer were monopolistic producers of urban services, as they had been prior to 1900 and even 1920. The choice available to unincorporated residents was no longer incorporation or annexation to meet urban needs, but was expanded to include the County as an efficient and large scale regional producer of basic services and special districts which allowed various combinations of services and service levels to be realized.

On the other hand, while the development of the County as a jurisdiction of metropolitan scope offered positive inducements to communities to remain unincorporated, it also resulted in the emergence of a policy, on the part of the County, which was designed to inhibit the formation of new cities. By 1930, and increasingly so by 1950, the County's position as a major producer of municipal services primarily depended upon maintenance of its unincorporated area clientele. Actions of the County reflected this dependency. In addition, the legislature modified the formal requirements to initiate petitions for an incorporation election in such a way that placing the question before the voters became more difficult and shifted the decision of calling an election from simply registered voters to property owners.

FORMAL AND INFORMAL BARRIERS TO INCORPORATION

The Board of Supervisors had adopted a laissez-faire attitude toward incorporation proposals during the 19th and early 20th Centuries. If a petition met the legal requirements, protesting property owners were eliminated from the boundaries, when possible, and the matter was placed before the affected voters. However, from the mid-1920's, several formal and informal methods were utilized to discourage or directly prevent the formation of municipalities. A number of avenues were open to the County in pursuing this *exclusionary* policy.

As an administrative agent of the state in processing incorporation petitions, the Board of Supervisors adopted a policy of scrutinizing the motivations of incorporation proponents, and questioning the capacity of a proposed municipality to finance adequate levels of urban services. Consequently, four efforts to organize cities were aborted in 1924 and 1925 when the Board eliminated territory from the proposed boundaries in such a manner that the number of residents in the remaining area did not meet the legal requirement of 500. A similar action was taken in 1932.

No specific authority was delegated to county supervisors to judge the viability of proposed cities in the Municipal Corporation Act. Neither was there any indication in the Act that the authority to delete territory was intended to be used to defeat an incorporation movement. Nevertheless, the power was available, if a board of supervisors chose to exercise it in this way. A modification of this policy was also used in 1925. The Board reduced the territory of the proposed City of Verdugo to a point that the proponents withdrew their effort, claiming that the remaining area would ". . . not permit of a practical or efficient city of the sixth class to function properly."

INCORPORATIONS ELECTIONS 1930–1950*

| | | ELECTION RESULTS | |
YEAR	COMMUNITY	Yes	No
1930	Downey	182	456
1930	Gardena	502	237
1931	East Los Angeles	5	416
1933	Garden City	462	8,429
1939	Palos Verdes Estates	215	208
1945	Willowbrook	267	345
1946	Willowbrook	339	448
1950	Baldwin Park	1,164	2,016
1950	Bell Gardens	768	1,608

* Figures adapted from data in Richard Bigger and James D. Kitchen, *How the Cities Grew* (Los Angeles: The Haynes Foundations, 1952), pp. 111–114.

In the early 1930's several efforts to form municipalities were negatively in-fluenced by the Board of Supervisors, and others were decisively defeated by the voters. Most of this activity centered in the densely populated East Los Angeles section of the County. A 1931 proposal sought to incorporate City Terrace. The boundaries described in the petition were irregular, and encircled a real estate venture so that it remained unincorporated but was protected from possible annexation by the City of Los Angeles. The Supervisors refused to call an elec-tion on the grounds that the petition was not submitted in good faith, and that the taxes which would have to be levied would amount to confiscation of prop-erty. No efforts were made to contest the authority of the Board to reject the petition in this fashion, although the County had no legal basis for so doing.

Another petition was rejected the same year, but was accepted for processing when the action was challenged. This petition sought to create a city two blocks wide and eighteen blocks long, directly east of Los Angeles, and was designed to prevent the expansion of the central city. The proposal was defeated at the polls by a vote of 416 to 5. Two additional efforts were made to organize cities with populations of 75,000 and 50,000 in East Los Angeles. In one case, a petition was submitted to the Board of Supervisors in 1932, but was never brought to a formal hearing. Strong local opposition developed during a pro-tracted dispute between proponents and county officials over the accuracy of the boundary description. The next year, a proposal to incorporate Garden City, which included much of the territory in the previous effort, was rejected by a vote of 8,439 to 462 by local voters.

Whatever the motives of the Board of Supervisors, residents of areas pro-posed for incorporation held a similarly negative view toward the organization of municipalities when the question was placed on the ballot. The owners of industrial and large undeveloped areas, as well as residential property owners, generally equated municipal status with higher tax costs without compensating social or economic benefits. As the Depression deepened in the early 1930's, this concern over protecting property from the higher tax rates associated with the support of urban services through a municipal corporation was reflected in actions of the state legislature to provide additional protection to landowners against having their property included in cities against their desires.

Two amendments revised the Municipal Corporations Act in the 1920's so that certain types of undeveloped land could not be included within the bound-aries of a proposed municipality without a specific request by the owner. A provision adopted in 1933, and still in force, had more far reaching con-sequences in modifying the ease with which an incorporation proposal can be initiated.

Rather than protecting certain types of land from inclusion in a municipality, the 1933 amendment gave property owners a method of vetoing the formation of a city. Prior to this change, incorporation proceedings were initiated by a petition containing the signatures of at least fifty qualified electors. Under this provision, a city could theoretically be organized without a single property owner favoring the action. The modified petition requirements stipulate that the document must be signed by at least 25 percent of the holders of title to land whose holdings represent at least 25 percent of the value of land within the proposed boundaries. The final decision is still in the hands of a majority of the voters in the area, but no election can be held without the affirmative approval of a substantial number of property owners.

The generalized opposition to incorporation among county residents, and the increased difficulty proponents faced in bringing the matter to a vote were reflected in the fact that only one proposal to form a city reached the election stage between 1933 and 1945. However, the tempo of the growth, particularly in the unincorporated areas, increased significantly in the 1940's over the previous decade, and possible benefits from municipal status were seriously considered in a number of sections with the end of World War II.

"SELLING" COUNTY SERVICES

County policy continued to be aimed at inhibiting the incorporation or annexation of its urbanized service areas. A recurrent point openly made by members of the Board was that the various incorporation proposals were not economically feasible, and that a community would actually be reducing its service levels by such action. The 1945 and 1946 incorporation efforts in Willowbrook led the Supervisor representing that area to observe, "They can't get enough money from legitimate sources to pay three policemen and they won't have any jail." The same Supervisor had to be reminded that unless a hearing were granted before the Board, the proponents could compel the County to process their petition by going to court.

A 1949 movement to incorporate the San Gabriel Valley community of Duarte caused Supervisor William A. Smith to comment that the "Assessed valuation of property in Duarte is not high enough to support an efficient city government." As a warning, the Supervisor pointed to several existing cities in his district as ". . . glaring indications of what could happen to county unincorporated territory financially unable to support a municipal government." During the Baldwin Park incorporation election campaign, Supervisor Raymond V. Darby advised the community that he did not believe that assessed valuation of the area was sufficient for "financial soundness" and stated that "It looks like you won't be able to raise enough city taxes to build a jail or hire a jailer."

Bell Gardens incorporation proponents ran into a similar attitude when they presented their petition to form a city in 1950. The Board expressed dissatisfaction with the adequacy of the tax base and, during the public hearing on the petition, one Board member responded several times to protests against the proposed city by suggesting that the opposition get out the vote on election day. The public hostility of County Supervisors to cityhood in the Willowbrook, Baldwin Park and Bell Gardens elections undoubtedly played a role in defeating the proposals at the polls.

In several instances, when a section of the County ran into serious service problems, the Board urged the use of special districts as an alternative solution to annexation or incorporation. This tactic was used in 1949 when the wealthy and semi-rural residential area of La Cresenta, faced with a water shortage, considered annexation to neighboring Glendale. With the support of Glendale, an annexation election was scheduled for December, 1949. During the last month of a hotly contested campaign, the County Supervisor from this area advocated the formation of a county-wide water district. The full Board of Supervisors immediately gave their support to the plan, prior to the annexation vote, and discussed an election on the question in January, 1950.

The impact of this proposal by County officials, ". . . coupled with statements as to the probability of admission to the Metropolitan Water District, and the immediate withdrawal of county services from the area," turned out to be "grist for the mills" of the anti-annexationists. The area rejected joining Glendale by a vote of 3,900 to 2,949. The county-wide water district was never formally presented to the voters, but a smaller district was formed in the area in 1950. Glendale added part of the section through annexations in the subsequent years.

Groups within the unincorporated territory considering incorporation were often in contact with the County requesting various types of data concerning the population or assessed valuation of their area, or the current tax rates and levels of service received. Because the County was the only jurisdiction which maintained most of this information, or had easy access to it, administrators were generally aware of and in touch with any incipient movements to form a city through contacts from the proponents themselves. These opportunities were used to stress two themes: that the quality of county services could not be duplicated by a small city; and that incorporation might result in the loss of future county financed improvements.

In 1946 and 1947, county analysts prepared reports on the feasibility of incorporation for Altadena, Downey, and Temple City when interest was expressed in these communities. The Altadena report pointed out a number of advantages and disadvantages to incorporation. Among the latter points mentioned were: incorporation "costs the taxpayers more money"; the quality and variety of services provided by the County are higher than "can be afforded by the smaller cities"; and that ". . . city residents continue to pay the general county tax rate thereby continuing their support of municipal services rendered by the county in unincorporated areas." The report also mentioned that county plans for developing golf links in the area would have to be discontinued under existing policies if the area incorporated. Similar points were presented in the other two reports.

Most county communications with groups considering incorporation or annexation were in the form of direct responses to information queries and public appearances before local meetings. The role of the County in the Bell Gardens incorporation effort in 1949–1950, which was opposed by the Board of Supervisors, illustrates the nature of community contacts by county administrators. In response to request for information from the Bell Gardens Betterment Association, departmental officials strongly voiced the benefits of unincorporated status. In correspondence, the Chief Engineer of the County Fire Department listed the personnel and equipment serving the area, stated that the cost of maintaining a fire department of the same size by a city of Bell Gardens "would be prohibitive," and concluded by commenting that ". . . by use of the various Districts' equipment on a mutual aid basis, a much better Fire Department is maintained than would be possible otherwise at a minimal cost to the tax payers."

Concerning Sheriff's services to the community, a letter to the president of the Association from the Captain of the East Los Angeles Station called attention to the fact that approximately $300,000 was allocated to the operation of the East Los Angeles Station, and ". . . nearly one-third of that cost was for services rendered in the Bell Gardens area." After pointing out that the personnel and equipment covering the community and the range of specialized services would otherwise be available only from the largest city, the letter ends with the comment that ". . . a locally maintained police department could not hope to give you the services you are now receiving from the Sheriff's Office."

Opponents of the incorporation in Bell Gardens utilized similar facts and figures concerning the levels of service received from the County, and argued that they could not be matched by local production. County administrators also appeared at a number of community meetings during the campaign to provide information on current and future services. Their presentations led a member of the Citizen's Committee for the Incorporation of Bell Gardens to complain that county officials were appearing at "all the mass meetings our opponents have had" and "talked against incorporation by talking taxes, taxes, taxes."

Incorporation supporters also charged that county employees were actively campaigning to defeat the proposal at the polls. The accusation was primarily leveled at fire district personnel who, as one proponent put it, were being brought in from other districts to "do their dirty work."

The actual involvement of county employees in organized opposition to incorporations during this period is difficult to document. However, there is little doubt . . . that fire district personnel were actively opposed to formation of new cities. The County had no arrangement for selling or providing the service through district membership to municipalities, and a reduction in the size of the existing service area was looked upon as a threat to job security.

22. The Case against Total Amalgamation in Metropolitan Toronto*

ALBERT ROSE

The creation of the Municipality of Metropolitan Toronto is one of the most important post-World War II metropolitan developments in the view of Albert Rose of the School of Social Work at the University of Toronto. Rose has been Vice-Chairman of the Metropolitan Toronto Housing Authority since 1956. He evaluates seven arguments advanced in favor of amalgamation of the 13 governments in the metropolitan Toronto area and argues against total amalgamation. Although he admits that each argument in favor of amalgamation contains an element of truth, the arguments are not sufficient reasons for dissolving the metropolitan federation.

The Municipality of Metropolitan Toronto presents a curious paradox as it approaches the beginning of its tenth year of operation as a federated government for a vast metropolitan area. The familiar expression "Nothing succeeds like success," has apparently been reversed in the case of Metropolitan Toronto, where substantial success is in some quarters considered to be a significant failure.

This peculiar logic is especially puzzling to a person like the writer, who has discussed many aspects of metropolitan government with authorities in this field. With very few exceptions there is widespread admiration throughout North America, the United Kingdom, and in Europe, both for the form of government inaugurated in Toronto on January 1, 1954, and for its achievements. There is, as well, a real understanding in these countries of the problems

* *Public Affairs Report* (April 1963), pp. 1–5.

that remain unsolved, and of the failure to attain perfection in providing services to a large and growing population.

Canada, quite frankly, has made few contributions to the development of governmental organization in a democratic society. It is not an exaggeration, however, to state that Metropolitan Toronto is widely regarded as one of the most significant political innovations developed anywhere in the postwar period. Nor is it extravagant to suggest that total amalgamation and the dissolution of the Municipality of Metropolitan Toronto will set back seriously the numerous efforts at governmental reorganization in metropolitan areas in the United States.

The arguments put forward in the recent wave of amalgamation fervor in Toronto have two aspects in common: (1) each argument has an element of truth, and (2) taken singly or together the arguments do not provide sufficient evidence to warrant sweeping away Toronto's metropolitan federation in favor of total amalgamation.

Basically, the proponents and opponents of amalgamation present an identical lineup to that which prevailed in the late 1940's and early 1950's. The amalgamationists, by and large, are the politicians of the City of Toronto who believe that the "one big-city" approach will best enhance the image of the city and serve its future development; the newspapers, which have never accepted Metro as anything but "a stage on the way to complete amalgamation"; the research specialists and bureaucrats who stand for apparently "neat and tidy" solutions for urban problems; and persons who honestly believe that perfect equality is conceivable within political and administrative compromises. These groupings overlap to some degree, of course.

The opponents of amalgamation, on the other hand, are the so-called "selfish" politicians of the suburban municipalities; a majority of the residents in those municipalities; and citizen groups and individuals who argue that there are important human values inherent in moderate- or small-sized local governmental units. These values—citizen interest, initiative and participation—are related to the capacity of the individual to comprehend and feel a part of that government which is in fact closest to him and his family.

It must be admitted that in the major metropolitan areas of the western world, particularly in the two most notable metropolitan federations, New York and London, the trend of political action and thinking is now on the side of decentralization. In New York City, which functions under a so-called "Borough System," the pattern has been one of successive centralization for more than a quarter-century. Under the Charter of 1938, the government of the City of New York is the single dominant governmental authority for the local affairs in the metropolis. The general plan of government has been a consolidation of the city, county, borough (five boroughs and five counties with identical boundaries exist within the City) and school activities. Today, New York City is trying to break down its huge governmental area into local community planning units and local school boards in a desperate effort to stimulate local interest and initiative.

Admittedly, the strength of this movement is in some doubt and the thinking has not gone far beyond the creation of local advisory committees. Nevertheless, the New York experience does illustrate the great difficulty involved in decentralizing a governmental giant once it is created.

The recommendations of the Royal Commission on Local Government in Greater London (1957–1960) have essentially the same basic meaning. The Commissioners wrote that "The Boroughs should be the primary units of local government and should perform all functions except those which can only be effectively performed over the wider area of Greater London." Legislation recently introduced into Parliament to implement the report of the Royal Commission will strengthen the attempt to create meaningful and viable boroughs for the most part with a population of 200–300,000.

THE ARGUMENTS OF THE AMALGAMATIONISTS

In Metropolitan Toronto, the proponents of amalgamation or merger of the thirteen municipalities into a unitary form of government make the following principal arguments:

1. The federated metropolitan government was born in a crisis of the late 1940's and early 1950's, when population was growing rapidly, when water was in short supply, and virtually non-existent in certain suburban areas, when sewage disposal was inadequate and thousands of septic tank installations posed a very real threat to public health and sanitation.

The emergent crisis, it is affirmed, has now been solved, largely by the creation of Metro, and there is now no compelling reason to maintain and continue a metropolitan form of government based upon federal principles. This argument is very difficult to accept as a piece of logical reasoning.

2. It is also argued that Metropolitan Toronto has not, as a government, solved some of the most important problems which it was designed to alleviate. In particular, the failure to create a reasonably adequate stock of public low-rental housing for families, and the failure to develop a widely accepted master plan for the Metropolitan Toronto Planning Area, are laid at the door of Metro.

This writer, who has some relevant experience in these fields, considers the failure in public housing to be a national problem, a national failure, even a North American tragedy. It is the product of many factors: indecision at the federal and provincial levels of government until this last year; the high cost of acquisition and clearance of blighted areas; the high cost of construction of public housing with union labor; the antiquated financial arrangements which result in an unpalatably high rental subsidy; the confusion between social and economic motives; and the continuing argument at all levels of government concerning the proper responsibilities of local federal-provincial housing authorities. Very little of this debacle can be attributed to the Municipality of Metropolitan Toronto.

As early as 1954, the writer argued for the creation of a single housing authority for the entire metropolitan area,[1] and this development is now a real possibility for the coming year. The failure to achieve this form of partial amalgamation is again not the responsibility of the metropolitan government alone, but is in part a failure by the federal and provincial governments to agree on what a metropolitan housing authority can and should do, as well as complications in the intergovernmental arrangements.

In the field of physical planning it was far too much to expect that Metro would solve all of the major problems created by more than fifty years of haphazard urban development. Also, Metro had only nominal control over the rapid growth of the three large townships, Etobicoke, North York and Scarborough. This responsibility was, in large measure, left by the Provincial Legislature to the local planning boards. If the draft comprehensive plan for the Metropolitan Toronto Planning Area is not formally "official" as yet, this is hardly the sole responsibility of the metropolitan government. The real problem was cited by Catherine Bauer Wurster in an address to the American Municipal Association in December 1957, when she said, "There appears to be a need for positive public policy on a number of new but basic issues, at least in general terms, before any final official plan can be prepared, adopted, and put into effective practice."

3.   The present system of divided jurisdiction in such fields as public health, fire protection, garbage collection and the like, is alleged to be more costly than would be the case in a series of further partial amalgamations or in a unitary system for the metropolitan area. In support of this argument, one newspaper has recently pointed to an increase of 41 percent in the cost of unified police administration in Metropolitan Toronto from 1957–1961 inclusive, by comparison with an average increase of 124 percent in the cost of fire protection in four area municipalities.

The writer submits that this is not a fair comparison. The provision of fire protection services in rapidly expanding municipalities, some of which are as large in area (twice as large in one case) as the City of Toronto, requires new fire stations, very costly equipment of many kinds, and vast increases in manpower. In the case of police administration it is even conceivable that the cost is higher than it would have been under the previous divided jurisdiction. Who knows? And can anyone state for certain that an amalgamation of the fire departments would have resulted in the required expansion of fire protection services at lesser cost?

4.   The general argument, of which the previous expression is a part, simply holds that the maintenance of Metropolitan Toronto as well as the thirteen area municipalities involves a good deal of costly duplication of departments, staffs and functions.

[1] *The Globe and Mail, Toronto,* December 11–12, 1954.

There may indeed be some duplication—for example, there is a Metropolitan Finance Commissioner, a City Finance Commissioner, and local treasurers in the area municipalities. Would a total amalgamation save a good deal of money? Not likely! Debentures in the amount of $100 million plus would still be required annually and the debenture debt must be administered; taxes must be collected from nearly 400,000 householders and thousands of businesses; and the present metropolitan-wide assessment responsibilities would be continued.

If the Toronto area were amalgamated, two things would happen over a range of municipal services. First, the senior officials would require additional remuneration by virtue of their substantial increase in responsibility in an amalgamated city. Second, a number of regional offices would be required, headed by properly remunerated deputy commissioners or supervisors. One must be optimistic indeed to foresee much saving in this process, and, in fact, the costs would be greater in the short run as the standards of service were applied uniformly and urban growth proceeded.

5.   Metro's creation has not resulted in full tax equality. Although there is a metropolitan assessment system and clearly far more equalization than there would otherwise have been, it is a fact that a residential taxpayer in some area municipalities pays about two thirds or three quarters of the taxes paid by a residential taxpayer on the same assessment in the City of Toronto and in certain other municipalities.

This is a serious anomaly. Moreover, the heavily taxed areas outside the City are not necessarily the beneficiaries of municipal services equal in standard to those in the City, or in some of the more lightly taxed suburbs, The answer to this problem may lie in total amalgamation—or it may not.

There is, however, a prior question usually put in the following manner: Should the average family in the three municipalities experiencing most rapid growth receive the same standard of municipal services, and at the same rate of taxation, as the average family in Leaside, where taxes are lowest, and in Toronto, where taxes are highest? If the answer is "Yes" it is argued that the principle of amalgamation is established. In the writer's view the answer is "No" unless the majority of families in the metropolitan area are willing to pay far more than the present level of taxation in the City of Toronto.

Another approach to greater equality lies in the proposal put forward in the Gathercole Report in 1960–1961, for the consolidation of the thirteen municipalities into four or five cities or boroughs in Metropolitan Toronto, one of which would be the City of Toronto.[2] Representation by population could be made fairly consistent with representation by financial interest. The "Borough of Toronto's" proportion of total population and assessment would exceed the combined population and assessment within each of the other Boroughs, but would steadily decline, reaching parity with them by 1970. Within these viable units of 200–300,000 current population, and the present City, there exists the strong possibility of

[2] Ontario. Department of Economics, *A Report on the Metropolitan Toronto System of Government,* prepared for the Special Committee of the Metropolitan Council on Metropolitan Affairs. 90p (mim) Toronto, November 1961.

achieving inter-municipal taxable equality—under Metro, while preserving the proven advantages of the Metropolitan Toronto governmental
federation.

6. Furthermore, it is emphasized that the system of representation in
Metro is faulty and seriously out of joint. Undeniably the Reeve of Long
Branch and the Reeve of Swansea represent some 11,000 and 9,600 people,
respectively, and have one vote each in Metropolitan Council, while the
Branch and the Reeve of Swansea represent some 11,000 and 9,600 people,
275,000 and 220,000 people, respectively, have the identical one vote each.

It is also sometimes forgotten that the City of Toronto, with 62 percent
of the total assessment and 56 percent of the total population in the
metropolitan area in 1954, was seriously under-represented in the original
Metropolitan Council. But by 1961, the City had dropped to 46.3 percent
of the total assessment and 41.5 percent of the total population. Thus, it
is now over-represented on the basis of these criteria.

In the writer's view, however, there is a good case for appreciably higher
representation for the central city in a metropolitan form of government
than its population and assessment would warrant. This case rests on the
position of the City of Toronto as the urban and financial core of the
metropolis and, frankly, on political grounds. Overrepresentation may be
an essential inducement if the politicians of the City are to accept a four-
or five-city plan as the next step in metropolitan political organization.

Nevertheless, despite the failure to date to modify the original schedule
of representation within the federated government, the problem is not
insoluble. Total amalgamation would not, in itself, solve the dual problem
of representation—that of the central city versus the suburbs, and that of
suburb versus suburb. The creation of one unified city would require the
mapping of new wards or constituencies based upon principles not yet
clearly enumerated by the proponents of amalgamation. Certainly this
would not be an easy process and within a decade might produce electoral
districts with as much variation in population as now exists within the
present city wards.

A better solution may well be possible in the four- or five-city proposal
and the continuation of Metropolitan Toronto. For the first decade the
City might well be granted three times the representation in the Metropolitan Council that each of the other new boroughs receives. Thus, in a
five-city federation, the City of Toronto would have three sevenths of the
members of the Council; in a four-city federation Toronto would have one
half of the members.

A transitional decade is recommended to enable us to see whether the
population and urban growth projected for Metropolitan Toronto will in
fact be realized. It is essential, as well, to observe where such growth takes
place within the metropolitan area.

7. Finally, it has been argued that, notwithstanding the achievements
of Metro, a unified city government would have produced identical results,
and probably at lesser cost. We shall never know! We do know that the
Ontario Municipal Board in 1953, in response to the City's (1950) application for amalgamation, indicated little confidence in the prospect of
progress if the City of Toronto were at the helm of a unified metropolis
with a unitary government.

TWO APPROACHES TO AMALGAMATION

The City has now once again applied formally to the Ontario Municipal Board for the amalgamation of the thirteen municipalities in the metropolitan area. It has not been made clear, however, that there are two fundamentally different approaches to total amalgamation.

The first approach, which the City requested in 1950 and presumably intends now, is nothing more than the annexation of the twelve suburban municipalities by the central city. The semantics are different, of course—"amalgamation" is a fine sounding word with a "voluntary" ring to it—but the result would be identical to the traditional annexations of the past. The local municipalities would be incorporated in the one "big city" of Toronto. Surely this is what the political leaders and senior officials have sought for nearly fifteen years, and if one accepts the concept and validity of the unitary approach there is nothing reprehensible about their intention.

The second approach—which many suburban representatives and citizens dislike as much as they do complete amalgamation—is a continuation of the process of consolidating specific municipal services under the administration of Metropolitan Toronto. Police administration and the licensing function were transferred from local municipal administration to Metro in 1957. Public welfare services and public housing are in the process of consolidation at the present time, and may become metropolitan functions in 1963.

What remains under local jurisdiction? The administration of public education, fire protection, public health, garbage collection, the local distribution of water and collection of sewage, local streets, local parks, and public libraries. This is by no means a negligible listing; but education, public libraries, and fire protection, at least, have been studied for possible consolidation. The first two—education and library services—have been the subject of full-scale examinations during the past two years.

If this process of successive centralization were to continue unabated, there would come a time, sooner or later, when the area municipalities would reach an untenable position of weakness. At this point the few remaining services could be consolidated and total amalgamation would be achieved. In this case, however, it would be the Municipality of Metropolitan Toronto, rather than the City of Toronto, which would emerge as the dominant government. The area municipalities would be incorporated in Metro.

THE CASE AGAINST TOTAL AMALGAMATION

In the writer's view, neither approach is acceptable. The case against total amalgamation rests on two bases: First, the proponents of amalgamation have failed to demonstrate that the weaknesses of Metropolitan Toronto as a form of government are sufficiently serious to warrant its dissolution in favor of the unitary approach; and the proponents of successive centralization have failed to demonstrate that many additional services require metropolitan administration. Public housing and public welfare services patently require consolidation because of a serious breakdown in progress in the provision of low-rental housing for families—the need to speak to the federal and provincial governments with "one voice" rather than several—and because of serious inequality in sharing the burden of public welfare assistance.

The need for consolidation in public housing and in public welfare has been demonstrated to the satisfaction of the Metropolitan Council, and in the case of housing, to the satisfaction of the Provincial Government as well. Legislation will be introduced to create a single metropolitan housing agency.

In a similar manner, when the need for consolidation in other services has been demonstrated, action may be taken. If there is any crisis, however, in the provision of fire protection, public health, garbage collection and other services, the public has been generally unaware of and unconcerned with the seriousness of the situation.

Public education is a rather different matter, however. We have been told by a special committee on the Metropolitan School Board "that by 1970 differences in the ability of local boards to finance their educational programs will have reached critical proportions." It remains to be seen whether the solution to this emerging crisis need be found in a consolidation of the educational function within a metropolitan administration and the dissolution of the local boards.

In the second place, total amalgamation does not promise the residents of Metropolitan Toronto any clear-cut series of solutions to the most pressing problems of community development. Financial equality, after all, even if accomplished, is a flaccid concept. The writer, a taxpayer in the City of Toronto, knows full well that the population of those municipalities in which tax rates are substantially lower than in the City is approximately 250,000 (including Etobicoke), one seventh of the metropolitan population. "Soaking" the so-called "rich" in Forest Hill, Leaside and Etobicoke would not reduce taxes for central city home-owners by a single dollar.

CONCLUDING COMMENTS

The real challenge in a modern metropolitan area like Toronto is the provision of a whole urban environment that is a *good* environment, and the chance for people to choose among several different types of conditions and influences. This means that we must develop political institutions which will promote and protect diversity.

Do we want this kind of diversity? If we do we must decide clearly which public services need to be uniform and which may be left to the administration of a meaningful and viable local government. We need to encourage local interest, local initiative and local participation.

The answer does not lie in the creation of a vast city of more than two million persons by 1970 and nearly three millions by 1980. The challenge lies in finding ways of strengthening of local government by reorganizing it into moderate-sized units. The seven small municipalities that now have 20,000 population or less can maintain their identity as neighbourhoods or electoral districts within the new boroughs or cities.

The relevance of the Toronto experience lies in the proof that a metropolitan government with certain specific areawide responsibilities can operate success-fully. Its success, however, depends upon common agreement that its functions are regional rather than local in nature, and upon an appropriate system of representation from its constituent units. It is not necessary or essential that each areawide service be assigned to a separate special district or administrative commission created for the purpose.

The Metropolitan Toronto plan does ensure a reasonably equitable sharing of the cost of metropolitan services through a system of levies upon the con-stituent municipalities. Nevertheless, a metropolitan form of government, like any other government, requires occasional adjustments—both in its method of representation and in its system of financing—if reasonable equality is to be maintained during these decades of rapid population growth and mobility.

23. Report
of the Royal Commission
on Metropolitan Toronto*

On June 20, 1963, H. Carl Goldenberg was appointed the Lieutenant Governor's commissioner to review the Municipality of Metropolitan Toronto. The order-in-council appointing Goldenberg designated him the Royal Commission on Metropolitan Toronto. On June 10, 1965, the

* From *Report of the Royal Commission on Metropolitan Toronto* (Ottawa: June 1965), pp. 24–25, 29–37, 169–82, 192–95, and 200–06.

commission released its report assessing the progress made by and the problems of the Municipality of Metropolitan Toronto.

The importance of this report should not be underestimated as it is having a major impact upon the metropolitan reform movement in the United States as well as in Canada. The report contains not only an excellent review of the metropolitan reform movement in the Toronto area, but also a penetrating analysis of the effectiveness of metropolitan federation. Although Commissioner Goldenberg concludes that total amalgamation is undesirable for the Toronto area, he does recommend the partial consolidation of the area's 13 municipalities into four cities.

SEEKING A SOLUTION

Although for about 25 years the City had been officially opposed to any move to annex surrounding municipalities, it was apparent to some that the seeds of future problems were being sown by the policy of "no further annexations." Even before the adoption of this policy, a bill had been introduced in the Ontario Legislature in 1925 seeking to establish a metropolitan area of Toronto. The bill died on the floor of the House.

In the 'thirties and 'forties, three reports recommended a reorganization of the area. In 1935, A. F. W. Plumptre, of the Department of Political Economy of the University of Toronto, urged unification of the urban sections, in a report to the Minister of Municipal Affairs. In 1949 there were two reports. In the first, the Toronto and York Planning Board recommended the unification of the City with the other seven municipalities lying between the Humber River and the Township of Scarborough. The second, by the Civic Advisory Council of Toronto which, at the request of the Mayor of Toronto, had set up a committee to study metropolitan problems, offered alternative proposals, one of which was the creation of a metropolitan form of government.

In 1947 the Town of Mimico applied to the Ontario Municipal Board for an order to create an area for the joint administration of such major municipal services as education, fire and police protection, administration of justice, health and welfare, planning, sewage disposal and public utilities, including transportation and main highways. No definite boundaries were set out in this application, except that the inner suburbs were to be included in their entirety together with "the urban sections" of Etobicoke, North York and Scarborough. A number of preliminary hearings were held and the Ontario Municipal Board finally ordered public hearings to open in January 1950.

Before the hearings could take place, there were new developments. On

January 16, 1950, the Hon. Leslie M. Frost, Prime Minister of Ontario, called together the heads of the thirteen municipalities which now constitute the area municipalities of Metropolitan Toronto and suggested that they form themselves into a Toronto Area Committee to consider four specific questions which he submitted to them. The committee's reply a few weeks later indicated that there was little hope of the municipalities settling their problems amicably among themselves.

Meanwhile, on January 18, 1950, Long Branch filed an application with the Municipal Board for the amalgamation of New Toronto, Mimico, Long Branch and Etobicoke. The situation was further complicated when, on February 2, 1950, the City of Toronto, reversing its long-standing policy of no further annexations, applied for an order amalgamating the City with all the surrounding municipalities, except the more rural parts of Scarborough and Etobicoke.

Faced with three different applications covering parts of the same area, the Ontario Municipal Board gave the City's application priority over that of Mimico and indefinitely postponed hearing the application from Long Branch. As it turned out, the last named application was never heard. The City's application, however, was held to be beyond the Board's jurisdiction because only parts of Scarborough and Etobicoke were included for purposes of the proposed amalgamation. This was remedied on May 15, 1950, when the City of Toronto applied for total amalgamation with the twelve surrounding municipalities.

The public hearings of the Mimico and the revised Toronto applications were held concurrently and commenced on June 19, 1950. They terminated one year later. On January 20, 1953, the Ontario Municipal Board, under the chairmanship of Mr. Lorne R. Cumming, Q.C., issued the historic report, known as the Cumming Report, which culminated in the creation of the Municipality of Metropolitan Toronto. . . .

THE MUNICIPALITY OF METROPOLITAN TORONTO ACT

The Government of Ontario acted quickly on the Report. Bill 80—"An Act to provide for the Federation of the Municipalities in the Toronto Metropolitan Area for Certain Financial and Other Purposes"—was introduced in the Legislature with a minimum of delay. On April 2, 1953, only six weeks from the date of the Report, "The Municipality of Metropolitan Toronto Act" received Royal Assent. Thirteen days later the first Metropolitan Council was sworn in. In the nine and a half months which followed, it prepared the plans for the change-over to the new system, and on January 1, 1954, the new metropolitan government commenced operations.

DISTRIBUTION OF POWERS

The Municipality of Metropolitan Toronto Act, 1953, referred to in this report as "the Metro Act", provided for a division of powers between the Metropolitan Corporation and the area municipalities along the lines recommended by the Cumming Report. In general, matters of area-wide concern were assigned to the Metropolitan Council or the quasi-independent metropolitan boards, while those of local concern remained the responsibility of the area municipalities. Two major changes in the division of powers were made in 1956, effective January 1, 1957, when the Act was amended to provide for unification of the police forces under a Metropolitan Board of Commissioners of Police and to transfer responsibility for licensing to a Metropolitan Toronto Licensing Commission. Civil defence and control of air pollution have also become metropolitan responsibilities. Accordingly, the distribution of powers is now as follows:

Powers of the Metropolitan Corporation

Assessment and Taxation. Assessment of real property, both metropolitan and local, throughout the area. On the basis of this assessment, the Metropolitan Corporation levies on the area municipalities for its requirements according to the proportion which the assessment of each bears to the assessment of the whole area.

Debenture Borrowing. Borrowing of money, subject to the approval of the Ontario Municipal Board, for the Metropolitan Corporation, the Toronto Transit Commission, any area municipality, and any board of public school trustees in the area, by the issuing of debentures on the credit of the Metropolitan Corporation.

Water Supply. Construction and maintenance of all works for the production, treatment and storage of water and all trunk mains; the wholesale distribution of water to the area municipalities, with power to fix wholesale rates and to set standards for local distribution systems in the area municipalities.

Sewage Disposal. Construction and maintenance of trunk sewer mains and sewage treatment works to provide a metropolitan sewage disposal system, and to set standards for local works connected to a metropolitan work.

Roads. Establishment of a metropolitan road system and designation of highways as metropolitan roads, with power to prescribe speed limits thereon and to control traffic over and to limit access to such roads.

Transportation. Construction, maintenance and operation by the Toronto Transit Commission of all forms of public transportation within the metropolitan area, except steam railways and taxis.

Education. Co-ordination of educational facilities in the area by the Metropolitan School Board, which also makes maintenance assistance payments to each local board in respect of every pupil.

Parks. Establishment of metropolitan parks and recreation areas and assumption, with the approval of the Ontario Municipal Board, of existing parks.

Health and Welfare. Provision of homes for the aged, hospitalization and burial of indigents, maintenance of neglected children, and postsanitorium care of tuberculosis patients.

Administration of Justice, etc. Provision and maintenance of a court house and a jail, and conveyance of prisoners; juvenile and family court; magistrates' courts; provision of Registry office and Land Titles Office accommodation.

Police. Police services throughout the metropolitan area under the Metropolitan Board of Commissioners of Police.

Licensing. Licensing of trades and businesses by the Metropolitan Toronto Licensing Commission.

Housing and Redevelopment. All powers of a municipality in the fields of housing and redevelopment.

Planning. Preparation of an official plan for the Metropolitan Planning Area by the Metropolitan Planning Board.

Air Pollution Control.

Civil Defence.

Powers of the Area Municipalities

Fire Protection.

Water Supply. Construction and maintenance of local distribution systems and retail sale of water to consumers.

Sewage Disposal. Local sewage collection and construction and maintenance of local sewage collection systems.

Garbage Collection and Disposal.

Roads. Construction and maintenance of local streets and sidewalks, including sidewalks on metropolitan roads.

Planning, etc. Planning by local planning boards in conformity with the Metropolitan Official Plan when it becomes effective; zoning.

Education. Operation of schools by the local board of education, the area municipality being responsible for costs above the metropolitan grants.

Recreation and Community Services. Local parks; recreation programmes; community centres and arenas; public libraries.

Traffic Control, etc. Traffic regulations on local streets; street lighting; municipal parking lots.

Housing. All powers of a municipality in the fields of housing and redevelopment.

Health and Welfare. Public health services; general welfare assistance and social work services; maintenance of non-wards.

Hydro-Electric Power. Local distribution.

Licensing and Inspection. Preparation and enforcement of building by-laws; marriage licenses; dog licensing.

Taxation. Levying and collection of taxes for local purposes, including the metropolitan levy.

Under this distribution of powers the Metropolitan Corporation and the area municipalities each have certain exclusive functions and share responsibility for others. The shared functions, such as water supply, sewage disposal and roads, fall under metropolitan jurisdiction in their area-wide aspects and under local jurisdiction in their local aspects. In the fields of housing and redevelopment, Metro and the area municipalities have equal powers.

METROPOLITAN COUNCIL

The Municipality of Metropolitan Toronto Act enacted the basic scheme and most of the recommendations of the Cumming Report with two major exceptions, the first affecting the composition of the Metropolitan Council and the second affecting education. The legislation accepted the principle of federation and separated the twelve suburban municipalities from the County of York for municipal purposes. Toronto, as a city, was already separate.

The Report had recommended a council of nine full-time members holding no local office, of whom four would be appointed by the Toronto City Council, four would represent the suburbs with one elected from each of four groups of suburbs, and the ninth would be the chairman to be appointed by the Lieutenant Governor in Council. The term of office was to be "not less than three years". The Report pointed out that, as the council was to be a taxing body, its members should be elected, but it saw serious objections to the direct election of the members of the first council.

The Act accepted the principle of equal representation of the City and the suburbs as a group, but in other respects departed from the recommendations. It provides that the powers of the Metropolitan Corporation are to be exercised by a Metropolitan Council composed of the following: from Toronto, the Mayor, the two of the four controllers who received the highest number of votes at the preceding municipal election, and the alderman from each of the nine wards who received the highest number of votes in the ward; from the suburbs, the heads of the council in each municipality. Each suburb is given one representative and one vote, regardless of population. The Council is thus composed of twenty-four members and the chairman, if he is not chosen from the Council membership. The term of office coincides with the term of local office, which was originally one year but, by an amendment to the Act effective in 1956, is now two years.

The chairman is the head of the Council and its chief executive officer. The first chairman was appointed by the Lieutenant Governor in Council but the Act provided that thereafter the Council was to elect one of its own members "or any other person" as chairman, originally for one year but now for two years. A chairman who has not been elected from among the members of the Council, votes only in the event "of an equality of votes"; if he has been elected from the Council, he has a second or casting vote in such a situation. The first chairman, Mr. Frederick G. Gardiner, Q.C., appointed by the Lieutenant Governor in Council in 1953 to hold office until the end of 1954, was re-elected by the Council at each election until his retirement in 1961, when he was succeeded by Mr. William R. Allen, Q.C.

Part VII of the Municipal Act requires all cities with a population of not less than 100,000 to have a board of control. The Cumming Report did not recommend such a board for Metro because the Metropolitan Council was not to be a municipal government in the ordinary sense of the term. The Council was given authority, however, to set up standing and other committees and, as early as May 1953, provided by by-law for the appointment of an executive committee composed of the chairman and four other members. In 1958 the Act was amended to give statutory authority for the establishment of an executive committee composed of the chairman and four or six other members of the Council, one-half from Toronto and one-half from the area municipalities. It also empowered the Council to authorize the committee to exercise any and all powers of a board of control under the Municipal Act, and such powers were duly conferred on the committee by by-law. Accordingly, the executive committee, now consisting of the chairman of Council, who is also chairman of the committee, and six members, prepares the annual budget, awards all contracts, nominates all heads and deputy heads of departments, and initiates policy proposals; it may only be overruled on the award of contracts and on nominations of officials by a two-thirds vote of the Council.

The Council has also established the following standing committees: welfare and housing, works, transportation, and parks and recreation. Each has seven members, including the chairman.

METROPOLITAN SCHOOL BOARD

With respect to education, the Cumming Report said that "the fundamental problem is to find an equitable method of financing capital and maintenance costs," and recommended that a portion of these costs be financed on a metropolitan basis. The powers were to be exercised by the Metropolitan Council which was not to assume "the functions of a metropolitan board of education": the local school boards were to retain almost all their powers. The Metro Act, however, created a Metropolitan School Board of 22 members constituted along the lines of the Metropolitan Council.

The Board is composed of the chairman of the Toronto Board of Education, the member from each of the nine City wards who received the largest number of votes in the ward, the ten chairmen of the suburban school boards,[1] and two representatives appointed by the Metropolitan Separate School Board,[2] one of whom must be from the City and the other from the suburbs. The chairman of the Metropolitan Board, like the chairman of the Metropolitan Council, is selected from among the twenty-two members or from outside.

The Act confers upon the Board the responsibility of co-ordinating the area's requirements for school accommodation and school sites. Each local school board must submit its proposals in this regard, with their estimated cost, for review by the Board, which may revise them before submitting a composite proposal to the Metropolitan Council.

The Metropolitan Corporation assumed all school debenture liabilities of the area municipalities outstanding on January 1, 1954. Debt created subsequently for the erection of new schools and the acquisition of lands for school sites was apportioned between the Metropolitan Corporation and the area municipalities, the former assuming the portion of school debt which is recognized by the Province of Ontario for legislative grant purposes. This policy was recently changed; the Metropolitan Corporation now assumes all debt incurred from January 1, 1964, for the municipal share of standard school construction costs under a ceiling cost formula, the area municipalities continuing to be responsible for all costs in excess of the ceiling.

The general legislative grants for school purposes, with a few exceptions, are paid to the Metropolitan Board, which makes maintenance assistance payments to each local school board in respect of each resident pupil in amounts which it determines annually for each category. The amount per pupil in each category must be uniform for each board within the area. The Act also confers on the Metropolitan Board the power to define the boundaries of attendance areas, to determine the charges to be made for non-resident pupils, including their transportation, and to fix the cost of special classes.

To meet its expenditures and obligations, the Board submits its estimates annually to the Metropolitan Council, which, in turn, levies the required amount

[1] The three lakeshore municipalities of Long Branch, New Toronto and Mimico have a combined school board; hence there are only ten suburban boards instead of twelve.

[2] This Board operates Roman Catholic schools pursuant to provincial legislation. Its representatives on the Metropolitan School Board do not participate in proceedings exclusively affecting the public elementary schools.

on the area municipalities. This levy, however, finances only a part of total school costs. The Act specifically preserves all the powers, duties and responsibilities of each local board of education which are not inconsistent with its provisions. Accordingly, each area board prepares and adopts its own current estimates to finance the additional expenditures for its own pupils and submits such estimates for levy by the local council.

METROPOLITAN TORONTO PLANNING BOARD

The Metropolitan Corporation is the designated municipality for the Metropolitan Toronto Planning Area under The Planning Act. This Act applies to it, subject to Part XIV of The Municipality of Metropolitan Toronto Act which excludes powers with respect to redevelopment, subdivision control, zoning and building by-laws, but authorizes agreements with area municipalities or others relating to conditions of approval of subdivision plans.

The Act provides that the Planning Board is to be constituted as under The Planning Act, except that the membership is at all times to include two persons recommended by the Metropolitan School Board.

As originally established in 1953, the Board consisted of fourteen members: nine appointed by the Metropolitan Council from outside its membership; three Council representatives—the Chairman of Metropolitan Council, the Mayor of Toronto and a suburban member of the Planning and Parks Committee (since renamed the Parks and Recreation Committee); and two representatives of the Metropolitan School Board. In 1957 the Board's composition was altered to include all of the foregoing (except the suburban member of the Planning and Parks Committee) and, in addition, four representatives from the fringe areas, the four chairmen of the standing committees of Council, a suburban councillor, and the chairman of the Toronto Transit Commission. The addition, in 1959, of a representative from the Separate School Board brought the Board to its present strength of 24 members.

For the purpose of representation on the Board, the thirteen fringe municipalities which are included in the Metropolitan Planning Area are divided into four districts, with one representative from each, as follows:

West District—Toronto Township, Streetsville, Port Credit.

North-West District—Toronto Gore Township, Vaughan Township, Woodbridge.

North-East District—Richmond Hill, Markham Township, Markham Village, Stouffville.

East District—Ajax, Pickering Township, Pickering Village.

As a planning board governed by the provisions of The Planning Act, the Board has the duty to prepare an official plan for the area and recommend it to the Council for adoption. After adoption by the Council, the plan must be submitted to the Minister of Municipal Affairs for his approval. Upon such approval the plan becomes official.

TORONTO TRANSIT COMMISSION

The Municipality of Metropolitan Toronto Act created the Toronto Transit Commission as successor to the Toronto Transportation Commission and conferred upon it full powers with respect to "the construction, maintenance, operation, extension, alteration, repair, control and management" of all forms of local public passenger transportation in the Metropolitan Area, except steam railways and taxis. The assets of the Toronto Transportation Commission, including the capital stock of Gray Coach Lines Limited held by it, and of the area municipalities in respect of public passenger transportation were vested in the new Commission without compensation to the former Commission or to any municipality, subject to assumption by the new Commission of all liabilities in respect of the property transferred.

Under the Act, the original commissioners were to be the three members of the former Toronto Transportation Commission and two members appointed by the Metropolitan Council, who were to be ratepayers and residents of an area municipality other than the City of Toronto. Except in the case of the first members, the term of office was to be five years and commissioners were to retire in rotation. The term was reduced to three years on a staggered basis in 1963, when the Metropolitan Council was also authorized to reduce the membership from five to three. The Commission still consists of five members who must be appointed on the affirmative vote of at least two-thirds of the members of the Council present and voting.

The salary of the commissioners is fixed by the Council, to which an annual financial statement and general report on operations must be submitted. The Commission may not acquire land to be paid for by borrowing without the approval of Council, and the debentures for all sums necessary to finance the Commission's undertakings are issued by Metro, the Council retaining "its authority with reference to providing the money required for such works" [sec. 116(e)].

While setting up these relationships between the Metropolitan Council and the Transit Commission, sec. 115(c) of the Act specifies that the Commission's "powers, rights, authorities and privileges shall not be exercised by any area municipality or its council or by the Metropolitan Corporation or the Metropolitan Council." It was originally intended that the Commission should be financially self-sustaining: sec. 116(1)(c) authorized it to fix tolls and fares so that its revenue "shall be sufficient to make all transportation facilities under its control and management self-sustaining, after providing for such maintenance, renewals, depreciation, debt charges and reserves as it may think proper." In 1962 the Act was amended to authorize the Metropolitan Corporation to contribute to the capital costs of the Commission with the approval of the Municipal Board (sec. 116a), and in 1963 to authorize contributions to operating costs [sec. 116a(2)].

METROPOLITAN BOARD OF COMMISSIONERS OF POLICE

Under the original distribution of powers, and until January 1, 1957, the police services remained a responsibility of the area municipalities. On that date all police services were unified under a Metropolitan Board of Commissioners of Police. The Board is composed of five members: the chairman of the Metropolitan Council; a member of the Council appointed by it, who, by custom, has always been the Mayor of Toronto; and three members designated by the Lieutenant Governor in Council, of whom one is a judge of the County Court of the County of York and two are magistrates.

METROPOLITAN LICENSING COMMISSION

A second change in the distribution of powers became effective on January 1, 1957, when licensing became a metropolitan function. The Metropolitan Licensing Commission was created with certain statutory powers, including, inter alia, the licensing and regulation of teamsters, cab owners and drivers, auctioneers, bill posters, driving schools and instructors, electrical workers, and plumbers. Its powers may be extended by by-law of the Metropolitan Council, under the provisions of any Act, to cover "the licensing, revoking of a license, regulating, governing, prohibiting or limiting of any trade, calling, business or occupation or the person carrying on or engaged in it . . ." (sec. 211(2)). A number of by-laws extending the Commission's powers have been passed.

The Commission was originally composed of the chairman of the Metropolitan Council or his delegate, and two magistrates designated by the Lieutenant Governor in Council. In 1963 the Act was amended to provide that the Commission shall be composed of the chairman of the Metropolitan Council or his delegate, and two members appointed by the Metropolitan Council who are not members of the council of an area municipality. The Commission elects its own chairman.

RELATED BOARDS AND COMMISSIONS

The Metro Act makes reference to boards and commissions created under other legislation on which Metro is represented or which are represented on Metro bodies. They include the Metropolitan Separate School Board, the

Metropolitan Toronto and Region Conservation Authority and the Toronto and York Roads Commission.

METROPOLITAN SEPARATE SCHOOL BOARD

The Metropolitan Separate School Board was created by a special Act, assented to on April 22, 1953, which set up a metropolitan area for separate school purposes. The area covers all the area municipalities, except Mimico and the Union Section in the south part of Etobicoke bordering on Mimico, which have retained their own separate school boards. There are no other local separate school boards.

The Metropolitan Board has complete administrative and financial control over schools under its jurisdiction. In this respect a pattern had been set by its predecessor, the Toronto and Suburban Separate School Board, created in 1941 with administrative and financial authority over separate schools in the City and the greater part of the suburbs. The assessment for separate school purposes, since the inception of Metro, is made by the Metropolitan Assessment Commissioner and the tax rate for separate elementary schools is uniform throughout the area under the Board's jurisdiction.

Members of the Board are elected by separate school supporters biennially by wards, with one member for each ward. The original Board consisted of fifteen members, of whom nine represented Toronto and six the suburbs. In 1956, an additional suburban ward was created, raising total membership to sixteen. Two more suburban wards were created in 1964.

The Board is represented by two members on the Metropolitan School Board who do not participate in proceedings affecting public elementary schools since The Separate Schools Act provides for education up to Grade 10. The Board is also represented by one member on the Metropolitan Toronto Planning Board.

METROPOLITAN TORONTO AND REGION CONSERVATION AUTHORITY

The Conservation Authorities Act, 1946, permitted a group of municipalities in a watershed or a group of watersheds to form a conservation authority for the purpose of carrying out a programme to conserve the natural resources of the area within its jurisdiction. At the inception of Metro four such authorities, the Etobicoke-Mimico, the Humber, the Don and the Rouge-Duffin-Highland-Petticoat Creek, had been formed. Recognition of the need for a regional approach and for a more substantial financial base, as well as the impetus provided by the disastrous flood following Hurricane Hazel in October 1954, led in 1957 to the amalgamation of the four authorities and the formation of the Metropolitan Toronto and Region Conservation Authority. . . .

The Authority is administered by 55 appointed members: 3 members, including the chairman, are appointed by the Province of Ontario, 26 by Metro, and 26 by member municipalities outside Metropolitan Toronto. The work of the Authority is financed by levies on the member municipalities and by federal and provincial grants. The annual municipal levy is based on population. Accordingly, the Municipality of Metropolitan Toronto contributes 92 per cent of the municipal share.

TORONTO AND YORK ROADS COMMISSION

Prior to the formation of Metro, the City of Toronto and the County of York shared in the costs of construction and maintenance of suburban roads in the County, each paying 25 per cent and the Province 50 per cent. The Toronto and York Roads Commission was established in 1916, with two representatives each from the City and the County and one from the Province.

The Cumming Report, taking cognizance of the financial implications to the County if the southern municipalities were separated from it, pointed to "the need for a special adjustment between the metropolitan area and the remaining county arising from the fact that the northern municipalities with less than fifteen per cent of the County equalized assessment would have to assume the County's portion of the cost of maintenance of nearly sixty per cent of the mileage of the existing county and suburban roads." Accordingly, implementing recommendations of the Report, the Metro Act provided that the Toronto and York Roads Commission be continued (sec. 104), and that all roads forming part of the county road system on December 31, 1953, other than those vested in a local municipality or assumed by Metro under the Act, continue to form part of the county road system as "suburban roads." Part VIII of The Highway Improvement Act, providing for the division of costs of suburban roads, was made to apply to the Metropolitan Corporation (sec. 101).

Metro thus became responsible for 25 per cent of the approved costs of suburban roads in the County, the expenditures on which are planned by the Toronto and York Roads Commission in co-operation with Metro's Roads Department and Planning Board. The composition of the Commission was also changed to provide for two representatives from the County, two from Metro, and a fifth selected by these four or, failing this, by the Lieutenant Governor in Council. . . .

CONCLUSIONS

The area of the Municipality of Metropolitan Toronto is 240 square miles, which, it is estimated, is developed to about two-thirds of its designated urban capacity under the proposed Official Plan. Its population in 1964 was approximately 1,750,000; the projected population is 2,040,000 by 1971 and 2,300,000 by 1980, and the urban capacity is estimated at 2,685,000. The fringe municipalities, with an area of 480 square miles, twice the area of Metro, have a population of about 180,000, with estimated increases to 257,000 by 1971 and 500,000 by 1980. Their estimated urban capacity is 960,000. Accordingly, the combined population of Metro and the fringe, with an area of 720 square miles, is now almost 2,000,000 and, if trends are maintained, will be approaching 3,000,000 by 1980. It is necessary to have regard to these facts and projections in considering an extension of the boundaries of the Metropolitan Area. It is true that Greater London now covers an area of almost 620 square miles, with a population of about 8,000,000, but the United Kingdom is a unitary state whereas Canada is a federation of provinces. In considering the potential size of Metropolitan Toronto, consideration must also be given to its place in the Province of Ontario.

There is no ideal size for a metropolitan area, and the forces contributing to this pattern of urban growth are not abating. It is now more than sixty years since H. G. Wells described the developing problem as follows.[3]

> You will find that many people who once slept and worked and reared their children and worshipped and bought all in one area, are now, as it were, "delocalized"; they have overflowed their containing locality, and they live in one area, they work in another, and they go to shop in a third. And the only way in which you can localize them again is to expand your areas to their new scale.

I am confident that if Wells had lived to witness "the metropolitan explosion" since 1945, he would have agreed that there are limits to expanding areas "to their new scale."

Metropolitan Toronto and its urban fringe form part of an urban belt which extends eastward to Oshawa and westward to Hamilton. A dividing line might be drawn on the east, but the belt to the west is unbroken; it can be said that the Toronto metropolitan region runs right up to the metropolitan area of Hamilton or that the latter is only a further extension of the former. It is clear that, for political and administrative reasons, Metro's boundaries cannot be extended indefinitely to encompass the extension of urban development. Subject to other regional adjustments in the interval, however, growing urbanization and interdependence point to an extension of Metro's boundaries in due course to include substantial parts of the urbanizing fringe units.

[3] H. G. Wells: "A Paper on Administrative Areas Read Before the Fabian Society," in appendix to "Mankind in the Making" (New York: Charles Scribner's Sons, 1904), p. 379.

An important test for the delimitation of urban boundaries is the need for the provision of integrated urban services. Accordingly, there would be justification for extending Metro's boundary northward, since urbanization on this boundary is dependent on Metro for water and sewage services. But, as has been shown, the area is still very largely rural and urbanization has been fairly effectively controlled and should continue to be regulated by a Metro Official Plan. On the basis of present projections, it will be some years before the municipalities on the northern fringe, even as a group with an area larger than Metro, would qualify, in terms of population, as a Metro area municipality. Moreover, the removal at this time of all or part of the southern six municipalities for municipal purposes from York County would seriously affect the financial position of the County and its remaining municipalities. Prior consideration should therefore be given to a reorganization of county government. In the meanwhile, the powers and the machinery are available, both at the provincial and the Metro level, to provide the services required for present and planned urban development. The Metro Act confers authority upon the Metropolitan Corporation to enter into agreements with outside municipalities in respect of water supply, sewage disposal and public transit. There are also the powers of the Ontario Water Resources Commission in the matter of water and sewage facilities. However, failing satisfactory arrangements to provide the required facilities, the appropriate built-up area north of Steeles Avenue in Vaughan and Markham townships should be annexed to North York without undue delay, with compensation to the townships and the County of York for loss of assessment, under the provisions of section 14 of The Municipal Act.

Metro's northern boundary should be reviewed from time to time in relation to the progress of urbanization. My recommendations are predicated on the relatively limited urban development envisaged in the proposed Metro Official Plan. If, more extensive urbanization is contemplated, with the consequent need for a wide extension of Metro services, incorporation in some form with Metro will have to receive serious consideration. As stated by Mr. Murray Jones, formerly Metropolitan Planning Commissioner, in presenting a brief for the County of York (Proceedings, pp. 845–846):

> . . . . the basic issue is a question of the timing of further extensive urbanization not presently contemplated . . . . Should it become necessary in the future to contemplate another extensive area of urbanization much larger than that now proposed, it would obviously have to result in a change in political organization for the simple reason that it would involve the creation of an extensive new system of "Metropolitan" services.

On the west, the Township of Toronto, with the largest urban growth in the fringe area, resembles more closely the growing area municipalities of Metro. The extension of Metro's boundaries to include the Township would have serious effects on Peel County. Prior consideration should be given to other forms of regional municipal reorganization in the area, such as the creation of a smaller "Metro."

Urbanization in the eastern fringe is still very limited. Pickering Township is experiencing the "spill-over" problems of a dormitory municipality adjacent to a large urban complex. The special situation of such municipalities should be officially recognized by the Provincial Government through appropriate adjustments in grants for municipal and school purposes.

If it were the sole test, the existence of a continuous urban area extending beyond its boundaries would justify extensions of Metro's limits. But, as has been shown, there are other considerations. If Metro's limits are to be extended, it is necessary to assure a viable pattern of municipal organization on its new boundaries. Accordingly, I have recommended that prior consideration should be given to municipal reorganization in the fringe areas.

REORGANIZATION OF METROPOLITAN TORONTO

In 1953 the Ontario Municipal Board reported that "the basic problem to be solved in the Toronto metropolitan area is indicated in the significant contrast between the underlying social and economic unity of the area on the one hand, and the illogical and inequitable but extremely rigid divisions of political jurisdiction and available taxable resources on the other." As a solution, the Board recommended the establishment of a metropolitan form of government based upon a federation of the thirteen area municipalities with powers divided between the latter and the new central authority.

METRO'S ACHIEVEMENTS AND CONTINUING PROBLEMS

The Municipality of Metropolitan Toronto came into being on January 1, 1954. It has realized its objectives in substantial measure. The many briefs submitted to the Commission were unanimous in their praise of Metro's accomplishments and its contribution to the remarkable growth and development of the Toronto area in the past decade. Thus, while proposing a basic change in the system, the City of Toronto, in its brief, said:

> In giving thought to the best form of government for the Toronto metropolitan area, the City of Toronto is well aware of the remarkable record of achievement which has been chalked up throughout the past decade by the Municipality of Metropolitan Toronto. In this brief we have no wish to play down Metro's accomplishments.

Notwithstanding these accomplishments, this report has shown that some of the problems described in the Cumming Report of 1953 persist and have grown. They flow from continuing "illogical and inequitable but extremely rigid divisions of political jurisdiction and available taxable resources." The area is divided into thirteen municipalities ranging from less than one square mile to seventy square miles in size, from 9,000 to 650,000 in population, and from $22 million to $2 billion in taxable assessment. As a result, in an area which is a social and economic unit, there are undue inequalities in the burden of financing essential services and in the range and standards of some of the basic services provided. While the equalizing influence of Metro has prevented far greater inequalities from developing, the spread between the lowest and highest taxed municipalities has tended to widen. Moreover, with population growth concentrated in the outer suburbs, inequalities in representation on the Metropolitan Council have grown to the point that reform is imperative. A system which gives equal representation to Swansea, with 9,300 people, and North York, with 340,000, can no longer be maintained.

In 1961 and 1962 three municipalities proposed changes which would affect the structure of Metro. On December 20, 1961, the Village of Long Branch passed a by-law authorizing an application to the Ontario Municipal Board for amalgamation of the three Lakeshore municipalities. On September 24, 1962, a by-law passed by the Town of New Toronto authorized an application for amalgamation of the Lakeshore municipalities and the Police Village of Malton with the Township of Etobicoke. On October 9, 1962, a by-law of the City of Toronto authorized an application for amalgamation of all the municipalities in the Metropolitan Area. The powers of the Board to hear such applications were rescinded as from April 26, 1963, by an amendment to the Metro Act, following a statement in the Legislature by the Hon. John P. Robarts, Prime Minister, that the Government of Ontario had decided to appoint a Commission to inquire into the structure and organization of Metropolitan Toronto.

The need for change was recognized in most briefs to the Commission, but no brief suggested a return to the pre-Metro forms of municipal organization in the area. The City of Toronto submitted that:

> Despite the weaknesses of Metro, its critics have not proposed turning back the clock. The degree of metropolitan unification which has been attained should in the opinion of all responsible observers be preserved. It is generally recognized that Metro has proven, as the Ontario Municipal Board had hoped, "a forward step in the solution of an extremely difficult problem" . . . . . *Change ought therefore to consolidate gains and build upon them* . . . . .

On changes in the Metro structure, the area municipalities were understandably divided. Most of the smaller units, while recognizing that some changes are necessary, urged that they be made within a continuing metropolitan

federation of thirteen municipalities. The larger suburbs also favoured continuation of the metropolitan system but with the area municipalities consolidated into a small number of "boroughs." The City of Toronto alone recommended amalgamation of the whole area into one city.

MAINTENANCE OF THE STATUS QUO

The arguments of the smaller municipalities in favour of the status quo are
twofold. There is, first, the sentimental desire to preserve their local identity,
with emphasis on the values of the neighbourhood area and community feeling,
of citizen interest and the responsiveness of local government. Secondly, it is
argued that the smaller units now provide a level of services which reflects the
needs and desires of the local residents whereas under any form of merger these
residents would have to pay higher taxes for a uniform level of services over a
wider area.

The desire to preserve local identity for its own sake is understandable. In
some cases it is naturally fortified by financial, economic and other advantages
which attach to the unit as a separate political entity. A local patriotism
develops and local boundaries are considered as fixed and permanent. The
resulting situation has been fittingly described by Dr. Luther H. Gulick, a noted
authority on municipal government and former City Administrator of New
York:[4]

> Finally, a fixed political boundary serves as the mediaeval wall behind
> which the employees of the governmental unit, including the local poli-
> ticians, are deployed, not only to perform their services, but to defend
> "their town" and themselves against the outside world; and this they do in
> all sincerity. Fixed boundaries thus create their own protection by raising
> up powerful political defenses, patriotic loyalties, fiscal rigidities, and
> bureaucratic mercenaries.

There is considerable nostalgia in the arguments for the preservation of all
existing local boundaries in the Metro area. The submissions bring to mind the
days before the widespread use of motor cars and the rapid spread of urbanization, when municipal boundaries were more realistic and each town was a clearly
recognizable entity, separate and distinct from its rural hinterland. The
neighbourhood, the local area in which each inhabitant knows a large number
of the others and is conscious of a considerable community of interest with
them, was the unit of local government. In areas which are largely rural, this
is still true. But in large integrated urban areas where the people are economically interdependent, working in one municipality and living and paying taxes

---

[4] Luther Halsey Gulick: The Metropolitan Problem and American Ideas (New York:
Alfred A. Knopf, 1962), p. 50.

in another, with large numbers moving from one unit to another every few years, the old concept of the neighbourhood as the unit of local government scarcely applies. This is the price of mobility. The nostalgic arguments for the preservation of all artificial boundaries in an urban complex such as Metropolitan Toronto have been largely invalidated by social and economic change.

It does not follow that with a change of boundaries a sense of community is or should be lost. It is an asset which can be preserved. The local neighbourhood does not disappear with the extension of municipal boundaries, nor should the patriotism which attaches to it. The brief of the City of Toronto says, with effect, that:

> When a former self-contained town or village is swept up in a metropolitan expansion, part of its character is lost whether or not it is stripped of its independent municipal status; and part of it remains even if its corporate entity has disappeared. Toronto people still talk of Yorkville, which was annexed in 1883, of Riverdale, which was absorbed a year later, of Rosedale, of the Annex, Sunnyside and Parkdale, each of which became part of the City of Toronto before 1890. The history of Toronto annexations contains many another familiar name including Deer Park, Wychwood, West Toronto, Balmy Beach, Dovercourt, North Toronto and Moore Park. The two latest were added to the City in 1912!

Having been "swept up in a metropolitan expansion," the Toronto area municipalities are, as such, no longer distinct and separate neighbourhoods but interdependent parts of a geographic, social and economic unit. It is in this context that we must look at the thirteen municipalities into which this integrated urban area is divided, the great variations in their size, population and resources, and the consequent disparities in their financial burdens and in the range and standards of some of the basic municipal services which they provide.

Reeve Edwin J. Pivnick, of Forest Hill, in his evidence before the Commission, acknowledged that (Proceedings, p. 329): ". . . co-operative action between component members of an amalgamated or federated system can be diminished significantly if the members are separated by fundamental disparities in economic resources." Co-operative action is also impeded by the gross inequality in representation on the Metropolitan Council inherent in the present structure which calls for one representative from each suburb regardless of differences in population.

It has been argued that to minimize the effects of an uneven distribution of resources more responsibilities should be assigned to Metro. This argument has merit; I have recommended an extension of metropolitan responsibilities in respect of education and certain other matters. But I have also recommended that important functions be left to the area municipalities, provided that the municipalities are regrouped into larger units which would make a fuller range of basic local services more widely and more equally available than is possible under the existing system. The alternative is to transfer responsibility for an increasing number of services to the Metropolitan Corporation. If this process is carried much further, however, it will be difficult to justify the continued existence of the individual municipalities. There will not be much left for them to do. In the words of W. A. Robson, Professor of Public Administration in the University of London:[5]

> Those who cling too tenaciously to the preservation of "historic" areas in a world where the traditional boundaries have become irrelevant can achieve their object only at the cost of depriving the "historic" areas of all administrative significance and vitality.

Having considered the submissions and the facts of the situation, I find that the case for the maintenance of the status quo in Metropolitan Toronto is not valid.

AMALGAMATION

The City of Toronto recommended amalgamation of the Metropolitan Area into one big city. While this recommendation was supported by a number of other briefs, it was opposed by the large bulk of the submissions to the Commission. The other area municipalities were of course unanimous in their opposition. . . .

Having expanded over a period of thirty years by absorbing newly built-up areas, Toronto, after the first World War, adopted a policy of "no further annexations." It was only in 1950 that it reversed its position by applying to the Ontario Municipal Board for an order amalgamating the City with the surrounding municipalities. The Board dismissed the application and recommended a form of metropolitan government for the area. In 1962 a City by-law authorized a new application for amalgamation.

The case submitted by Toronto to the Commission is based on three main grounds: that amalgamation "offers the most complete and direct cure to current problems of taxation, representation and organization;" that "an outright merger is the simplest and most logical governmental arrangement, offering the best prospects for continuing achievement;" and that such a merger "is entirely practical and readily attainable." The brief submits that, with the elimination of thirteen municipal councils and the related boards, commissions and departments, substantial savings in administrative costs would be effected, although it admits that additional expenditures would be necessary "to eliminate differences

[5] W. A. Robson, in "A Century of Municipal Progress" (London: George Allen & Unwin Ltd., 1936), p. 458.

in service standards that could not be tolerated within an amalgamated municipality." It alleges that the Metro system involves duplication of effort and
"adds to the cost of administering local government services;" one big city could
introduce economies of scale. With respect to its own position in the area,
Toronto complains that the creation of Metro has locked it "inside its existing
boundaries with no opportunity to expand but a responsibility to assist the
suburban municipalities with their expansion;" that it "is bearing more than its
fair share of the cost of services as a consequence of its central location;" and
that, as a result of "planning by assessment" in the suburbs, it is subject to
unfair competition for high-grade commercial and residential development. The
City maintains that amalgamation, with centralized control and uniform tax
rates, would eliminate city-suburban tensions and consolidate the gains flowing
from the degree of unification already attained under Metro.

There is much that appeals in the case for amalgamation. With local government shared by Metro and thirteen municipalities, the area is highly over-
governed, and the variations in size and resources of the units are reflected in
wide disparities in tax burdens and in services. Amalgamation offers a solution
which would eliminate thirteen local governments, equalize tax rates, consolidate administration, and prepare the way for uniformity of services. To many
persons this is a simple straightforward answer to Metro's problems. But "neat
and tidy" solutions to complex problems of government are not necessarily
applicable or practical.

The City's case assumes that municipal services and tax rates should be equal
throughout the 240 square miles of the Metro area. This assumption fails to
recognize that there are differences between the inner ring of developed municipalities with high population densities and the three developing outer townships
with large areas of agricultural and vacant land and relatively low density of
population. I have said in this report that the citizens of the thirteen municipalities are entitled to more equality in the range and standards of basic services
than the present fragmented system of government permits, but this does not
mean that there must be complete equality in respect of all services regardless
of the different requirements of developed and developing areas. At this stage,
there is room for some diversity in services and therefore in tax rates.

The City submits that total amalgamation will mean more efficiency in
administration. In relation to administration by thirteen units of varying size
and resources, this argument has validity. However, such savings in costs as may
be effected would soon be more than offset by the increase in expenditures to
raise the standards of services to a common level. In respect of Metro, no proof
was submitted of unnecessary duplication of effort or that the metropolitan
system has added considerably to the costs of local government. It has been
shown . . . that Metro's expenditures on general government, including the costs

of assessment for all the area municipalities, have ranged from only $1.01 to $1.15 per $1,000 of taxable assessment. Considering the growth of the area and the consequent expansion of municipal services since 1953, costs would have risen whatever system of local government prevailed.

While economy and efficiency in administration are necessary, they should not be the sole test of representative government. The recent report of the Royal Commission on Greater London points out that: "Local government is with us an instance of democracy at work, and no amount of potential administrative efficiency could make up for the loss of active participation in the work by capable, public spirited people elected by, responsible to, and in touch with those who elect them."[6] The report goes on to say, however, that "it is always necessary to bear in mind that unless local authorities are so constituted as to be able to undertake all the functions appropriate to local government there will always be the risk that more and more functions will be taken away from local government and given to ad hoc bodies or to central government."[7] Total amalgamation of the Metro area would mean centralized administration with necessary decentralization of some local services through the establishment of divisional offices responsible to the central office. In my opinion, the requirements of both democracy and administrative efficiency will be better satisfied if the administration of such local services, as distinct from area-wide services, is, as far as possible, in the hands of local officials responsible to local elected representatives in municipalities properly constituted to meet the needs of the Metropolitan Area.

The population of the Metropolitan Area in 1965 is greater than that of seven of the ten provinces of Canada and approximately equal to the population of the eighth, British Columbia. Total amalgamation would therefore create a city with a population of more than 1,750,000 in 1965 and a forecast population of more than 2,000,000 by 1970 and about 2,500,000 in the early 1980s. On the matter of bigness, the Toronto brief says that in 1963 there were 41 cities, "single municipal entities," which were larger in population than Metro: "The number included five cities in the United States and one in Mexico, nine in Europe, five in South America, two in Australia and the remaining twenty in Asia." This is scarcely a valid argument for total amalgamation in Toronto; I doubt that its citizens would want to pattern their municipality on or face the problems of any of the cities to which the brief has reference. It is relevant to note that the municipal reorganization of Greater London which became effective on April 1, 1965, took the form of a new metropolitan government, with a

---

[6] Report of the Royal Commission on Local Government in Greater London, op. cit., p. 59.

[7] Ibid, p. 61.

great reduction in the number of local authorities, and that in Los Angeles, a report in 1961 also recommended a metropolitan government for area-wide functions.[8]

The Toronto brief submits that: "A unique requirement of government at the local level is to accomplish periodic adjustments of the units of government in response to the growth of urban areas." I have said that increasing urbanization in the fringe areas points to an eventual extension of Metro's boundaries. The City admits that "the extent of urban development which needs to be enclosed may be a factor in deciding which is more practical, amalgamation or federation. If federation should be continued, the most likely way of adding territory would be to take in some further municipalities and to give them the status which now applies or is then assigned to local municipalities within the present boundary line. If we amalgamate, the outer boundary could be extended by adding whole or part municipalities which would thereby be brought into the enlarged city." On this point, I agree with Controller William L. Archer of Toronto, who, in his brief, said:

> . . . . . The brief from the City of Toronto has raised the question of the location of our outer boundaries. It is my submission that in those cases where it becomes necessary to alter the outer boundaries of Metropolitan Toronto, it can be done more easily through a district system than through a totally amalgamated system. The essential point of our system of government in this area is that we must retain a high degree of flexibility for the future. The rigidity of total amalgamation would place restrictions on the future growth and development of our area and make it difficult, if not impossible, to develop regional government for the urbanized area that exists between Oshawa and Niagara Falls.

Toronto submits that: "It is generally recognized that Metro has proven, as the Ontario Municipal Board had hoped, 'a forward step in the solution of an extremely difficult problem.' *Change ought therefore to consolidate gains and build upon them.*" The brief does not prove that consolidation of the gains under Metro calls for the dissolution of the metropolitan system and total amalgamation of the area. Reeve True Davidson, of East York, in her evidence before the Commission, said, with effect (Proceedings, p. 1567):

> I think that there is no reason to have amalgamation. You don't have to put the baby out with the bath water. There is no reason why we shouldn't retain the Metro system while getting rid of the inequitable— nobody denies the present representation is inequitable, and that there is a wide variation in the tax rate, although I don't object to some variation in the tax rate. I think this is reasonable so that people can have what they want and can pay for.

[8] Metropolitan Government for Los Angeles: A Workable Solution (March 1961).

CONSOLIDATION

All briefs submitted to the Commission praised the achievements of Metro and the large majority favoured the continuation of metropolitan government with a consolidation of the area municipalities into a smaller number of units, usually referred to as "boroughs." The number suggested ranged from four to eight.

For the reasons already set out in this report, I have concluded that, notwithstanding the impressive accomplishments of Metro, there are certain continuing problems which call for a reorganization of the municipal structure in the area. Accordingly, I have rejected the maintenance of the status quo. While recognizing some of its advantages, I have also rejected total amalgamation. I do not find that a case has been made for the dissolution of the metropolitan system of government. It is my conclusion that continuation of a metropolitan federation with a consolidation of some of the area municipalities will best meet the requirements of government and of continued growth of the Metropolitan Area.

In recommending a metropolitan government based on the principle of federation, the Ontario Municipal Board, in the Cumming Report of 1953, said that "one of the great virtues of any federal scheme is its flexibility and the comparative ease with which it can be adapted to changed conditions and the realities of a particular situation." In my opinion, the continuing rapid growth of the Metropolitan Area in the 1960s makes it essential to maintain such flexibility. This must be a basic consideration in a reorganization of the municipal structure of the area.

Having proposed a new form of government which involved many adjustments, the Cumming Report, as a practical consideration, sought to avoid drastic changes which were not immediately necessary. However, it did foresee changes in due course and pointed out that:

> They [the municipalities] are not in the position of sovereign states entering a federation on a contractual basis and the scheme of federation now proposed will not be comparable to a rigid written constitution to be amended only by mutual consent. Necessary changes can and will be made as the need arises by the act of the legislature which is at all times the only source of the powers which are being discussed.

The Board's comments, in 1953, on the existing boundaries of the area municipalities are particularly relevant. The Cumming Report anticipated a regrouping of municipalities when it said that:

> The need of future changes in the boundaries of the city and the twelve suburbs . . . must not be overlooked. In many cases these boundaries have been the result of purely arbitrary decisions or the result of temporary influences and do not now conform to natural or logical divisions of com-

munity interest. It is also quite possible that within some of the larger municipalities the process of further division by separate incorporation may continue as in the past.

I have concluded that a regrouping is now necessary.

My recommendations for a consolidation of area municipalities are not based on theories as to the "optimum" size of a municipality in terms of population. Much has been written on this subject and the briefs to the Commission made many references to such writings, but there is no agreement on the "optimum," and the figures vary widely with the criteria applied. I agree with the Royal Commission on Greater London that "there is no special virtue in any one figure." In fact, it cannot be said that there is one optimum size for municipalities. What may be the appropriate size of constituent units of one metropolitan area will not necessarily be appropriate to another with different characteristics derived from its own history, geography, population composition and economic development. The "metropolitan problem" is general, but it must be dealt with on the basis of the facts of each particular situation.

In briefs submitted by area municipalities to justify the preservation of existing units, there was frequent reference to the principles of democracy. I hold that a democratic solution for the problems of a metropolitan area is one which is based on the needs of the larger community rather than on the special interests of particular sections within that community. The situation in Metro must therefore be viewed in the context of one geographic, social and economic unit divided into thirteen municipalities which vary greatly in size and resources, with consequent disparities in tax burdens, in the range and standards of services, and in representation on the Metropolitan Council. There is the core city, fully developed, which is the financial, industrial, commercial and cultural centre, providing services which benefit all parts of the area. There is the inner ring of nine developed suburbs, of which some are not in a position to provide the range and standards of services required in a modern urban complex, while others, with large industrial and high class residential assessment, are able to provide local services with considerably less tax effort than their neighbours. There are, finally, the three large and populous outer suburbs which are still in the stages of development and, therefore, face problems which are different from those confronting the developed City and inner suburbs.

By far the bulk of population growth in Metro's first ten years took place in the three outer townships. This trend is continuing and, according to projections, will continue into the 1980s, as shown in *Table 1*. It is forecast, on the basis of existing local boundaries, that by 1980 the proportion of Metro's population residing in the City and the inner ring will have declined according to the following tabulation:

SOLUTIONS FOR METROPOLITAN PROBLEMS

DISTRIBUTION OF POPULATION IN METRO (PERCENTAGE)

YEAR	CITY AND 9 INNER SUBURBS	3 OUTER SUBURBS
1953	77.9	22.1
1963	56.2	43.8
1971 (forecast)	49.3	50.7
1980 (forecast)	44.6	55.4

TABLE 1

METROPOLITAN TORONTO: POPULATION FORECAST 1971 AND 1980

MUNICIPALITY	1963 POPULA-TION[1]	PER-CENT OF TOTAL	1971 POPULA-TION[2]	PER-CENT OF TOTAL	1980 POPULA-TION[2]	PER-CENT OF TOTAL
Toronto	630,339	38.1	670,000	32.8	680,000	29.6
North York	307,584	18.6	450,000	22.0	515,000	22.4
Scarborough	240,371	14.5	345,000	16.9	485,000	21.1
Etobicoke	177,537	10.7	240,000	11.8	275,000	11.9
York	126,311	7.6	137,000	6.7	137,000	5.9
East York	70,176	4.2	77,000	3.8	84,000	3.6
Forest Hill	21,126	1.3	25,000	1.2	23,000	1.0
Leaside	18,453	1.1	24,000	1.2	28,000	1.2
Mimico	18,150	1.1	20,000	1.0	20,000	.9
New Toronto	11,785	.7	14,000	.7	15,000	.6
Long Branch	11,129	.7	14,000	.7	14,000	.6
Weston	9,983	.6	13,000	.6	12,000	.5
Swansea	9,371	.6	11,000	.5	12,000	.5
Metro Total	1,652,315	100.0	2,040,000	100.0	2,300,000	100.0

[1] Annual Report of Municipal Statistics, Province of Ontario, 1963.
[2] Metropolitan Toronto Planning Board 1963 (Forecast based on existing boundaries).

Considering the growth and development trends of the area and the problems created by the inequitable division of political jurisdiction and taxable resources, I find that the thirteen diverse municipalities—one city, four towns, three villages and five townships—should be consolidated into four cities.

A FOUR-CITY SYSTEM

The City of Toronto and the inner suburbs of York Township, Forest Hill, Leaside, East York and Swansea are linked by geography and common interests. They are mature and developed areas, and, except for Forest Hill and Leaside, face common problems of renewal and redevelopment. With each municipality seeking to improve its tax base independently, they compete for development and redevelopment projects, which are accordingly dealt with on a piecemeal basis and without regard to sound planning in the overall interests of the area. The current disputes over the proposed densities of building projects in York Township are an example of the conflict of interest under the existing fragmentation of authority.

The six municipalities are highly interdependent. Leaside, for example, with the highest rate of average annual earnings and the lowest tax rate in the Metro area, derives its economic strength from a high assessment base divided equally between industrial plants and dwelling units of above average values. Located in the heart of the Metropolitan Area, its factories draw their manpower, in the main, from Toronto, East York, and other municipalities. Leaside, therefore, requires a minimum of such services as welfare; the City, East York and the other areas provide most of the employees for its industries and the municipal services for them and their families.

A look at the map shows the artificial boundaries which separate each of the five suburbs from the City of Toronto. Each is a political unit, but in terms of geography and of social and economic interdependence they are all parts of the City. It is only logical that they should be merged with it politically. A consolidation of the five suburbs with the City of Toronto will strengthen the core upon which the strength of the Metropolitan Area as a whole depends. It will make possible the coordination of planning for urban renewal and redevelopment by one planning body operating under one local council. It will also eliminate the unfair disparities in financial burdens and inequalities in the range and standards of services in the area of 54 square miles covered by the six municipalities.

The three outer suburbs are actually three large cities; in fact, they rank in population with the largest cities in Canada. Among Ontario municipalities, North York ranked second, Scarborough fifth and Etobicoke sixth, in 1963. They meet the tests of viable and effective local government in terms of size, population, resources and scale of operations. As urban entities, the municipal status of township is no longer appropriate to them. North York, Scarborough and Etobicoke should continue to be area municipalities of Metro and the status of each should be changed from township to city.

The remaining four suburbs of the inner ring, Weston and the Lakeshore municipalities of Long Branch, New Toronto and Mimico, share the problems of the inner group. However, they are not linked to the City geographically like the others. The geographic ties of the Lakeshore municipalities are with Etobicoke. It is relevant to note that in September 1962, the Town of New Toronto applied for amalgamation of the three municipalities with Etobicoke.

I find that such a consolidation is logical and warranted by the existing situation.

Weston is geographically linked with North York and there is a history of inter-municipal agreements between them. For these reasons and in the interests of administrative efficiency, I find that Weston should be consolidated with North York.

Accordingly, I recommend that the area municipalities of Metropolitan Toronto should be consolidated to form four cities, as follows:

The City of Toronto, consolidating the City of Toronto, the Township of York, the Village of Forest Hill, the Town of Leaside, the Township of East York, and the Village of Swansea. (Area: 54 square miles).

The City of North York, consolidating the Township of North York and the Town of Weston. (Area: 69.1 square miles).

The City of Scarborough. (Area: 70 square miles).

The City of Etobicoke, consolidating the Township of Etobicoke, the Village of Long Branch, the Town of New Toronto, and the Town of Mimico. (Area: 47.9 square miles). . . .

THE METROPOLITAN COUNCIL

Under the recommended four-city plan, the population of Metropolitan Toronto as has been shown, would be distributed as follows:

	1964	1971
Toronto	900,513	944,000
North York	351,891	463,000
Scarborough	253,292	345,000
Etobicoke	238,635	288,000
Total	1,744,331	2,040,000

This distribution provides a basis for equitable representation on Council within a metropolitan federation.

I reject the suggestion made in a number of briefs that representation should be determined by assessment as well as population. This is a theory which is long outdated. It is incompatible with the principle of representation by population. In modern democracies representatives are elected to represent people, not dollars. As stated by Reeve True Davidson of East York, in her brief, "a democratic belief in the significance of the individual, regardless of his wealth or poverty, forbids acceptance of the theory that financial interest should be regarded as justifying special representation."

Metro Council is now composed of twenty-four members and the chairman. Considering the need to provide reasonable representation for each of the proposed cities, I recommend that the membership of the Metropolitan Council should be set at twenty-six, with the following representation for each of the cities:

City of Toronto	13
City of North York	5
City of Scarborough	4
City of Etobicoke	4
Total	26

On this basis, the representation of each city would reasonably approximate its percentage of the total Metro population, as shown by the following comparisons:

	PERCENTAGE OF TOTAL COUNCIL MEMBERSHIP	PERCENTAGE OF TOTAL METRO POPULATION	
		1964	1971
Toronto	50.0	51.7	46.3
North York	19.2	20.2	22.6
Scarborough	15.4	14.5	16.9
Etobicoke	15.4	13.6	14.2

The average population represented per member of Metro Council would be as follows:

	1964	1971
Toronto	69,270	72,615
North York	70,378	92,600
Scarborough	63,323	86,250
Etobicoke	59,658	72,000
Average	67,089	78,461

The overall average should serve as a guide on population and representation when the incorporation of fringe municipalities into Metro is considered.

I recommend that, to maintain reasonable equity, representation on Council should be reviewed every ten years on the basis of the last Census of Canada.

To maintain the link between Metro Council and the area councils, I recommend that the representation of each city on the Metropolitan Council should be composed of the mayor and of metropolitan councillors elected directly by each ward or by a combination of wards, the councillors to serve on both Metro

Council and the respective city councils. This proposal is described in more detail below.

THE CHAIRMAN OF METROPOLITAN COUNCIL

The Metro Council may elect as chairman one of its own members or any other person. If elected from outside the membership of Council he has no vote "except in the event of an equality of votes"; when elected from Council he "has a second or casting vote." Mr. F. G. Gardiner, Q.C., the first chairman, whose dynamic leadership has become legendary, held no elective office when he was originally appointed by the Lieutenant Governor in Council nor when he was thereafter elected and re-elected by Council. His successor, Mr. W. R. Allen, Q.C., was a member of the Board of Control of Toronto when first elected chairman; he resigned from the Board following his election and held no elective office when re-elected for a second term. It has been urged that the responsibilities of the post call for the election of the chairman by the citizens of Metro at large; alternatively, it has been suggested that, if he is to be elected by the Council, he should be chosen only from among its members.

The chairman is in law and in fact not only the head of Council but also the chief executive officer of the Metropolitan Corporation. He is the only member of Council who is required to devote his full time to Metro. As the head of the government of a federation of municipalities, he must be impartial. He must also be sufficiently independent in relation to local politics to be able to face pressures and to fight on issues where the area-wide interest may conflict with a local interest. There is no doubt that the independence of the chairman has contributed in large measure to the successful operation of metropolitan government in Toronto. I doubt that he could retain his independence if he were required to be elected at large; an election in an area of 240 square miles, with a population of 1,750,000, would have to be financed by large business enterprises or by a political party. The fact that the mayors of big cities in the United States are elected at large is not very relevant; they are as a rule the candidates of a party. Moreover, they are elected as heads of individual municipalities and not as chief executive officers of municipal federations.

While I find more merit in the submission that the chairman should be elected from among the members of the Council, I do not think that the requirements of the office and the experience of Metro justify such a limitation. As briefs to the Commission made frequent reference to English local government, it may be pointed out that municipal councils in England are composed of elected and non-elected persons: councillors, elected by popular vote, and a certain number of aldermen who are chosen by the councillors and not by the electors. The council as a whole elects the chairman, who qualifies if he is a councillor or alderman or is eligible for election as a councillor. The Greater London Council, created by the London Government Act, 1963, following the report of the Royal Commission on Greater London, is composed of one hundred directly elected councillors and sixteen aldermen chosen by the councillors. The chairman, who is chiefly a presiding officer, is elected by the Council but does not have to be a councillor or an alderman himself.

Considering the operation of Metro under its first two chairmen and my recommendation for the direct election of metropolitan councillors, I recommend no change in the provisions of the Metro Act governing election of the chairman of Metropolitan Council. If a metropolitan councillor representing one of the consolidated cities is elected chairman, he should be free to decide whether he is in a position to retain both posts. If, however, the mayor of a city is elected chairman and were to retain both posts, it would be difficult for him to remain impartial in the event of a conflict of interest between his city and Metro. Accordingly, I recommend that the Metro Act should be amended to provide that on the election of the mayor of a city to the office of chairman of the Metropolitan Council, the office of mayor of the city shall become vacant. . . .

SUMMARY OF RECOMMENDATIONS

REORGANIZATION OF METROPOLITAN TORONTO

1. The system of metropolitan government should be maintained, with a consolidation of the thirteen area municipalities into four cities, as follows:

> The City of Toronto, consolidating the City of Toronto, the Township of York, the Village of Forest Hill, the Town of Leaside, the Township of East York and the Village of Swansea.

> The City of North York, consolidating the Township of North York and the Town of Weston.

> The City of Scarborough.

> The City of Etobicoke, consolidating the Township of Etobicoke, the Village of Long Branch, the Town of New Toronto and the Town of Mimico.

2. The transfer of assets from the amalgamating municipalities to the amalgamated cities should be effected without compensation to any area municipality but subject only to the assumption and payment by the amalgamated cities of the relative outstanding capital indebtedness.

3. The cities of North York, Scarborough and Etobicoke should continue to be considered townships for the purposes of provincial road grants.

4. With the introduction of the four-city system, the partial graded exemptions in Toronto and New Toronto should be abolished in stages over a five-year period by reducing the percentage of exempted assessment by ten percentage points in each year, with provision for assistance in the case of affected owners and tenants who show need.

5. In integrating municipal staffs, the new authorities should offer employment to all employees who had permanent status on the first day of April in the year preceding the effective date of the reorganization. Existing wage and employment standards should, as far as possible, be protected.

THE METROPOLITAN COUNCIL AND PROPOSED CITY COUNCILS

1. Representation on the Metropolitan Council should combine direct election of metropolitan councillors with representation of the area municipalities.

2. The Metropolitan Council should be composed of 26 members, with the following representation for each of the four cities:

Toronto	13
North York	5
Scarborough	4
Etobicoke	4

3. Each city should be represented on the Metropolitan Council by the mayor and by metropolitan councillors elected directly by each ward or by a combination of wards, the councillors to serve on both Metropolitan Council and the respective city councils.

4. The existing provisions of The Municipality of Metropolitan Toronto Act governing the election of the chairman of Metropolitan Council should not be changed, except to provide that on the election of the mayor of a city to the office of chairman, the office of mayor of the city shall become vacant.

5. Representation on the Metropolitan Council should be reviewed every ten years on the basis of the last Census of Canada.

6. The four cities should be divided into the following number of wards:

Toronto	12
North York	8
Scarborough	6
Etobicoke	6

7. The division into wards should be made by the Ontario Municipal Board, by virtue of its authority under section 13 of The Municipal Act. The Board

should aim at a reasonably approximate equality of population per ward and should also endeavour, as far as possible, to retain the whole of an amalgamating municipality within a single ward or within contiguous wards.

8. Each of the city councils should be composed of the mayor, to be elected at large and to be ex officio a representative on Metropolitan Council; metropolitan councillors, to serve on both Metropolitan Council and city council; and aldermen, to serve only on city council.

9. Aldermen and metropolitan councillors should be elected on the following basis:

 Toronto: one alderman and one metropolitan councillor from each of the twelve wards.

 North York: two aldermen from each of the eight wards and one metropolitan councillor from each combination of two contiguous wards.

 Scarborough: two aldermen from each of the six wards and one metropolitan councillor from each combination of two contiguous wards.

 Etobicoke: two aldermen from each of the six wards and one metropolitan councillor from each combination of two contiguous wards.

10. Each city council should have an Executive Committee composed of the mayor, who should also be the chairman, and four members elected by the council from among its members. The Executive Committee should exercise the powers conferred by The Municipal Act on a Board of Control.

11. The municipal franchise in the four cities should be uniform.

12. The term of office of members of the four city councils and of the Metropolitan Council should be increased to three years.

METRO'S BOUNDARIES AND THE FRINGE AREAS

1. Before considering extension of Metro's boundaries, the Province should give consideration to the position and function of the counties and to municipal reorganization in the fringe areas, including the possible creation of a smaller "Metro" on the western fringe.

2. Failing satisfactory arrangements by Metro and the Ontario Water Resources Commission to provide the required water and sewage facilities on the northern fringe, the appropriate built-up area north of Steeles Avenue in Vaughan and Markham Townships should be annexed to North York without undue delay, with compensation for loss of assessment to the townships and the County of York.

3. The Provincial Government should formally recognize the special situation of dormitory municipalities adjacent to Metro by appropriate adjustments in grants for municipal and school purposes.

METROPOLITAN PLANNING

1. A Metropolitan Official Plan should be adopted without undue delay. Adoption of the plan should be followed by the preparation, jointly with the local municipalities, of more detailed district plans and the enactment of the necessary changes in zoning by-laws. The plans should be subject to periodic review.

2. The Municipality of Metropolitan Toronto Act should be amended to declare more explicitly the responsibility of the Metropolitan Corporation, as the designated municipality, for the general direction of the physical development of the Metropolitan Planning Area, with powers:

(a) To establish basic zoning standards and categories

(b) To participate with an area municipality in redevelopment and urban renewal

(c) To enact a uniform building by-law and to establish uniform engineering design standards

(d) To review development applications and proposals and to make recommendations thereon to the provincial agency

(e) To secure the conformity of local official plans and zoning by-laws in the Metropolitan Planning Area with the Metro Official Plan, reserving to the municipalities a right of appeal to the Ontario Municipal Board. The procedures to ensure conformity of plans should be prescribed by regulations under the legislation.

3. The Planning Act should be amended to permit municipalities to transfer the functions now vested in local planning boards to a Planning Committee of Council with power to co-opt. The planning staff in area municipalities should be constituted a civic planning department.

4. The law should provide for a representative of a municipality, which is not otherwise directly represented on the Metropolitan Planning Board, to attend and to be heard when matters originating from, applying to or of particular concern to such municipality are under consideration.

5. In the absence of other regional planning machinery, the area covered by Brampton and its vicinity should be included in the Metropolitan Planning Area and should constitute a fringe district entitled to representation on the Planning Board.

METROPOLITAN AND LOCAL SERVICES

1. *Transit.* The chairman of the Metropolitan Council should ex officio be a full member of the Toronto Transit Commission.

There should be a more formal coordination in overall transportation planning between the staffs of the Transit Commission, the Metropolitan Planning Board and other agencies, in order to ensure that proper consideration is given to all forms of transportation required to meet the present and prospective needs of Metro and the surrounding area.

2. *Roads.* The design of access to metropolitan roads should require the approval of Metro authorities, and Metro should assume appropriate major local arterial roads.

The Metropolitan Corporation should be authorized to assume roads on Metro's boundaries as metropolitan roads.

The Province and Metro should coordinate expressway construction to meet the overall requirements of both transportation and local development.

3. *Traffic management.* The traffic engineering services of the Metropolitan Area should be unified under Metro.

Metro should establish an area-wide parking authority with power to operate parking facilities directly or to enter into a contractual arrangement for their operation by the Toronto Parking Authority.

4. *Public housing.* The Ontario Housing Corporation should act as a single agency on behalf of the federal and provincial governments in dealing with the Metropolitan Corporation in respect of all further low rental housing developments in the Metropolitan Area, with Metro assuming the remaining municipal financial responsibility therefor.

5. *Health and welfare.* The Metropolitan Corporation should take steps to provide a metropolitan public emergency ambulance service and should consider a contractual arrangement with the City of Toronto under which the City would operate the service.

A Metropolitan Board of Health Officers, composed of the health officers of the four cities, should be formed to coordinate the public health policies of the municipalities and to advise on health and sanitary inspection matters.

It should be the aim of the four cities to make health and welfare services equally available to individuals and families with the same needs, no matter where they live in Metropolitan Toronto.

6. *Waste disposal.* The Metropolitan Corporation should assume responsibility for all waste disposal in the Metropolitan Area.

7. *Sewer renewals.* The Metropolitan Area as a whole should share in financing the municipal costs of the necessary trunk sewer renewal programmes in the core area.

8. *Parks and recreation.* The Metropolitan Corporation should exercise responsibility for the development of the waterfront for park and recreational purposes.

9. *Police.* The police function should not be divided between Metro and the area municipalities, but more effort should be made to improve relationships between the police force and the area municipalities.

10. *Administration of justice.* The need for a properly staffed and serviced Metropolitan Juvenile and Family Court, with court facilities in each of the four cities, is sufficiently immediate to warrant the necessary increase in Metro's budget for this purpose, pending a review of the sharing of costs of the administration of justice between the Province and the Metropolitan Corporation.

11. *Licensing.* The four cities should assume responsibility for the licensing of local businesses which are tied to a specific location, as distinct from metropolitan-wide businesses and activities which should continue to be licensed by the Metropolitan Licensing Commission. The Commission should set minimum standards for local licensing where required.

Consideration should be given to an arrangement between the four cities and the Licensing Commission under which, the municipality having made the decision, the license would be issued on its behalf and at its request by the Commission, with the fee paid to the city concerned.

The law should require approval by the Metropolitan Council of license fees adopted by the Licensing Commission.

12. *Fire protection.* Under a four-city system, fire protection should remain the responsibility of the area municipalities, with an effective mutual aid agreement under which each could request assistance from one or all of the others when necessary.

Where centralization is necessary, as in the case of a central communications system, the system should be operated by the City of Toronto under a contractual arrangement.

The fire chiefs of the four cities should constitute an area committee to advise on matters of mutual concern affecting the fire fighting services of the area.

13. *Libraries.* The operation of libraries should remain a local responsibility in each of the four cities, with coordination by a Metropolitan Library Board. The recommendations of Report No. 1 (1962) of the Special Committee on Library Services appointed by the Metropolitan Council to study and report upon the Shaw Report should, as far as possible, be implemented.

EDUCATION

For public schools, the educational structure in Metropolitan Toronto should be reorganized as follows:

1. The Metropolitan Area should be divided into eleven school districts, with boundaries fixed on the basis of criteria for determining the viability of school districts. The proposed boundaries are set out in Chapter XII.

2. An elected central board, to be called the Metropolitan Toronto Board of Education, should have overall responsibility for school finance and for the development of an acceptable and uniformly high metropolitan standard of education. The administrative responsibilities of the central board should be limited to matters relating to area-wide policies, including teachers' salary scales, to coordination of mutual services, and to the provision of services which can best be provided on a metropolitan basis.

3. Local elected boards, to be called District Education Councils, should operate the schools and administer the school programme.

4. The central board should be composed of two trustees elected at large in each school district at elections held on the same day as the regular municipal elections, and two representatives of the Metropolitan Separate School Board. The chairman should be elected from among the members. The term of office should be three years.

5. The remuneration for members of the central board should be raised to a figure more commensurate with their responsibilities and the additional responsibilities of the chairman should be recognized by a higher remuneration.

6. Each District Education Council should be composed of the two trustees elected to represent the district on the central board, one trustee appointed by the Separate School Board, and eight district trustees elected at large in the district. The chairman should be elected from among the members. The term of office should be three years.

7. A Director of Education should be the chief executive officer of the Metropolitan Toronto Board of Education and a District Superintendent should be the principal officer in each school district, reporting directly to the former.

8. Educational finance should be coordinated by the central board and a uniform tax for education established throughout Metro. The central board should secure all tax revenue for educational purposes from the Metropolitan Council through the uniform levy.

9. District education councils should be allocated a fixed percentage of their total budgets to enable them to add to their programme if they desire to provide special equipment or a special service or to undertake educational experiments which are not included in the area-wide budget.

10. The Metropolitan Corporation should assume the local school debt of the area municipalities outstanding on December 31, 1963.

24. Government Proposals
for Reorganization
of London Government*

A Government White Paper, issued in 1961, accepted the basic recommendations of the Royal Commission on Local Government in Greater London 1957–1960, but decided to have larger and fewer boroughs and concluded that a two-tier education system would not function well. The White Paper describes the broad intentions of the Government for the restructuring of the system of local government in the greater London area.

THE ROYAL COMMISSION

1. The Royal Commission on Local Government in Greater London was set up in December, 1957:

> to examine the present system and working of local government in the Greater London area; to recommend whether any, and if so what, changes in the local government structure and the distribution of local authority functions in the area, or in any part of it, would better secure effective and convenient local government; and to regard, for these purposes, local government as not including the administration of police, or of water, and the Greater London area as comprising the Metropolitan Police District together with the City of London, the Boroughs of Dartford, Romford and Watford, the Urban Districts of Caterham and Warlingham, Chorley Wood, Hornchurch, Rickmansworth, and Walton and Weybridge, and the Parish of Watford Rural in the Watford Rural District.

Their report was made in October, 1960 (Cmnd. 1164).

2. After an exhaustive consideration of the administration of the main local government services, and of the general functioning of local government in the areas, the Royal Commission summed up their conclusions in these words (paragraphs 695, 696):

> Where things are working well our inclination is to leave them alone. We do not believe that London's problems can be solved merely by improving the machinery of government. Our inclination is to recommend changes only where they appear to be essential.

* From *London Government: Government Proposals for Reorganization* (London: Her Majesty's Stationery Office, 1961), pp. 2–12.

In spite of these predilections the facts we have found to exist and the inferences we feel bound to draw from them drive us to the conclusion that, judged by the twin tests of administrative efficiency and the health of representative government, the present structure of local government in the Review Area is inadequate and needs overhaul.

3. The Commission's criticisms of the present system fall under two main heads. First, they found that a number of vital functions—notably town planning, traffic, roads and overspill—which at present are the concern of many different authorities, require a broader treatment than can be given to them under the present system. Second, they found that for a variety of reasons the status and responsibilities of boroughs and urban districts have seriously declined; and they expressed the belief that the health of local government required the rehabilitation of these authorities.

4. The Commission's main recommendations, which were unanimous, may be summarised thus:

(a) The conception of an upper and lower tier of authorities should be replaced by the conception of the Greater London borough as the primary unit of local government, performing all functions which can be performed within its own limited area; and a directly elected Council for Greater London as a unit of local government performing functions which can only be or can better be performed over the wider area of Greater London.

(b) The appropriate range of population for a Greater London borough should be 100,000 to 250,000 and, wherever practicable, existing boroughs and county districts should be retained or amalgamated without change of boundaries.

5. The Commission recommended that the principle to be followed in assigning functions was that those to be performed by each type of authority should be as far as possible self-contained without overlapping or duplication. Their report contains detailed proposals for distributing functions. They considered that the boroughs' responsibilities should include housing, the Greater London Council having some concurrent and supplementary powers: personal health, welfare and children's services: environmental health, other than refuse disposal: roads, other than main roads: and libraries. They should also have an important part in the administrative discharge of education and planning functions. The Council for Greater London should be the education and planning authority, with some functions in these fields undertaken by the boroughs on lines to be laid down by statute, and the authority for traffic, main roads, refuse disposal, fire and ambulance services. They should also have concurrent or supplementary powers in respect of housing, parks, open spaces, entertainments, main sewerage and sewage disposal, and land drainage.

6. The report suggests the broad lines on which amalgamation of boroughs should take place, but the Commission made it clear that they had taken no evidence specifically on this, and that their recommendations were provisional.

GOVERNMENT'S MAIN CONCLUSIONS

7. The Government have carefully studied the Royal Commission's report, and the views of the 100 and more local authorities and others who have commented on it.

8. The Government's main conclusion is that the Commission were justified in their criticism of the present structure of local government in Greater London, and that their broad design should be adopted as the basis for improving it. In particular the Government endorse the view that the boroughs ought to become the primary unit of local government; and that a new, directly elected, authority should be set up to administer functions which require to be dealt with over the whole of Greater London.

9. This conclusion is subject to two important qualifications of the Commission's plan. One is that the boroughs ought to be larger, and therefore fewer, than the Commission proposed. The other is that the structure recommended by the Commission for education is not considered to be satisfactory. On education the Government do not agree that the two-tier system proposed would be likely to work well. They think that, given larger boroughs, education could and should, over the greater part of the area, become a borough service. In the heart of London, however, the Government consider that the best arrangement would be to have a large education authority for an area comprising several boroughs. . . .

10. Coming back to the broad design, the Government entirely agree with the Commission that Greater London has a recognisable civic unity and shape, largely because it has grown outwards from a single centre. But its local government structure, inherited from the days when London was much smaller, in no way reflects that unity. The major services are administered by six county councils and three county borough councils, and three systems of local government exist side by side. They are: single-tier government in the county boroughs, two-tier government of the normal pattern outside the present administrative county of London, and a unique two-tier system within the administrative county, in which most of the important local government functions vest in the county council.

11. London has clearly outgrown the system of local government devised to meet the vastly different physical and social conditions of the last century. This great town now faces immense problems of congestion, of traffic, of land

shortages, and of major redevelopment. All of its citizens are "Londoners," not only those who live within the City and the 28 metropolitan boroughs. Greater London is their city and all are involved in what happens to it.

12. The Royal Commission were convinced that, unless some method could be found within the framework of local government to tackle the pressing problems of Greater London, the central Government would increasingly supersede the local authorities. They thought that that would be disastrous for local government, and they were right. That is the answer to those who say that a system of local government which recognises Greater London as a unit for some purposes is not local government at all. In the Government's opinion it is the only way to enable Greater London to enjoy an adequate measure of responsible self-government.

13. There is now an opportunity to carry out effective reorganisation which will bring London government into harmony with the physical features of the metropolis, and will fit it to face the new problems presented by changing social conditions and the ubiquitous motor vehicle. The Government are convinced that if this opportunity is not now grasped, local government will wither in the capital city where, in the past, it has been strongest.

14. The Government have been impressed by the wide recognition among the local authorities concerned of the need for some change. True, many would adopt a different and less radical solution than that proposed by the Commission. But about the same number, while having reservation on some points of detail, accept the Commission's broad plan.

15. The feature which attracted the greatest support was the conception of the borough as the primary unit of local government. The Government are sure that this is the right principle. It is a serious defect in the present organisation that many of the boroughs, and especially the metropolitan boroughs, have no real responsibility for the running of the local and personal services. The system proposed by the Commission would place personal, preventive and environmental health services, welfare and children's services, and housing, in the hands of one authority, local enough in character to enable local knowledge of the area and of its living and working conditions to be brought to bear. This would not only greatly enlarge the scope of the borough councillor, but would also make for more effective administration of these closely linked social services. The Government regard this as a key feature of the Commission's plan, and one well designed to attract into local government more men and women of real ability, by making sure that there are worthwhile jobs for them to do. If any re-organisation of local government does not secure this it will fail of its purpose.

16. The principal alternative plan is one, sponsored chiefly by the county councils of Essex, Kent, London, Middlesex and Surrey, for an indirectly elected

joint board for an area a good deal wider than that reviewed by the Commission, and the retention of the existing county and county borough councils. The board would have responsibilities in town planning for drawing up a master plan to which the local planning authorities would be required to conform, covering such regional questions as the main road framework, target populations, the level and main disposition of employment: for laying down the main considerations for dealing with traffic: for planning and co-ordinating refuse disposal: and for planning and co-ordinating programmes for over-spill. The powers of this joint board would be mainly advisory in character, and meanwhile somewhat greater powers would be conferred on or delegated to the boroughs.

17. The Government believe that a plan on these lines would not begin to meet the needs of the situation. For a start it ignores—or denies—one of the fundamental assumptions on which the Royal Commission's Report was based. This is that the built-up areas outside the County of London are, now, more properly a part of Greater London than of the Home Counties to which historically they belong. But that apart, this plan would surely confuse responsibilities. The authority which has to deal with the planning, traffic and road problems of Greater London must exercise a real responsibility, and must be able to secure that its plans are effectively carried out. A largely advisory body, with powers mainly of co-ordination and supervision, would be likely to achieve very little. The overall authority must be an executive body if it is to be effective, although no doubt it would be right that it should in some matters act through the agency of the borough councils. The Government also believe that this authority, for full effectiveness and bearing in mind the powers and responsibilities which it will carry, ought to be directly elected. A joint board as envisaged would entail a third tier of responsibility, and this would only further confuse the already confused local government pattern in the area. County councils would be sandwiched between the joint board and their boroughs and districts, while the latter could not be given the responsibilities which, in the Government's view, they ought to have.

18. The Government recognise that the abolition of the present county pattern in the London area will present formidable problems of organisation. Their concern is to get the best administrative structure for local government. When that is settled they will give consideration to such related matters as the arrangements for the administration of justice, for the lieutenancies and for sheriffs. In general they wish to emphasise that they propose to make only changes which are needed to achieve their main purpose and matters consequential to it. These proposals should not affect any existing cultural, social, sporting or other associations or loyalties which may be based on the traditional counties. They are, however, convinced that London needs a form of local government organisation to match its present physical shape and state.

They are convinced, too, that this organisation must be one which recognises the unity and cohesion of the area, and which would combine ability to handle those issues that demand a comprehensive view of the whole area with the capacity to grapple effectively with the many and complex local problems. The Government believe that, provided these conditions are met, the new structure will provide fuller opportunities for really worthwhile local government service.

THE BOROUGHS

19. The Royal Commission suggested that the boroughs should fall within the population range 100,000 to 250,000, and provisionally proposed a pattern comprising 52 new boroughs (including the City). The Local Government Act, 1958, provides that, in so far as the constitution of a new county borough outside the metropolitan area is affected by considerations of population, the Minister should presume that a population of 100,000 is sufficient to support the discharge of the function of a county borough council. This does not mean, however, that larger units would not be better if they could be set up without loss of convenience. Larger units would mean more work for each authority in all the personal services, and so make specialisation in staff and institutions more efficient and economical. In addition, larger units would be stronger in resources and so better able to secure the major redevelopments which many boroughs now need. They would be better able to maintain and improve the standard of their services and to undertake their development as circumstances may require. Moreover the very nature of London—continuously built-up at high densities, with a comprehensive system of transport and a population which in many of its daily activities pays little regard to local boundaries—distinguishes it from the typical county borough. Hitherto, London has suffered in its local administration from too great a proliferation of not very strong authorities. The aim now should be to create units which, while retaining their local character, are well equipped to provide a fully adequate standard of local services. In a closely-knit area such as London, the Government believe that this object can best be assured by aiming at a larger minimum population and rather fewer boroughs than suggested by the Commission. They consider that this will make not only for higher standards, but also for greater economy in administration.

20. The Government's general conclusion about the size of the boroughs is that it would be desirable to aim at a minimum population of around 200,000 wherever possible. Some boroughs might be substantially larger than this. They propose shortly to circulate, as a basis for consultation with the local authorities, an illustration of how larger boroughs might work out.

21. The Government agree that the term "metropolitan borough" should now be abandoned; they propose the title of "London Borough." The Commission suggested that the constitution of the borough councils should follow that of municipal boroughs outside London, and the Government agree with this view.

22. The Government agree with the Royal Commission in thinking that the boundaries and status of the City of London should remain unchanged, and that it should receive the additional powers given to boroughs in the London area.

THE GREATER LONDON COUNCIL

23. The Government agree that the Greater London Council should be directly elected. They propose to adopt the Commission's plan that its members should serve for three years and retire together.

24. The Commission proposed that election should be based on Parliamentary constituencies. On the present structure this would give a membership of about 110. Many authorities have criticised this proposal, and argue that representation would better be based more directly on the boroughs. This is a matter which will require further examination in the light of the pattern of boroughs which emerges, and the Government reserve their decision on it.

25. The Government agree generally with the principles applied by the Commission in deciding which areas they should recommend for inclusion in the Greater London administrative area. When consultation takes place with the local authorities about the borough pattern, there will be opportunity for any peripheral authority to make known its views about its inclusion in or exclusion from the London area. The districts left out of the London area will be brought within the ambit of the Local Government Commission, who will then of course be able to consider, among other things, Watford's claims for county borough status.

FUNCTIONS

26. The following paragraphs set out the Government's broad proposals with regard to the administration of particular functions; many matters of detail will naturally require further consideration.

PERSONAL HEALTH AND WELFARE SERVICES AND CHILDREN'S SERVICES

27. There was no doubt in the Commission's mind that these services, with the exception of the ambulance service, should all be organised on as local a basis

as possible; they recommend that they should become a borough responsibility. The Government agree with this conclusion. They concur also in the belief that positive advantages will follow from the concentration of responsibility for these services, and other associated ones such as housing and environmental health, in the hands of the same authorities.

HOUSING

28. The Government accept the Royal Commission's main conclusion that housing is essentially a borough service. New boroughs ranging upwards from around 200,000 population should be able to handle all aspects of their housing problems (including slum clearance) which can be solved within their own boundaries.

29. The Government think, however, that it would be right to confer reserve housing powers on the Greater London Council. That body should be solely responsible for arrangements for overspill outside the area. They should be empowered to build within the area if and only if that is necessary to help a borough unable to solve its own problems, or to secure development in accordance with the development plan. The Council should not build within the area except with the consent of the council of the borough in question, or of the Minister if the two councils are unable to agree.

30. The Government concur in the Commission's proposal that houses in Greater London at present owned by the London County Council should pass initially to the Greater London Council. They also consider—a point not touched on by the Royal Commission—that in the first instance the houses owned by the London County Council outside Greater London would have to be transferred to the new Council. But in time all these houses ought, in the Government's opinion, to be transferred to local ownership and management.

TOWN AND COUNTY PLANNING

31. The Commission's main proposals were that the Greater London Council should be responsible for the preparation and periodic review of the development plan for the whole area, although, subject to some qualifications, the borough councils should be responsible for dealing with individual planning applications. The Government agree that this general scheme of working is right.

32. The need to have one plan for the whole of Greater London was the point on which there was the most complete agreement among the authorities in their comments on the Commission's report. The alternative proposals put forward by the county councils envisaged a master plan prepared by a joint planning board—a set of general principles, within the framework of which

the present planning authorities would prepare their own development plans. The Government do not believe that this scheme would prove effective. It is true that the county councils who sponsored the joint board scheme also urged the need to look at a much wider area than that adopted in the Royal Commission's proposals; and it is true, too, that the influence of London spreads far beyond the continuous built-up area. There is however a clear distinction between the nature of the planning problems in the main built-up area—which clearly must be looked at as an entity for planning purposes—and those in the areas beyond. The two react on each other, but they can be handled separately.

33. A number of detailed matters connected with the part which the borough councils should play in planning, both in the build-up of the overall plan and in the handling of individual planning applications, need further consideration, and on these the Government have yet to reach final conclusions. In particular, further examination will be given to the proposition that it may be desirable to define special areas and within those areas to specify the kinds of development calling for reference to the overall authority.

34. The planning powers so far considered are those dealing with overspill, the development plan and the control of land use. Planning authorities also have powers to carry out comprehensive redevelopment, and that raises the question whether the Greater London Council should have any function in this field. Clearly the borough councils can be left to deal with most of such development entirely within their own boundaries—certainly in so far as it is of a fairly normal character, such as the clearance and fresh layout of obsolete development and minor improvement to the road pattern. But where major schemes are concerned, entailing perhaps exceptionally heavy expenditure, on occasion traversing borough boundaries and usually involving major road improvements and affecting traffic conditions over a wide area, it may be necessary for the Greater London Council to carry out the work. In the Government's view they should have powers to do so, but (as in the case of housing) exercisable only with the consent of the borough councils concerned or, if there is no agreement, of the Minister.

TRAFFIC AND HIGHWAYS

35. As with planning, there was widespread agreement that traffic management and the construction of main highways raised urgent problems which could be solved only in the context of Greater London as a whole. The essential recommendations of the Royal Commission in this field were that one authority should be responsible for traffic management throughout Greater London, and that the same authority should be responsible for the construction, improvement, maintenance and lighting of all main roads.

36. The Government accept both these recommendations in principle. A number of detailed matters will require consideration, especially the question of the complementary functions of borough councils, but in the Government's view there is no doubt that ultimate responsibility for traffic management and main roads should be placed on the Greater London Council.

37. The Commission differentiate between "main roads" (by which they mean those chiefly used by through traffic) and other roads, and recommend that within Greater London this distinction should replace the existing road classification. All main road work should then rank for grant. The Government intends to give further study to these proposals, and also to the extent to which main roads in the Greater London area should or should not be designated as trunk roads under the direct responsibility of the Minister of Transport.

EDUCATION

38. The proposal of the Royal Commission was that education functions should be divided between the Greater London Council and the boroughs. The Government appreciate the considerations which led the Commission to this proposal: that it is most important to give to the London boroughs an effective role in education; but that to divide the whole metropolitan area up into 50 or so self-contained units would result in a too fragmented system, especially in the heart of the area, where schools and institutions have been provided without regard to borough boundaries, and where the free movement of pupils across these boundaries has been one of the strengths of London's educational system.

39. The Government do not feel able to accept the division of the services between the two different types of authority. This is a system that can be made to work, but, as the Royal Commission themselves pointed out, it has not always worked very satisfactorily, and the Government believe that it would be wrong when reorganising the local government system in Greater London deliberately to legislate for a divided responsibility in the educational field.

40. As already indicated, the Government's view is that there should be assigned to the boroughs services which can be effectively provided at the local level, and to the Greater London Council those functions which require to be planned and co-ordinated over the whole built-up area. Following this principle, they are satisfied that it would be wrong to entrust to the Greater London Council the function of carrying out the whole education services for Greater London; the area is far too large to form a single education unit. Moreover, their proposal to organise the area in larger and fewer boroughs than the Commission envisaged makes a big difference. The Government believe that, given larger boroughs, it would be satisfactory that over the greater part of the area education should become a borough service.

41. They do not think, however, that this would be right in the centre of London, where the absence of administrative boundaries and the consequent complete freedom of choice for pupils and students, is of special value. Here they would wish to see one education authority for an area much larger than can be envisaged for the individual boroughs. It might well be that a central area with a population of the order of 2 million would be appropriate.

42. The precise definition of the area to be covered by the central London education authority depends very much on the pattern of the boroughs in the centre. The Government propose that this should be further considered in the course of the consultations about the borough structure referred to in paragraph 20.

43. The Government would wish to take the views of the local authorities concerned before deciding what form the education authority for the central area might take, and the extent to which the boroughs might be associated with it.

44. So far as higher education outside the universities is concerned, the Minister of Education has recently proposed that the colleges of advanced technology should be transferred from the control of the local education authorities to direct grant status. The remaining arrangements for higher education will be subject to review in the light of any recommendations that may be made by the Committee on Higher Education under the chairmanship of Lord Robbins.

YOUTH EMPLOYMENT SERVICE

45. The Government propose that the organisation of the youth employment service should be on the same pattern. The central London education authority, and the boroughs in outer London, would provide the service unless any of them opts not to do so, in which case it would be provided in that area by the Minister of Labour.

ENVIRONMENTAL HEATH SERVICES

46. The Government agree with the Royal Commission's conclusion that, subject to certain exceptions, the environmental health services should be the responsibility of the borough councils. In the Government's view there is a clear case for making the Greater London Council responsible for refuse disposal (as distinct from collection), and they agree with the Commission's proposal on this point. Further thought needs to be given to the allocation of responsibilities for main sewerage and sewage disposal, for land drainage and for certain major parks and open spaces.

AMBULANCE SERVICE

47. The Government agree with the Commission's recommendation that the Greater London Council should be responsible for the ambulance service; the area for the efficient operation of the ambulance service is very much larger than that appropriate to the other health and welfare services.

FIRE SERVICE

48. The Government also agree that this service can more effectively be organised over a wider area, and should be the responsibility of the Greater London Council.

OTHER SERVICES

49. These are not mentioned individually in this paper and some of them will need to be discussed with the local authorities concerned before final conclusions can be reached. While the Government agree with the principle which animated the Commission's approach, namely, that as many functions as possible should be performed as locally as possible, they also recognise that there may be services other than those mentioned in this Paper which need to be exercised over or on behalf of the whole of Greater London.

INTELLIGENCE DEPARTMENT

50. The Commission recommended that the Greater London Council should set up a first-class intelligence department for continuous research into the many interlinked problems of Greater London as a whole, a department which should serve not only the authority itself but also the borough councils, the central Government and the public. In the Government's view there is a clear need for such an intelligence department, and they fully endorse the Commission's proposal.

FINANCE

51. Obviously the financial implications of any reorganisation of local government must be carefully considered. In the Government's view the financial arrangements should follow consequently on changes which are necessary for other reasons. It would be premature at this stage to set out detailed proposals on finance. There are many factors which make a reliable estimate of the finan-

cial consequences of reorganisation impossible at the present time. The probable effect on rate resources of the general revaluation for 1963 will not be known until 1962. The future cost of services when they fall to be carried out by altered or enlarged local authorities cannot be very closely estimated. For these reasons the Government have not yet reached a final conclusion on the Commission's proposal that the counties of Essex, Hertfordshire, Kent and Surrey should, for a limited period, be granted financial relief in respect of the severance of parts of those counties.

52. The Government appreciate that the reorganisation proposed would involve considerable reduction in the resources of Surrey, Essex and Kent, but they see no reason to dissent from the Commission's view that each of these counties would remain financially viable. Compensation for added burdens resulting from boundary adjustments has caused considerable difficulty and friction in the past, and the statutory provision for it was repealed by the Local Government Act, 1948. The Government would be reluctant to revive the principle of compensation for added burdens, though they will consider when further figures are available whether an exception should be made for the counties affected by the reorganisation of London Government.

53. The Commission noted that the average rate resources per head of population were higher in Greater London than in the rest of the country. But they recommend that a scheme of rate equalisation should be introduced to reduce the disparity between rates in the central area and those which may have to be levied by some of the other boroughs in Greater London. The Government agree that a scheme is needed. Further study will be necessary before the details can be settled.

FUTURE STEPS

54. The legislation required to give effect to these far-reaching proposals will of necessity be extremely complicated, and there are many matters which will need to be explored with the local authorities before legislative proposals can be presented to Parliament.

55. This White Paper sets out the Government's broad intentions. They are proceeding now with a detailed study. It is not possible at this stage to say when a Bill giving effect to the proposals will be presented to Parliament, but the aim will be to make it possible for the new authorities to be elected in the autumn of 1964 and to take over from the existing authorities in April, 1965. In the case of those councils which will be wholly replaced by the new authorities, the Bill will provide for the cancellation of elections which would otherwise have intervened between the passing of the Bill and the date when

the new authorities take over. It is the Government's desire that the change over should be made at the earliest practicable date, partly because it is very difficult for the existing authorities to carry on once it is known that changes are impending, and partly also because the Government believe that the changes proposed will provide, for this great city where more than 8 million people live, a more effective and a more firmly based system of local government, better fitted to meet the needs of the future.

25. The New Government in Greater London*

L. J. SHARPE

L. J. Sharpe, lecturer in public administration at the University of Oxford, reviews the opposition to the London Government Act of 1963, assesses the criticism of the plan of government, and draws lessons which may be applicable to the United States. Sharpe is also the former research director of the Greater London Group, an interdisciplinary research group at the London School of Economics.

Local government reform is loved by no one. In the abstract most people of reasonably progressive outlook are in favor, but, faced with concrete proposals, enthusiasm wanes. We may all want reform, but for someone else. The London reform was no exception. Certainly at the opening stages most local authorities and professional bodies in the area were against the plan.[1]

Perhaps the potentially most serious political opposition came from the outer London Conservative Members of Parliament who, like their constituents, were appalled at the idea of being absorbed into a new London. This opposition was most vehement in Surrey. The exclusion from the plan of some of the peripheral boroughs and districts before the Act was passed, effectively silenced most of this opposition, however.

The bulk of the opposition to the Bill was confined, during the later stages of the reform process, to the Labour Party and in particular the London Labour

* From *Public Management* (April 1966), pp. 96–99.

[1] For an excellent account of the political aspects of the London reform, see Frank Smallwood, *Greater London: The Politics of Metropolitan Reform* (Indianapolis: Bobbs-Merrill, 1965).

Party and various professional associations. For them the plight of the leafier suburbs was not at stake but the London County Council—the star in Labour's crown.

The County of London had remained in Labour's hands for almost thirty years and even during the darkest days of the 1950's, when the Party's fortunes were at their lowest nationally, had loyally returned a Labour majority to County Hall. Since the government in power was Conservative any scheme which involved its abolition was inevitably viewed as tantamount to gerrymandering— one of the worst of all crimes in a two-party system. Moreover, the London County Council enjoyed a high reputation for many of its services and was especially esteemed for its education and housing.

Thus the reform could be seen in Labour's eyes as manipulation for short-term political ends and at the same time as an attack on the social services. Little wonder then that the London Bill's passage through Parliament was one of the most contentious of the 1959–64 session.

Despite these fears the Labour Party won a handsome victory at the first GLC election and has a majority on 20 of the 32 borough councils. Gerrymandering apart, how far was the opposition to the Act justified? The following is a brief outline of my own view of some of the salient arguments put forward against it.

CRITICAL VIEW OF THE NEW LONDON

The need to create a single, metropolitan-wide body in Greater London for planning, highways, and associated services was, I think, unanswerable. There is little doubt that the over-all quality of these services, particularly traffic management, will show a marked improvement over the next decade as a direct result of reorganization.

This does not mean that the proposed GLC is perfection. I would like to see, for example, as has been suggested by some critics, the Council's powers on the housing side strengthened so that it can build anywhere in the area on a concurrent basis with boroughs. And there would seem to be scope for streamlining the proposed somewhat cumbersome joint machinery for planning which has been criticized in some quarters.

Nevertheless, looking purely at the engineering services, the new machinery meets a clearly felt need, and it is unfortunate that discussion about it has become mixed up with questions of regional government, which is very much in intellectual vogue in Britain at the moment. The GLC will not be a regional authority, and its creation has very little bearing on the argument for or against a regional authority for the much wider southeast England area.

Turning to the more personal services, on which have focused perhaps most of the informed criticism of the new scheme, I think it can fairly be said that the assumption explicit in the new set-up—that they should be as close as possible and responsible to the populations for whom they are provided—is sound.

Certainly it seems clear that in the health and welfare field rigid departmentalism, which tends to develop *pari passu* with increasing size, defeats the purpose of many of the services. For in the last analysis they are intended to serve one basic unit, the family. The problem is, how close must the services be to the client? The Commission thought that a borough population of 250,000 was about the maximum, the Government a third of a million. I would favor a higher maximum.

There is of course no scientific basis for determining optimum population in these matters; inevitably any choice tends to be a balance of advantage struck between the competing needs of accessibility and functional efficiency. Those who place a higher premium on efficiency will demand a higher maximum.

In a continuously built-up area the need for accessibility is less than a discrete provincial town. In a built-up area local loyalties are weaker, the population is more mobile, and intricate administrative patterns that are unsupported by observable, physical differences tend to confuse and frustrate. For these reasons I think functional efficiency should play a larger part in the determination of the size of the lower tier in London than it might elsewhere.

Another source of criticism of the new set-up has focused on the welfare and child care services in the poorer inner areas of London. While one recognizes the need for reasonably uniform boroughs over the whole area, all armed with the same set of functions and powers, there are a number of special problems in the core city which suggest that complete uniformity may be inappropriate.

For the welfare and child care services there are strong arguments for areas wider than any individual borough. This is because the inner area has a higher proportion of working-class residents who tend to need more welfare services. Because of the anonymity which it offers to unmarried mothers, the core city has special child-care problems too. Adequately trained staff for the health and welfare services are in short supply throughout Britain, but in the unsalubrious areas of inner London they would be very hard to come by for borough employment.

Another problem arising out of the insistence upon uniformity of functions for the boroughs concerns the central area. This is an area which is somewhat bigger than the central business district to allow for future expansion. Here there is a strong case for the GLC exercising all planning functions since this is the dominant service center for the whole metropolis. It houses all the great institutions of state, and it is the preeminent shopping and cultural center.

But more important, it is the great office zone providing employment for well over 1,300,000 people every day. It is the area which lies, literally and metaphorically, at the root of the commuter problem. Any development plan for the whole area must give it very special attention, and in view of the inevitable pressures from powerful commercial and other interests, it requires a strong countervailing planning body.

When we speak of the metropolitan area problem we are in fact talking about transit. Yet the Greater London Council will have no transit functions since the whole of the transit system in London is outside local government and forms part of the nationalized system. The only link between it and the Greater London Council is a very minor requirement in the act that the GLC must consult the London Transport Board over street repairs. If London's new government is to succeed in its allotted task, a much stronger link must be forged.

IMPLICATIONS FOR THE U.S.

Are there any lessons to be drawn from the London experience which might be applicable to the United States? Probably very few for two very good reasons.

The first is the power that can be exerted by the central government in Britain. If the national government really wants to do something in Britain it can usually do it without conceding too much. In this case the government did want to act and, although it had a few tricky rapids to negotiate, the remarkable thing is the similarity of the London Government Act to the original Royal Commission report.

Second, the status of local government in Britain and conceptions of democracy are different from those of the United States. There is little conception in Britain of making legislative change, even when it involves the abolition of political institutions, subject to the concurrence of the electorate. Parliament devised the existing local government system, so Parliament can change it.

Thus the London scheme did not have to run the gauntlet of a local referendum, which would be obligatory for a reform scheme of this character in the United States and would, if we are to believe Professor Scott Greer, kill such a scheme stone dead.

Two aspects of the reform saga are, I think, of some importance to the American reader. The first is that it shows that thorough-going reform is possible, that local government institutions are not immutable despite the intransigence of vested interests and the general public's indifferences. An example is perhaps worth a shelf full of well-intentioned tomes on the metropolitan area problem.

It must also be emphasized that throughout the reform process there was a meaningful debate being conducted about the relationship between area and function, about the competing demands of local democracy and functional efficiency, about the respective roles to be played by national and local government.

And these arguments influenced the shape of the reform. It was not the mere resolution of the demands of competing groups and interests.

One final point. The Greater London Council is the first purpose-built local authority we have had in Britain in the sense that its jurisdiction and powers were largely determined by the services it will perform. Yet except for the research and intelligence department, its internal structure has been fashioned on strictly traditional lines.[2]

Despite the fact that one of its primary purposes will be coordination of related services, it will operate under horizontal functional committees manned by elected councillors and advised by professional officers. Apart from the clerk of the council, who is the chief legal officer and administrative head, there will be no central managerial focus.

However, a special committee was set up by the central government in the spring of 1964 to look into the whole question of management in local councils in England and Wales. Already one local authority, Newcastle-upon-Tyne, has anticipated the committee's findings and is creating a more closely integrated administrative machine, headed by a chief administrator formerly with the Ford Motor Company in Britain. It may well be that the reform of London government is yet to be completed and that a new pattern of internal administration will take shape to match the new over-all structure of government.

26. A Most Unusual Organization*

Metropolitan problems which transcend state boundaries are extremely difficult to solve. To date, the special district has been principally relied upon to solve functional metropolitan problems in an interstate area.

The largest metropolitan special district is the Port of New York Authority created, in 1921, by an interstate compact entered into by the states of New York and New Jersey with congressional approval. The authority is responsible for the development and operation of a number of major

---

[2] See L. J. Sharpe, *Research in Local Government: The Role of the Research and Information Unit of the G.L.C.* Greater London Paper No. 10, London School of Economics, 1965.

---

* *Forbes* (March 1, 1966), pp. 50, 53–55, and 57; (March 15, 1966), pp. 6–7. Reprinted by permission of FORBES Magazine.

transportation facilities including airports, bridges, terminals, and tunnels.

The Port of New York Authority has been criticized strongly for its pro-automobile and anti-mass transit bias. The excerpt from *Forbes* is a hard-hitting attack upon the Port of New York Authority and the Triborough Bridge and Tunnel Authority.

The twelve commissioners of the Port of New York Authority reacted to the *Forbes* article by sending a letter to the editor which refuted certain points contained in the article, but failed to comment upon the charge that the authority is pro-automobile and anti-mass transit.

The outfit was formed in 1921. It had no assets, no reserves, no operating income. Today its physical assets are estimated at $1.5 billion, its funded debt is over $850 million. Its bonds are AA-rated, its net operating revenues are running at $80 million a year. (It doesn't have a private army, but it has its own police.) A tribute to vision, dedication and hard work? Only partly.

The "company" is the Port of New York Authority, and its phenomenal growth is due, not quite so much to business acumen, as to the fact that it has a monopoly to charge a toll on every motor vehicle that rolls over or under the Hudson River, in or out of New York City; to charge a fee on every airplane that lands or takes off at LaGuardia, Kennedy and Newark airports. Unlike private businesses, the PA pays no taxes and has the right of eminent domain. Unlike a government, it need never face the electorate.

Obviously, no private corporation can compete with it. This would not cause too much consternation if the Port Authority restricted itself to activities in which private enterprise was disinterested. But it doesn't. It often competes directly with private business.

From the standpoint of the states of New York and New Jersey, and especially of the City of New York, the situation is even more dismaying. The Authority can do things which frustrate their own plans and which cost them money. They're almost helpless to prevent it. Right now New York City's new Republican mayor, John Lindsay, is finding this out as he struggles to unify his city's chaotic transportation.

What is this powerful outfit and how did it get that way? When the Authority was founded it was given the general and unspecific task of developing the terminal and transportation facilities of the entire New York port area—roughly, within a circle having a radius of about 25 miles from the Statue of Liberty. (The Authority was established by acts of the legislatures of both states, and approved by the U.S. Congress.)

In its formative years the PA stuck mostly with the transportation facilities that were its prime moneymakers: bridges, tunnels and airports. These made the PA a real beneficiary of the auto age, and later of the air age. As its tax-free profits piled up, it built more facilities to bring cars, trucks and airplanes into New York. Finally, its air and automobile facilities made so much money that the Authority—like many another corporation with vast resources—is now diversifying.

It is not, however, diversifying into transportation as its charter would seem to require. The PA shows no interest in helping unsnarl Manhattan's strangulating traffic. Instead, with the tax-free, eminent-domain advantages that private corporations don't enjoy, the Port Authority has moved into real estate on a scale that would make William the Conqueror pale with envy.

At the lower tip of Manhattan, the PA proposes to build a World Trade Center. It will be housed in twin 110-story skyscrapers, *each* higher than the Empire State Building (1,350 feet compared with 1,248 feet). *Each* will contain more than twice as much space as the world's largest private office building, the Pan American World Airways building that now dominates mid-Manhattan (5 million square feet compared with 2.4 million).

It is expected that 50,000 persons will work in these buildings and that 80,000 will visit them each day. In addition to its office space, the Trade Center will include a major hotel, the Manhattan Terminal of the Port Authority Trans-Hudson railroad system (formerly the Hudson & Manhattan Railroad), plus arcades, exhibition galleries, shops, restaurants and parking garages.

ADDED WOES

The present estimated cost of this monster is $525 million (up $250 million from an initial estimate four years ago). The PA's critics are quick to point out that this amount of money could completely refurbish New York's dilapidated subway system; it could rehabilitate its shockingly run-down commuter railroads several times over. Either of these projects would help ease Manhattan's transportation woes. The Trade Center, on the other hand, will certainly aggravate them.

Listen to the figures: Critics have pointed out that the 130,000 persons who will be in the building on a working day will be poured into a part of the city already so jammed that people have to walk in the streets. They will have to get to it by subways so crowded—at rush hours—that it is sometimes impossible to get aboard.

One of the PA's distinguished critics is Adolph A. Berle, professor at Columbia Law School. He thinks the PA's building project will pile up woe for an already hard-pressed city. "I have not yet seen and do not think that there has yet been made," he has said, "any statement of the cost of this proposition to the

City of New York. [Because of crowds] this will require structural changes, additional police to direct traffic, probably new facilities. It certainly will require a tremendous amount of additional water just to service the building. If, to the cost of operating this proposed building, there were added the indirect costs which will be imposed on the city to service it, it is a question whether this investment would be attractive at all."

A VICTIM

The idea for a World Trade Center in New York is not exactly new, but the explanation of how this came about at this particular time and place is interesting. Until 1927, the privately owned Hudson & Manhattan Railroad, which links New York and New Jersey, was a moneymaker, carrying 113 million passengers a year. Then, the Port Authority got control of the Holland Tunnel. The tax-free competition sent H&M's passenger traffic plummeting to under 30 million and the H&M went into the red to a tune of $6 million a year.

In 1962, the New York and New Jersey legislatures ordered the Port Authority to take over the railroad and keep it operating. The PA kicked and screamed. PA Executive Director Austin Tobin said at the time that the H&M's "financial problems are formidable and they are all written in red ink." He added that "its operating problems are entirely new to our experience." To placate him, the two states granted the PA the right to build the Trade Center. It was a wonderful idea for the Authority. The Trade Center is expected to bring in $26 million a year, which will make up for the H&M's losses four times over.

The Trade Center will be built on the lower western tip of Manhattan, and the twin 22-story H&M Terminal buildings, which already occupied part of the site, will be torn down. (The PA had mentioned a figure of $20.5 million for the H&M buildings and other assets of the railroad. Only a few weeks ago a New York State Supreme Court judge recommended a $70-million settlement— a decision the PA intends to appeal.)

Even if the PA beats the price down, the Trade Center bids fair to be the most expensive office building ever erected, in both absolute and relative terms. Although its present estimated cost is $525 million, there are those who say it will end up at more than $700 million. With its 10 million square feet of space, this averages out to $52.50 a square foot by the PA's own estimates, or $70 by its critics', in contrast to the current going figure for a major new skyscraper in New York, which is roughly $35 a square foot. The PA, of course, proposes to finance this new venture as it has all past ones, by issuing tax-exempt bonds —and this has raised further resentment among private real-estate men in the city.

They have organized the Committee for a Reasonable World Trade Center, which is supported by such big realty names as Lawrence Wien, Harold Uris and Seymour Durst. Says Robert Kopple, head of the committee: "If private builders want to put up a building, we raise $25 million and get a bank to go along for another $25 million. Then we go out and sell leases. When we have signed leases for, say, 10% of the building, we turn them over to the bank and get another advance. But the bank wouldn't give us another dime without those signed leases locked in its vaults. The PA has so much money and so much power it can go ahead on promises."

EMPTY SPACE

Some of the promises are pretty good; in fact, the PA expects to fill 60% of its space on promises. The PA itself will move in, from its 15-story building on Eighth Avenue; the U.S. Government will move in its Customs Service and some other installations; the State of New York will move in its offices; a number of foreign governments and foreign and domestic shipping concerns will come along. The first thing that worries New York real-estate men today is the effect that all this space-to-be-vacated will have on the market; the second thing is how the PA will fill the 4 million square feet it still has to rent after all the official and quasi-official space is filled.

Said Kopple: "If they get caught in a bind, we're afraid of what they could do to rents. The going rate is $6.50 or $7 a square foot in a new building. But they don't pay any taxes, that's 75 cents a square foot off. Interest at 3.25% instead of 5.25%, that's $1.25 a square foot. No income taxes, that's another $1.25. They could rent for $3.50 a foot if they wanted to. They say they'll rent at competitive rates, but we haven't been able to get them to tell us what competitive rates mean. The only released figure they have published has been the rental to the Federal Government for the customs house—and that is a minimum of $3.57 a square foot."

TELLING THEM OFF

When the PA was founded in 1921 it was the first of its kind in the U.S. (The model for it was the Port of London Authority.) Now almost every fair-sized port in the U.S. has its own port authority.

There are many people who feel that the PA should stick to its last. One rival, the Port of Philadelphia-Camden, now handles more foreign trade than New York does. Since 1947 foreign trade has grown over 200% for

Philadelphia-Camden while New York has grown only 77%. In defense of the New York Port Authority it must be said that the lack of growth has been relative, not absolute. That is, New York has about held its own in tonnage, but has failed to benefit from the over-all growth in foreign trade.

But there is no getting away from one fact: While the New York Port Authority was busying itself with plans for diversifying, its rival port authorities were sticking strictly to their knitting by concentrating on shipping and transportation facilities.

It might be expected that this sort of loss of position—whatever the reasons for it—might have caused a public outcry and led to public and political pressure on the New York PA. Yet the simple fact is that through the years, during which it has become powerful and arrogant, the PA hasn't lost many battles. It is responsible to the governors and legislatures of the two states by the terms of its founding, and it is presumably also responsible to Congress, which has final authority over all compacts entered into between the states. But it has seldom been called to account for the way it handles its money, and, on the few occasions that it has been, it has reacted like a bear with a sore ear.

In 1960, for example, New York's Democratic Representative Emanuel Celler wanted to prove that the PA's George Washington Bridge and Holland Tunnel had paid for themselves many times over, and that the tolls should be eliminated. Tobin more or less told Celler that it was none of his business, for which the House cited him for contempt. (The case was later dismissed, and Celler now refuses even to discuss it.)

The following year, when the New Jersey State Senate decided it wanted the same figures, Tobin submitted them. The figures showed that, up to 1960, the PA had invested a total of $202 million and that it had gotten its money back plus interest and had a net profit of $92 million. The tolls, however, remained.

In the early 1930s, when the Authority was still struggling with its financial teething problems, the two state legislatures had given it the power to pool its revenues. This enabled the PA to use the surplus from the George Washington Bridge and the Holland Tunnel to cover the deficits of facilities that weren't paying *their* way. This built the PA a vastly larger credit base for its bond offerings. It gave it the means for expanding almost indefinitely.

Outside of the Celler hearings and the New Jersey Senate action, the PA's operations have largely gone unquestioned. The actual legal process involved provides that the PA is required to submit to each of the two governors proposals for projects it intends to undertake, and the governor has ten days in which he may veto the project. Actually, no governor of either state has ever vetoed any major project the Authority has suggested.

HAVING ITS OWN WAY

This giant corporation without stockholders, this vast government without voters handles enormous sums of money and dispenses huge amounts of patronage.

A single project in 1962, building a second level on the George Washington Bridge, cost $145 million. True to his pro-automobile, antimass-transportation bias, Tobin refused to listen to suggestions that the new level be used for a high speed mass-transportation system. He was deaf to arguments that this could carry far more people at rush hours with far less congestion than autos could. He argued that motorists paid for the project and so motorists alone should benefit. There were a good many people who thought that Tobin was dead wrong, but there was nobody to blow the whistle on him.

Over the years—to 1971—the PA figures on spending $500 million for improving facilities in such installations as Kennedy and LaGuardia airports. This is not counting the half-billion dollars for the World Trade Center buildings and continuing to refurbish the H&M. Not one cent has been budgeted for subways or other forms of mass transportation. Only the largest corporations have capital budgets to match the $1-billion program, for which the Port Authority will have to account to no one.

In terms of assets, the PA would rank among the top 25 U.S. corporations. In 1955, it had a net income of $35 million after interest and operating expenses, on a gross income of $69 million. In 1964, it had a gross of $167 million and a net of $63 million. True, the PA's obligation has increased, too. Its debt now totals over $850 million, up from $280 million a decade ago; it covered its interest charges 8.46 times in 1955 vs. 4.1 times in 1964.

"However," Tobin said in a recent public statement, "even at a coverage of 1.80 we will be earning about $60 million in net revenues after mandatory long-term debt service. This, it seems to me, offers a considerable safety factor for our bondholders."

Yet this growing burden of debt has given the PA an excuse to back away from participation in the mass-transit projects New York City so badly needs. But the excuse is not a very convincing one: The PA's surplus, roughly equivalent to earned surplus in a corporation, now stands at around $800 million, and there are very few railroads in the U.S., even the most prosperous ones, which have an interest coverage that could compare to the PA's. Even in 1971, with the World Trade Center under way and with all the new borrowing now projected, the PA's total debt service, including amortization, will come to only about $75 million, leaving a balance, a "net profit," of $60 million.

END OF THE LINE?

The Port Authority has been able to buffalo state legislatures and governors in the past. There are indications, however, that the PA's almost total independence may be coming to an end. In Albany, the Senate Committee on the Affairs of the City of New York, headed by Senator Thomas J. Mackell, has issued a 130-page report blasting the PA, the Triborough Bridge & Tunnel Authority and the New York Transit Authority for their collective failure to solve the mass transportation problem in and around New York City.

There is no corporate relationship among any of these authorities. There is an indirect and highly personal one, however. The turbulently truculent Robert Moses, chairman of the Triborough Authority, generally espouses Tobin's causes. Moses, New York's commissioner of practically everything, is an old hand at constructing anything that will move automobiles, and a superb empire builder to boot.

Moses' Triborough empire, in fact, is almost the equal of Tobin's PA. To build his Triborough Bridge & Tunnel Authority, he started in 1934 with the old Triborough Bridge Authority, added the Henry Hudson Parkway Authority, the Marine Parkway Authority, the New York City Parkway Authority and the New York City Tunnel Authority. He has ended up today with a corporation with some $860 million in assets and 1964 revenues of $45 million. Moses' Triborough Bridge & Tunnel Authority is a great bridge-and-tunnel builder—the newest and brightest diadem adorning its brow is the Verrazano-Narrows Bridge (toll: 50 cents) over Lower New York Bay. The only basic difference between Moses and Tobin is that Moses operates entirely within New York, while Tobin is bi-state. (Moses never thinks small; even before the Verrazano bridge was finished, he was talking of a $6\frac{1}{2}$ mile bridge over Long Island Sound, connecting Bayville in Nassau with Port Chester in Westchester County.)

Moses may, in a way, have established a precedent for Tobin's concept of the World Trade Center, for ten years ago Moses built the New York Coliseum, an exhibition hall which includes a 20-story office building. Just exactly what a bridge authority was doing building an exhibition hall with a commercial office building has never been determined.

At the moment, both Tobin and Moses have their troubles. State Senator Mackell, since issuing his 130-page report, has introduced legislation that would forbid the PA to go ahead with its Trade Center until the plans can be reviewed by the legislatures of the two states. The legislatures gave the PA the go-ahead in 1962, but Mackell argues that Tobin's project has grown so much since that it needs to be reviewed.

As for Moses, his potential problems have grown worse since the frightening

New York subway strike. The subways are deteriorating, both financially and physically, and they are far more vital to the city than Moses' bridges and Tobin's buildings.

New York's Mayor Lindsay has already proposed legislation that would bring the Triborough Bridge Authority and the New York Transit Authority more directly under his control by appointing an over-all transit coordinator, and by using some of Triborough's $35-million-a-year profit to pay costs now borne by the city.

Bob Moses immediately took this proposal on. Lindsay's idea, he remarked, was "poorly advised" and sprang "from panic, not logic." What he meant, of course, was that when Lindsay learned his way around he would know enough to leave Moses and Tobin alone. Lindsay got off easy. Moses has told off presidents of the United States in sharper words than those. (Lindsay learned fast. He had also proposed that members of the Authority be made dismissable "at the will of the appointing official." Moses called this idea "fantastic," and Lindsay withdrew it four days later.)

Tobin and Moses, moreover, have powerful friends. Most powerful among them are the building trade unions which are licking their chops over the prospect of thousands of highly paid jobs. Tobin has a powerful supporter for his World Trade Center in David Rockefeller, president of the Chase Manhattan Bank and younger brother of the New York Governor. Comforted by this kind of support, Tobin and Moses show no willingness to subordinate their private empires to the greater good of New York City.

A TRUCK IN THE VAULT?

However all this comes out—the lesson of the unchecked growth of the PA and its cousin, the Triborough Bridge Authority, has not been lost on other communities. The lesson is clear: Unchecked, the privileges of collecting tolls and operating free of income taxes are potentially dangerous. As one businessman put it: "It's like being permitted to drive a truck through the Chase Manhattan's vaults and then to be able to laugh at the cop who tries to stop you."

SIR: As commissioners of the Port of New York Authority we are completely familiar with its operations and policies but we do not find in your article (FORBES, Mar. 1, p. 50) any resemblance to the organization we know so well.

The article ignored what the Port Authority really is: a governmental agency of the states of New York and New Jersey consisting of a board of 12 commissioners, six appointed by the governor of each state. It is the commissioners who set the policy of the port authority and who at each annual meeting appoint the Executive Director to serve for a term of one year. The commissioners have manifested their confidence in Austin Tobin by re-electing him each year since 1942.

The article ignored what the World Trade Center really is: a public port development project which the legislatures of the two states have *directed* the port authority to undertake.

The article states that the port authority "has a monopoly . . . to charge a fee on every airplane that lands or takes off at LaGuardia, Kennedy and Newark airports." The fact is that the port authority makes such charges to support an investment of public funds of over half-a-billion dollars and that, as a result of these charges, the metropolitan airports are operated at no cost to the general taxpayers of the area.

The article states: "In 1962, the New York and New Jersey Legislatures ordered the Port Authority to take over the [H&M] railroad and keep it operating. The PA kicked and screamed." The fact is that the legislatures authorized and directed the port authority to undertake the Hudson Tubes-World Trade Center project *after* the port authority had developed and submitted a financial plan to the legislatures outlining how it could undertake the rehabilitation of the railroad without destroying the authority's credit.

It mentions an investigation of the port authority undertaken by the New Jersey State Senate in 1961 but does not mention the comprehensive report on the port authority thereafter submitted by that committee. The members of the committee, after completing their investigation, unanimously sponsored the legislation in New Jersey authorizing and directing the port authority to undertake the World Trade Center Project, the same project which your article cites as "proof" that the port authority is exceeding its powers.

S. SLOAN COLT
JAMES C. KELLOGG, III
HOWARD S. CULLMAN
GERARD F. BRILL
JOHN J. CLANCY
CHARLES W. ENGELHARD
ALEXANDER HALPERN
DONALD V. LOWE
JOSEPH A. MARTINO
BAYARD F. POPE
BEN REGAN
W. PAUL STILLMAN

Commissioners of the Port of New York Authority

New York, N.Y.

27. A Limited-Function
Metropolitan Government
for the Bay Area*

One of the most interesting recent metropolitan developments was the passage of a resolution by the Board of Supervisors of the City and County of San Francisco pointing out the problems caused by a proliferation of special districts and calling for the creation of a limited function metropolitan government for the Bay Area. The proposal is unique in that the metropolitan government, basically a multipurpose special district government, would be a unit of local government instead of a state-operated special district government and would not replace any units of general purpose local government.

Whereas, The Association of Bay Area Governments, being aware of the evolutionary developments which have taken place in the Bay Area since the end of World War II and the fact that during the past 17 years five single-purpose area-wide governmental special districts have been created, with others in prospect, has undertaken a one-year study to reconsider its own basic policies concerning the proliferation of special districts and its own future; and

Whereas, The vital interests of the citizens of San Francisco and their government are directly involved in the future growth and development of the nine-county Bay Area and the solution of the increasing number of serious and complex regional problems which confront the area; and

Whereas, Specific additional area-wide needs that illustrate the reality of the danger of proliferation of special districts, include: (1) a proposed Bay Area greenbelt district; (2) a proposal for area-wide airport planning and financing; (3) suggestions concerning the need for an area-wide agency to locate and operate major refuse disposal sites for the cities and counties of the Bay Area; (4) the proposal made by Mayor John F. Shelley to ABAG in 1964 concerning the need for providing a maximum choice in housing throughout the Bay Area for families of all income levels and all ethnic groups to relieve the continuing trends that adversely affect non-white and low income citizens and the future of the central cities; (5) proposals for unified control of the bridges and ports of the Bay Area; and

---

* Resolution approved by the Board of Supervisors of the City and County of San Francisco, April 11, 1966.

Whereas, Developments begun during the postwar period seem to be converging, and districts which originated separately now find that the effective operation of each depends on the others, which increasing interdependence would indicate that the time has come to participate in the creation of a long-needed government by, of, and for the Bay Area community, which will strengthen, not disrupt or replace, the existing system of city and county government in the Bay Area, while at the same time enabling the critical needs of the metropolitan community to be provided for effectively, in a democratic way; and

Whereas, The City and County of San Francisco as a member of ABAG and a participant in the proposed study of the future of the Bay Area, has an obligation to provide leadership in the formation of constructive policies aimed at the solution of area-wide governmental problems; now, therefore, be it

Resolved, That the following shall be and it is hereby established as the basic policy of the City and County of San Francisco as to the creation of means to fulfill future governmental needs of the Bay Area, and such policy shall guide the city's delegate to ABAG:

GENERAL POLICY GUIDELINES

Recognizing the danger inherent in piecemeal creation of what has been described as "a fragmented super-government for the Bay Area," San Francisco favors establishment of a unified, limited-function, metropolitan government, which is a genuinely local Bay Area government, and not a state agency performing local governmental functions. San Francisco also favors the grouping together of all present and any essential new Bay Area functions under a single limited-function Bay Area government, with less than total consolidation of all special districts acceptable initially in order to get the framework of the new government established.

San Francisco is not committed to any detailed particular form of metropolitan, limited-function government and to preclude premature dissention or disagreement concerning details, will favor discussion of metropolitan governmental needs at the level of general principles until firm agreement on this level is achieved. Normal differences regarding form may then more easily be ameliorated.

Existing area-wide governmental functions which should be unified as soon as possible include: (1) air pollution control, (2) bay water pollution control, (3) bay conservation and development, (4) area-wide transportation planning, (5) comprehensive Bay Area development planning. Eventually, the Bay Area

Rapid Transit District should become an integral part of the unified Bay Area government.

BROAD PRINCIPLES

1. The Bay Area government must have an entirely local Bay Area political constituency, that is, it must not be a state agency with some local representation on the governing board.

2. The functions of the new government must be restricted to those essential area-wide functions that are not and apparently cannot be handled adequately by the city and county governments of the Bay Area.

3. The Bay Area government shall replace no local general purpose government, that is, all existing city and county governments will continue and, in fact, will be more firmly established for the future as a result of the creation of the limited-function Bay Area government.

4. The Bay Area government's legislative body must be composed of members directly elected to it. The duties of the Bay Area legislative body will be complex and demanding; it will not be possible to continue the transition arrangements of the postwar period which placed city and county elected officials or their appointees on the governing bodies of the area-wide special purpose districts.

5. Whatever method of organizing the Bay Area legislative body is decided upon, it must be in accord with the principle of equal representation. There will be issues facing the Bay Area government, such as the bay conservation issue, that will require the urban population of the Bay Area to have a direct majority.

6. The existence of the Bay Area government should preclude the creation of any additional separately-established metropolitan special districts in the future.

7. A merger of metropolitan Bay Area functions is necessary now as an alternative to the present and future proliferation of special districts. This proliferation is not only an obstacle to an informed and interested electorate, but it diffuses our financial resources and political energies. Proliferation will make it practically impossible for the citizens of the Bay Area, as voters in a democracy, to understand and exercise effective control over the work of the increasing number of special districts. A unified, limited-function Bay Area government is needed to make democracy work at the metropolitan level and to strengthen the tradition of city and county home rule and self-government in the Bay Area.

Further Resolved, That the City and County of San Francisco shall support the above-stated policy and principles at the meetings of the General Assembly, the Executive Committee, and, in particular, the Goals and Organization Committee of ABAG; and, be it

Further Resolved, That the City and County of San Francisco shall support the continued existence of ABAG, whether or not the results of the study of its Goals and Organization Committee recommends the creation of a unified limited-function metropolitan government. If ABAG does support the establishment of such a government, in addition to fostering cooperative enterprises on important matters where there is general agreement, ABAG will be needed to openly and forcefully oppose the unnecessary expansion of the new government. If ABAG does not support the establishment of the new Bay Area government, the City and County of San Francisco will continue to press for further consideration of the proposal.

Further Resolved, That the City and County of San Francisco will make special efforts to maintain liaison with the existing Bay Area Transportation Study Commission and the Bay Conservation and Development Commission as the work of the ABAG Study Committee progresses, and will encourage their concurrence in the recommendation that the creation of a unified, limited-function metropolitan government is the most effective governmental framework within which the permanent functions of their organizations could be carried out.

Further Resolved, That copies of this resolution be forwarded to the Honorable Edmund G. Brown, Governor of California, members of the State Legislature, and officials of the federal government, with the request that they consider the policies and principles set forth herein to the end that all officials and agencies who will be affected by the proposed creation of a unified, limited-function metropolitan government may be apprised of the status of the ABAG study and the position of the City and County of San Francisco on the future governmental needs of the Bay Area, and with unanimity of purpose may join in a concentrated effort toward the accomplishment of the goals and principles incorporated herein.

INTERJURISDICTIONAL COOPERATION

Governmental feuding may appear to be a characteristic of metropolitan areas, yet their development has been accompanied by interjurisdictional cooperation in the form of interlocal provision of services on a contract basis, metropolitan planning, and metropolitan councils of government.

INTERLOCAL CONTRACTING

Interlocal contracts for the provision of services have existed for many years, but have been given greater prominence as a method of solving certain metropolitan problems as the result of the development, in 1954, of the Lakewood Plan. Like the commission-manager plan in Dade County, Florida, the Lakewood Plan involves the county, in this instance the county of Los Angeles. Instead of providing all services itself, the new city of Lakewood contracted to have nearly all of its services provided by the county of Los Angeles. Lakewood's lead has been followed by cities incorporated in Los Angeles County since 1954. Reading 30 describes the services offered by the county and the alternatives to entering into a contract with the county available to a city.

The Lakewood Plan is still in the stage of development and modification. Among the more interesting developments have been the appointment by Los Angeles County of a County-City Coordinator, an

Assistant Chief Administrative Officer, to assist officials of cities contracting with the county for the provision of services, and the organization
in 1958 of the California Contract Cities Association. Although a number of observers credit the Lakewood Plan with relieving certain metropolitan pressures, other observers oppose the provision of services by
interlocal contracts because it perpetuates the fragmented system of
local government.

METROPOLITAN PLANNING

The first type of metropolitan planning was conducted by single
purpose special districts which had been organized to solve a particular
area-wide problem. Comprehensive metropolitan planning is principally
a post-World War II development. A few isolated instances of earlier
comprehensive planning may be cited: the most famous is the Regional
Plan for New York and Its Environs which was sponsored by the Rus-
sell Sage Foundation and completed in 1929.

Urbanization has made regional planning imperative if costly mis-
takes are to be avoided and problems transcending local political
boundaries are to be solved. Its objective is to end haphazard growth
by drafting and implementing a comprehensive and coordinated plan
to guide the development of the metropolitan area. A special effort is
made to rectify the unplanned heritage of the past. Possessing only
advisory powers, a planning commission must work closely with local
governments, state agencies, federal agencies, and private organizations
whose activities and programs affect the development of the area. To
be successful, the commission must persuade the other organizations
to plan and execute their programs within the framework of the comprehensive plan. A profile of an average planning agency is contained
in Reading 28.

Although planning commissions are established under provisions of
a state enabling act, the federal government primarily has been responsible for the growth of area-wide planning by using conditional grants-
in-aid to persuade local governments to organize metropolitan planning
commissions. The importance of such planning is emphasized in President Johnson's message to Congress contained in Reading 12. A local
government within a metropolitan area becomes eligible to receive

federal grants for specified projects—airports, highways, hospitals, libraries, open space land projects, sewerage facilities and waste treatment plants, transportation facilities, water development and land conservation projects, and water supply and distribution facilities—only if its grant applications are reviewed by a metropolitan planning commission. Advocates of planning are convinced the development of plans will act as a stimulus to cooperative action as the realities of area-wide problems are brought into focus and a framework is provided for conjoint action. Reading 29 describes the benefits of metropolitan planning.

METROPOLITAN COUNCILS OF GOVERNMENT

Metropolitan or regional councils of government, which seek to overcome the forces of separatism and to facilitate the resolution of area-wide problems by means of interlocal cooperation, trace their origin to the Metropolitan Boroughs' Standing Joint Committee, created in 1912 in the greater London area, to effectuate cooperation between the boroughs and act as liaison between them and the higher authorities.

The failure to achieve a major restructuring of local governments in most metropolitan areas and the ever increasing magnitude of metropolitan exigencies led in the 1950s to the creation of councils of governments in the United States. The Supervisors' Inter-County Committee in southeast Michigan, organized in 1954, generally is recognized as the oldest council in the United States although the Cuyahoga County Mayors and City Managers Association was organized in 1933 to promote intergovernmental cooperation among 57 municipalities in the Cleveland area. The Supervisors' Inter-County Committee's establishment was followed by the organization of the Metropolitan Regional Council in the New York City area in 1956 and the Metropolitan Washington Council of Governments in 1957. In 1966, the *Metropolitan Area Annual* listed 18 active and ten inactive metropolitan councils in the United States. By August 1967, the number of active councils had increased to 50. The advantages and disadvantages of a council of governments are evaluated in Readings 31 and 32.

One reason for the relatively slow increase in the number of councils of governments in the United States prior to 1966 was the problem of finance. Although a council is relatively easy to form, financing has proved to be a problem. However, a sharp increase in the number of councils is one immediate product of the federal Housing and Urban Development Act of 1965 which makes financial aid available to organizations composed of public officials who represent political jurisdictions within a metropolitan area. To be eligible for a federal grant, a council must consist primarily of elected representatives of municipalities and counties rather than officials of special agencies and authorities. A grant, in an amount not exceeding two thirds of the cost of the work, may be made to a council to undertake studies, collect data, develop regional plans and programs, and engage in other activities designed to provide solutions for metropolitan problems. The remaining one third of the cost of the work must be met by the council in the form of cash or professional and technical services contributed by the jurisdictions comprising the membership of the council.

The purpose of the new federal grant program is to encourage the formation of councils of policy and decision makers representing the local governmental units within a metropolitan area and enable them to develop and implement programs for the coordinated development of the area. In consequence, councils are undertaking regional planning and in a few areas the abolition of an independent metropolitan planning commission and the transfer of its functions to the council of government is under consideration.

28. The Metropolitan
Planning Agency:
A Profile
of the Average*

A composite picture of a metropolitan planning agency is contained in this excerpt from the *National Survey of Metropolitan Planning*. The survey was prepared by the U.S. Housing and Home Finance Agency for the Senate Subcommittee on Intergovernmental Relations, which believes that metropolitan planning, among other things, can coordinate federal programs. The questionnaire used in the survey grew out of an earlier one used by the National Municipal League, the results of which were published in the July 1962 issue of the *National Civic Review*.

How is the average metropolitan planning agency structured, and what does it do? Admittedly, no one agency represents the typical operation. It might be informative, nevertheless, to present a profile of the average agency, based on the study findings. The reader should be aware that this is a highly generalized version, constructed by totaling the responses of all agencies—multijurisdiction, city-county and county agencies, serving different sized populations and representing different regions—to specific questions, and then determining an average response. Here, then, is the composite:

The average metropolitan planning agency is about nine years old, and serves a (1960) population approximately the same as that of Tulsa, Oklahoma, or Tampa, Florida (275,000), and an area slightly larger than Rhode Island (1200 square miles). It was established by local resolution under a state enabling act, with comprehensive planning as its primary purpose.

The agency has a 16-member commission, with each person serving for four years. Members are selected by the governmental bodies represented on the commission. There is a fairly even sprinkling of elected and appointed public officials, but most of the commission members are lay citizens. County and city governments are heavily represented, with limited representation of the state, townships, and special districts.

The average agency's area of jurisdiction is generally similar to the SMSA it

* From *National Survey of Metropolitan Planning* (Washington, D.C.: Government Printing Office, 1963), pp. 24–25.

serves. Its boundaries were determined by the jurisdictions represented on the commission, and action to revise the boundaries is subject to agreement by the participating units. A government may secede from the commission by merely giving notice of its intention to do so.

In 1963, the agency had a budget of $136,000, about the size of the planning budget for St. Louis, Missouri, or Oakland, California. This money comes from several sources, with the largest donors being the federal and county governments. Contributions from city and state governments are considerably smaller. Private sources contribute even less, while direct taxing power as a source of revenue is almost minimal. The greatest portion of funds goes for staff salaries; less than 10 percent goes for payments to consultants. The agency has a staff of 13, six of whom are full-time professionals.

Most of the revenue is spent on long-range planning operations and general administration. A bare 7 percent goes toward local technical assistance. The planning program concentrates on general planning studies, including population and economic analyses, land-use studies, transportation studies, and some activity in the fields of zoning and subdivision control. The agency has probably prepared some kind of comprehensive development plan. Occasionally, it conducts studies on flood control, storm drainage, water pollution, waste disposal, and other area-wide environmental problems.

The average agency is required by statute to adopt a comprehensive plan, but the statutes do not authorize other area-wide agencies to adopt this plan. Coupled with this limitation, there is a lack of any mandatory requirement for local governments to refer their plans, codes, or capital improvement programs to the metropolitan planning agency for review. However, the agency sometimes reviews or comments on local, state, or federally supported projects within its jurisdiction, the referral being up to the discretion of the submitting body.

Although it does not spend much out of its own pocket on local technical assistance, the agency does provide a wide range of services to local governments, sometimes on a reimbursable basis. Most frequently these services consist of general planning advice and information, although the agency will occasionally prepare a comprehensive plan, review zoning and subdivision cases, or prepare special studies for a locality.

Another important phase of the average metropolitan planning agency's program is public relations. Activities are usually recorded in an annual report. Relations with the press are maintained through the issuance of occasional press releases covering agency highlights, results of studies, and résumés of commission meetings. The agency may also issue a newsletter. The staff is kept busy during the year with numerous speaking engagements before citizen and business groups, and some participation in television or radio programs. Occasionally the agency may hold a conference, sponsor an educational clinic, or prepare an exhibit on metropolitan planning. The agency feels that its chief public support comes from chambers of commerce, citizens' planning and development groups, and the League of Women Voters.

Considerable time is spent by the average agency in assisting and working with other public bodies. Apart from providing certain technical services to local governments, the agency usually maintains some working relationship with regional non-planning units in the area and with state agencies. It generally provides planning advice and information to special districts, among the most important of which are health, recreation, school, sanitary, and water districts. On sporadic occasions, it might even undertake a special study for a particular special district.

Relations with state agencies are uneven. Where a state planning agency exists, it might provide the metropolitan planning agency with data or advice. Rarely is the metropolitan planning agency asked to advise on the state planning program. The average agency does provide other state departments, principally the state highway agency and, to a lesser extent, the state recreation and health agencies, with special kinds of information related to their programs.

The director, when asked to appraise agency weaknesses, points to limited public support for metropolitan planning, insufficient power, and inadequate funds and staff. He fells that the agency's technical program is sound, and that good relationships exist with other governmental units.

29. Who Benefits
from Metropolitan Planning?*

In 1963, the Senate Subcommittee on Intergovernmental Relations contracted with the Joint Center for Urban Studies of the Massachusetts Institute of Technology and Harvard University for a study of the objectives of metropolitan planning, and its status and effectiveness. Although a planning agency generally has only advisory powers, the excerpt from *The Effectiveness of Metropolitan Planning* describes how a planning agency can help to assure the proper development of a metropolitan area by increasing public cognizance and understanding of area-wide problems and bringing local officials together in a quest for their solution. Reading 33 predicts that greater reliance will be placed upon metropolitan planning to facilitate the resolution of area-wide problems.

* From *The Effectiveness of Metropolitan Planning* (Washington, D.C.: Government Printing Office, 1964), pp. 9–20.

. . . The studies and recommendations of metropolitan planning agencies are generally addressed to three levels of government—local, state, and federal— and to the citizens of the metropolitan area at large. These four major clients of metropolitan planning each use planning services in different ways and derive different benefits from them.[1]

LOCAL GOVERNMENT

Metropolitan planning offers local units of government three distinct advantages: general technical assistance, metropolitan studies and projections as background for local decisions, and an opportunity to participate in decisions affecting both the region and the local community.

In many urban areas where metropolitan planning is now under way, the professional staff of the metropolitan agency is called upon for advice and assistance to local communities. Effective local government has come to depend more and more upon technical expertise in such fields as building and housing codes, subdivision regulations, zoning, urban renewal, and the preparation of community master plans. Considerable technical knowledge is required not only for the effective regulation of local development, but also for participation in a number of federal and state programs of assistance to local governments. Most small communities cannot support a technically qualified staff on a permanent basis, but may hire consultants from time to time or may turn to state or metropolitan agencies for help. Many metropolitan planning agencies furnish this type of aid at cost or as an unpaid service, and local governments have been quick to recognize the advantage of having a reservoir of technical skills available to them.

METROPOLITAN BACKGROUND FOR LOCAL DECISIONS

Local plans and decisions affecting community development rest inevitably on estimates of what the future will bring in terms of population, housing demand, industrial growth, and tax base. Planning for school systems, for example, requires projections of school-age population and of local resources that will

---

[1] Other investigators have concentrated their attention on the responsibilities of these clients to assume leadership in seeking solutions to metropolitan problems rather than on the separate benefits derived. See, for example, the Commission on Intergovernmental Relations (Kestnbaum), "A Report to the President for Transmittal to the Congress" (Washington, D.C., 1955), pp. 52–54. An effective statement of the responsibilities in each sphere is presented by the Advisory Commission on Intergovernmental Relations in its report on "Governmental Structure, Organization and Planning in Metropolitan Areas" (Washington, 1961) and in its third annual report (Washington, 1962).

be available to help meet school-bond obligations. These projections must incorporate a view of population growth and change within the metropolitan region. Trends in migration from central cities to suburbs must be studied in order to reach a realistic estimate of future school needs in any particular community; detailed studies of the metropolitan housing market are of great value for local governments that must estimate their own future share of metropolitan population. But few communities can afford to make such studies, or have a technical staff that can do the job. Local economic forecasts also require a realistic estimate of the region's economic prospects, as well as studies of the distribution of industry within the metropolitan area. In the absence of metropolitan economic studies, local estimates are often based mainly on optimistic expectations; the sum of industrial growth charted in local community plans tends to be far in excess of reasonable metropolitan growth prospects. Here, too, the regional studies that are needed are beyond the financial and staff resources of any single community.

In short, informed local decisionmaking requires appraisal of the community's prospects for future growth and change, and these prospects depend upon the future of the metropolitan area. Forecasting the region's future is a complex task involving demographic and economics techniques as well as the skills of land-use planners. No single community is likely to have the funds or staff for such an effort, but all local governments in an area could benefit substantially from a joint project to develop the necessary projections. Metropolitan planning agencies typically carry out studies of this kind, and experience has been that local governments repeatedly request reports and data on regional studies as background for their own planning.

LOCAL PARTICIPATION IN STATE DECISIONS

Local governments also stand to derive another kind of advantage from metropolitan planning: a more effective voice in decisions affecting the region and their own communities. State agencies are the main decisionmakers in such fields as highway location, regulation of commuter railroads, and acquisition of open space for regional parks. Decisions about regional transportation facilities and open space can have a major impact upon the development of a community, by affecting its desirability for residence and industry, and by changing local circulation and opportunities for land development. Local governments often take strong positions on the location of new regional facilities, particularly when these lie within their own boundaries, but communities acting alone and lacking a regional perspective may have little success in arguing their positions with state agencies. If a new highway is to be built, for example, the preferred locations of those communities through which it must pass may add up to a series of ill-matched road fragments, rather than a coherent highway alinement meeting modern standards of design.

If the state is to be given a reasonable alternative to consider, local preferences must be coordinated with one another to produce a consensus that will also allow the facility to function properly. A metropolitan planning agency can take the initiative in eliciting local views, organizing a cooperative effort, and working out the necessary compromises to produce a reasonable plan. The state highway agency itself could, of course, play a similar role, but the metropolitan planning agency is likely to be more sensitive to local views, either through local representation on the planning council, or in any case through its familiarity with the many aspects of metropolitan development aside from the particular facility under consideration by a specialized state agency.

STATE GOVERNMENT

The states also have a stake in metropolitan planning, for they can derive substantial benefits both from the technical studies and the interlocal cooperation that such planning would foster. State legislatures and operating agencies make many decisions affecting metropolitan development, but their decision must often be made without careful consideration of the impact they are likely to have upon the region. Metropolitan planning agencies can serve as staff extensions of state executive agencies and of the state legislature, giving advice on the probable effects upon metropolitan development of such state measures as highway construction, park acquisition, housing programs, and tax policies involving local governments. This type of technical advice is particularly important for the implementation of state policies concerning economic development, education, recreation, transportation, and housing—for such policies must be worked out to an increasing extent within the states' urban areas. As metropolitan planning staffs develop a body of technical studies and projections, they will become valuable adjuncts to state legislative bodies and operating agencies, as well as to local councils and departments.

RESOLVING STATE-LOCAL CONFLICTS

Aside from providing improved information to guide state decisions, metropolitan planning agencies can also promote an informed resolution of conflict between state and local points of view in matters relating to metropolitan development. The problem of arriving at a consensus of local views on the location of new highways has already been mentioned: a metropolitan agency that can take the initiative in lining up local agreements on alternative route alinements will surely facilitate the work of the state highway department. Recent experience in metropolitan Boston illustrates another type of problem to which a metropolitan planning agency would address itself. Rail commuter service on the Old Colony Line of the New Haven Railroad came to a halt several years ago, and the state had to purchase the right-of-way at a low cost for a public transit operation. Several governors and a succession of legislative commissions wrestled with the problem of finding ways to continue service on this line, but the communities to be served were unable to come to an agreement about how to finance a new commuter operation, or how it should be related to the Metropolitan Transit Authority, which operates the network of public bus and rail lines in the Boston area. No solution is yet in sight, and commuters from the area formerly served by the Old Colony Line have switched to the automobile, adding new congestion to the region's overworked highway system. There is no assurance that an effective metropolitan planning organization could have found an acceptable solution, but the skills of a professional planning team would surely have produced a wider exploration of alternatives to consider, and would have furnished considerable assistance to the hard-pressed agencies that were working on this problem.

THE FEDERAL GOVERNMENT

Federal activities in urban areas have increased to the point where the federal government is now a key partner in metropolitan development. The President's budget for 1963 proposed federal expenditures of approximately $4 billion for capital investments under the major community development programs—an amount twice the level of corresponding federal outlays in 1960 and more than four times the 1958 level.[2] A study by the Housing and Home Finance Agency found that in 1962 the programs of 12 federal agencies generated over $100 million in public and private expenditures in the Atlanta metropolitan area alone.[3]

As the United States has become an increasingly urban nation, federal concern for national development has naturally evolved into a series of programs focusing on the metropolitan regions where most Americans live and work, and where the centers of economic activity are located. Federal agencies are heavily involved in metropolitan housing programs, urban renewal, the construction of highways, hospitals, and mass transit lines, airport and harbor development, and a number of other programs that influence the growth of metropolitan areas. Although local and state governments generally initiate and manage these proj-

[2] See Norman Beckman, "Our Federal System and Urban Development," *Journal of the American Institute of Planners,* XXIX (August 1963), 152–167; pp. 155–156.

[3] Statement of Robert C. Weaver, Administrator, Housing and Home Finance Agency, before the U.S. Senate Subcommittee on Intergovernmental Relations, Dec. 14, 1962.

ects, federal agencies must review them to be sure that they meet appropriate standards for federal assistance and that they further the objectives of Congress in establishing federal aid programs. Metropolitan planning can furnish important help in this review of local projects.

ESTABLISHING PROJECT FEASIBILITY

A basic question in reviewing locally proposed projects is that of feasibility: can the project be carried out as planned, within the proposed cost limits? In the case of urban renewal projects, an estimate of feasibility requires a study of the demand for land that is to be made available to private investors. Local renewal authorities are required to conduct such studies, but they frequently concentrate their attention on their own small part of the metropolitan land market. Thus, many renewal projects in the separate communities of a metropolitan region may all count on attracting the same investment capital. In actuality, the amount of investment that will be made in land to be used for new housing or retail outlets will depend upon metropolitan-wide demand for these facilities. If local renewal authorities overlook new investment going on concurrently in other parts of the region, or fail to consider metropolitanwide demand, they can easily overestimate the market for their own land. The many square miles of cleared land standing vacant in renewal areas around the country attest to the prevalence of high hopes among renewal agencies, rather than to the soundness of metropolitan land market studies.[4] Review of such projects by metropolitan planning agencies can supply much of the missing metropolitan perspective, and can alert federal agencies to the fact that the sum of investment anticipated for all proposed projects within an area may be many times greater than the investment capital that is likely to materialize in the entire metropolitan area.

MEETING FEDERAL OBJECTIVES

Another important question in reviewing locally proposed projects is the extent to which they will be used. The volume of traffic that a highway will serve, or the number of visitors who will use a new recreation area, is an important consideration in deciding whether a project is worth while. Here, too,

---

[4] Nationwide information on the reuse of land cleared for urban renewal projects is not readily available, but it is common knowledge that one of the greatest difficulties of urban renewal is to find developers who will rebuild cleared sites. According to a recent study, of the 18,912 acres of land acquired for urban renewal, only 7390 had been resold by the end of 1962. (Gurney Breckenfeld, "The Many-Fingered Federal Puppeteer," *House and Home,* XXIII (June 1963), 118.

the use of a facility can best be predicted on the basis of metropolitanwide studies of traffic patterns and recreation trends. Federal agencies are far removed from the scene, and seldom have the time or staff to conduct their own studies of the metropolitan area. Local authorities, on the other hand, seldom take the entire metropolitan area as their province to study; their legal responsibilities are to local governments, and not to the entire area. Federal highway legislation recognizes the significance of metropolitanwide traffic patterns and requires comprehensive transportation plans for whole urban areas. Metropolitan planning agencies will be particularly well qualified to conduct such studies, not only for transportation but also for the many other facilities for which federal aid is available.

The effects of federally aided projects upon the metropolitan region are also relevant in a review of local proposals; certain effects may defeat the objectives of the federal programs that are involved. Federal aid for urban renewal, for example, has as one of its main purposes the elimination of slums and the improvement of housing conditions. To safeguard these aims, federal law and administrative policy require that people displaced from renewal areas must be relocated in sound housing. Local renewal authorities must furnish evidence that decent housing is available for relocation within the metropolitan area, but the reports of local authorities are often poor substitutes for a study of the metropolitanwide housing market. Various local agencies may each lay claim to the same vacancies as resources for relocation; vacant units within one locality may be counted as relocation reserves in the reports of several different renewal authorities. In addition, unless the total metropolitan housing demand is taken into consideration, a simple count of vacancies may fail to reveal that families other than those to be displaced by urban renewal are likely to occupy them. It has become increasingly clear from a series of relocation studies that urban renewal often shifts slums rather than eliminating them, clearing old housing within project areas but causing overcrowding or the occupancy of substandard housing elsewhere in the region.[5] Metropolitan housing studies, which should be conducted as part of the work program of a metropolitan planning agency, would make possible a more realistic overall assessment of an area's housing resources, and would furnish the basis for a comprehensive attack on the problems of slums. Particular renewal projects could be reviewed in the light of such studies, and modifications could be indicated where the metropolitan picture reveals inadequacies in the supply of relocation housing.

[5] See Peter Marris, "A Report on Urban Renewal in the United States," in the *Urban Condition,* ed. Leonard J. Duhl (New York: Basic Books, 1963), pp. 113–134; and U.S. Commission on Civil Rights 1961 Report, "Housing" (Washington, 1961), pp. 89–92, 143–144, 148.

A metropolitan planning agency can also serve as a useful clearinghouse in bringing about greater coordination of federal programs within the area. Without effective coordination, different federal agencies may work at cross-purposes in metropolitan development. Federal housing programs that promote suburban growth may at the same time overload federally aided highways, or, by failing to take advantage of locations where newly planned highways can handle the traffic effectively, housing programs may create premature demands for additional federal highway aid. A planning agency, by calling attention to these effects of federal programs, could bring about greater economy in the administration of these programs, with increased local and federal benefits.

COORDINATING FEDERAL AND LOCAL ACTION

Aside from making possible a more sensitive federal review of local projects, metropolitan planning can provide a number of other benefits that will help insure optimum use of federal aid. The success of federally aided projects often depends in part upon action by a number of local governments in guiding future development of the metropolitan area, but in the absence of metropolitan planning there is usually no provision for coordinating local action for this purpose. A new highway, for example, will generally pass through many municipalities within an urban region; each of these municipalities can influence the development that occurs along the highway by means of zoning and other local measures. If locations near the highway prove attractive for industry, local communities may all stimulate the development of industry along the highway. Industrial plants generate traffic, and the result of unchecked industrial development may be to overcrowd the highway so that it no longer serves the purposes for which it was intended, while other parts of the highway system remain under-utilized. One of the responsibilities of a metropolitan planning agency would be to study the impact and the use of major new facilities, and to make local governments aware of the effects their own actions have on the use of the region's resources and services.

Metropolitan planning can help bring about a coordination of federally aided projects with local actions of many kinds. One important aspect of this coordination is to be sure that locally sponsored projects do not work at cross-purposes with federally aided undertakings. Improper planning of local streets, for example, can clog the interchanges of federally aided highways with traffic unable to enter or leave the highway at adequate speeds. Many facilities receiving federal aid require adjustment of the local circulation system to provide adequate access. Other local regulatory action may also be desirable to protect the investment in new facilities; special zoning may be required to keep tall structures out of approach zones to airports, or to regulate new development close to federal highway interchanges. The problem of protecting interchange areas has already given rise to legislation proposed in the Pennsylvania legislature (senate bill 542, 1963 session, Local Government Highway Interchange Protection Act). This bill would authorize local governments to adopt ordinances which would apply only to areas around the interchanges of local roads with major highways, or to modify existing local zoning to provide for interchange protection by appropriate regulation of land uses and establishment of setback lines. Where a local government fails to establish an interchange ordinance, a newly created state interchange protection commission will administer such an ordinance.

Metropolitan planning agencies would act in similar situations, serving as channels of communication between federal bodies and local governments, assisting in the review of locally proposed projects, and suggesting appropriate local action to accompany federal investment in community facilities.

Aside from the coordination of projects, metropolitan planning can contribute to the federal interest in urban development by helping to coordinate the operating policies of federal agencies with those of local governments. Communities often follow established policies with respect to assessments, water and sewer extensions, street improvements, and the operation of school and recreation systems—all of which have considerable influence on the pattern of development. Federal agencies also follow established policies concerning the issuance of mortgage insurance, the provision of grants and loans for public works, and the conservation of land and water resources—which also have considerable impact on the development of the same communities. The effects of both sets of policies will of course be significantly greater if they work jointly toward particular objectives in community development than if they follow independent guidelines. A recent conference called by the Administrator of the HHFA produced many suggestions for the codifying of such policies into an "urban development policies instrument," to insure that all relevant federal and state programs are coordinated with local policies at the point of impact in local areas.[6]

The work program of a metropolitan planning agency should include a coordinating role in bringing local policies affecting land development into harmony with one another within a metropolitan area, and in promoting agreement with federal policies affecting the development of the same area. The metropolitan planning agency can also pinpoint bottlenecks which obstruct sound development and help bring joint local-federal programs to bear upon their

[6] F. Stuart Chapin, Jr., "Taking Stock of Techniques for Shaping Urban Growth," *Journal of the American Institute of Planners,* XXIX (May 1963), pp. 76–86. This paper was given originally at the 1962 HHFA Administrator's Conference on Problems and Needs of Urban Expansion.

removal. Effective coordination will require reaching a consensus on the desired pattern of development, and this consensus should ultimately be reflected in a metropolitan plan. Laying the groundwork will be difficult, but the planning agency would begin consultations with local governments, as well as with federal and state agencies, in an early stage of its operations. In the absence of a metropolitan planning agency, consultations are likely to be haphazard and are likely to deal mainly with single programs rather than with the entire range of relevant policies. Both the comprehensiveness of metropolitan planning and the clear assignment of responsibility for initiating consultations to the metropolitan agency, will provide a means of making federal policies more effective by relating them to the shared objectives of all levels of government in shaping the growth of metropolitan areas.

THE METROPOLITAN AREA

The people living and working in a metropolitan area will derive obvious benefits from the increased effectiveness of federal, state, and local governments and the private sector in making decisions that affect metropolitan development. The benefits are not merely those of more efficient government and more informed decisionmaking, however; they also include the many advantages of making metropolitan development subject to conscious public choices, rather than a byproduct of the operations of many independent governments and public agencies.

Much debate has recently been generated about the advantages and shortcomings of the new patterns that are now emerging in our metropolitan regions, with the spread of low-density suburban housing, the decentralization of employment and retailing, the shift from public transportation to the private automobile, and the rapid consumption of open space for urban development. Critics have pointed to the high cost of this prevalent form of metropolitan growth, with huge investments in roads, schools, and utilities in the suburbs while existing facilities in the central cities are underutilized. Economic studies of the New York metropolitan region[7] indicate that under present growth patterns, each new household in the region in the next 20 years will require a minimum investment of $16,800 for capital facilities, not counting private utility investments; the total required for all new households from 1960–1985 is expected to be more than $28 billion. Highways are by far the most expensive item in these estimates: their cost per additional household amounts to $7350 of the total $16,800. More compact patterns of development could save substantially

[7] These studies are reported in Regional Plan Association, Bulletin 100, "Spread City" (September 1962).

on capital costs simply by reducing the need for new highways, in addition to other possible savings that would result from greater use of existing facilities.

Other interpreters of metropolitan development maintain that current growth patterns are worth their high cost—that they meet the preference of most metropolitan citizens and produce an environment satisfactory to them. Raymond Vernon[8] has pointed out that middle-income families today, with considerable spending power at their disposal, are eager to satisfy a hunger for land in quarter-acre, half-acre, and even larger lots for new single-family homes. Although both direct and indirect costs are high, and long commuting is frequently necessary, the majority of families nevertheless take satisfaction in the progress and improvement they have made by leaving the more crowded living conditions of the inner cities. Edward C. Banfield and Morton Grodzins, in their study of government and housing in metropolitan areas,[9] also grant that present suburban growth is expensive and could be cheaper if governments in metropolitan areas acted jointly to plan for growth and services. But they, too, see advantages and satisfactions in the present system of growth: Because development controls and service policies are established independently by each local government, the consumer finds a wide range of alternatives to choose from. He can spend his housing dollars in a community where service levels and taxes are high, where they are both low, where building codes permit cheap types of construction, or where they are more restrictive. If people are willing to pay an added cost to live in an independent suburb that follows its own particular policies, Banfield and Grodzins see no reason to object. They pose only two questions: Are the people who live in such communities actually bearing all of the extra costs, and are they aware of them? The projections and cost estimates that go into a metropolitan planning program would certainly increase public awareness of the cost of present development patterns, and would provide a basis for more informed decisions by both citizens and governments.

Economic questions are not the only issues in the present debate about metropolitan development in the United States. Banfield and Grodzins see the values of autonomy, diversity, and maximum individual choice in the diffused decision-making that now determines how our urban regions grow. Critics of this system, such as Luther Gulick[10] and Robert C. Wood,[11] center their argument on the

[8] Raymond Vernon, "The Myth and Reality of Our Urban Problems" (Cambridge, Mass.: Joint Center for Urban Studies of Massachusetts Institute of Technology and Harvard University, 1962).

[9] Edward C. Banfield and Morton Grodzins, "Government and Housing in Metropolitan Areas" (New York: McGraw-Hill, 1958).

[10] Luther H. Gulick, "The Metropolitan Problem and American Ideas" (New York: Alfred A. Knopf, 1962).

[11] Robert C. Wood, "Suburbia: Its People and Their Politics" (Boston: Houghton

inability of decentralized decisions either to realize the full potential of what the metropolitan environment might become, or to cope with the many un-pleasant byproducts of urban growth that require concerted action for their solution: slums, traffic congestion, air and water pollution, inadequate parks, racial and economic segregation. As Wood has described the metropolitan scene, individualism shades easily into self-interest and a failure to come to grips with common problems: "The sense of responsibility of freemen to one another and the recognition of common purposes that constitute a persuasive part of the American creed are lost, and the spectacle ensues of a simple scramble to the top for the best market baskets of local government services."[12]

PUBLIC CHOICES IN METROPOLITAN DEVELOPMENT

Conflicting views about the merits of current metropolitan growth patterns have never been tested against actual public opinion; the conditions that produce present patterns are, by and large, not now subject to effective citizen control. Metropolitan planning may or may not work to alter the present directions of metropolitan growth, but it will work to coordinate independent decisions that affect this growth, and it will promote joint action to deal with metropolitan problems. Its function will be one of presenting the issues to governmental bodies, stimulating a public discussion of alternative patterns of development, and bringing the entire subject of metropolitan growth within the scope of gov-ernmental policy decisions. The citizens of a metropolitan area can have a voice in the area's development as their governmental representatives come to grips with the choices that they can exercise through joint public action to shape the nature of urban development. Nongovernmental interest groups—chambers of commerce, citizen housing associations, and the many civic groups that organize to have a voice in government decisions—would also enter the discussion of what kind of metropolitan area would be most desirable, and how it might be achieved.

The contributions of metropolitan planning to the metropolitan area itself would consist of three major activities. First, the planning agency would work to make public action more effective in influencing the development of the urban area. This work will consist largely of taking the lead in setting up con-sultation between governments and public agencies that can have considerable impact on the region's growth if they coordinate their policies and work for mutually acceptable objectives. Second, the metropolitan planning agency would provide an informed basis for making decisions about the area. It would carry

Mifflin, 1958); and Robert C. Wood, "Metropolis Against Itself" (New York: Committee for Economic Development, 1959).

[12] Robert C. Wood, "Suburbia: Its People and Their Politics," p. 288.

out studies and projections of the region's future potentialities, forecast the impact of particular actions and policies, suggest ways of coping with problems, and present alternative patterns of development for the decision of local, state, and federal governments. Private developers, too, armed with such information, would be able to make more rational plans for current and future investments. And third, the planning agency could help bring private citizens into the decisionmaking process, by making them aware of metropolitan problems and soliciting their views on possible solutions. An effective metropolitan planning agency would give the urban citizen opportunities to make choices about his future environment, rather than leave these choices to the separate operational decisions of local governments and public agencies that typically focus on their own immediate objectives rather than on the future of the metropolitan region.

THE URBAN FUTURE WITHOUT EFFECTIVE METROPOLITAN PLANNING

The current development of urban regions has proceeded in the absence of effective metropolitan planning. The results have been far from disastrous: essential services have been provided, housing has been built to take care of expanding population, businesses and industries have grown, and incomes have risen. State governments and special metropolitan districts and authorities have been active in building highways assuring adequate water supplies and sewage disposal, improving harbors and airports, and operating park systems. The American governmental system has indeed responded to the most serious challenges of urban growth, and a major part of this response has been increasing federal assistance in community development. As a result, the most pressing needs have been met, and few real crises have been allowed to develop.

Part of this picture of urban growth—though not yet a very important part—has been the start of metropolitan planning. . . . it is clear that present efforts, while commendable in themselves, are mostly too new and too limited to have had much effect on the patterns of metropolitan growth. There are a few noteworthy exceptions, such as the Regional Plan Association in New York. A privately supported civic association, it has successfully promoted a pioneer plan for the New York region prepared in 1929, and has recently sponsored a major research project, the New York Metropolitan Region Study, with support from the Ford and Rockefeller Foundations. One or two other regions have also had well-supported and impressive metropolitan planning efforts, but the typical metropolitan planning agency has only a small staff and inadequate resources to conduct necessary research, prepare plans, or to speak effectively for metropolitan interests when development decisions are made.

The shortcomings of our present system of urban development have not been disastrous, but they have nevertheless been serious. Metropolitan governmental districts and authorities that were created to provide specific services generally perform well in the functional areas for which they have responsibility, but many have proven to be unresponsive to political control by metropolitan area residents, and unwilling to coordinate their programs with those of other government agencies. Thus, highway authorities and mass transit authorities often pursue unrelated policies, with the result that the overall transportation needs of the area are poorly served.[13]

The pressures of metropolitan growth are unlikely to diminish. Most likely we shall continue to cope with them by a series of improvised governmental arrangements that will provide necessary services and forestall major crises. But unless we strengthen means for metropolitanwide policymaking and governmental coordination—such as more effective metropolitan planning—this "muddling through" approach will leave us with a mounting accumulation of unsolved problems, and with metropolitan areas that will fall far short of the potential that they could realize, despite the very high costs of our urban growth.

Metropolitan planning agencies that are inadequately equipped to work on the most difficult problems will make some contribution toward solving less complicated and less controversial ones. Such agencies can be expected to take a part in the advance planning of some water and sewer systems, for example, and in identifying areas suitable for regional parks. Problems of traffic congestion, mass transportation, industrial development, housing, and urban renewal require more elaborate studies and involve more sensitive issues. These are the problems least susceptible to attack by the "muddling through" system of metropolitan development.

In an interview conducted as part of this study, an Atlanta journalist pointed to this kind of shortcoming in the present program of the Atlanta Metropolitan Planning Commission. He felt that the commission should tackle some of the most difficult regional problems, particularly the problem of finding adequate living space for the Negro population. This arose from a conviction that the problem will have to be approached regionally, because housing is needed in outlying areas as well as in the central city.

When Mayor Frank P. Zeidler, of Milwaukee, was once asked how the fragmentation of government in metropolitan areas affects the housing situation, he replied in a similar way:

> The housing problem is in the central core of the cites. Here the people are packed in densities upwards of 10,000 persons per square mile and in

---

[13] The limitations of metropolitan governmental districts are discussed in general terms in John C. Bollens, "Special District Governments in the United States" (Berkeley: University of California Press, 1961), pp. 88–92; and with specific reference to the New York region in Robert C. Wood, "1,400 Governments" (Cambridge: Harvard University Press, 1961), pp. 114–172.

many cites with densities many times that. As the houses deteriorate there is no method to move the people around and clear the sites.

The cites are surrounded by suburbs with zoning restrictions that restrict residence to the upper income groups or that restrict the number of families per acre. Consequently, the pressure between the masses of people in the city seeking to go outward and the suburb exclusiveness creates a continual area of conflict.

The central cities contain the minority groups which the suburbs fiercely resist. The present types of minorities resisted are Negroes, Puerto Ricans, and Mexicans.

The minority groups entering the big cities for work cannot find sufficient living space and crowd into the slum areas which are the only places that will receive them. Here they are exploited by high rents for dwellings which are not repaired by rapacious landlords. In addition, families crowd in and overuse the structures so that the life expectancy of the structure is greatly diminished. The patterns of living of many minority families tend to aggravate the unsanitary and dilapidated conditions of living.[14]

Thus the by-products of urban development by independent decisionmaking may include a denial of adequate housing opportunities for many citizens. Metropolitan planning can promise no quick solution to such a problem, but it is likely to increase public recognition of the issues involved, and to bring together government officials in a search for regional solutions.

Most of the accumulating metropolitan problems are likely to consist of inconveniences, inefficiencies, and unrealized opportunities. Yet, as population pressures continue to mount in urban areas, and as demands for land and services increase, new areas of social conflict could develop and pose more critical challenges for public policy. In either event, an early strengthening of metropolitan planning would provide a means for recognizing and anticipating many problems, for taking joint action to deal with them, and for extending public policy beyond the level of alleviating problems and into the realm of working to achieve positive goals in metropolitan development. . . .

[14] Quoted in Banfield and Grodzins "Government and Housing in Metropolitan Areas," pp. 85–86.

30. The Lakewood Plan*

ROBERT O. WARREN

In Reading 21, Robert O. Warren records the development of Los Angeles County as a producer of Municipal services. In this reading he describes the services offered by Los Angeles County to contract cities— the Lakewood Plan—and points out that a city has several alternatives to entering into a contract with the county. The city can provide its own services, purchase services from another city, enter into a contract with a private firm for the provision of services, or join a special service district. Consequently, a city is in a position to bargain with the county and considerable bargaining occurs.

The interpretations of the contract system presented here can be no more than hypotheses at this stage and should be considered as such.

BARGAINING, ACCOMMODATION AND MARKET PRESSURES

Los Angeles County represents only one of several options available to a city for the production of public goods and services. Apart from the County, a contract city can potentially produce services itself; purchase them from another jurisdiction, such as a municipality; enter into a joint management arrangement; and, in some instances, participate in a self-governing special district or buy services from a private firm. In the last case, firms offer such services as animal regulation, engineering, planning and street sweeping.

The fact that a contract city has the legal authority to withdraw from service agreements with the County does not mean that a city actually can withdraw or, if it can, that it will. There is a consensus among County and city administrators that certain Lakewood Plan cities have such marginal tax bases that the relative capital and operating costs of establishing municipal departments for many services would be unacceptable to the community. Conversely, in other cities, the potential costs of exit from County services are far less prohibitive. It is primarily these units that tend to behave competitively in the sense of evaluating

* From *Government in Metropolitan Areas: A Reappraisal of Fractionated Political Organization* (Davis, Calif.: Institute of Governmental Affairs, University of California, 1966), pp. 224–33. Footnotes in original omitted.

County services against alternatives and bargaining for modifications in service arrangements and prices. As will be seen, the exposure of the County to market-like forces does not require that all municipal purchasers act competitively, but only that such a policy is pursued by some.

Contract cities usually take two types of costs into account in judging the County as a producer. All things equal, a community will seek the lowest economic cost for obtaining a service at a stipulated level. This is basically a question of price and involves quantifiable variables. All things, however, are not always equal. City decision-makers also give weight to social costs which involve values that are presently difficult or impossible to quantify. In planning, for example, a city might look upon the handling of most contracts with local residents by County rather than city personnel as a cost. Whether or not this cost is balanced by the costs or values foregone of not contracting for the service will determine if the County is retained.

In attempting to evaluate market choices, Lakewood Plan cities can seek information about production costs from the County and often have a price or unit cost available for comparing the County against other arrangements. At the same time, whatever the response of the County in cost and performance reporting, cities have an independent capacity to develop and interpret data. Benefit-cost studies can be made through their administrative staffs or hired consultants. At a more gross level, the charges for a County service can be compared with the estimated costs of production in traditionally organized cities of similar size and characteristics. Bids from private firms also can provide a measure against County prices.

A city that wishes to modify the charges for a County service faces a relatively inflexible pricing system. By law, the County is required to charge an amount that will cover all production costs. But even with this constraint, there are possibilities for lowering a price. This can result from greater production efficiency induced by competition in general or from bargaining for the elimination of specific cost factors. Similarly, short of withdrawal, cities can seek the reallocation of the component parts of a service between the County and municipality as a means of reducing economic or social costs. This latter type of negotiated change is illustrated in several modifications made by the Road Department in the issuance of street construction permits.

The Department initially issued permits and inspected street construction work as a single package. However, one city manager concluded that the service would be more responsive to local needs if permits were issued by the city, but inspection was continued by the Road Department. Under existing arrangements, there were reporting problems, and individuals desiring permits were required to travel to downtown Los Angeles, often a considerable distance, where permits were issued by the County.

The immediate response to the proposal at lower levels of the Department was negative on the claim that it was administratively unfeasible to separate the issuing of permits from inspection as well as undesirable for control purposes. When no modification could be obtained the matter was taken to the County-City Coordinator's office by the city. The Coordinator has no authority to direct a department to take any action, but can raise policy issues with agency leadership and exercise some degree of informal influence. In subsequent negotiations, with the Coordinator favorably disposed toward the city's position, the top level of the Road Department was more responsive to the idea than lower echelons had been and an adjustment was made. However, this new arrangement presented other problems for cities.

After several municipalities had adopted the innovation, it was found that the low volume of permit requests made the cost of processing applications quite high for a city. A compromise was finally worked out whereby a city can issue permit applications and collect the fees while the County processes the requests and mails the approved permit to the resident.

Road Department administrators feel that even if cities follow this plan they will have greater expenses than those that leave both functions with the County. However, it is conceded that individuals are saved from extended trips to Departmental offices, and that a city is allowed better control over information and relations with local residents.

This pattern of interaction suggests that the Coordinator's office is a potential source of influence upon operating agencies for at least a re-examination of long established and unquestioned procedures. In this sense, the office serves as an agent to facilitate experimentation which otherwise might be viewed as unfeasible or undesirable within the value framework of a departmental bureaucracy.

The components of other services have been divided between the County and cities with less procedural problems. In planning, some cities employ their own personnel for handling requests for zoning changes, public information contracts and routine staff work for city planning commissions, while utilizing the Regional Planning Commission for specialized studies and master plan work. Several municipalities, especially larger ones, have found that local production of certain public works functions is less costly than contracting with the County. Thus, one city has set up a Department of Public Works which performs routine street maintenance, curb repairs, street sweeping and some engineering functions, but obtains building inspection, major engineering work and traffic signal maintenance from the County.

Another consequence of competition for the County involves pricing policy. The Road Department again provides an example with its street sweeping contract service to cities. As of 1963, eleven of the twenty-nine post-1950 cities utilized either private firms or had decided to provide street sweeping through local production. Some dissatisfaction with the price of Road Department developed in Lakewood soon after incorporation. A bid was obtained from a private firm, but County service was continued. In 1956, Frank Aleshire, then City Manager of La Puente, stated that he could not get adequate cost data from the Road Department in terms of either curb-mile or man-hour cost units and, subsequently, the City contracted with a private firm. The City of Paramount also contracted with a private firm on the grounds that reliable cost estimates could not be obtained from the County.

Another alternative was utilized in the City of Norwalk. The City Administrator called for bids on street sweeping, and also developed an estimate of the costs of local production. Five bids by private firms ranged from $44,000 to $56,000 annually; the County estimate was $62,000; and the figure for Norwalk to produce the services was $32,000. Norwalk chose the last alternative.

In discussing these withdrawals Road Department Officials have emphasized that they are not in competition with cities or private firms for street sweeping contracts. It is pointed out that, whereas a private company can make a firm bid, the Department can only make estimates which might be subject to revision in order to recapture full costs as the law requires. County cost estimates are based on the productive work-hour unit rather than on a curb-mile unit, which some city administrators prefer. This unit is justified on the grounds that the Department is concerned with the measurement of costs for cleaning streets rather than for "one-run" sweeps.

Even with the loss of some cities the Road Department has retained eighteen post-1950 communities for street sweeping on a contract basis and, in the process, has made certain responses to its competitive position. A flat price for street sweeping has been replaced and charges are now broken down on the basis of component operations so that a municipality may accept or decline some of the more specialized and consequently more costly elements. This has allowed a city several price options. The Department has also installed improved odometers and time meters on its equipment to provide more precise data upon which to base cost estimates for services to cities.

These modifications apparently have had the effect of making the Department's prices more competitive. A private firm has periodically submitted bids to the City of Lakewood. In a 1958 evaluation of the County's charges by the City, they were found to be lower than those proposed by the private bidder. But in reporting on the subject to the City Council, the City Administrator commented that, "We feel the very fact that the Dickson Company is in the field has had a tremendous effect on the County operation and it has greatly improved." . . .

The bargaining power of a city to obtain modifications in service arrangements necessarily differs with the degree to which a county agency finds a withdrawal undesirable. This is particularly true when the matter at issue involves basic departmental policy. For example, prior to 1959 several cities un-successfully sought to reduce the cost of law enforcement by modifying the unit purchased. The standard unit which the Sheriff offered was a one-man patrol car during the daylight shift, and a two-man car for the remainder of a twenty-four hour period. Presuming no flexibility in the price, charges could still be reduced by lowering production costs. With this intent, proposals were made by cities to purchase the services of vehicles with one rather than two deputies for the twenty-four hour period, thereby cutting labor costs by approximately one-half.

Such requests ran counter to County policy and were initially rejected. Experiments had been made with one-man patrol cars in the early 1950's, but the results were found to be unsatisfactory from an enforcement point of view. However, a major policy change was eventually made in the face of the possible contract termination by the large and strategically located City of Norwalk.

In June of 1958, the Norwalk City Council voted to extend the Sheriff's contract for only six months, pending a re-evaluation of law enforcement al-ternatives. The City Administrator strongly favored a city police department on the grounds that such a move would give more responsive and less costly protection to the community. A private firm was hired to make a survey of existing service levels and costs and the estimated costs of operating a pro-fessionally adequate city police department.

The survey report was issued in November, 1958. It concluded that charges for law enforcement by the County for the equivalent of a sixty-seven man police department would be $423,360 annually, and that a comparable city force of sixty-nine employees would cost approximately $665,000 per year. However, no recommendation was made and it was pointed out that the cost figures did not take into account the questions of quality, responsiveness and local preferences.

At the time the withdrawal was being discussed, the Norwalk Sheriff's Station served as headquarters for a Patrol Division which contained 62.54 square miles and a total population of 240,546, including the contract cities of Bellflower, Dairy Valley, Lakewood, Paramount, Pico Rivera, and Santa Fe Springs. Sheriff's officials looked upon the possible withdrawal not only as likely to create serious operational problems, but also as a threat to the organi-zation's commitment to maintain its contract cities and to the development of a consolidated county-wide system of law enforcement. There was a fear that a "domino-effect" might result, with other cities following suit, if one large municipality were to end its contract.

In describing the agency's view of the Lakewood Plan, one official states that:

> In April, 1954, when the first Contract Law Enforcement Services of the Sheriff's were offered to Lakewood, the eyes of public servants and taxpayers alike focused on the operation of the experimental plan. With specific

reference to law enforcement, much of the success in Lakewood and other contract cities is due to the fact that the Sheriff's personnel wanted the plan to work.

The goal of the Sheriff's Department to retain its municipal buyers is closely related to a belief that a unified system of law enforcement is desirable for the total county area. One study indicates that, "County officials concerned with Contract Law Enforcement are of the opinion that eventual consolidation of all law enforcement services in Los Angeles County will result."

Within this set of values, the potential loss of Norwalk was viewed as a "basic test" for the future of the Sheriff's role in Lakewood Plan and the region. After a series of vacillations on the part of the Norwalk City Council, a decision was made, in the first part of 1959, to continue with the Sheriff. The patterns of influence, which affected this decision are complex and have not been adequately studied. However, it can be indicated that the County was actively involved in formal negotiations to maintain the contract service.

The City of Norwalk was able to gain a major policy concession concerning the use of one-man patrol cars in renegotiating its contract. During the early part of 1959, a series of meetings were held between the City Administrator and representatives of the Sheriff and the County-City Coordinator in which the municipality sought greater flexibility in the type of patrol car unit it could purchase. One county official recounts that the Department was able to "salvage" its contract with Norwalk:

> . . . through initiating an alternative plan, after an infinite number of meetings and newspaper battles. The basic difference was the provision of one-man traffic units instead of two-man traffic cars.

According to the Norwalk City Administrator, the new arrangement allowed the City to purchase a slightly higher level of service for 1959-1960 at $37,000 less than had been paid for law enforcement the previous year. This was accomplished by making greater use of one-man cars for service. The Sheriff agreed to allow the use of these units around the clock, provided that a basic number of two-man cars was utilized in non-daylight shifts.

Along with an economic saving, the City Administrator claims that communication between himself and the Station Commander has improved, and that more attention is now paid to Norwalk as a community rather than simply as a part of a service area. During the withdrawal controversy, the Sheriff's Department adopted a policy that all County patrolmen serving Norwalk would be residents of the City, and the Station Commander emphasized that:

> . . . although the men are working for the County, they definitely will have the community's interest at heart not only from the standpoint of trying to be good lawmen, but also because they reside and have civic pride and interest in Norwalk.

These examples of bargaining and accommodation indicate that the County has had to make accommodations to subsets of consumers. However, there is no guarantee that the County can or would be willing to take account of all contract city preferences. Cases also exist of cities withdrawing from County service arrangements. These instances provide some indications of the conditions under which stress and breaks can occur in this voluntary relationship.

TABLE 1

MAJOR COUNTY SERVICES TO POST–1950 CITIES*

DEPARTMENT OR DISTRICT	CITIES (29)
District Attorney	
City Prosecuting Services	29
Engineer	
Building Inspection Services	25
Engineering Staff Services	27
Industrial Waste Regulation	24
County Fire Department	
Fire Protection	27
Health Department	
State Health Law Enforcement	29
City Health Ordinance Enforcement	28
County Public Library	
Library Services	21
Pound Department	
Animal Regulation	27
Regional Planning Commission	
Planning and Zoning Services	19
Road Department	
Street Maintenance and Construction	26
Bridge Maintenance	24
Street Light Maintenance	24
Street Sweeping	18
Traffic Signal Maintenance	27
Traffic Striping and Marking	23
Sheriff	
Law Enforcement Services	26
Traffic Enforcement	24

* Figures from *Services Provided to Cities by the County of Los Angeles, July 1, 1963.*

CORE LAKEWOOD SERVICES AND PROBLEMS OF STABILITY

A review of the major municipal services produced by the County for post-1950 cities is contained in Table 1. In only three instances, library, planning and street sweeping, do fewer than twenty-three of the twenty-nine cities obtain these services from the County. However, County officials tend to view the viability of the Lakewood Plan in terms of the mix of services it produces for cities rather than the number. On this basis, the Fire and Sheriff's departments and the Library are considered to be core components and the loss of municipal customers from these functions is looked upon as potentially threatening to the County's general position.

Thus far the County Public Library has proven to be the most vulnerable of these three services to the loss of municipal clientele. Six new cities have set up local libraries and a number of other district members have considered similar action. The withdrawals, for the most part, reflect tendencies which were apparent in the decisions of Signal Hill and Vernon to leave the district in an earlier period. Five of the cities have predominately industrial or agricultural land use patterns. As indicated in Table 2, they have well above average assessed valuations and relatively small populations. The income redistribution effect of the district's tax structure was the primary motivation for utilizing other means of production. Local property within these cities, subject to the district's uniform property tax, contributed amounts well in excess of the value of services received by the communities.

. . . The difference between the revenue contributed and the value of services received in each of these communities was so great that virtually no ground

TABLE 2

POST–1950 CITIES WITHDRAWING
FROM LOS ANGELES COUNTY PUBLIC LIBRARY

CITIES	POPULATION*	PER CAPITA ASSESSED VALUATION
Commerce	9,555	$25,709
Dairy Valley	3,508	5,954
Industry	778	54,868
Irwindale	1,518	11,542
Santa Fe Springs	16,342	5,218
Downey	82,505	1,887

* Source: U. S. Bureau of the Census.

existed for accommodation. The County could not find an acceptable alternative basis for allocating costs and the cities would not agree to the benefit-cost discrepancy inherent in the district's uniform tax levy.

In spite of the loss of these municipalities, the Library has retained twenty-one of the twenty-seven contract cities it served as unincorporated territory. But even apart from the extreme benefit-cost gaps in the above cases, the County has faced a general problem of justifying the tax costs of district membership to other municipalities. A particular difficulty has existed in identifying and communicating the value of indirect benefits to cities.

31. Cooperation in Metropolitan Areas through Councils of Government*

JOHN K. PARKER

John K. Parker, manager of the Systems Division at the Fels Institute of Local and State Government of the University of Pennsylvania, has drawn a composite picture of the organization and functions of a metropolitan council of governments based upon a study of seven councils in the United States. Parker summarizes the advantages and disadvantages of a council, and concludes it is the only practical means by which officials of the various governmental units collectively can guide the development of a metropolitan area and resolve its problems. Reading 33 generally agrees with this conclusion.

ORGANIZATION OF COUNCILS

A summary of the findings of a recent study of the seven existing councils of governments will provide a general understanding of how these cooperative mechanisms are organized and how they function. For convenience, the results of the study are summarized in the form of a typical or "model" council of governments.

* *Public Management,* October 1963, pp. 223–25.

AREA CHARACTERISTICS

The model council may be located in a metropolitan area of any size. The number of counties, municipalities, inhabitants, and square miles encompassed may vary, as may the number of states involved. (Present councils range from 150,000 people living in one city and two counties to 18,000,000 people living in 16 major cities and 21 counties in three states.)

MEMBERSHIP, PURPOSES, AND POWERS

The model council is composed of an equal number of members of the governing bodies of each of the counties and municipalities in the metropolitan area. Affiliation and withdrawal is by resolution of each local governing body. The purpose of the model council is to study and determine means of solution of area-wide problems of common concern to local governments and, generally, to promote intergovernmental cooperation. The model council is an advisory body which has power only to recommend action. Each member government must itself decide to act (or not act) in accordance with the recommendations.

INTERNAL ORGANIZATION

In addition to the general membership which meets semiannually, the model council has an executive committee which meets monthly. The executive committee appoints standing policy committees and takes action as empowered by the general membership. The executive committee is composed of one representative of each county, each major city, and of the smaller municipalities as a group.

Policy committees are organized for each major functional interest of the model council (transportation, planning, etc.). At least one technical advisory group (TAG) assists each policy committee. TAG's are composed of administrative and technical officials of local governments, state and federal agencies, and other persons whose organizations or personal qualifications may contribute to solution of problems under study. TAG's are vital to the functioning of the model council. They not only provide expert knowledge to aid policy committees in their studies but also enhance continuing administrative cooperation.

STAFF SERVICES

The staff of the model council consists of an executive director, an assistant, and a secretary. The staff ensures effective communications among members and committees, performs specialized research, handles correspondence, provides administrative services to committees, and takes action as directed to assist in carrying out programs of the council.

Financing is by voluntary contributions of member governments assessed on the basis of population. Annual costs are approximately one cent per capita, depending on the size of the area.

PROGRAMS

The model council's programs will change as various problems become of greater or lesser interest to member governments. Relatively permanent programs include transportation, planning, parks and open-space acquisition, public safety, air and water pollution abatement, uniform codes and standards, and government operations and research.

IMPLEMENTING RECOMMENDATIONS

The major means by which the model council implements recommendations is through joint cooperative action by all or most of the local governments in the metropolitan area. Cooperative action is facilitated as both the elected and appointed officials of the governments concerned have participated in developing the recommended course of action.

The ability of the model council to "speak with one voice" for the metropolitan area also enhances cooperation from state and federal agencies and legislatures, as does the participation of state and federal agency officials in the work of the technical advisory groups.

No single "model" council of governments will meet the needs of all metropolitan areas. Of the present councils of governments, those in the larger metropolitan areas most closely resemble the "model" council just described. These include the Supervisor's Inter-County Committee in the Detroit region, the Association of Bay Area Governments in the San Francisco Bay Area, the Metropolitan Regional Council in the New York region, the Regional Conference of Elected Officials in the tri-state Philadelphia region, and the Metropolitan Washington Council of Governments in the National Capital area. It is interesting to note that only the Detroit council currently enjoys the active participation of all the counties in the area. While participation of all eligible governments is the goal of each council, it is not essential for effective action. As one official has noted, the nonparticipants simply get a "free ride" and share in the benefits of the activities of the council of governments without sharing in the work load.

NO MAGIC SOLUTION

The formation of a council of governments offers no magic solution to the difficult problems involved in providing effective, efficient, and responsible government in a metropolitan area. Among the disadvantages which have been attributed to councils of governments are the following:

(1) They do not offer a means of redistributing tax resources in the metropolitan area.

(2) They have no coercive power to enforce their decisions.

(3) There is no legal requirement for local governments to join the council and no legal bar to withdrawal.

(4) They cannot take effective action on an area-wide problem if a majority of members oppose the proposal.

(5) They may delay the formation of a true metropolitan government. (Sometimes this argument is reversed, and councils are criticized because they may hasten the formation of a metropolitan government. Neither argument is supported by evidence.)

The advantages of councils of governments, which seem to have accounted for their rapid spread during the past nine years, include the following:

(1) They are relatively easy to form, requiring only that the governing bodies of a substantial proportion of local governments in the area wish to form a council.

(2) They provide a mechanism for studying problems, obtaining and reconciling the views of the various local governments in the area, and taking joint action when a course of action is decided upon.

(3) They provide a policy body of elected officials which can provide guidance to regional organizations concerned with metropolitan area development. These may include research organizations, authorities and special districts, interstate agencies, and regional planning bodies.

(4) They provide the means of representing the needs of the metropolitan area as a whole to state and federal agencies and legislatures.

Whether or not the advantages of councils of governments outweigh the disadvantages is largely an academic question. At present, they seem to offer the only feasible means for elected and appointed officials to combine their efforts to guide the growth of the more complex metropolitan areas and to alleviate the problems which have been inherited from the past.

32. ABAG Appraised*

In one of a series of reports on metropolitan problem solutions made possible by a grant from the Ford Foundation, the Institute for Local Self Government reviews the first five years of the Association of Bay Area Governments (ABAG), one of the most active metropolitan councils of governments. Although ABAG has been accused of hampering the creation of an area-wide government, the report concludes it has become a permanent organization which will have a major impact in the Bay area

BACKGROUND

More than four million people live in the San Francisco Bay Region. It is one of the nation's major metropolitan urban areas, approximately 7,000 square miles in size. By conservative calculations, ten million people will live here in 1980. It is in the midst of what will be a lengthy period of turmoil and transition, characterized by rapid urbanization with its tremendous forces of physical, economic, technological, cultural, and social growth and change. The region is confronted with many complex problems which overlap boundaries of the individual units of government and communities which are its constituent units. Regional planning, water and air pollution, transportation and mass transit, automation and technological unemployment, physical and social blight in the center and sprawl at the perimeter are but a few examples drawn from a list that is both frightening and challenging in magnitude and seriousness.

The Bay Area's efforts to deal with area-wide problems have been hampered because responsibility and authority is split and shared among numerous units and levels of government which are not structured for concerted regional action. The responsibility for meeting area-wide governmental needs and producing the level of services demanded by the rising expectations of all citizens in the Bay Area is shared among and within the nine counties (Alameda, Contra Costa, Napa, Marin, San Francisco, San Mateo, Solano, Sonoma); nearly 100 municipalities, and approximately 500 special districts, excluding school districts and those which perform non-urban functions. Various state and federal agencies and numerous commissions and boards operate in the area, each concerned with segments of governmental services and functions.

* From *ABAG Appraised: A Quinquennial Review of Voluntary Regional Co-Operative Action Through the Association of Bay Area Governments* (Berkeley, Calif.: Institute for Local Self Government, Claremont Hotel Building, 1965), pp. 3–7 and 52–60.

There is an abundance of governments. The relatively strong position, governmental power, and provision of services such as welfare and health by county governments in California underlies all considerations of area-wide actions. In California, the county is very much more than the administrative arm of the state, as it is frequently elsewhere. However, where so many share responsibility and authority, no single entity is sufficient to do an effective job on a regional basis. While the actions of the various units and agencies occasionally have been complementary, they are rarely co-ordinated and, not infrequently, have been in conflict.

Paradoxically, the abundance of governments has been, by and large, that of "good government." Regional problems, however, have proved in many cases to be only extensions of urban problems. ABAG came into existence not solely because of inefficiencies, but rather because the strength and experience of local governments in the Bay Area provided leadership prepared to undertake regional problem-solving through their own organization designed to overcome difficulties aggravated by a lack of co-ordination.

Through the years, there have been numerous attempts to create regionally-based, special-purpose governmental structures for dealing with area-wide problems. Several have been only partially successful because they lacked jurisdiction in all nine counties. Separate, regional governmental units now exist for controlling air and water pollution, rapid transit, water supply and sewage disposal, some regional parks, and bridge crossings of the Bay. Two state agencies recently came into existence which, however, are not primarily service-oriented. They are designed to study regional problems: The Bay Area Transportation Study Commission, and the Bay Conservation and Development Commission.

However, such organizations do not alter the conditions of divided and shared responsibility. They are reflective of the overall picture of fragmentation. Only one, the Water Pollution Control Agency, which is a regional arm of state government, has jurisdiction in the whole nine-county area. The two recent additions (BATSC and BCDC) are not envisioned as permanent agencies but are temporary in nature, primarily for research and study purposes, although the BCDC does have police powers to prevent further filling of Bay tidelands during its studying lifetime. Most have jurisdiction over only a small portion of the region and *no two have the same boundaries.* Most are limited by law to a single purpose; none is general in purpose. Their authorities and responsibilities overlap and are layered between the authority and responsibility of other local governments, and of state and federal agencies. The lines between them are, at best, hazy. The Bay Area's regional special districts and authorities do not constitute a co-ordinated approach to area-wide governmental needs.

Based upon well-established traditions, "home rule" is more than a legal maxim or philosophic concept in the Bay Area. It is a basic fact of local government life in California in keeping with American local government's mainstream. It is responsible, in large part, for the strength of the local governments and their effectiveness in solving local problems, locally.

In this tradition and against this background, Bay Area county and municipal officials have devised the first truly comprehensive, multiple but limited-purpose, regionally-based institution for developing co-operative, co-ordinated approaches to area-wide problems. ABAG has been termed by the United States Advisory Commission on Intergovernmental Relations as ". . . one of the most significant recent developments in local government in metropolitan areas." ABAG is now five years old. It has generated widespread interest in its affairs by producing an impressive record of activity and accomplishment. This report critically evaluates its current and potential usefulness as a system of governance for responding to regional needs, determining regional objectives, and executing programs for their implementation.

ABAG has been praised by some as the only politically practical approach to ultimate development of a multi-function, limited-purpose, democratically-structured metropolitan government for the Bay Area. ABAG has been condemned by some as an inadequate, self-serving instrument of city and county officials which will fail to achieve its ambitious goals and which will delay and hamper the creation of "more adequate institutions," perhaps a "super-government." Whatever its merits and demerits, after five years of operation, ABAG appears here to stay. It will have a substantial influence upon the future pattern of regional governmental organizations in the Bay Area. Its implications have great significance for the metropolitan regions in California and elsewhere in the United States. A counterpart, the Southern California Association of Governments (SCAG) has already been formed and it is, likewise, the prototype for a possible similar organization arising in the San Joaquin Valley.

The Institute for Local Self Government, in fulfillment of responsibilities under its Ford Foundation grant, believes it important to make the results of ABAG's experience "available in useable form in sufficient time to be of value to other communities which confront similar circumstances." . . .

A SUMMARY APPRAISAL OF ABAG

After five years of operation the question of ABAG's becoming "an effective instrument for regional problem solving, strengthening the theory and practice of home rule and initiative as it harnesses and focuses local governments on regional problems whose causes and effects transcend the jurisdiction of its individual members" may no longer be valid. The question may now well be: "*How* can it do so?" While the experts were debating the theory of voluntary cooperative effort on the part of local governments in the Bay Area, the facts of ABAG's existence and its policy and program evolution overtook the debate. The organization's future now lies in the answer to the question of how successful it is in implementing its planning decisions in fulfillment of its expanded role.

Operating as it does, in an area of heavy influence of the University of California at Berkeley, it may be well to turn to three eminent professors who have been interested in the development of ABAG. Professor T. J. Kent, chairman of the Department of City and Regional Planning, a councilman in Berkeley and a delegate to ABAG's General Assembly, believes that ABAG's planning decisions were in error. Although he supports the concept of home rule and advocates a permanent place for ABAG in the future of Bay Area government, he predicts and recommends the gradual development of a two-level system in which regional problems would be shifted to a "unified, limited-function federation of local governments; largely controlled by cities." He describes ABAG as a "voluntary association" which can "never perform the painful acts of government."

Kent would attack the regional planning problem by creating a single purpose special district with power to tax but lacking the police power with which to enforce its decisions. He predicts only the following permanent functions for ABAG:

"1. To strengthen the city and county governments of the Bay Area so that everything that can possibly be done locally will be done locally and will be done well.

"2. To explore and foster voluntary cooperative solutions for all area-wide problems that can be dealt with effectively in this way.

"3. To support the creation of a unified, limited function government in the metropolitan Bay Area to deal effectively with those relatively few major public needs that definitely cannot be provided for by voluntary cooperative action.

"4. To oppose, openly and forcefully, all attempts to transform the limited function Bay Area government into an all-purpose government."

Professor Mel Scott, also of the University of California's Department of City and Regional Planning, while he has not addressed himself to the question of ABAG's future in specific terms, believes that it is not the appropriate agency to undertake regional planning.

Scott seems to doubt the sincerity of the city and county legislators who support ABAG as a regional planning agency. He says that "if 70 or more city and county governments comprising the Association of Bay Area governments truly wish to control regional affairs and to provide strong leadership in regional planning and development, they will seek to wrest more of the power of decision from the state and federal governments. These local governments will also take steps to integrate multi-county special districts, each of which is doing some form of single function planning without maintaining close liaison with other similar districts. Since the cities and counties of the Bay Area do neither of these things, their professions of dedication to the principle of home rule are unconvincing."

Although Scott assumes that ABAG, with assistance from federal and state governments, will develop a regional plan for the Bay Area which "respects technical findings about the Bay and promotes over-all interest of the region, the state, and nation," he advocates formation of a new metropolitan authority to assume the regional planning function on a permanent basis. He proposes a permanent San Francisco Bay Conservation and Development Commission created by federal, state, local compact to control the development of the Bay and its environs. The Commission would be a review board for permits to fill Bay waters and construct shoreline and other projects both public and private and it would regulate the use of shore area and Bay waters by exercise of the police power. It would also be a developing and operating agency with power to levy taxes, issue revenue and general obligation bonds, and to acquire land by eminent domain to carry out projects which localities and private owners could not execute. Cities, counties, other agencies of local government, and private interests would be bound by the decisions of the Commission, while state and federal governments would possess veto powers in extraordinary situations.

Although Scott did not indicate the extent of area to be included within the jurisdiction of the proposed commission, it must be presumed to include the greatest part of the area normally included within the nine-county concept of the region. The topography, geology and pattern of urban development would require jurisdiction over many aspects of private and public life in a broad area. It must be presumed that such a commission would become, in fact, *the* regional planning agency for the Bay Area.

It is unrealistic to expect any but a negative reaction to Scott's proposal on the part of local government officials and legislators. They, as Scott implies, may not be able to "prevent the establishment of such a commission even if they wished." Still, they are not likely to accept gracefully a suggestion which origi-nates outside their own organization, which conflicts fundamentally with their own concepts of regional planning as expressed in the ABAG program, and which is presented with the threat that if they do not act, "the governor must."

Local government officials in the Bay Area tend to view the ABAG approach as a politically feasible one in the evolutionary development of a governmental entity, possessing multiple but limited functions. They believe ABAG is capable of bringing regional authority to bear upon area-wide problems and that it is politically viable, representative, and consistent with the traditional and valued

American concepts of democracy with its emphasis upon effective local government institutions.

Perhaps the most balanced of the professorial views comes from Professor Victor Jones, Chairman of the Department of Political Science at the University of California, a leading student of metropolitan problems and, for a long time, an advocate for the creation of multipurpose metropolitan governments. Jones has latterly described voluntary metropolitan associations as ". . . the most promising development in our American federal system." Writing in April, 1962, he gave the following reasons for this conclusion:

1. They indicate that local elected officials are becoming more aware than they were a decade ago of "the metropolitan implications of some of their problems, needs and activities."

2. The forum which they provide is good, "provided the discussion is about real and important matters and steps have been taken to define the issues, identify different ways of dealing with them and bring to bear upon the discussion a body of organized and relevant information."

3. They can participate in the discussion of federal-state-local or state-local policies as an equal partner with federal and state agencies. They can "insist that the side-effects on local government of particular programs are as important as the efficacy of the program itself."

4. They appear to be a "necessary and viable first stage of the emergent federalism of metropolitan communities."

Speaking specifically of ABAG, he said: "With the organization and development of ABAG, I see for the first time in thirty years of observation and inquiry the promise of an evolutionary, limited, federated metropolitan government. Let those who fear it will be nothing but a debating society help it come to play a more active and positive role in governing the Bay Area. At the same time, let those who fear that it will grow into a monster of super government help it remain cautious in assuming any function that the community does not consider to be properly metropolitan in scope or in nature. Both must remember, however, that the alternatives are not the black and white of a simple, consolidated metropolitan government or of no metropolitan government at all. The American people operating through municipal and county governments will prevent the first extreme. The same American people, if they think it necessary to by-pass local government, will operate through state and federal governments to see that metropolitan problems are solved. If local governments are by-passed often enough, the cumulative effect may be greater than the outright abolition of counties and cities. If the concept of home rule is not broadened to cover the metropolis so that local government can participate as an equal partner in governing the metropolis, then local government, as we have known it, will wither away. ABAG, alone, is in a position to make the concept and practice of home rule into a viable government for the Bay Area that can work with cities and counties and with the state and federal governments."

In an address to ABAG's General Assembly in February, 1963, William L. Slayton, Commissioner, Urban Renewal Administration, Housing and Home Finance Agency, presumably representing the federal government's concern with regionalism, called for a "metropolitan federalism—a federalism of local governments under a concept of limited association for the pursuit of common objectives." Since that time, the Housing and Urban Redevelopment Act of 1965 has emphasized Slayton's words by making additional federal financing available to ABAG. A two-third grant authorization for most, if not all, of its regional programs is now available from the federal government with the stated congressional objective to "encourage the establishment and continued operation of organizations of policy and decision makers, representing the various local governments within a metropolitan area, so that they may develop and carry out programs for the coordinated development of the area." ABAG is clearly eligible for what promises to be very large grant programs.

Also under the terms of a 1965 act, federal grants to local governments for water filtration plants, underground storage basins, storm sewers, water lines and water impoundments will not be made after July, 1968, unless they are consistent with a program for a unified or "officially coordinated" area-wide water or sewer facilities system as part of the area's comprehensively planned development, which in the words of a House Committee "would minimize waste and unnecessary costs which are the result of unplanned and haphazard construction of basic community facilities." ABAG, having undertaken the role of a regional planning agency for the Bay Area, can expect its reviewing and coordinating functions in regional planning to be spurred by these actions. Aside from any policy deliberations by its General Assembly or Executive Committee by the last quarter of 1965, congressional action has clearly strengthened and opened broad new areas of financial support.

What is apparent from this quinquennial appraisal of ABAG is that ABAG's future probably will lie somewhere between the viewpoints outlined above. The Association is well on the way to developing into an effective device for dealing with regional problems. Perhaps this is the least and the most that can be expected of it. It has conclusively demonstrated that it can stimulate and guide factual analyses which are essential first steps to reasonable regional action. It has proved its worth as a desirable public forum for debate and consideration of vital issues, and it has developed organizational machinery for successfully considering and adopting meaningful alternatives for policy considerations.

We have not yet developed in America generally accepted criteria for an effective and desirable system of regional governance that would fully satisfy the interests of the state, the federal government, the citizens of the region and the politically elected leadership in it. As ABAG moves into areas where it will be forced to make difficult, basic, and controversial decisions involving the vested interests of its members, there will be an evolvement and refinement of such criteria. That much is clear from the record of the first five years. Whether a voluntary association of local governments can oversee, coordinate and implement its decisions through the cooperative action of its county and city constituents, regional special districts, federal and state agencies, and the many non-governmental roles it has to play and still be supported and thrive as a meaningful element in its region's life is a question that perhaps can best be answered at the end of the next five years.

Certain it is that the ABAG experiment is in the main current of American political thought. It is an inspiring story based on American traditions of politically responsible democratic problem-solving. Viewed one way, ABAG is an extension of local government resources—political, legal, financial—to problems of a region. It may well be called an experiment in "regional home rule." It has proved that locally elected, mostly part-time officials can serve their local governments and at the same time, their region. They have taken the time to fulfill their interests. They have developed broad perspectives and they have been willing to relate regional to local responsibility in their actions.

PART FIVE

The Future
Metropolis

It is believed that voters in most metropolitan areas will continue to reject proposals for a revolutionary restructuring of the governmental system of the metropolis. Interest, therefore, in discovering ways of solving area-wide functional problems within the existing framework of local government has been stimulated. This approach to solving metropolitan problems is supported by several political scientists who tend to feel that it matters relatively little with respect to the development of the future metropolis if we have a system of fragmented local government. The system may be maladroit, yet it has not collapsed and has met, albeit not in the most satisfactory manner, the basic service needs of the metropolis.

Local political boundaries may be anachronistic, but they have not prevented the development of cooperative mechanisms to facilitate the resolution of pressing regional problems. The spread of the cooperative movement among units of local governments has been fostered by two developments. First, service inadequacies have prompted local governments to hold frequent discussions in order to plan joint action and the pooling of resources to provide services on an area-wide basis. Second, the federal and state governments, by means of various conditional grant-in-aid programs, are fostering interlocal cooperation and regional action. In consequence, artificial political boundary lines are beginning to be obliterated with respect to certain governmental functions.

Great reliance currently is being placed upon metropolitan planning and metropolitan councils of governments to foster cooperative inter-local action to solve area-wide problems. The consensus approach permits the resolution of certain metropolitan problems and the satisfaction of certain area-wide service needs without necessitating a fundamental change in the basic structure of the system of local government. However, this approach may not be the ideal political mechanism for the solution of area-wide problems.

It would be a mistake to underestimate the difficulty of securing area-wide action by the cooperative approach which is subject to the vagaries and whims of each governmental unit. The fact that the various units of local government within a typical metropolitan area have common problems does not guarantee they will be able to agree upon a common course of remedial action. If they are motivated by narrow self-interest and the spirit of localism is strong, attempts to secure a consensus for action will prove fruitless. Should a municipality with a key location refuse to cooperate with the other units of local government, effective metropolitan action may be frustrated. The initial enthusiasm for inter-local cooperation may be replaced by hard bargaining and total inaction in a number of cases. Furthermore, interlocal cooperation may be unable to respond quickly enough to cope with exigencies created by a rapidly changing metropolitan environment.

Interlocal cooperation will solve successfully noncontroversial problems, and it is reasonable to predict that conjoint action will be a prominent characteristic of the government of the metropolis in the future. The success of the voluntary approach undoubtedly will depend heavily upon the support it receives from the federal and state governments. And the degree to which the approach is successful will affect the prospects of implementing a major restructuring of the government of the metropolis as advocated by reformers.

The development of megalopolises and the increasing seriousness of central city problems in several areas of the United States are two major developments pressuring the state and federal governments to play a greater role in the government of the metropolis. In a number of states, less emphasis may be placed upon the creation of a metropolitan government and more emphasis may be placed upon the assumption by the state government of responsibility for the solution of certain area-wide problems.

As metropolitan areas expand toward and merge with each other to form a megalopolis, the inadequacies of the consolidated metropolitan government and the two-tier approaches become obvious. Only the federal and state governments have the necessary authority and resources to solve the problems which transcend the boundaries of SMSA's and states. A partnership approach involving a federal-state compact probably will be relied upon to a greater extent in the future and will be an important part of the government of the metropolis.

The only general prognosis which may be advanced is a mixed one. That the government of the metropolis has a potpourri of problems cannot be denied, yet it should not be judged on the basis of unrealistic standards which do not accord the values of a fragmented governmental system proper recognition. It would appear to be reasonable to conclude that continued tinkering will change significantly the nature of the governmental system of the metropolis over a period of years.

33. Changing Directions*

HENRY J. SCHMANDT

The changing attitude toward metropolitan reform during the past ten years is surveyed by Henry J. Schmandt, Chairman of the Department of Urban Affairs at the University of Wisconsin at Milwaukee. Schmandt points to the shift of decision-making powers affecting metropolitan areas to the state and federal governments and large corporations. He prognosticates that these external pressures will force the local governments in a metropolitan area into a continuing dialogue about area-wide goals and policies.

Despite large outpourings of reformist activity, survey commission studies and reorganization referenda, the governmental face of the metropolis looks little different today than it did two decades ago. If anything, the pattern has become even more diffused and complex with the addition of new municipalities and special districts. Yet strangely enough, less is heard today about metropolitan governmental reorganization than at any time in the recent past. The dire forebodings of those who warned of imminent catastrophe unless drastic action was taken to redesign the urban polity have now become faint echoes. Only an occasional plea continues to be heard for broad-scale changes—for the holistic solution or grand design—in the metropolitan governmental system while attention has shifted to partial and incremental remedies.

The history of the metropolitan reorganization movement is one of steadily declining aspirations. During the first few decades of the present century, reformist rationale generally assumed the indispensability of political unification. Although recognizing the argument for local rule, it saw little reason for granting administrative autonomy to what it regarded as neighborhoods or sections of a single community. By 1930, however, consolidation had been largely abandoned as a practical reform while the emphasis had shifted to various forms of local federalism. And by the end of the 1950s, the movement had veered further in the direction of lesser remedies, with "voluntary cooperation" becoming the popular nostrum.

The most revealing indication of the lessened interest in major structural reorganization is the precipitous decline in the popularity of metropolitan study

* *National Civic Review* (November 1965) pp. 530–34.

commissions. Only a few years back such bodies were the highly vaunted carriers of the reform cause, the college of physicians prescribing for the governmental ills of the metropolis. The movement reached its peak during the five-year period from 1953 to 1958 when more than 65 metropolitan commissions or survey groups were established. Today, there are less than a handful in operation and few if any new creations are contemplated.

What has brought about the shift in emphasis and change in attitude during the past ten years? Four factors help to explain this phenomenon: (1) the long history of failure to effect major change, (2) growing awareness of the complexity of the problem, (3) the new orientation of urban research, and (4) the continuing shift of power upward to higher levels of government.

HISTORY OF FAILURE

The first factor—the unimpressive record of reform accomplishment—requires little comment. Other than the Miami and Nashville successes, both of which can be explained largely by atypical circumstances, no major change in the existing governmental pattern of any American metropolitan area has taken place during the last decade. This continued lack of success has dulled the enthusiasm of the civic activists who have spearheaded the reform cause. At no time a grassroots movement and almost universally lacking support from local government officials and political leaders, the crusade ground to a halt when community notables and good government groups began to lose interest. Metropolitan reformers had originally assumed the existence of widespread latent support for governmental restructuring among the citizen body. When they finally became convinced of the fallacy of this assumption, they reluctantly concluded that change could be accomplished only through regular political channels and with the support or acquiescence of local officialdom. To proceed on this basis required a dilution of the reform prescriptions.[1]

METROPOLITAN COMPLEXITY

The second factor—a changed attitude toward metropolitan reorganization—reflects a greater appreciation of the problem's complexity on the part of both civic activists and academicians. Until recent years, reformist dogma had been based on a simplistic view of the metropolis and the problems which afflict it.

[1] See in this connection Henry J. Schmandt, *The Milwaukee Metropolitan Study Commission: Metropolitan Action Studies No. 3.* Indiana University Press, Bloomington, 1965.

Those who called for change were virtually unanimous in their diagnosis: too many governments, overlapping jurisdictions, duplication of services, wasteful and inefficient operation. To them, the answers were apparent; research was required only to document the case and provide ammunition to sell the product.

By the end of the last decade, a new note was finding its way into the debate. Observers of the metropolitan scene were beginning to ask whether the pluralistic pattern of local government was really the villain in the play and whether the commonly proposed forms of area-wide government were really worth fighting for. Political scientist Edward Banfield struck this note when he said: "That there are 1,071 independent local governments in the New York area may not be as bad as it is made to sound. Perhaps there should be even more."[2] In similar vein, Charles Adrian wrote that most of the needs and problems discussed in metropolitan survey commission reports are not crisis situations but part of the ordinary problems of living in a wealthy, changing, complex nation.[3]

The passage of time, moreover, has brought a reaction to the old prescriptions even among seasoned veterans in the field. What seemed self-evident to many of them as late as the 1950s now appears highly problematic. Luther Gulick recently described the changing perspective in his characteristically eloquent fashion:

> The answer is not as easy and simple as most American reformers thought as recently as five or ten years ago. When we first faced the problem of urban explosion, it was natural to seek a solution of emerging governmental difficulties through the direct application of simple measures such as annexation of the suburbs, consolidation, public utility extensions and the simple direct enlargement of the boundaries of the local government. Where this approach encountered difficulties, we turned to "authorities" and other special districts and created state commissions without much thought as to where this might lead us. Thus we met what we thought were simple problems with simple, direct answers.[4]

But when the simple, direct answers produced few results, the civic activists either withdrew from the arena or acceded to the voluntarism of local officialdom.

URBAN RESEARCH

The third contributing element—the new urban research—is a correlate of the second. As late as 1957, political scientists were being chided for their

---

[2] "The Politics of Metropolitan Area Organizations," *Midwest Journal of Political Science* (May 1957), pages 77–78.

[3] "Metropology: Folklore and Field Research," *Public Administration Review* (Summer 1961), page 149.

[4] *The Metropolitan Problem and American Ideas*. Alfred A. Knopf, New York, 1962, page 119.

failure to study seriously the impact of urbanization on local governmental institutions.[5] Today, however, such a charge would be less valid. During the past decade, a new breed of political scientists has appeared on the urban scene. Highly critical of their predecessors' preoccupations with governmental structure and administrative management prescriptions, they have called for empirical testing of long-held assumptions. In their eyes, the classical metropolitan studies and recommendations which emerged from them were based on nothing more than what Coleman Woodbury has referred to as "folk political science," plausible, often repeated, but without any firm empirical foundations. Their frontal attacks on the citadels of orthodoxy served to cast further doubts on the basic assumptions of the metropolitan reform movement and to dissipate the aura of legitimacy in which it had been cloaked.

The changing orientation of urban research is evidenced not only by the work of academic scholars but also by the type of studies now prevalent among local agencies and committees, both public and private. The 1958 *Digest of Metropolitan Surveys* listed a total of approximately 50 local and regional studies then underway, with almost 40 of them involving governmental reorganization. In contrast, the 1964 tabulation showed some 160 studies, less than ten of which could be referred to as reorganization oriented.[6] The remainder dealt with the broader social, economic, transportation, planning and developmental aspects of the metropolis. The direction of "applied" research, in other words, indicates a growing realization by many in the urban field that the most crucial problems of the metropolis—race relations is one, for example, and poverty another— are at best peripherally related to local governmental organization. As a result, the currently predominant trend is to accept the present governmental pattern as a given and to seek ways to accommodate the problems of the day within its general framework.

THE SHIFT OF POWER

The fourth and final factor—the upward thrust of power—is a reflection of the diminishing degree of control that local areas have over their own destiny. With the increase in societal scale, many of the crucial decisions relating to the metropolis are made by agencies outside its borders: in Congress and at the state capitol; in the Department of Housing and Urban Development, the Bureau of Public Roads and Department of Health, Education and Welfare; in

---

[5] R. J. Daland, "Political Science and the Study of Urbanism," *American Political Science Review* (June 1957), page 491.

[6] *Digest of Metropolitan Surveys, 1958 and 1964*. Graduate School of Public Affairs, State University of New York, Albany.

344 THE FUTURE METROPOLIS

the state highway commission and other state administrative agencies; and in the board rooms of national corporations.

As this trend has developed, local interests and local governments have turned increasingly to federal and state levels for assistance. The old conviction that metropolitan areas could solve their own problems if only their governmental structure was properly organized has given way to the belief that salvation lies primarily in help from above. This reliance, although bemoaned by many, is regarded by others as the most realistic means of achieving a higher measure of order in the metropolis despite its fragmented governmental system. The federal government, for example, is now administering over 40 separate programs of financial aid for urban development, over a half of which have been enacted since 1950. A number of these have performance standards incorporated in them and several, such as highway and open space aids, are geared to metropolitan planning.

There is little question but that the present direction will continue, with increasing pressure being placed on local policy-makers to enlarge their perspectives. The annual reports of the Advisory Commission on Intergovernmental Relations, perhaps the best barometer of current thinking in the urban governmental field, underscore this trend. Among the commission's recent recommendations are ones which would require review of certain federal grants in aid by metropolitan planning agencies, favor general purpose units of local government over special purpose districts as federal aid recipients and a general admonition that the national government "must be prepared to accept, as a permanent and continuing responsibility, the stimulation and support of state and local efforts to achieve an effective and orderly pattern of metropolitan area development."[7]

THE SHAPE OF THE FUTURE

During the past decade, the concept of intergovernmental cooperation has gained in favor while other approaches to metropolitan government, including the two-tier remedy, have received less attention. In practice, the voluntaristic path has represented more a defense of the status quo than a serious effort to meet the needs of the modern metropolis. Its use in most instances has involved little more than joint action of limited scope by two or more local units in minor and non-controversial matters.

[7] Advisory Commission on Intergovernmental Relations, *Sixth Annual Report,* Washington, D. C., January 31, 1965.

Yet the retreat from more comprehensive remedies to the lesser concept is not without its promising features. Both the national and state governments are almost certain to bring increasing pressure on urban governments to effect greater administrative coordination and more orderly development. Responsible local officials, moreover, are beginning to realize that, in view of the upward shift of power, they must mobilize in self-defense if they are to retain a voice in critical developmental decisions affecting their communities.

In sum, if the trends which have been manifest during the past decade continue, as they are likely to do, we can expect the future to bring:

1. Incremental rather than major alterations in the existing governmental system, including the gradual assumption of more urban-type functions by the county;

2. More concern with the study and resolution of social, economic and physical development problems within the governmental pattern as it is presently constituted;

3. Accelerated efforts to develop intra-area policy and planning mechanisms of a voluntary nature as typified by the Association of Bay Area Governments (ABAG) and by regional planning agencies such as those in the northeastern Illinois, southeastern Wisconsin and the Minneapolis-St. Paul areas;

4. Increased state intervention in metropolitan affairs both indirectly through grants in aid and directly through enlarged controls over such areas as municipal incorporation, annexation, air and water pollution;

5. Greater use of federal grant programs to induce cooperative planning and development by local units;

6. Increased efforts to effect changes in state and local tax structures to eliminate the serious fiscal inequities which are common among local units in metropolitan areas.

In the last analysis, it really matters little to the shaping of the modern metropolis and to its proper functioning whether we have one or fifteen fire departments, whether some duplication of services exists or whether water is supplied by one special district and sewage disposal by another. Such a fragmented service pattern does raise problems of coordination, efficiency and citizen control (the last is frequently exaggerated), but it is unlikely that these drawbacks will render the system dysfunctional. What is important is that there be some institutional mechanism—whether in the form of inter-municipal councils, regional planning commissions or other yet-to-be-devised instrumentalities—for bringing together all relevant public agencies—local, state and national—in a continuing consideration of area-wide developmental goals and policies. The subtle controls of external pressures will increasingly force the governmental units of metropolitan areas in this direction.